STRUGGLE FOR THE WORLD

DESMOND DONNELLY

STRUGGLE
FOR THE
WORLD
The Cold War: 1917-1965

As the nature of foul weather lieth not in a shower or
two of rain but in an inclination thereto of many days
together, so the nature of war consisteth not in actual
fighting but in the known disposition thereto during all
the time there is no assurance as to the contrary. All
other time is peace.

THOMAS HOBBES, *Leviathan*

ST. MARTIN'S PRESS · NEW YORK

I would like to thank Messrs. Cassell
for permission to reproduce extracts from
Sir Winston Churchill's *The Second World
War*, and Associated Newspapers Ltd.
for permission to reproduce A. J. Cummings's *News Chronicle* article

To

ERNEST BEVIN *and* DEAN ACHESON

*Two men who stood when Earth's
foundations fled*

CONTENTS

CONTENTS

MAPS

PREFACE

I first thought of writing this book when I was climbing down a rickety metal staircase at the back of a hotel in Alma Ata. I was not on a spying mission. I was going to discuss international politics and co-existence with a group of staunchly patriot young Russians. Yet I felt very conspicuous in the gathering dusk as I made my way down to the yard that lay at the rear of the hotel, which also had an exit that was not visible to the main hotel entrance. I had given my word that I would only keep my appointment if my "interpreter" was not aware of the meeting. I knew that everything I did, however small, was being reported upon by the dogged and humourless young woman who had been attached to me in Moscow and who never left my side except when I went into my hotel bedroom. At that moment she was sitting in the hotel foyer, stoically reading a grubby book and imagining that I was safely in my room writing letters. Outside, on the veranda near the main entrance, drinking a glass of "peevo," was a gentleman who reported on my interpreter. What a ridiculous way to behave, I thought to myself. How did this situation come about? Where and when will it end? Have there been moments in time when the mutual suspicions of East and West could have been resolved?

The last thirty years have seen greater changes in the pattern of human affairs than at any time since the fall of the Roman Empire. They have been more rapid even than those when Jenghiz Khan's forces swept the great land mass that lies between the shores of the Pacific Ocean and the banks of the River Oder that so nearly constitute the boundaries of the Communist world to-day. The British Empire, which in size and influence far exceeded the great Empires of Greece and Rome, has been liquidated. The United States and the Soviet Union have emerged as super-powers trailing satellites of varying degrees of willingness behind them. A man named Mao Tse-tung accomplished one of the great marches of history— greater even than Hannibal and Xenophon—and proclaimed the Chinese People's Republic from the balcony of the red Tien An Men in Peking. The development of modern technology has made

9

a nonsense of all previous defence concepts and will continue so to do.

In Europe itself there has been a profound human and political change. The European Civil War—as the historians of the future will describe the conflicts that spanned the years from 1914 to 1945 —is now over. It has been replaced by the wider civil war of the inhabitants of the earth, known as the Cold War. The old enmities have been or are in the process of being buried—to be replaced by new fears, appetites, and the Communist drive for world domination. Within the Communist lands themselves there are new forces stirring. As the fires of revolution have begun to burn lower in Russia, the flames are rising yet higher in China.

The canvas of this great challenge—the supreme challenge of this harsh and terrible twentieth century, the bloodiest and most turbulent era of recorded history—is world wide. The ordeal is far from over. Ahead lie new challenges and ordeals, calling for courage, more courage, implacable purpose and endless prudence. At one moment, there is a bold dramatic picture attracting the attention of all mankind. At another, there are almost imperceptible and minute threads of dispute.

Yet history is not a series of episodes, nor of individual appetites. It is a broadly connected process and an aggregate of desires. The Communist revolution, followed by the Western reaction to it, coincidental with the sudden emergence of Afro-Asian nationalisms, cannot be seen as events of themselves, unconnected with all that has gone before; any more than Hitler's attempt to succeed where men like Alexander of Macedon and Napoleon failed before him, can be regarded in isolation. For both Hitler and Lenin to seize power and to pursue policies aimed specifically at world domination, the conditions had to be propitious.

The Cold War has its origins in the struggle for power in Central Asia between the rival imperialisms of Britain and Russia in the nineteenth century. There was that strange period of history known as "The Great Game" when names such as Samarkand and Bokhara acquired a magical ring and men attempted to get to Central Asia, and gave their lives in the process, in order to stake out their respective nations' influences. Late in the nineteenth century, Roberts, when Commander-in-Chief, India, occupied many of his dispatches with the Russian "capacity for intrigue"— or "subversion" as latter-day cold warriors have called it. So the struggle was there—and so was the traditional doctrine of mutual suspicion—before ever the Red Flag floated over the Winter Palace on that cataclysmic day in 1917. Similarly, the tensions and future struggles in the Orient, which will intensify from now on, have their roots in geo-political conflicts that have gone before.

In writing about the story of this, the greatest issue of all human history, I have been faced with the twin problems of compression and emphasis. There have had to be many omissions, notably the detailed story of the Yugoslav break with the Soviet Union and the interminable and sometimes incomprehensible disarmament negotiations, except in so far as they thread into the basic tapestry of conflict. I am only too conscious that there have had to be many more omissions. For the author, it has been a great and rewarding experience of self-education extending over many years. I must have read over a thousand books in my quest for background, and scrutinised innumerable documents. I have consulted many people —some famous and some unknown—who have given me freely of their valuable time and advice. To these I owe debts that I can never repay. To mention them all would be impossible. Therefore my selection must be arbitrary. There are, in particular, two friends who figure in these pages and whose encouragement has been unstinting: in Britain, the Rt. Hon. the Earl of Avon; and in the United States, the Hon. Dean Acheson. I am deeply indebted to the librarians of the Foreign Office and the Royal Institute of International Affairs. The basic framework of research was undertaken for me brilliantly by Mrs. Jennifer Bourdillon, who is now the Headmistress of a famous girls' school. I owe much to Mr. Mark Bonham Carter, whose sympathy and intelligent appreciation of issues have always been at hand. His help has far exceeded the bounds of the normal author and publisher relationship. Finally, I owe most of all to Miss Sheila James, who typed and re-typed manuscripts and who never wearied of the many tasks of research. Without her loyalty, this book would have been impossible.

I emphasise that the opinions expressed are my own. The deficiencies and faults are my responsibility. As I wrote every page, at the back of my mind have been the vast and terrible issues involved in the story. These are not the chronicles of remote history. They are the passions and struggles of life, love, liberty and death involving all of us living, and the generations to come.

The story is not yet concluded; and in certain instances it is only just beginning. At the end there must be co-existence or no existence; peace and fulfilment or nuclear war—and the long silence of universal death in the calm days that go on and on as the bones whiten in the noonday sun.

The goal is peace. The cherished heritage is freedom. The involvement is total. Every human being, to a greater or lesser extent, is a participant in the events which have their origins in the story I have sought to unfold. I have no place for those who, in future, seek to evade or to avoid. For Milton has said it three centuries ago: "I cannot praise a fugitive and cloistered virtue unexercised and unbreathed that never sallies out and sees her adversary but slinks out of the race where the immortal garland is to be run for, not without dust and heat. . . . That which purifies us is by trial and trial is by what is contrary."

DESMOND DONNELLY

Roch,
Pembrokeshire
February, 1965

PART ONE

PROLOGUE

CHAPTER I

THE BOARDING PARTY

A deluge with an unseaworthy Ark. The timbers were rotten and most of the crew not much better. The Captain was suited for a pleasure yacht in still waters, and his sailing master had been chosen by his wife, reclining in the cabin below. The rudder was seized by a disorderly rabble of counsellors, drawn at random from Dumas, soldiers, sailors, and workers' committees, political organisations of every colour and creed, who had spent most of their time and energies in quarrelling as to the direction in which the ship ought to be sailed until, at last, it was captured by a piratical crew who knew their destinations.

David Lloyd George

A small man with a reddish-grey beard sat working in a room lined with books. The room was not large. The bookshelves gave it a comfortable, warm atmosphere, the atmosphere that one might associate with the study of a distinguished professor, holding a chair in one of the great universities of Eastern Europe. But there was also an Eastern European, almost Slavonic, feeling about the place.

The room itself lay down long, dilapidated, uncarpeted corridors, which had not seen the glistening wet of a paintbrush for many a long year. To get to it, you had to pass through a quadruple cordon of guards. Three successive varieties of pass were essential. Sentries stood with fixed bayonets at the strategic points, covering you as you presented the relevant pass for the particular checkpoint in this great rabbit warren of buildings.

Whoever you were, however eminent your name or well known your face, you still had to have those three different passes to get through the armed cordons to the man in the book-lined room. There were only five exceptions to this rule—the man's wife and his four sisters who lived with him. These people, together with his cats, were the only living creatures with whom he was in constant and daily contact.

The man himself was decidedly homely, if not ugly. He had a bald pate and slightly squinty eyes. His broad nose, thickish lips and unkempt beard gave him the appearance of a bulldog. At first glance, if it had not been for the book-lined room, you might have passed him for a bluff sea-captain doing a shore job. There was also the man's wide forehead, showing that he ought to be a thinker. It redeemed his face from the heavy, almost brutish quality that it might otherwise have had.

His dress was nondescript. He wore a slightly soiled white collar. Even a soiled white collar was a rarity in Russia in those days. He had a dark brown business suit and a black tie. His trousers were stuffed into knee-high boots of thick felt, the warmest kind of foot covering.

When he spoke, he was unhesitating, like someone who knows his own mind. Even when he spoke to foreigners in English, although his English was a little slow, he was very sure and precise. People who went to see him for the first time after he had moved into the book-lined room were nearly always surprised by his approach. He appeared at once to be the practical man. He gave his views realistically, analytically but never fanatically, or even dogmatically. As one newspaperman put it following an interview at the time: "Most of his words would have fitted comfortably into the mouth of a British Conservative Prime Minister."

This was Lenin as he sat in the Kremlin Palace of Justice. The year was 1920. The World War was over. The Intervention had ended. The Russian Civil War was over. The seat of government was now in Moscow. At last he was in office *and* in power.

Here was the extraordinary man who had just turned the world upside down; and because of whom human affairs could never be the same again. Despite his appearance, he was first and foremost a professional revolutionary. He had never followed any other occupation. In and by revolution, he had lived. He was a striking instance of a purpose that from early youth had marched unflinchingly towards a chosen goal, undisturbed by weariness or intellectual doubt, knowing no compunction. The staggering goal that he had set himself was world-wide revolution, to cross the seven seas and to engulf the five continents.

Nineteen-twenty was also the year of great transition for Lenin. Behind him lay the desperate struggles that had taken him and his little group thus far towards the tasks of implementing the theories

in which they believed. How did he get thus far? And where was
his Odyssey to lead?

The true home of Marxism was Germany. When Marx had written
Das Kapital he had been writing with his thoughts upon the German
proletariat which was living in one of the growing industrial areas of the world. Thus, by 1914 and because of Marx's
influence, the German Social Democratic party had become the
leading Marxist party in the world. Its Russian counterpart was
relatively weak, trailing far behind– so much so that Lenin was to
say in 1918: "The absolute truth is that without a revolution in
Germany we shall perish."

It was the accident of events in 1917 that gave Lenin his chance.
War, as the giant locomotive of history, suddenly pulled more
strongly in Russia than in Western Europe. And the Russian
revolution stemmed specifically from the military defeats inflicted
by Germany upon Russia in that year.

It was also war—and the total preoccupation of the Western
Powers with waging war—that was largely responsible for the first
of the many instances of the West's failure to understand what was
happening in Russia. To appreciate much that came later, it is
therefore necessary to examine the thoughts and moods of early
1917, when Russia was in the process of being defeated. Her human
lifeblood was running out, unstemmed by the tourniquets that
proper statesmanship would have applied in such circumstances.
The Russian ruling class was in disintegration. The nation was
spiritless.

The Allied leaders were anxious and disturbed—particularly
Lloyd George. On the British Prime Minister's pressure, a military
conference was convened in Petrograd for January, 1917, to find
out what was happening on the Eastern front and what support the
Western Allies might expect from Russia in the year then beginning.

The British delegation was led by Lord Milner, and included
Sir Henry Wilson, a distinguished soldier. France was represented
by M. Gaston Doumergue, then Minister for the Colonies, an
ex-Premier, a future President and again to be Premier. He took with
him General Castelnau, one of France's greatest soldiers. Upon
arrival, the British and French missions were depressed in the
extreme by what they saw. After a few days, Wilson wrote in his
private diary: "It seems as certain as anything can be that the
Emperor and Empress are riding for a fall. Everyone—officers,

merchants, ladies—talk openly of the absolute necessity of doing away with them. . . . They have lost their people, their nobles and now their army, and I can see no hope for them; there will be terrible trouble one day here." Yet, extraordinary though it may appear in retrospect, and despite Wilson's assessment, Milner and Doumergue thereupon promptly convinced themselves that all would be well.

Milner reported to the British Cabinet: "As far as the purely political aspect of the matter is concerned, I have formed the opinion that there is a great deal of exaggeration in the talk about revolution, especially about the alleged disloyalty of the army. That the army should be very dissatisfied with the way in which the war has been conducted is only natural." Doumergue went further. In an interview with *Le Matin* he said: "I have brought back an excellent impression from my journey. It is clear from all the conversations I had and all that I saw that Russia is filled with unanimous will to pursue the war to a complete victory." Thereby Milner and Doumergue joined the long and still growing list of travellers to Russia who have been taken in by the so-called "delegation technique."

A few days later came the deluge. Revolution broke out in the streets of Petrograd and chaos spread rapidly throughout the country.[1] An enormous red flag now floated over the Winter Palace, which had been the stronghold of the Tsars since Peter the Great and which had so recently afforded hospitality to Milner and Doumergue. It was in the midst of this catastrophe and chaos that Lenin returned to Russia from Switzerland, where he had been in exile. The German Government now agreed to permit him and his group to cross Germany to Russia, and their reason was simple. Lenin was opposed to Russia continuing the war against Germany.

The Western leaders totally misunderstood what was happening. President Wilson, in a speech to Congress, said: "Does not every American feel that assurance has been added to our hope for the future peace of the world by the wonderful and heartening things

[1] Russia, prior to the Revolution of 1918, adhered to the Julian calendar. On the other hand, most Western countries in modern times have followed the calendar instituted by Pope Gregory XIII in 1582. The difference between the two calendars was thirteen days at this point. Thus the Russian February and October revolutions took place in March and November according to the Gregorian calendar, Russia adopting the Gregorian system by Soviet decree in February 14th, 1918.

that have happened within the last few weeks in Russia? . . . Here is a fit partner for a league of honour."

There was a great deal of anxiety amongst Lenin's party as it crossed Germany, and also amongst the Bolsheviks in Petrograd, as to the reception that Lenin would receive on arrival. They need not have worried. A huge crowd packed the square in front of the Finland Station in Petrograd. Banners fluttered and several military bands stood by. At last, as Lenin's train steamed in, very late, the "Marseillaise" blared forth. When he stepped down on to the platform, Lenin was wearing a round cap and looking frozen. For a second he stood there bewildered.

When the party had left the station they had a better chance to take stock. They were still a long way from power. They represented only a small minority amongst the many turbulent movements going on around them, and they had played only a small part in the decisive act of ejecting the Romanovs.

The most important single fact that now and throughout 1917 propelled the Bolsheviks forward to a position of real power was the decision taken by Kerensky and those associated with him in the Provisional Government that replaced the Tsar to continue the war against Germany. The mood of Russia was well past such thoughts of Kerensky. Her people wanted to be out of the war, at whatever political cost. Lenin stood, clear and unequivocal, for taking Russia out of the war.

Matters were carried a stage further by the complete failure of Kerensky's last attempt at a military offensive in July. Another armed uprising broke out in Petrograd and 400 people were killed before it was put down. In the confusion of events it led to a bitter reaction against Lenin. He was openly labelled as an agent of the Germans. At that moment it looked as though the Bolsheviks would never achieve power, and Lenin became very depressed. The situation was transformed, however, by one of the bizarre events that punctuate the story of the Russian Revolution. An attempt was made by the big industrialists and landowners—now thoroughly alarmed—to replace Kerensky, the Socialist, by a military dictator whom they could trust. The person they chose for the role was the Commander-in-Chief of the army, General Kornilov, who has been described as "a man with a lion's heart and the brains of a sheep." Kornilov's simple soldier's feeling had been sickened by the intrigues and indecisions at the centre of government. When he broke finally with Kerensky, in September, 1917, he attempted

19

to march upon the capital. It was a ridiculous venture because Kornilov's troops melted away in the face of political agitators who came out to meet them.

The revolutionary cauldron now boiled faster.[1] The Bolshevik's cry—"Peace, Land, Bread"—was their greatest single asset and its simple message evoked a human response. On 25th October[2] Kerensky declared "A State of Insurrection" and denounced Lenin as "a State criminal."

The State could survive no longer. At 10 a.m. on 26th October[2] Lenin's colleague, Trotsky, issued a proclamation stating that the provisional Government had fallen and power had passed to the Soviets. The collapse was general and by seven o'clock only some of the Ministers of the Provisional Government and a garrison in the Winter Palace held out. At 1 a.m. on 27th October[2] the final stage began. At 2 a.m. the Red Guards, who had infiltrated the corridors, rushed the inner room where the Civilian Ministers were meeting. It was all over. Perhaps the most apt comment was made by Philip Jordan, the negro butler of David R. Francis, the American Ambassador. Writing home, he stated: "On last Tuesday [he meant Wednesday] the Bolsheviks got the city in their hands and I want to tell you that it was something awful."

One immediate difficulty was to face the Bolsheviks—on 12th November Russia was due to go to the polls to elect the Constituent Assembly that had been promised by Kerensky, and the Bolsheviks found that it was too late to stop the election. It was the ideal of the freely elected Parliament for which Russia had hoped for more than a generation. The Bolsheviks in office, to their chagrin, polled only 9.8 million votes out of 41.7 million, or 24 per cent. The clear winners were the Social Revolutionaries with nearly 21 million votes or 50·8 per cent of the total. Not even in their strongholds of Petrograd and Moscow did the Bolsheviks command a majority. On Lenin's orders the Assembly's first meeting was postponed until January. The Bolsheviks were already learning the dangers that a system of free elections held for them.

The first act of the new Bolshevik Government, taken upon the

[1] The events leading up immediately to the Bolshevik seizure of power in the October Revolution are told magnificently in a book by an American, John Reed, *Ten Days That Shook The World*. John Reed was a very young Harvard graduate with pro-Communist views. His classic of reporting played a significant part in influencing liberal public opinion in the United States. He died in Russia of disease in 1920.

[2] Julian Calendar dates.

day of the October Revolution, was to announce a Decree of Peace. The concept behind this document is of profound importance. From it stemmed much of the new Bolshevik Government's early conflict with the Western Powers because of their opposing attitudes towards the continuance of the war. The immediate prospect created by Russia's intended withdrawal from the war was that Germany would be able to transfer her huge military forces on the Russian front for a last and overwhelming attack in the West. The Russian Decree of Peace was drafted by Lenin personally. It was a call for *general* peace. The Decree itself was made available at once to the foreign Press correspondents in Petrograd and then broadcast by radio. It began: "The Workers' and Peasants' Government, created by the Revolution of 24th-25th October and based upon the Soviets of Workers', Soldiers' and Peasants' Deputies, proposes to all the warring peoples and their governments that they immediately enter into negotiations for a just, democratic peace. A just or democratic peace, such as the majority of the workers and the toiling classes of the warring countries, exhausted, tormented and ravaged by the war, are yearning for—the sort of peace which the Russian workers and peasants have demanded in the most definite and insistent way since the overthrow of the Tsarist monarchy— this sort of peace would be an immediate peace without annexations, without the seizure of foreign territories and without the incorporation of foreign peoples and without indemnities. . . ." It continued: "The [Russian] Government considers that it would be the greatest of crimes against humanity to continue this war only to determine how strong and rich nations should divide among themselves the weak peoples they have seized. . . ."

The reason for Lenin's position about the war must be explained. Lenin himself had always belonged to that section of the European Socialist movement which had consistently opposed war. He regarded it as a conflict from which no gains could come to the workers. Yet Lenin did not want peace as an end for humanitarian reasons, as a pacifist would. He wanted peace because he thought that only by peace could he spread the universal social revolution in which he believed. Even more specifically, he did not want peace at all unless it was accompanied by revolution.

Universal revolution was Lenin's overriding thought. And because of the original Marxist belief that the real base for the world revolution had to be established in an industrial country like Germany, the Bolsheviks in October and November, 1917, still looked upon their success in Russia as a preliminary stepping-stone to the other revolutions that must come elsewhere. Lenin's call to peace, in his own mind, was the call to world revolution which he and his colleagues considered both inevitable and immediately in prospect. But Lenin soon found that his hopes for general peace and wider revolution were not going to follow as he had expected. Outside Russia his dramatic Decree of Peace was virtually ignored. The Bolsheviks recoiled with shock. They could not wait. They had to deal with their own problem immediately and were at once forced to sue for a separate peace with Germany. Thus the awful spectre of a separate Russian peace that had haunted men in London and Paris was now on the point of becoming a reality, and it filled the Western Powers with despair.

The formal Soviet-German negotiations were one of the strangest confrontations in the long history of wars and defeats.[1] The doctrinaire and totally inexperienced zealots of the most extraordinary government of this century were meeting the representatives of the *ancien régime*, who were in a strong position. The German and Austrian delegations were bland and charming. Their friendliness and fraternisation quickly disarmed Joffe, the leader of the Soviet delegation, so much so that Trotsky, who had been appointed Commissar for Foreign Affairs, decided to take over the leadership of the Soviet delegation himself and to put a stop to this heretical and inhibiting behaviour.

Trotsky's arrival at Brest-Litovsk, a few days after the conference began, changed the atmosphere, as he ordered an immediate stop to private entertaining, and insisted that the Soviet delegation had all its meals separately in its own quarters. But even Trotsky could not alter the nature of the German demands, in the forefront of which was the separation from Russia of Russian Poland, and the Baltic provinces of Lithuania and Kurland. The Germans also refused to recognise Russian authority over the rich grainlands of the Ukraine, and they fostered, instead, a separatist Ukrainian movement. The claims were a very serious threat to the new Bolshevik Government, whose dilemma was clear. If they accepted the terms, their acceptance would gravely discredit the régime and could even destroy it: if they refused, the Germans could impose their will by force.

Trotsky asked for an adjournment to consult his colleagues, and

[1] A vivid account of the Brest-Litovsk Conference is given by Sir John Wheeler Bennett in *The Forgotten Peace*.

travelled back to Petrograd. As Trotsky crossed the Russian positions and saw for himself the empty Russian trenches from which the soldiers had deserted in thousands, he received a salutary lesson in the realities of power politics. Whilst it was soon to be lost upon him, it was accepted by others in his government in the years that were to follow, for power became their foremost preoccupation.

Lenin, as consistent as ever for peace, was in favour of accepting the German demands, whatever the cost. Others in the Central Committee, led by Bukharin, advocated their rejection. Trotsky himself took a middle position: the Bolsheviks should decline to sign the peace and also decline to make war. His famous phrase, ringing down the years, was: "Neither war, nor peace." When the grim, humiliating proposals were put to the vote, the result was an astonishing success for Bukharin, whose plan received thirty-two votes. Trotsky's "neither war, nor peace" got sixteen votes. Lenin was outnumbered.

As the Bolsheviks were split, Trotsky's defeated proposals provided some basis for a meeting point for the different factions. The Commissar for Foreign Affairs returned to Brest-Litovsk and, not surprisingly, he was met by implacable German insistence. Abiding by the terms of his mandate, Trotsky was forced to break off all negotiations on 10th February, 1918. The atmosphere at the final session was bitter. The Germans lost their suave, patronising manner in a flash. This was not what they had come to Brest-Litovsk for, and they ordered the immediate resumption of hostilities. Their armies started to advance upon Petrograd, meeting no opposition from the empty Russian trenches. The logic of Lenin's peace position had become unassailable. There was no alternative. The Bolsheviks therefore took the heart-rending decision to capitulate. On 3rd March, 1918, the Soviet negotiators signed even more savage terms than those they had declined so recently.

The Treaty of Brest-Litovsk caused consternation amongst the Western Allies. The long winter of 1917-18 would be over in a few weeks and the weather would soon be suitable for the great German offensive upon the Allied positions. With the aid of the reinforcements that would be coming from the East, there would now be the strong possibility of a German break-through to Paris. Such was the appalling prospect arising out of the Russian capitulation— as seen from the West. From this dire anticipation was to stem the Allied intervention in the Russian Civil War, which was still going

23

on, as the Bolsheviks had not yet succeeded in establishing themselves in some parts of their vast country.

To be fair to them, the Bolsheviks were, at the time, also concerned to avoid appearing as the accessories of Germany's apparently approaching victory. They had, therefore, taken what steps they could in their pitifully weak bargaining position to get guarantees from Germany that German troops would not be transferred from one front to the other. Unfortunately for them—and for the Western Allies—they were in no position to back their arguments.

Immediately the Treaty was signed Germany proceeded to transfer two million men to the West. There were several theories in London, Washington and Paris as to how to deal with the situation. Some Western leaders considered active military intervention in Russia, in order to try to bring Russia back into the war. Others suggested military aid for those elements that were prepared to continue the war. Apart from efforts to keep Germany's Eastern forces diverted, there was also the problem of the considerable Allied dumps of military stores at Archangel and Vladivostok. Diplomatically, there was the further problem that the Western Allies did not recognise the Bolshevik Government and their missions had no formal contact.

As a consequence of the peculiar circumstances, the Allies relied more and more for their contacts with the Bolsheviks upon unofficial "agents," each of whom was a character whose story subsequently became part of the legend of the revolution. The American agent, Lieut.-Col. Raymond Robins, as he was then known, had been in command of the American Red Cross Commission to Russia. The Frenchman, Jacques Sadoul, had come to Russia as part of the French Military Mission. He was a Socialist who identified himself more and more with the Bolsheviks, and in later years he was to become a rigid Communist. Britain's man, Bruce Lockhart, had been the Acting Consul-General in Moscow. All three men were soon close to the Bolshevik leaders. None of the Western agents can be described as being in any way personally hostile towards the great political movements with which they now had to deal, and they were soon supporting the view that the best way of dealing with the problem of continuing the war against Germany was by working through—and not against—the new Bolshevik Government.

The first acts of Allied intervention in Russia, which in the instance were necessitated by the demands of the war, took place in circumstances of great confusion. In 1917, the British had a naval squadron stationed at Murmansk, where it had protected the supplies to the Archangel military store dump before the Russian collapse. After Russia's withdrawal from the war the British naval officers ashore established friendly relations with the socialist-controlled Murmansk Soviet, a body which became extremely alarmed by the danger of the Germans advancing upon the town and seizing it. So, with the collaboration of the Murmansk Soviet, the British took over the defence of the port.

The situation at the time was such that it was natural that there should be misunderstandings on all sides. For instance, the Murmansk Soviet received a telegram from Trotsky at the height of the Brest-Litovsk crisis: "You must accept any and all assistance from the Allied Missions and use every means to obstruct the advance of the plunderers." Even more astonishing, three months after the ratification of Brest-Litovsk, President Wilson in Washington had the impression that the Soviet Government had given its endorsement to the joint defence plans at Murmansk and was continuing to do so. In reality the situation was different, because the Soviet Government— now moved to Moscow—was both alarmed and angered by the Murmansk situation. Furthermore, they had apparently forgotten that they had condoned the arrangement in the first place.

Whilst the Allies—still thinking in military, and not political, terms—were considering what further steps they might take in the East to divert German forces from the Western Front, Britain sent a small force to strengthen her Murmansk unit. It landed on 23rd June, 1918. A group promptly set off on a railway train on the line going south to reconnoitre. About a hundred miles from Murmansk it met another train, laden with Soviet troops, coming north to assert Moscow's authority over the Murmansk Soviet. Discussions took place between the rival trains, made more difficult because the Red Commander seemed drunk. To the British the situation looked delicate. The British commander, taking no chances, promptly rounded up the Russian forces, and the two trains went south together. Two more trainloads of Moscow troops were met on the way, and they, too, were arrested by the British, who proceeded to secure the line as far south as Kem.

When news of these events reached Moscow, there was even greater anger amongst Lenin and his colleagues. Fiery telegrams passed between the heads of the Bolshevik Government and the Chairman of the Murmansk Soviet, a merchant seaman named Yureyev. Lenin personally warned Yureyev, and Yureyev replied: "It is all very well for you to talk that way, sitting there in Moscow." Yureyev then telegraphed to Trotsky's successor as Commissar for Foreign Affairs, Chicherin: "Comrade, has life not taught you to view things soberly? . . . If you know a way out of our condition, tell it to us." Chicherin replied angrily: "Tell the Admirals [meaning the British] who put you up to this that in the event of an armed intervention . . . they will encounter a popular uprising." Completely unmoved, Yureyev cabled back yet again: "You said that some sort of admirals put me up to this, but this is not true—they did nothing of the sort. . . . I can say that I have the impression that Count Mirbach [the German Ambassador in Moscow] is standing behind your back." Not surprisingly, it was the end of the Murmansk Soviet's relations with the Bolshevik Government. Yureyev was formally denounced as "an enemy of the people." "The Intervention" proper had started.

President Wilson, hesitant and bemused, was now persuaded to agree to an Allied expedition to Russia under British command. The British put forward the extraordinarily optimistic belief that they could recruit enough anti-Bolsheviks in the Murmansk-Archangel area to form an anti-Communist Russian force loyal to the Allies. They also considered, quite mistakenly, that the whole operation could be undertaken by a relatively small force. Without waiting for the Americans, they moved (together with some French troops that had arrived at Murmansk) upon Archangel on 2nd August, 1918, and took it. Simultaneously, another separate Allied intervention was taking place in Vladivostok. This had different origins. It began really out of an uprising of some thousands of Czech prisoners in Siberia who were in transit for Vladivostok and who were joined by Russian anti-Communist elements. As a result of the Czechs' initiative, Soviet authority in the area collapsed, to be replaced by anti-Bolshevik Russians led by Admiral Kolchak. And President Wilson, who had a sentimental attachment to the Czechs—he liked to patronise little peoples and admired Masaryk—decided upon a joint American-Japanese intervention in order to help the Czechs.

About eight thousand American troops were dispatched to Vladivostok, which, like Archangel, was at that time one vast Allied military dump. Japanese troops promptly joined in the venture for

separate reasons, unconnected with Wilson's idea of helping
the Czechs. At the back of Japanese thinking was really the idea
that Japan might in this way consolidate her position in Manchuria.
The American troops, together with the Japanese, took over the
railway line as far inland as Lake Baikal. Some skirmishes
took place with the Bolsheviks but the military encounters were
brief and limited—Masaryk's Czechs had, in fact, cleared the
way.

As soon as the British heard of Wilson's decision to intervene in
Siberia, orders were sent to Hong Kong to dispatch a battalion—
the 25th Battalion of the Middlesex Regiment—which was under
the command of a Labour M.P., Colonel John Ward.

The summer of 1918 drew to its conclusion. The German drive
for Paris was halted and turned back. As the Americans and
Japanese were establishing themselves and securing the eastern
section of the Trans-Siberian railway, the Great War ended. The
convulsions of popular feeling, stemming from the horrible carnage
in the trenches and the apparent pointlessness of all the war's
suffering which had first gripped Russia the year before, engulfed
Germany. The Kaiser, like the Tsar, was swept away. Imperial
Germany, like Imperial Russia, tottered and then crashed. And
the German Government that took its place was moderate—
socialist in outlook. Indeed, at first sight, it was not unlike the
Kerensky Government. The Bolsheviks, in particular Lenin,
promptly assumed that this was the unfolding of their cherished
dream of world revolution based upon Germany.

The ending of the war in November, 1918, brought the Allies to
the first watershed in their relations with the Bolshevik régime.
"The Intervention"—muddled and half-hearted as it had been—
no longer had its initial *raison d'être* of association with the war.
For the Bolsheviks it was a watershed too. Lenin and his colleagues
in Moscow now had the hope that the Allies would leave; and the
ending of the war had brought other blessings for the Communists.
The immediate consequence of the German defeat had been to
remove the threat of the German plans for the Ukraine and the
rest of the Brest-Litovsk Treaty's terms.

The Allied leaders who met at Versailles were disunited on the
issue of Russia. Lloyd George was strongly against proposals to
commit Western forces to a prolonged major campaign against the
Bolsheviks. Wilson, whose country had become involved in intervention in Russia by a series of reluctant or misconceived ventures,

was uncertain. Only Clemenceau remained implacable in his hostility towards the new Soviet régime.

As for the Soviet Government, it made repeated attempts to make contact with the Western statesmen, as the great men dispensed destiny in Paris. Most of these Soviet attempts to establish a channel of communication failed, partly because the Western leaders were reluctant to negotiate with the Bolsheviks, about whom they were at loggerheads themselves, and partly because of the effectiveness of the White Russian supporters at Versailles. These latter were untiring in their lobbying of the Western delegations in a manner that was to be repeated thirty years later by the "China Lobby" in the U.S.A. They spoke constantly of fictitious successes by the anti-Bolshevik forces in the Russian Civil War. And the Allies, uncertain as to their lines of action, took the easier course of sending arms and money to the White Russian leaders—Admiral Kolchak in the East and Generals Wrangel and Deniken in the South. The Bolsheviks, who knew that the White Russian forces could not survive without Allied help, nevertheless persevered in their attempts to come to some accommodation with the Allies. They offered considerable concessions, including an amnesty to all their White Russian opponents in the Civil War. These offers were turned down.

As the Versailles Peace Conference drew to its close, the White Russian successes also began to be questioned. Kolchak began to suffer major reverses. His decline became so rapid and catastrophic that it ended with his capture and execution, and no optimistic propaganda could overcome this last fact. Kolchak's collapse settled the fate of Allied intervention. One by one, the various Allied expeditionary forces were withdrawn. Those in the Archangel region and the French troops around Odessa were the first to go, in 1919. The Americans, operating from Vladivostok, left in the spring of 1920. The British Labour M.P., Colonel John Ward, who had been in command of the Middlesex Regiment, had left a little earlier—in mid-1919—but not before he had been so outraged by Communism as he saw it that he conducted a strenuous political tour through Siberia, addressing public meetings about Red iniquities to bewildered Russian audiences who did not understand English. The major reason for the Allied decision to withdraw was the fact that the expeditionary forces were manifestly inadequate for there to be any hope of success. These forces would have had to be reinforced very considerably for them to have made any real impact upon the situation in such a vast country, and the war-weary Allied Governments and peoples were not prepared to undertake this. The withdrawal did not stem from Allied military reverses, as subsequent Soviet legend has it, for they were few. Nor was it the result of any agreement with the new Soviet régime.

After the defeat of Kolchak's White Russian forces, military aid continued to be sent to Wrangel and Deniken, but gradually the Bolshevik Red Army, organised by Trotsky, established supremacy on that front also, as it had done against Kolchak. By the end of 1920 these White Russian ventures were defeated as well.

Since the Russian Revolution there has grown up a great folklore about "The Intervention", what happened at the time and the part that it is said to have played in the subsequent thinking and attitudes of the Soviet leaders. On the Communist side, "The Intervention" confirmed the worst suspicions about the attitudes of the capitalist powers towards the Bolshevik Revolution. It undoubtedly left scars upon the Soviet psychology that have been made indelible by the distorted history and propaganda of the passing years. And, in the short term, it led to the immediate re-doubling of Lenin's efforts to promote the wider revolution, in which he thought he saw the only real hope for the survival of the Russian Soviet State.

Even before the Allied intervention was over, practical plans for turning Russia into the base for the coming European revolution were in being. Lenin's first hope had been that the moderate Socialist régime that had taken over in Germany after the November revolution would develop rapidly into something akin to the Bolsheviks. He had particular faith in the left-wing section of the German Social Democratic party—the Spartacists—whose leaders, Karl Liebknecht and Rosa Luxemburg, started with views akin to his own. However, Lenin was quickly disillusioned by the German moderate Socialists. The left-wing Liebknecht-Luxemburg group, splitting from the Social Democrats, thereupon founded the German Communist party, upon which Lenin now pinned his hopes. There was also great excitement in Moscow when news was received of the establishment of left-wing régimes in Hungary and Bavaria. For a brief period, the Bolsheviks even contemplated sending troops to Hungary to support Bela Kun's revolution.

Lenin's hopes of favourable developments in Germany and Hungary were short-lived. The Hungarian régime collapsed within a matter of weeks. Disaster also struck the German Communists in

January, 1919, through abortive insurrection. A revolutionary group seized various public buildings in Berlin on 4th January and attempted a *coup d'état*. It was a weak and poorly organised rebellion that was easily put down by the German Army and an organisation known as the Free Corps, a forerunner of the Nazis. In the course of these events, Liebknecht and Rosa Luxemburg were clubbed to death by rifle butts and their bodies dumped in the Landwehr canal. Finally, as if this were not enough, Eisner, who was leader of the Communist movement in Bavaria and the first Prime Minister of Bavaria after the German November revolution, was assassinated, and his régime disintegrated rapidly.

Lenin now took another step of far-reaching importance. He had decided earlier to create a special body for the promotion of his concept of the world revolution. Indeed, ever since the Second International, he had been determined upon this course, as he saw this as the only way to bring the World Communist movement under his personal control. Accordingly, the Bolsheviks summoned a founding congress for a Third International to meet in Moscow in March, 1919. It was not a propitious moment. Kolchak's forces were still advancing. The Bolsheviks controlled only parts of Russia. They were largely cut off from the rest of Europe. Before the congress could meet, Liebknecht and Luxemburg had been murdered. The result was that, out of the thirty-eight "delegates" attending the congress, thirty-six consisted of Russians, or foreigners resident in Russia. And only two had managed to make the hazardous journey from the outside world. One of these was Eberlein, the representative of the German Communist party. He had been instructed by Luxemburg to vote against the establishment of a Third International, really because Luxemburg profoundly distrusted Lenin's basic idea. But with Luxemburg's death, the one voice of opposition to Lenin from any Communist of international standing had now been stilled and Eberlein allowed himself to be won over. In this way the Communist International (or Comintern) came into being. A vital point was that all its decisions were binding upon all the parties who belonged to it. The reason was obvious—it provided Lenin with direct control of the World Communist movement that he had been determined to achieve. And in later years, the Comintern was to become a significant vehicle for Russian external policies.

This, then, was the situation as Lenin sat in his room in the Kremlin Palace of Justice, faced by the realities of governing a country that was exhausted by world war, followed by civil war. The task before him was immense.

The Bolshevik régime had to meet three major crises. First, there was a grave shortage of food. A combination of war, drought, and Marxist agricultural theory had resulted in a disastrous harvest. Millions were in danger of starvation. Secondly, Lenin, the practical man, realised that his régime needed foreign credits and trade in order to rebuild its industrial life. Here, his major obstacle was international confidence and the recognition of his government. He could see that there was no short cut to either of these ends readily at hand. Finally, there was growing disillusion amongst Russian workers with the Revolution itself. Hardships and ruthless political dictatorship that the Russian masses had accepted in civil war or when the régime was being threatened by "Foreign Imperialists" could no longer command the same unquestioning obedience.

Though Lenin was now in command of the Russian ship of State, his crew was untrained and the seas mountainous—and the great hulk was still very unseaworthy. It was a prospect to daunt the bravest and ablest man. Lenin was brave, dauntless and able.

CHAPTER 2

SOCIALISM IN ONE COUNTRY

A State without a nation, an army without a country, a religion without a God.
T. R. Fyvel

It is difficult now to recall the searing tragedy of the great famine that swept Soviet Russia almost as soon as the civil war was over. Travellers from the West described how they saw mile upon mile of fields burnt dry by the blazing rays of the sun. At almost every railway station on the line from the West, crowds of sick and starving men and women stretched out their hands and implored help in the name of Christ. Desperate people wandered across the country in packs in search of food, disease travelling with them as their constant companion. An epidemic of superstition swept the Russian people. In the night, women would plough furrows around their villages to the accompaniment of incantations, or leap naked over heaps of burning wood, in the belief that the cholera would not pass through fire, or over furrows, into their villages.

It was, in addition, a terrible and bitter awakening for Lenin and his new government whose original promise to the Russian people had been embodied in the Bolshevik slogan, "Peace, Land, Bread." Lenin was forced under pressure to promulgate his so-called New Economic Policy—the "N.E.P." Major concessions were made by him to private enterprise on the grounds that they represented a tactical retreat in order to make a future advance.

It is true that one major reason for the famine itself was the cruel drought. Yet everybody knew that there was another and more important reason for the tragic situation. It was the Bolshevik's attempt to reform agriculture; which in its turn stemmed from the farming theories of Marx, the townsman. The principle of collectivisation—or farming co-operatives—was resisted fiercely by the millions of individualistic peasantry and small farmers. They refused to co-operate, and food production fell as a result.

At first, Lenin was most unwilling to admit the existence of the food crisis. Yet, as the famine extended, there could be no hiding the magnitude of the human disaster. Nevertheless, the Bolshevik authorities themselves would not acknowledge the farming failure or appeal directly in their own name for help from the Western nations. They preferred to cause appeals to be issued through the mouths of famous Russian intellectuals such as Maxim Gorky or the ballerina, Anna Pavlova.

Fridtjof Nansen, the Norwegian explorer and humanist, appeared before the League of Nations at Geneva to reinforce these Russian appeals. Addressing the General Assembly he said: "I do not think that you will strengthen the Soviet Government by showing the Russian people that there are hearts in Europe. . . . But supposing it does strengthen the Soviet Government," he asked, "is there any member of this Assembly who is prepared to say that rather than help the Soviet Government he will allow twenty millions of people to starve to death? I challenge this Assembly to answer the question!" This great European thereupon carried his appeal out to the public on a massive lecture tour, evoking an amazing response of goodwill from the Western peoples. For example, when he came to Manchester Nansen was met by an audience of several thousands. The Free Trade Hall, with its associations with Cobden and Bright, was packed. Overflow meetings were organised hurriedly. Nansen told his story without emotion in his harsh Norse voice "with one hand in his pocket, in severe English. . . . After his introduction, most of the lecture was given in the dark while slides and films were shown on the screen. Here and there was the sound of sobbing." By the following week-end, the readers of the *Manchester Guardian* had subscribed £30,000 in the currency of the day. The story is indeed a manifest refutation of the allegations of implacable Western hostility that have now become the accepted pattern of Soviet history.

Nevertheless, by far the most important response to Russia's plight had to come from governmental level—private generosity could never be enough. The United States Government, despite its reservations about the political nature of Bolshevism, led the way in help—as it was to do again, over twenty years later, at the time of Lend-Lease. The American Relief Administration under the direction of Herbert Hoover, a future United States President, co-ordinated and administered most of the funds that were provided. Eventually, Hoover had over 18,000 soup kitchens or feeding stations operating all over Russia. It was estimated that his Relief Administration's efforts alone were responsible for saving eleven million people. When these and other efforts came to an end, the Bolsheviks formally expressed appreciation of the great services rendered by Americans and the other Western countries, but more recently the story has been twisted by Soviet historians who now describe these rescue operations as a massive attempt by the capitalists to penetrate the Soviet Union and overthrow the Revolution.

Lenin's next problem in 1920—it was one that had been with him from the outset—was foreign credit to make possible his plans for industrial expansion. He needed international recognition, for credits and recognition went hand in hand. Further, these problems were all interconnected with the basic decision of what to do about Russia's foreign debts, arising partly from the war and partly from the Bolsheviks' confiscation of large foreign holdings inside Russia.

The Bolsheviks' task was eased by one accident of history. The British Prime Minister of the day, David Lloyd George, happened to be the first man from the working classes ever to hold his office. And although Lloyd George had travelled a very long way from the humble shoemaker's cottage at Llanystymdwy, and was now the leader of a Tory coalition, he still retained his basic radicalism and his sense of identification with under-privileged peoples. Here was a man who was certainly not prepared to support a policy that was intended permanently to isolate the Soviet State. Lloyd George, however, had his difficulties. Apart from having to carry his Tory colleagues with him, he had to contend with the resistance created even amongst open-minded Liberals by Lenin's concept of world revolution and use of the Comintern as an instrument of Russian foreign policy—they were such surprising departures from all previous codes of international behaviour. In Western eyes, the use of a particular political party—the Communist Party—in another country to further the aims of one's own foreign policy and to appeal over the heads of that country's recognised leaders was an offence against the accepted codes of patriotism. Yet, seen from the other side, the Soviets saw no reason why they should adopt the conventions of capitalist diplomacy in order to help sustain capitalism and hold back world revolution.[1]

[1] The preamble to the Soviet Constitution, laying down the preconceptions of Soviet foreign policy as seen by Lenin and his colleagues, shows most clearly

There was still another difficulty. Lloyd George's determination to give the emerging Russian Government and people a chance was complicated by the Bolshevik concept of the purposes of trade. The straightforward slogan "Business is business" had no place in the Communist mind. To the Communists, all things had to have a political purpose. Of course, Lenin wanted trade for economic reasons. But he saw trade primarily as a political instrument and proposed so to use it, in order to obtain political recognition.[1]

Despite these various problems, Lloyd George persisted with his intentions. As early as 8th November, 1919, he made a speech at the Guildhall commending the end of the Intervention, which had caused a sensation. Next, he persuaded the Allied Supreme Council to lift the prolonged economic blockade of Russia on 16th January, 1920. As Lloyd George's aims unfolded, there was a mounting crescendo of bitter opposition from British Conservative circles, and it says much for the intrepid skill and inner conviction of the Prime Minister—completely dependent as he was upon the Tory Party in Parliament—that he did not deviate from his course.

Finally, when a Soviet delegation, led by Krassin, arrived in London in May, 1920, and was received by Lloyd George personally, the political atmosphere was so charged with suspicion that a satirical editorial appeared in the *Manchester Guardian*: "The

---

how the Bolsheviks viewed all international affairs. It states: "Since the time of the formation of the Soviet republics, the States of the world have been divided into two camps—the camp of capitalism and the camp of socialism.

"There—in the camp of capitalism—national enmity and inequality, colonial slavery and chauvinism, national oppressions and pogroms, imperialist brutalities and wars.

"Here—in the camp of socialism—mutual confidence and peace and the brotherly collaboration of peoples."

[1] A set of instructions for Soviet foreign trade delegations signed by Bukharin illustrated the Bolshevik view. "Trade interests must always serve the interests of Communist propaganda . . ." stated Bukharin. "The Soviet Government proposes to its foreign representatives to enter into negotiations with foreign firms on the question of commercial contracts. In all negotiations . . . the question of a State guarantee should always be raised before the order is acknowledged. (Note this point should always be raised at the end of the negotiations.) Bearing in mind the fact that none of the Great Powers has recognised the Soviet Government, no guarantee could ever be given and the foreign capitalists concerned will have to refuse the orders. Simultaneously, special Communist comrades should agitate in the factories and amongst the workers of the firms concerned, explaining to them that their owners have refused large orders from Russia because their governments do not want to trade with Russia."

blow has fallen. A Bolshevist real-life representative of Lenin has spoken with the British Prime Minister face to face. A being upon two legs and bearing the outward appearance of a man was seen to approach 10 Downing Street yesterday, to ring the door and gain admission. Mr. Lloyd George has seen him and lives. Not only does he live but he motored off afterwards to help enthrone an archbishop. We trust that the archbishop will receive a double portion of archiepiscopal anointment to avert the evil influence." And Churchill, who had refused to meet Krassin, speaking privately to Curzon, the Foreign Secretary, a few hours after the interview with Krassin, asked with a grimace: "Did you shake the hairy hand of the baboon?"

The Anglo-Soviet negotiations were hard, despite Lloyd George's goodwill. There were profound suspicions on both sides. After nearly a year of argument and recrimination in London, an Anglo-Soviet trade agreement was signed on 16th March, 1921, granting, in effect, *de facto* but not *de jure* recognition of the Soviet Government by Britain. Debts and claims were postponed for a permanent settlement that was to come later. Significantly, there was a clause barring "official propaganda" by the two countries against the institutions of the other. Unofficial representations were also exchanged. It was a major event, coming as it did in the midst of all the economic misery and famine then sweeping the Soviet Union.

Soviet-German relations had also been developing. They had moved a long way from the point at which Imperial Germany had collapsed, and Lenin had been sitting in his book-lined room in the Kremlin awaiting the second German revolution that would replace what he considered to be Germany's "Kerensky Government" of Social Democrats. By 1921, Lenin was beginning to realise that his hopes of a German Communist government would not mature overnight. Meanwhile, for the Germans, smarting and humiliated by the attitudes of the Allies, new prospects were also dawning. They had started to realise the advantages there could be in German-Soviet co-operation, if both countries were going to live in a world of implacable Allied hostility.

Thus there then began, quite early, an important period of German-Soviet harmony. Trotsky, who was Commissar for War at the time, appreciated the German needs for certain military arrangements. With the agreement of Lenin and his principal colleagues, he put out feelers. The Germans responded, and eventually a German military mission was dispatched to Moscow. Complementary military training arrangements were developed, with the Germans providing the technical experience and the Soviets making available the training grounds, far from the prying eyes of the Allies. The Germans under this arrangement even built a Junkers aircraft factory in the Moscow suburb of Fili. Considerable secrecy covered the clandestine Soviet-German projects. And, paradoxically, these Soviet-German military arrangements, that continued for several months, even after Hitler seized power in 1933, were used by Stalin to form part of a massive indictment against Trotsky and alleged Trotskyists.

The second facet of Soviet-German co-operation—the political— was much slower to develop. At first, the President of the Weimar Republic, Ebert, would have nothing to do with the suggestion. But a German pressure group known as "The Easterners" sprang up. And, eventually, the next German Administration cautiously came round to more of a pro-Russian attitude during the winter of 1921-2.

The climate was now propitious for a historic event. It came about in a curious way. Partly on Lloyd George's initiative, the two great "Outsiders" of Europe—Germany and the Soviet Union —had been invited to an international economic conference to be held at Genoa in April, 1922. For the Allies it was to be an important departure, but unfortunately the prospects for the conference suffered a setback when the French Government vetoed any discussion of reparations—at that time the major issue of European economic rehabilitation. This left little to discuss at the conference, except the economic problem of Soviet Russia.

As a preliminary there had been talk of a "consortium" to rescue Russia, but the prospect had frightened Lenin, who feared it implied another form of the Intervention. He and his colleagues had, therefore, arranged for the Soviet delegation led by Chicherin, the Commissar for Foreign Affairs, to break its journey in Berlin for political talks with the Germans. During this brief halt, Chicherin persuaded the Germans to draft headings for a Soviet-German political agreement, although the Germans refused to sign it in advance of the Genoa Conference.

Chicherin's tactics in his opening speech at the conference were skilful. Lenin, he recalled, had already offered concessions to foreign interests in order to develop the natural resources of the Soviet Union. He continued: "The Russian Government is ready

37

to open its frontier deliberately and voluntarily for international transit trade, to grant for cultivation millions of acres of fertile land, to grant rich timber, coal and mining concessions. . . ." One might have concluded that the Soviet Union was opening its doors freely. In fact, it was only a manœuvre of Lenin's, still obsessed by his belief that the Allies would intervene again in Russia. Lenin's intention, with this offer, was to establish a lobby of foreign capitalists with their interests committed to the maintenance of the Soviet Government who had granted them their concessions. At this point, the French and British delegations played into Chicherin's hands. France had been persistently obstinate about Germany. And now, together with the British, the French began private talks with the Soviet delegation, deliberately excluding the Germans. It was a fatal blunder. There were other miscalculations, too, all of which substantiated Chicherin's submission to Walter Rathenau, the German Foreign Minister, that a Soviet-British-French alignment was imminent. By these means, Chicherin manœuvred Rathenau into accepting the agreement that the Germans had hitherto regarded so reluctantly.

The Treaty of Rapallo—so named because it was signed at Rapallo upon Easter Sunday, 16th April, 1922—exploded upon Allied opinion as the first warning shot that could signify the opening of the Second World War. When Ribbentrop and Molotov penned their signatures to another Soviet-German pact seventeen years later, many said that the processes of history that are more continuous than commentators and politicians sometimes concede had already been sketched out in the pattern first established at Rapallo. The Treaty was innocuous in itself. It agreed to the exchange of ambassadors and the establishment of normal relations. Its significance was that it broke the ring—for both countries—of universal hostility and accorded to each a greater flexibility in foreign policy.

For a brief period, until the end of 1923, Soviet-German political relations were exceedingly close. They underwent a change when the Streseman Government in Germany abandoned the passive resistance policy towards the Allied occupation of the Ruhr and sought to create a better atmosphere towards the Allied Powers. The Soviet leaders thereupon reverted to their familiar general practice of using the local Communist party as the specific instrument of Russian foreign policy, and encouraged the German Communist party to undertake a further armed uprising against the

German State in October, 1923. The armed revolt was easily put down but the effect was a severe shock to the intimate political relations that had grown up since Rapallo, although the military co-operation remained unimpaired. Gradually, with patience, the links were mended again, but they never achieved the same strength and warmth as they had in 1922 and early 1923.

At home the Soviet Government was under constant strain. In May, 1922, Lenin, overworked and tired, had a stroke and he did not return to work until the end of November. Meanwhile, he had appointed Stalin General Secretary of the Communist party, much to the resentment of Trotsky, who was so angry that he declined Lenin's well-intentioned proposal to appoint him his own formal deputy. Although he apparently made a remarkable recovery, Lenin was never again the same driving force that he had been in the early days of Soviet power. The following year he was again stricken. Finally, he became paralysed, and he died after a long illness on 21st January, 1924.

The effect of Lenin's illness and death upon the course of Soviet policy will always be a question mark. Coming at that particular time, it certainly facilitated the accumulation of power in Stalin's hands and the downfall of Trotsky. During the months of Lenin's decline, Stalin had been steadily gathering in the reins of power, while the behaviour of Trotsky had served to strengthen Stalin's position.

For all his remarkable talents, Trotsky was a person of many deficiencies. Where Lenin was attractive, Trotsky was antipathetic. Trotsky's bristling crop of black hair, his feverish gaze, intensified by his eyeglasses, and his fierce, abrupt gestures, showed his brittle personality. The spacious and sumptuous office in which he used to sit—in such marked contrast to Lenin's unpretentious surroundings—added to the image of an imperious man. He was an easy target for Stalin, and in the week immediately before Lenin's death severe criticism of Trotsky was openly expressed at the party's Thirteenth Congress. As Lenin lay critically ill, Trotsky, himself not well, had left for a holiday in the south. He heard of Lenin's death only from the coded telegram Stalin sent him as his train was in a siding at Tiflis. It was a deeply personal blow. "Lenin is no more," he said. "The words fall upon our minds as a giant rock falls into the sea." Yet the puzzling fact is that Trotsky did not return at once to Moscow, and Stalin shrewdly advised him that there was no need for him to do so.

Meanwhile those who had waited in the endless queue to pass by Lenin's body as it lay in state recalled that it was impossible not to feel the extraordinary warmth with which he had come to be regarded and the pride of everyone who had been able to claim that he had actually seen him. For over a year he had dragged out his slow days in a living death. Now the bowl was broken and he was gone.

The new leader, Stalin, was a very different personality from either Lenin or Trotsky. Whereas Lenin had been a man of compelling brilliance, familiar with the languages and traditions of Western Europe, always ready to indulge in argument and dialectic, Stalin's main experience had been in organisation in the underground movement in Russia itself. He knew little of the outside world. He was by nature and training a cautious, suspicious and conspiratorial man. In manner, he also gave the impression of secretiveness. Stalin was only too conscious of his lack of stature within the world Communist movement, and for this reason he feared and disliked Trotsky in particular—as he was later to fear and dislike any other form of dialectical debate or deviation, including Titoism. His character led him always to seek to divide his enemies by oblique means rather than by direct confrontation. His strength lay in his quality of controlled courage and in his remarkable abilities as an organiser and master of detail.

Almost simultaneously with Lenin's illness and death there were changes in the political leadership of Britain. Lloyd George fell from power and he was replaced by a Tory administration led by Bonar Law.

Baldwin succeeded Bonar Law and was defeated at a General Election in December, 1923.

Ramsay Macdonald was now called upon to form the first minority Labour Government in British history, and Macdonald was committed already to granting *de jure* recognition to the Soviet Union. From the first, the British Labour Party had been sympathetic towards the Soviet Union, though it had never met with reciprocity. Instead, the Bolsheviks had always been particularly scathing about British democratic socialists. Trotsky had once called Macdonald "a banker's clerk" and the official Soviet Press had been consistently and bitterly hostile. *Izvestia* had even pronounced the comprehensive judgment: "The Labour Party includes such undesirables as persons professing religious convictions, Anglicans, Catholics and members of various sects, also Privy

Counsellors and Colonel John Ward." Nevertheless, Macdonald was not to be diverted. He formally announced *de jure* recognition of the Soviet Union on 2nd February, 1924.

The British step began a diplomatic avalanche. Italy followed suit on 8th February. A number of other countries, including Japan and France, did likewise within the year. But not the United States of America; that country was still most hostile towards the activities of the Comintern and the Soviet Government's failure to meet Imperial Russia's debts and the claims for American-owned property that had been seized by the Bolsheviks. Following *de jure* recognition, Britain invited Russia to send a delegation to London to discuss certain outstanding issues, including the settlement of claims. Macdonald opened the conference at 11.30 a.m. on 14th April, 1924, at the Foreign Office with the words: "Our first duty will be the liquidation of the past." But events were to belie his good intentions. Bargaining over the Russian debts was hard and protracted. Pressure groups developed. Eventually an emasculated Anglo-Soviet Treaty was signed and laid before Parliament.

In October of that same year, the Labour Government fell. It was defeated over a quite separate issue, but the whole Russian issue was injected into the General Election by the famous "Zinoviev Letter."[1] The situation could not have been more embarrassing for Macdonald and his colleagues, already on the defensive against the Conservative charges of weakness towards Communism.

Baldwin's new administration indicated at once that it did not intend to proceed to ratify the Anglo-Soviet Treaty—all the previous year's work having come to nothing. Relations between Britain and Russia now deteriorated rapidly, till the crisis of the Arcos incident of 12th May, 1927. This was a raid by the British police

---

[1] The true facts behind the Zinoviev Letter have never been established. On 24th October, 1924, in the midst of the Election, the head of the Northern Department of the British Foreign Office, J. D. Gregory—it is not clear whether he was acting on Macdonald's instructions—addressed a sharp note to the Soviet Chargé d'Affaires in London, protesting against a letter alleged to have been written by Zinoviev, the head of the Comintern, to the British Communist Party.

The letter, already published in the *Daily Mail*, was supposed to have been written by Zinoviev, and was savagely critical of the British Labour leaders. It instructed the British Communists to establish cells in the armed forces and to promote revolutionary action. Subsequently both Macdonald and the Soviet Government stated the letter had been a forgery and no original was ever produced.

41

upon the premises of Arcos Ltd., an official Soviet trading company, and also upon the offices of the Soviet Trade Delegation housed in the same building. The British Government accepted responsibility, agreeing that the raid had been carried out only after consultations amongst the Home Secretary, the Foreign Secretary and the Prime Minister. Later statements in Parliament by the Home Secretary, Joynson-Hicks, and by Baldwin made vague accusations of the premises being used for political conspiracies, but no substantive evidence appears to have been discovered. Nevertheless, Britain proceeded on 26th May, 1927, to sever all official relations with the Soviet Union, and these relations were not to be resumed until Labour was once more back in office after the 1929 General Election.

What were the factors motivating Soviet foreign policy as it had developed thus far? The basic formula ever since Lenin's day had been the incompatibility of the two worlds—capitalist and socialist —which made the worst conflict inevitable. Stalin, every bit as much as Lenin and Trotsky, believed that one day the capitalist world would be forced to wage war upon the Russian citadel of revolution. The guiding thought behind Chicherin's diplomatic manœuvres was constantly to postpone the day of armed attack until such time as the Soviet Union would be strong enough to withstand it. A reading of the columns of *Pravda* over this period shows that these were times when the Bolshevik leaders were seemingly in almost daily fear of the outbreak of war.

Chicherin, isolated by the major Western Powers, had promoted a series of treaties with Russia's immediate neighbours—amongst them, the Baltic States of Latvia and Estonia, to undermine the leadership of Poland; in the Near East with Turkey and Persia; further afield with Afghanistan. His intention was to establish a *glacis* of defence in the event of war. The old French concept of the *cordon sanitaire* in reverse was clearly in his mind. In the mid-1920s, Stalin, Chicherin and later Chicherin's successor, Litvinov, also became increasingly concerned at the prospects of growing rapprochement between Streseman's Germany and the Western powers. They were particularly alarmed at moves to bring Germany into the League of Nations and by the Locarno Treaties of 1925, which guaranteed Germany's western frontiers and provided for mutual security arrangements amongst France, Poland and Czechoslovakia. In this spirit, Chicherin embarked upon a policy of offers and threats in secret talks with German representatives. At one stage, he offered a full-scale Soviet-German alliance directed specifically against Poland in terms that had a later parallel in the Molotov-Ribbentrop pact. But Streseman refused to allow himself to be deflected from his purpose, though he made some lesser concessions to Soviet pressures.

But France was once more instrumental in getting Chicherin out of his difficulty. Supported by Poland, France vetoed Germany's entry into the League of Nations. And Streseman thereupon agreed to the so-called Berlin Treaty of 25th April, 1926, which specifically recalled the Rapallo Pact, and provided for neutrality if either Russia or Germany were attacked.

The year 1927 saw the launching of the first Soviet Five-Year Plan. It also marked the beginning of a period of Soviet withdrawal into relative isolation and the reduction of external activity by the Comintern. It indicated Stalin's growing preoccupation with internal and economic problems. Soon he was to be involved, deeply and irrevocably, in the great and ruthless drive for collectivisation, which compelled over a hundred million peasants to leave the land and which drove millions of Russians to school to be taught to read and write. The enormous benefits of Soviet industrialisation were to be proved a generation later. Yet, at the time, the cost in misery and suffering was to be tremendous. Millions endured terrible hardships to build blast furnaces and great steelworks. Tens of thousands died in the process. Stalin drove relentlessly on. Finally, the tragedy was to reach out into his own home in November, 1932, when his wife, Nadia Alliluyeva, committed suicide.

The period from Lenin's death until the early 1930s has come to be associated with the doctrine of *Socialism in one country*. It was a stage in Soviet development during which Stalin gradually reversed Lenin's *New Economic Policy*—the tactical retreat by easement after the economic disasters of the Intervention and civil war. It was during this period too that the personal conflict with Trotsky passed the point of no return, and Stalin, crushing all other opposition, turned the Soviet Communist party from the autocracy of Lenin's day, in which some discussion of issues had been permitted at the top, into a monolithic Stalinist tyranny.

Stalin himself advanced the doctrine of *Socialism in one country* as part of the indictment of Trotsky. Hitherto no leading Soviet personality had questioned Lenin's earlier belief that the success of the

43

Russian revolution would be dependent upon widening the Communist base in Europe. Indeed this had been the justification for the activities of the Comintern and the support that was given to the abortive uprising in Germany. Stalin had also committed himself, in lectures on the *Foundations of Leninism* in 1924 to the view that the final victory of the Russian revolution was conditional upon world revolution.

In early 1925 it had become apparent even to the most optimistic Communists in the Kremlin that the prospects for other revolutions in Europe were receding. Equally, despite the absence of international support, the Russian revolution had survived. In these circumstances, and in order to address himself to the great tasks before him inside Russia, Stalin's case for going back upon the thesis of his 1924 lectures was valid and understandable. In fact, he did not repudiate the idea of world revolution at all and held to this basic belief to the end of his life. Instead he developed the thought that Russia should first be fortified as the citadel of the world revolution, in order to support any advances at a later stage.

Trotsky, on the other hand, accused Stalin of giving up the aim of world revolution. His contention that the Russian revolution was thereby betrayed by the right wing of the Soviet Communist party, led by Stalin, became an obsession with him. In truth, there was less theoretical difference between Trotsky and Stalin than one would now suppose and their real differences were more of temperament. Trotsky did not reject *Socialism in one country*, any more than Stalin rejected the world revolution. It was really a matter of priority—in Stalin's view the establishment of socialism in Russia must come first; and in Trotsky's opinion the world revolution took precedence.

Gradually, Stalin's view prevailed. Stripped of all his offices, Trotsky was finally expelled from the Communist Party on 14th November, 1927, and he spent his later years in exile until he was murdered in 1940, in Mexico City, by one of Stalin's agents.

The second great upheaval of this period took place at the Sixth Congress of the Comintern in 1928 when the so-called "right opposition" to the speed of industrialisation was crushed and Bukharin was stripped of his influence. From this point onwards there was no free discussion, either inside the Soviet Communist Party or in any of the world Communist parties. The Stalinist bureaucratic revolution of 1927-8 led directly to the collectivisation famine of the 1930s, the great purge, the Molotov-Ribbentrop Pact and to the situation in 1946 in which total world war became a possibility. Thus Stalin had seized complete power and the wishful thinkers in the West who discussed, from time to time, whether the Soviet Union was becoming less or more liberal, completely missed the point. Whatever tactical shifts of policy there were subsequently, the Soviet Union had become a totalitarian state.

Yet it seemed, during this early period of Stalin's growing supremacy, that the problems of Soviet-Western relations had reached the point of being gradually resolved. We now know the most desperate decade in the history of European diplomacy was only about to begin.

CHAPTER 3

STALIN'S SECRET DECISION

I know the German nation loves its Führer; I should, therefore, like to drink his health.
Joseph Stalin

Hitler came to power on 30th January, 1933.[1] A strange creature stood in the place of the dead Weimar Republic, the like of whose countenance mankind had never before seen. Before the creature lay dead, burning amongst the ruins of Berlin twelve years later, a world war had to be fought. And Stalin was as slow as anybody to grasp the significance of the event that had taken place in Berlin on that January day. Indeed, the Soviet leader actually welcomed Hitler's seizure of power. He regarded it as a victory over the German Social Democracy which was the principal obstacle to the success of the German Communist Party in his thinking. Soviet-German relations continued largely as before. Soviet foreign policy remained on its previous course, suspicious of and defensively hostile to the Western democracies.

The Comintern, taking note of the way in which the German Communist Party had joined with the Nazis against the Social Democrats at the critical period of Hitler's advance to power, passed the following resolution in Moscow on 1st April, 1933: "The Praesidium of the Executive Committee of the Communist International, having heard the report on the situation in Germany, declares that the policy carried out by the Executive Committee of the Communist Party of Germany . . . up to and during the time of the Hitlerite coup was absolutely correct." There was a reason for the Comintern's resolution. The Communist Party of Germany had already virtually ceased to exist soon after Hitler's accession. Hitler had staged a barefaced operation on the night of 27th February. By some means, that remain in doubt to this day, the

---

[1] A vivid account of the occasion and of the events leading up to it are given by Alan Bullock: *Hitler, A Study in Tyranny.*

great Reichstag building had been set on fire. A crazed Dutch Communist named Van der Lubbe had been found in the building. Hitler had at once used the Reichstag fire as the excuse to attack the Communist Party, and from that moment on it had become, in effect, a proscribed body. Constitutionally, he was unable to prevent it from putting forward candidates in the March elections, held immediately after he had become Chancellor, yet the Communist deputies who were elected were never permitted to take their seats. A month after the Comintern meeting, on 26th May, 1933, Hitler ordered the occupation of the Communist Party's buildings, and the confiscation of all its assets. And the German Communist Party thus extinguished, as a result of the policy it had followed on Stalin's instructions, it was essential for the Comintern to pass its exonerating resolution as quickly as possible.

There is a simple answer to the riddle as to why Stalin condoned Hitler's coup—Russian self-interest. Although Stalin saw the German Communist Party being destroyed before his eyes, he considered that it was to his advantage to continue to maintain Soviet Russia's good relations with the new Nazi Government, and indeed to improve them, as the earlier goodwill had evaporated somewhat in the last days of the Weimar Republic. The Soviet Government summed it up thus: "In spite of their attitude towards Fascism, the people of the U.S.S.R. wish to live in peace with Germany and consider that the development of German-Soviet relations is in the interests of both countries." Litvinov stated the same point in even clearer terms in an address to the C.P.S.U. Central Committee on 29th September, 1933: "We of course sympathise with the sufferings of our German comrades, but we Marxists are the last who can be reproached with allowing our feelings to dictate our policy." In that sentence of Litvinov's there is a lesson to all those well-meaning Westerners who, failing completely to understand the Communist mind, have toadied to Soviet officials in the belief that in this way they are improving East-West relations. Similarly, these same misguided people have never understood that the Communist mind is perpetually preoccupied and fascinated by power and largely indifferent to other considerations.

Soviet-German trade at this time proved an interesting political barometer. Exports to Germany, as a proportion of total Soviet exports, went up from 17.3 per cent in 1933 to 23.4 per cent in 1934.

The 1929 British Labour Government had re-established relations with the Soviet Union, and by 1933 the only remaining great power that had declined to recognise the Soviet Union was the United States. At the root, the reason was America's hostility to all that the Soviet Government represented in the world. There were also the practical problems of debt settlement between the U.S.A. and the U.S.S.R., similar to those which had been faced by the British Government twelve years before.

Franklin Roosevelt, who took office as American President in 1933, had a very different approach to international affairs compared with his Republican predecessors. To some extent Roosevelt—despite his upper-class background—was the American equivalent to Lloyd George. He had similar generous sympathies and he operated, at times, in the same way, relying upon his own charm and personality to overcome obstacles and opponents. The first informal Soviet-American contacts took place at the Soviet Embassy in London during the 1933 World Economic Conference called to consider the great slump. Finally, after letters had passed between Kalinin and Roosevelt, Litvinov travelled to Washington in November, 1933. There was an unhappy exchange at the outset of negotiations, but an agreement was reached on 16th November involving a decision by the United States Government to recognise the Soviet Union. In this agreement Roosevelt insisted that Litvinov sign a mutual pledge on hostile propaganda. The debt negotiations were left over for later discussion, as were those with Britain.

Stalin, through his mouthpiece, Litvinov, now turned his attention to the League of Nations. He was fully aware of the relative unimportance of United States recognition. Nor, it must always be remembered, was the United States even a member of the League of Nations. This, in itself, restricted the U.S. role in international politics. By this time—early 1934—Stalin was also beginning to have second thoughts about Hitler, now firmly in power. He had received reports of talks by the Nazis about the Ukraine as the area of possible German *Lebensraum*. This could only mean one thing: Hitler was bent on rejecting the traditional German policy since Rapallo.

In this new and developing attitude Stalin was helped, to a considerable extent, by France; in particular by the policy of the French Foreign Minister, Louis Barthou. Barthou's original plan, conceived before his approach to Stalin, had been to establish an Eastern Pact to guarantee the existing frontiers in the area of Eastern Europe, grouping together Germany, Russia, Czechoslovakia, Poland and the Baltic States on the basis of a guarantee by France of the European borders of Russia, and by Russia of the Eastern frontiers of Germany. Unfortunately, both Poland and Germany opposed this proposal and Barthou was forced to drop it. So Barthou concentrated upon Stalin and here he met with a different reception.

As a preliminary to a Franco-Soviet Pact, Barthou secured the admission of the Soviet Union to the League of Nations as part of his pattern of collective security. It was a historic moment when Litvinov arrived at the Palais des Nations. Immediately the Soviet Minister was at home. He spoke its language. He soon established himself at Geneva as one of the League's outstanding figures. Stalin could not have had a better advocate in the great international forum of the 1930s.

Barthou then proceeded with the proposal for a Franco-Soviet pact as a mutual guarantee against aggression. What might have developed yet further is only a matter for conjecture because on 9th October, 1934, Barthou was assassinated.

It was a cruel blow to the policies for which Barthou stood and it was made all the worse because Barthou was succeeded by Pierre Laval, who profoundly distrusted Soviet Russia and who had also regarded Britain as a worthless ally. But Stalin had gone too far in his new thinking on Soviet foreign policy to be deterred by Laval. By now he had decided upon a major change in Soviet policy—the result of his realisation of Hitler's true significance. For his part, Laval was concerned not to disclose his long-term intentions too quickly, and so he continued with Barthou's overtures towards the Soviet Union. He signed a protocol in December, 1934, with Litvinov, at Geneva, pledging the two governments to continue with their efforts to create the Eastern Pact, and Western optimism ran high.[1]

Negotiations for the Franco-Soviet Pact went on through the early months of 1935. In April, Litvinov had to return home for consultations with Stalin and the negotiations were continued between Laval and Potemkin, the Soviet Ambassador to France, who successfully concluded the process. The Franco-Soviet Pact itself was signed by Laval and Potemkin on 2nd May, 1935. The central point of the Franco-Soviet Treaty and the main issue of controversy in the 1938 Czech crisis that reached its watershed at Munich was Article 2. This said: "In the event of France or

[1] For a detailed account of Laval's policies, see H. Torres, *Pierre Laval*.

the U.S.S.R., in the circumstances specified in Article 15, paragraph 7, of the League of Nations Covenant, being the object, in spite of the genuinely peaceful intentions of both countries, of an unprovoked attack on the part of a European State, the U.S.S.R. and reciprocally France shall immediately give each other aid and assistance."

The way was now open for the associate pact between the Soviet Union and Czechoslovakia. It was signed in Prague by Benes and Alexandrovsky, the Soviet Minister, exactly a fortnight later. Its provisions were identical *except for the protocol stating that the pledges of mutual assistance would only be honoured if France also went to the help of the country that was attacked.* In this way Stalin cunningly insured against the danger that he already foresaw—that France and Britain might encourage Hitler to strike eastwards and so to create the situation in which the Russian leader's worst fears were realised —the Soviet Union facing the whole might of German attack whilst France and Britain stood aside. This saving protocol in the Soviet-Czech Pact was to be his political escape route at the time of Munich and the basis for perpetual recriminations against France.

Concurrently with Litvinov's activities on the diplomatic level, Stalin—once he had been alerted to Hitler's purpose—had also been using his traditional weapon, the obedient Communist parties of the West, from early 1934 onwards. The first major indication, at this internal Communist party level, of Stalin's intentions came in France. Hitherto, the French Communists had been following their traditional line of attacking the Social Democrats, with Leon Blum as their principal target of abuse. Then, on 6th February, 1934, ugly scenes took place in Paris both inside and outside the French National Assembly, when neo-fascist elements staged riots directed at the newly-elected Daladier Government. There were strikes and counter-demonstrations against the rioters on 12th February, and to everyone's surprise the French Communists made common cause with the other elements of the French left, including the Social Democrats. It was clear that a change of policy was actually taking place. It was the *Front Populaire*. And the new policy soon moved so fast that the Communists were accepting political allies far to the right of Leon Blum.

The next year, 1935, was the decisive year for the new Communist policy—and not only for Communist policy. In France the *Front Populaire* achieved successes in the May Municipal Elections.

In July, the Seventh Congress of the Comintern, meeting in Moscow, gave its formal endorsement to the new Communist position. Simultaneously, European affairs became more grave. First, in the early autumn of 1935, Mussolini launched his attack upon Abyssinia. The League of Nations, created specifically to meet such a situation, was proved to be an ineffective instrument, because neither the British nor French Governments really intended to stop Mussolini's venture. Secondly, in March, 1936, Hitler ordered the reoccupation of the Rhineland, which had been demilitarised under the Treaty of Versailles.

These two events—Abyssinia and the Rhineland remilitarisation—represent the decisive period of European history between the two wars. If Mussolini's Abyssinian expedition had been seriously challenged by Britain and France, appeasement of the dictators would never have begun. If Hitler had been forced by Britain and France to evacuate the Rhineland, his drive eastwards—involving Austria, Czechoslovakia, Memel, Danzig and Poland—might have been prevented. As for Stalin, having seen Britain and France acquiesce tamely to the remilitarisation of the Rhineland, he knew that Hitler had satisfied his last major territorial demand in the West and, from then on, he would be looking east.

The storm in Europe continued to gather. In July, 1936, a military revolt took place against the legally-elected, if ramshackle, Republican Government of Spain. The military party, led by General Franco, was supported immediately by Mussolini and Hitler, who both sent large quantities of munitions accompanied by military advisers. Very soon they also put in troops. As the intensity of this Spanish War increased, the emotions of liberal opinion throughout the Western countries—particularly in Britain—became increasingly committed to the Spanish Republican cause. Spain was a symbol.

Britain and France both adopted a policy of "non-intervention" in the Spanish Civil War. Paradoxically, this favoured the Spanish rebels beause it meant that supplies comparable to those being sent to Franco's forces by Hitler and Mussolini were now denied to the Republican side. Stalin, in July, 1936, still under the impact of German remilitarisation of the Rhineland, hesitated. His first instinct was to stand aside. He accepted the Anglo-French formula for non-intervention before leaving Moscow for a holiday. But during August and September, a decision to intervene in Spain was taken by a plenary session of the Central Committee of the Soviet Communist Party whilst Stalin was out of Moscow.

As the Central Committee saw it, if the Franco forces won quickly and completely, then France would have Fascist Powers on three sides. Thus a Franco victory would have spelt disaster for the policy of anti-Hitler alliances and the *Front Populaire* upon which Stalin had already embarked and from which, as yet, he had not withdrawn publicly. Clearly—so they argued—something must be done to avoid the Republican debacle that threatened. Once the Soviet decision to intervene in Spain was taken, the Soviet Government acted with astonishing energy, although it was always careful not to involve itself officially. War materials and advisers were collected and dispatched as quickly as possible. In fact, though not in name, the Soviet Union now took over—for a brief period—the conduct of the civil war on the Spanish Government side. Secret police, counter-espionage, political commissars and censorship were all managed under the direction of Soviet agents. Soviet aid enabled the Spanish Republican Government to survive through the winter of 1936-7. Then, in early 1937, the scale of Italian and German intervention was stepped up to the point at which Stalin could not match it from his distant base without undertaking a commitment greater than he was prepared to accept. Stalin, therefore, decided to abandon the Spanish Republicans. He gradually withdrew back into the isolationism that had been his chief characteristic before the rise of Hitler. The Soviet Union's brief and tentative flirtation with the radical forces in the West was now over and any prospect of an effective alliance was finished. True, Litvinov continued to make speeches advocating collective security as he had done before, using with great skill the League Assembly at Geneva as his platform. On the surface, also, the changes in Soviet policy appeared small. Yet in practice, Stalin cut back his assistance to the Spanish Republicans, whose Government was now doomed to a lingering death.

The belief held at that time, especially in Western liberal circles, was that Stalin's sudden retreat from the *Front Populaire* was due specifically to his disillusionment with the negative attitudes adopted by the Western Powers towards Fascism. In particular, Britain and France were blamed. Yet how did Stalin himself view the international prospect over the vital period from Mussolini's invasion of Abyssinia in 1935 to the point at which he turned his back upon collaboration with any forces in Western Europe, abandoning the *Front Populaire* policy and allowing the Spanish Republicans to sink?

Stalin could see, from 1935 on, that there was no doubt about the long-term intentions of the Fascist dictators. He probably knew —as is now known from captured Nazi documents—that a secret German mission had gone to Tokyo in the autumn of 1935 to secure Japanese support for Hitler's and Mussolini's plans for expansion. (This was the forerunner of the Anti-Comintern Pact signed by Germany, Italy and Japan on 25th November, 1936.) The thought would not have escaped a suspicious man like Stalin that one obvious consequence of the Berlin-Tokyo-Rome axis was that Japan might find it easier to satisfy her own expansionist desires in Soviet rather than Chinese territory. Finally, it was common knowledge in Russia that anti-Communist thinking did not stop with the signatories of the Anti-Comintern Pact. There were certain members of the British and French Governments, and their immediate circles, who regarded Hitler as a vigorous bulwark against Communism, to be supported as such.

There is now evidence that immediately after the Rhineland re-militarisation and possibly even *before* the outbreak of the Spanish Civil War, Stalin had decided upon yet another major change in Soviet foreign policy. Acting with the greatest secrecy and stealth in late 1936, Stalin instructed the Soviet trade representative in Berlin, Kandelaki, to make overtures to the German authorities for a German-Russian rapprochement. Kandelaki failed in his first bid to make contact with Hitler because Hitler himself rejected the idea out of hand. On Stalin's instructions, Kandelaki tried again in early 1937. The details of these bizarre proposals and the actual circumstances in which they came to be made have never been told. They first came to light through the defection of a Soviet official named Krivitsky, who was later murdered in the U.S.A. in strange circumstances. Krivitsky's extraordinary story of a Soviet-Nazi rapprochement was only confirmed after the end of the Second World War, when a personal dispatch to Schacht from Neurath (at that time Hitler's Foreign Minister) dated 11th February, 1937, fell into Allied hands. On both occasions, Kandelaki was rebuffed by Hitler, who could not bring himself to come to terms with Stalin.

His overtures thus rejected, Stalin was forced to wait. He was good at waiting. And so he prepared himself for a situation of maximum freedom of manœuvre in his foreign relations. First came the gradual reduction of Soviet aid to the Spanish Republican Government from early 1937 onwards. Next he recalled the Soviet

Ambassador—Jacob Surtis, who, being Jewish, was not a suitable negotiating instrument in Russo-German relations. As if to prepare internal Russian opinion for a possible change, the indictments in the famous series of "Purge" trials then going on no longer drew a distinction between the Fascist powers and the Western democracies, as they had done earlier. When Surtis's successor as Soviet Ambassador in Berlin, Merekalov, was appointed shortly after the Austrian *Anschluss*, the Russian Press censor, after reference to a higher authority, passed for publication abroad a story by a foreign correspondent to the effect that "Moscow would soon be approaching Berlin for an improvement in relations." Immediately afterwards, a major speech by Litvinov on collective security, whilst released for publication abroad failed to appear in the Soviet Press. Taken separately, these and other events were not of sufficient import to prepare the world for what was to come in 1939. But seen collectively, they present a discernable pattern.

What lay behind Stalin's decision to come to terms with Hitler? Stalin's first thought, ever since his accession to power, had been to secure the citadel of revolution before proceeding to other ventures. After his slow awakening in 1934 to the threat to the Soviet Union posed by Hitler, he studied, with genuine alarm, *Mein Kampf* and Hitler's overt plans for German expansion to the east. It was at this point that Stalin considered collaboration with the Western Powers and he made his tentative attempts at the *Front Populaire*. The failure of Britain and France to make any kind of a stand against Mussolini's invasion of Abyssinia confirmed both Stalin's admiration for force and his long-standing contempt for the fibre of democracies. Even so, Stalin would not have considered that Abyssinia was a vital British or French interest in the same way as the re-militarisation of the Rhineland. It was the weakness and vacillation in London and Paris over the week-end of 7th March, 1936, that may have made up Stalin's mind, and the subsequent facts point to this conclusion. The Soviet leader knew from *Mein Kampf* that the Rhineland represented Hitler's last territorial claim in the West. Everything else that Hitler wanted lay to the East—Austria, Czechoslovakia and Poland—along the road to Moscow and the great "Anti-Communist Crusade."

The logic of Stalin's approach to this dilemma was sound. If the Western Powers would not act even when their own vital interests were involved, how much less likely were they to show resolution when their vital interests were not involved? Therefore,

he decided that he had to look to his own security. He must attempt
to make common cause with Hitler—at least until they had both
disposed of the British and French empires—in the hope that by
then he would be strong enough to show the Nazi leader that the
interests of their two countries were mutual. Events were to show
that Stalin's judgment and interpretation of the situation was right
up to a point, and Chamberlain's misconceived actions supported
the Soviet leader's thinking for over the next two years. Stalin's
major difficulty, which he was unable to overcome until it suited
Hitler's grand strategy, was to establish the essential relationship
with the Nazis. His major miscalculation was his complete failure
to grasp the importance of the slowly awakening public conscience
in the democracies which made itself felt over Czechoslovakia only
after the event and which acted so irrationally—to Stalin's way of
thinking—when Poland was attacked. His greatest mistake, however, was to misjudge Hitler's insatiable appetite for world domination that led Germany to attack Soviet Russia in 1941. He *never*
understood that last decision. But all this lay in the future.

The immediate situation was that Stalin in 1936, the suspicious,
calculating defender of what he conceived to be Russian national
interest had determined to return to the policy of German-Soviet
understanding despite Hitler's proclaimed intentions of attacking
Communism—indeed because of them. This was the origin, on
the Soviet side, of the Molotov-Ribbentrop Pact three years later.
Stalin persisted with the policy of Soviet-German rapprochement
throughout 1937, whilst the world still regarded Soviet Russia as
the leading anti-Fascist power unaware of his secret decision and
cynical scheming.

When Chamberlain succeeded Baldwin in May, 1937, there was
a change in British foreign policy. Whereas Baldwin had been
lethargic and insular in his approach to foreign policy, Chamberlain
possessed a strong distrust of Russia, a genuine horror of war and
an opinionated sense of mission. Chamberlain's destiny, as he saw
it, was to reach a *modus vivendi* with the Fascist dictators, which he
considered to be the best way to prevent the outbreak of a second
world war. And there is no doubt that Chamberlain was backed
by a substantial body of anti-Russian opinion in Britain which was
also friendly towards Hitler and Mussolini.

Stalin now felt confirmed in his decision to come to terms with
Hitler; and the Nazi leader was not slow to take advantage of the
new situation. With his western frontier secured increasingly by

British appeasement and French hesitation, Hitler had already turned his attention to expansion eastwards and decided to absorb Austria. On 12th February, 1938, he had called the Austrian Chancellor, Schuschnigg, to Berchtesgaden. Under the threat of invasion, he had forced Schuschnigg to sign a "protocol" of "friendly association."

Schuschnigg, however, was determined to make one last effort to save the independence of Austria, and he announced suddenly that he was intending to hold a plebiscite throughout Austria on 13th March. Hitler reacted with equal swiftness, ordering the immediate invasion of Austria to take place on 12th March, and large numbers of German troops and Austrian Nazis were in possession of Vienna on the morning of Sunday, 13th March, 1938.

The seizure of Austria by Germany on 13th March meant that Czechoslovakia was the country next in the line for Hitler's eastward advance. Not having established contact with Hitler, Stalin tried apprehensively to make a return to his earlier policy of allying himself with the Western Powers against Hitler. An official Soviet statement was issued on 15th March to the effect that in the event of a German invasion of Czechoslovakia and if France were to go to the assistance of Czechoslovakia, the Soviet Union would do likewise. This was a direct reference to the Franco-Soviet-Czech Pacts of 1935. On 18th March Stalin took another step. He had notes delivered to the British, French and American Governments proposing a four-power conference to consider ways to prevent further aggression. Chamberlain, in the House of Commons, promptly brushed aside the Russian proposal on the overt grounds that this would establish "exclusive groups of nations . . . inimical to the prospects of European peace." His private view, however, went much further: "You have only to look at the map to see that nothing that France or we could do could possibly save Czechoslovakia from being overrun by the Germans. . . . Russia is 100 miles away . . . we could not help Czechoslovakia—she would simply be a pretext for going to war with Germany."

Although Chamberlain's decision was taken on too narrow an assessment of the position, on the facts of geography he had a case at that time that cannot be ignored. It was reinforced when Bonnet, the French Foreign Minister, asked Litvinov in Moscow on 12th May just how the Soviet Union proposed to send Soviet troops to Czechoslovakia without the agreement of either Poland or

Rumania. "Litvinov said that the U.S.S.R. would not act without the consent of these countries; it was up to France, which had treaty relations, to secure their consent." After this, Bonnet did in fact approach the Rumanian Foreign Minister, as it was considered that he would be easier to deal with than his Polish counterpart, but Bonnet found him totally opposed to any such suggestion.

After the Soviet proposal of 18th March had been turned down by Chamberlain there came a series of articles in the Soviet Press and statements supporting Czechoslovakia. They were met by an equally clear assurance from Daladier, the French Prime Minister, on 12th June, that France's engagements towards Czechoslovakia "are sacred and cannot be evaded." However, Chamberlain always had other ideas. He proposed to Benes that he might send an investigator to Czechoslovakia "to promote a friendly compromise." And on 26th July, 1938, Chamberlain announced to the House of Commons that he was sending Lord Runciman to Prague.

On 2nd September, Payart, the French Chargé d'Affaires in Moscow, called on Litvinov, asking what aid Russia would give Czechoslovakia against a German attack, having particular regard to the difficulties of crossing Polish or Rumanian territory. Litvinov shrewdly countered by asking what were the French intentions. As Payart said nothing, Litvinov, who felt safer, proceeded to declare that the Soviet Union intended to fulfil its obligations although it recognised the practical difficulties imposed by geography. The Soviet Foreign Minister, therefore, proposed that the Council of the League of Nations would be invoked under Article 11 of its Charter, on the grounds that there was a danger of war and that Rumania should be approached with the authority of the League. Litvinov urged speed. He also proposed staff conversations, to take place immediately, amongst Russia, France and Czechoslovakia.

On 7th September, the French Ambassador in London saw Halifax to ask what would be the attitude of the British Government in the event of a German attack on Czechoslovakia. Whilst Chamberlain and Halifax were still considering the British answer, Bonnet asked Phipps, the British Ambassador in Paris: "To-morrow Hitler may attack Czechoslovakia. If he does, France will mobilise at once. She will turn to you saying, 'We march: do you march with us?' What will be the answer of Great Britain?" Without waiting for Halifax's answer to be relayed from London,

Bonnet left for the League Council in Geneva on 9th September, which was to be followed by the full League Assembly on 12th September. Litvinov arrived in Geneva almost simultaneously with Bonnet, bringing a large and impressive delegation, including the Soviet Ambassadors in Berlin, Rome, London, Paris and Stockholm.

Twelfth September, 1938, was a crucial day. There was ominous tension in Prague. The French and Soviet delegations stood by in Geneva. The British answer was expected hourly. Hitler was due to speak at Nürnberg in the evening at the end of the great Nazi Party Annual Rally. In the morning, the British Cabinet approved Halifax's answer to France, to be sent through Phipps to the Quai d'Orsay. It deserves to be studied by the reader of this book as if he were a member of the French Cabinet of the day waiting to receive it: "I naturally realise of what importance it would be to the French Government to have a plain answer to such a question. But, as you pointed out to Bonnet, the question itself, though plain in form, cannot be disassociated from the circumstances in which it might be posed, which are necessarily at this stage hypothetical. Moreover, in this matter it is impossible for His Majesty's Government to have regard only to their own position inasmuch as in any decision they may reach or action they may take, they would in fact be committing the Dominions. Their governments would quite certainly be unwilling to have their position decided for them in advance of the actual circumstances of which they would desire themselves to judge. So far, therefore, as I am in a position to give any answer at this stage to M. Bonnet's question, it would have to be that while His Majesty's Government would never allow the security of France to be threatened, they are unable to make precise statements of the character of their future action, or at the time which it would be taken, in circumstances that they cannot at present foresee."

Daladier—in the absence of Bonnet—immediately sought clarification of the actual nature of British help, if France's security were, in fact, threatened. According to Bonnet later, it was to be two infantry divisions, not motorised, and 150 aircraft. This was to be all Britain could produce within the first six months of war.

Hitler spoke on the same evening, his actual speech being relayed by almost every radio network in Europe. His harsh voice fell like a whiplash across the huddled shoulders of millions, as they sat by their radio sets, sometimes not needing the translators to tell them what was being said. The baying of the great Nürnberg crowd, assembled under the stars, provided a vast Wagnerian chorus in the background. Hitler warned the Western Powers against intervention. He violently attacked Bolshevism. He flayed Benes and the Czechs. His words meant only one thing: War!

The French Cabinet assembled on 13th September to consider the situation. If it came to war, they now knew they could count upon no significant military support from Britain. As to the Russian attitude, there were still important question marks despite Litvinov's apparently firm declaration, because the policies of the buffer countries through which Soviet assistance would have to reach Czechoslovakia were still in doubt. There were also grave apprehensions in France about Soviet military efficiency. The "Purges" had taken their toll at the highest levels of command. The Soviet road and rail system, the French Cabinet was also told, was so awkward and primitive that it might be months before a single division could reach Bohemia. In these circumstances, the only decision taken that day by the French was to postpone mobilisation and to seek a conference. And Benes, in Prague, was told that France was reconsidering her attitude. On the same night, 13th-14th September, Daladier contacted Chamberlain to tell him that the French Government believed a joint approach should be made immediately to Hitler, suggesting a personal meeting between Hitler, Chamberlain and Daladier. Unknown to Daladier, however, Chamberlain had already decided to act alone.

On his own initiative, without even telling the Cabinet, Chamberlain had telegraphed Hitler at 11 p.m. on 13th September, proposing to fly next day to Germany. As Chamberlain said himself, "I sent the telegram and told the Cabinet next morning what I had done." It was an astonishing action and it showed the reliance he also had placed in Soviet expressions. Hitler could hardly believe his eyes when the message was brought in to him. *"Ich bin von Himmel gefallen"* ("I fell from heaven"), he said with a chuckle, when recounting the story to a foreign diplomat.

The Soviet Government was not told in advance of Chamberlain's proposal. Nor was the Soviet Government informed in advance of any steps taken by the British and French Governments from this point on. The Soviet attitude was expressed four days later in a violent attack upon Chamberlain and Franco-British policies in *Pravda*. It ridiculed Chamberlain's hopes of appeasing Fascism and warned that his policy would not avert war. Instead, it advocated that France should stand firm with Czechoslovakia, a policy that *Pravda* claimed would be decisive in bolstering Czechoslovakia, regardless of what Britain did. Most significantly, no mention was made of the possibility that the Soviet Union might herself become involved in the conflict, or that she had any commitments to Czechoslovakia.

Chamberlain left for Berchtesgaden on 15th September. He returned on 17th September convinced that only the cession of the Sudeten areas to Germany would stop Hitler invading Czechoslovakia. Benes, beside himself in anguish and desperation, approached Alexandrovsky, the Soviet Minister in Prague, on 19th September. Alexandrovsky told him that if France honoured her obligations, the Soviet Union would do likewise. In the event of France dishonouring her signature, Benes was advised by the Soviet envoy, "to appeal to the League." Upon Germany being branded by the League as an aggressor, Russia would come to her aid regardless of what the other Powers might do, although the precise form of the aid was not made clear. With these Soviet assurances in his pocket, Benes rejected Chamberlain's proposals for cession.

There followed a macabre scene at two o'clock in the morning of 21st September, when the British and French Ministers in Prague called on Benes. They told him that there was now no question of arbitration. They urged him to accept the Franco-British proposals "before producing a situation for which France and Britain could take no responsibility." This amounted to informing Benes that he had been deserted. Faced with the appalling situation, the Czech Government gave way next morning, "yielding to unheard-of pressure" as it was stated in the public communiqué.

The Russians apparently knew little or nothing of the situation in Prague during these twenty-four hours, and the Czech decision to capitulate had not been announced when Litvinov rose to address the League Assembly on 21st September. He began: "One of the oldest, most cultured, most hardworking of European peoples, who acquired their independence after centuries of oppression, to-day or to-morrow may decide to take up arms in defence of that independence. Such an event as the disappearance of Austria passed unnoticed by the League of Nations. Realising the significance of this event for the fate of the whole of Europe and particularly of Czechoslovakia, the Soviet Government, immediately after the *Anschluss*, officially approached the other European Great Powers with a proposal for an immediate collective deliberation on the possible consequences of that event." Litvinov continued: "To our regret, this proposal, which if carried out could have saved us from the alarm which all the world now feels for the fate of Czechoslovakia, did not receive its just appreciation. . . . When, a few days before I left for Geneva, the French Government for the first time inquired as to our attitude in the event of an attack on Czechoslovakia, I gave in the name of my Government the following reply: 'We intend to fulfil our obligations under the Pact, and together with France to afford assistance in the ways open to us. Our War Department is ready immediately to participate in a conference with the representatives of the French and Czechoslovak War Departments, in order to discuss the measures appropriate to the moment. . . .'" Nobody there in the Palais des Nations knew that it was to be Maxim Litvinov's last major speech on the stage of international politics which he had trodden with such skill and control.

Meanwhile Chamberlain, armed with his Czech capitulation, was preparing to set out for Godesberg on the second of his three journeys to see Hitler. Apparently the Nazi dictator was astonished that the principle of cession had been accepted. He decided to press for more and produced a completely new set of proposals, involving yet greater Czech concessions. Chamberlain described the new demands as "a totally unexpected situation," and after much acrimony, the British Prime Minister retired across the Rhine to his own hotel near Königswinter. Whilst Chamberlain was still in Germany, on the actual day upon which the negotiations with Hitler had broken down (23rd September), Litvinov had a lengthy meeting in Geneva with the British delegation, Earl de la Warr, the Lord Privy Seal, and R. A. Butler, the Foreign Under-Secretary. Astonishing as it may seem, it was the only formal Anglo-Soviet consultation of the whole Czech crisis. Litvinov repeated his now familiar assurances about Czechoslovakia, provided always that France did likewise. He also proposed that there should be a three-power conference amongst Russia, France and Britain, and he offered to come to London for it.

That same night, Britain and France informed Czechoslovakia that they could no longer "take the responsibility of advising them not to mobilise." Czech mobilisation followed at once. The situation was now hardening and on 25th September Benes rejected the Godesberg terms. Next day the British Government issued a warning to Hitler: "If, in spite of all efforts by the British Prime Minister, a German attack is made upon Czechoslovakia, the immediate result must be that France will be bound to come to her assistance and Great Britain and Russia will certainly stand by France." This was the first mention Britain had made of the possibility of the Soviet Union as an ally, and such was Bonnet's opinion of Chamberlain that it was immediately suggested to the Press by the Quai d'Orsay that it was a forgery.

To return to Chamberlain himself: he had arrived back in London on 24th September and had dispatched one last appeal to Hitler through his personal adviser, Sir Horace Wilson. On 27th September he broadcast to the nation: "How horrible, fantastic, incredible it is, that we should be digging trenches and trying on gas-masks here because of a quarrel in a far-away country between people of whom we know nothing! . . . I would not hesitate to pay even a third visit to Germany if I thought it would do any good. . . . I am myself a man of peace to the depths of my soul; but if I were convinced that any nation had made up its mind to dominate the world by fear of its force, I should feel that it must be resisted. . . ."

Shortly after delivering his broadcast, Chamberlain received Hitler's reply to the last appeal he had sent via Sir Horace Wilson. Hitler offered to join in a guarantee of the new frontiers of Czechoslovakia and was willing to give further assurances about the method of carrying out the plebiscite in Sudetenland. Here, so Chamberlain thought, in his current frame of mind, was a glimpse of hope. He felt there was no time to lose. Again without consulting the French, the Russians or even his Cabinet colleagues, the British Prime Minister drafted two personal messages. To Hitler he telegraphed: "After reading your letter, I feel certain that you can get all the essentials without war, and without delay. I am ready to come to Berlin myself at once to discuss arrangements for transfer with you and representatives of the Czech Government, together with representatives of France and Italy if you desire." At the same time Chamberlain telegraphed to Mussolini informing him of his offer to Hitler.

Unknown to Chamberlain, Daladier and Bonnet were also thinking along similar lines. They had already instructed the French Ambassador in Berlin, François-Poncet, to suggest to Hitler that some extension of the Sudetenland territory be handed over for immediate occupation. While François-Poncet was actually in

Hitler's presence, delivering the message on 28th September, a telegram arrived from Mussolini urging Hitler to accept Chamberlain's offer. Hitler immediately cabled Chamberlain and Daladier, inviting them to Munich, together with Mussolini, for a meeting on the following day, 29th September.

The story of the Munich Conference and its outcome has been told frequently in detail. For the purpose of this narrative, it is necessary to emphasise only one point. As has been made clear by the account of events so far, the Soviet Union was virtually excluded by Britain and France from all consultations that led up to the crisis, with the exceptions of the French inquiries on 12th May and 2nd September, and the Anglo-Soviet talks in Geneva on 23rd September.

Even more extraordinary, in the course of two long speeches in the subsequent House of Commons debate on Munich, Chamberlain made no mention of the Soviet Union. Yet from the very beginning of Hitler's threat, following the Austrian *Anschluss*, the Soviet Government had spoken in the accents of collective security, and Litvinov's speech to the League Assembly on 21st September was the most forthright statement on the whole Czech crisis made on behalf of any nation. Nevertheless, the query remains: Were these public pronouncements of Soviet Russia genuine expressions of intended action or were they political manœuvres? Were they designed merely to demonstrate the inanity and folly of Chamberlain and the craven indecision of the French, principally Bonnet? In each Soviet statement there were always uncomfortable reservations that aroused doubts and suspicions in British and French circles.

The decisive answer must be military. By what means could Soviet aid reach Czechoslovakia? Vavrecka, the Czechoslovak Minister of Propaganda, in a broadcast on 30th September, immediately following the signing of the Munich Agreement, pointed out: "We had to consider that it would have taken the Russian Army weeks to come to our aid—perhaps too late. . . ." In fact, there were two railways from the Soviet Union which passed through Rumanian territory. And the German reaction was significant. At no stage, throughout the whole Czechoslovak crisis, did Hitler attach weight to the possibility of Soviet intervention. Count Schulenburg, the German Ambassador in Moscow, reported that there was no Soviet military activity and that there was a clear policy by Stalin not to prepare the Soviet people for conflict.

After the dramatic activity of the spring and summer, the winter of 1938-9 brought a lull in international affairs. Governments in all the European capitals were adjusting themselves to the new situation that had arisen out of the Munich Agreements. Nearly everybody realised that European affairs had entered a new and a historic phase but there were different opinions as to what the future held for its peoples.

CHAPTER 4

IDIOT'S DELIGHT

Stalin, the architect of peace. . . . By signing the non-aggression pact with Germany, Russia smashed the Fascist war-making alliance. Rulers in other lands stood aghast at the ease with which this master stroke of diplomacy was accomplished. *Tribune*, 1st September, 1939

The Soviet Union, after Munich, was isolated. Czechoslovakia had passed under German influence. Hitler was gathering his country's strength for the next advance eastward, including the occupation of Prague and the total dismemberment of Czechoslovakia. France, after Munich, appeared even more divided and defeatist than before. The British Government alone retained some of its overt, brittle confidence. Yet, beneath the surface, the British public, in a curious way, had resolved that appeasement was dead and that Munich had symbolised the extreme limit of Western retreat. This last point was not understood by the Fascist dictators any more than it was by Stalin.

On 9th March, 1939, Chamberlain delivered an amazingly optimistic talk to Parliamentary lobby correspondents at Westminster. He thought that the prospects of peace were better than ever before. He foresaw a disarmament conference before the end of 1939. Five days later there was a different story. Chamberlain had to tell the House of Commons: "The occupation of Bohemia began at six o'clock this morning. The Czech people have been ordered by their government not to resist." He added that in his opinion the guarantee that Britain had given Czechoslovakia under the Munich Agreement was no longer valid.

Chamberlain was due to speak at Birmingham Town Hall on 17th March, two days after. Most people expected him to accept Hitler's seizure of Czechoslovakia with the best grace possible. To everyone's amazement, however, the British Prime Minister appeared on the Birmingham platform as a man outraged. Now he felt cheated, humiliated and very angry. He had thrown aside his prepared speech which had been mostly on home affairs. Instead, he challenged Hitler. "I am convinced," said Chamberlain, "that after Munich the great majority of the British people shared my honest desire that that policy should be carried further, but to-day I share their disappointment, their indignation. . . ." He ended: "No greater mistake could be made than to suppose . . . this nation has lost its fibre, that it will not take part to the utmost of its power in resisting such a challenge if it ever were made."

Following on the German seizure of Prague (and the seizure of Memel on 19th March) Chamberlain's first idea was "to get a declaration signed by the four Powers—Britain, France, Russia and Poland—that they would act together in the event of further signs of German aggressive intentions." But he soon dropped this project because of Polish opposition, even though France agreed with his plan and Russia also had by now accepted (provided France and Poland did likewise). Again Chamberlain hesitated about negotiating with the Soviet Union. "I must confess," he wrote on 26th March, "to the most profound distrust of Russia. I have no belief whatever in her ability to maintain an effective offensive, even if she wanted to. And I distrust her motives, which seem to me to have little connection with our ideas of liberty, and to be concerned only with getting everyone else by the ears. Moreover, she is both hated and feared by many of the smaller states, notably by Poland, Rumania and Finland."

Chamberlain, therefore, decided to proceed without Russia. The British Cabinet sat long on 29th March and met again next day. A decision of great consequence was taken at these meetings and put into operation at once. The British Ambassador in Warsaw, Sir Howard Kennaird, later that same day, 30th March, was discussing a Polish Note with Beck, the Polish Foreign Minister, when an urgent message from Downing Street reached him. The Polish Minute records it thus: "During this conversation, the Secretary of the British Embassy, Mr. Hankey, called, bringing Sir Howard an instruction from his Government to ask the Polish Government whether they had any objection to a British Government guarantee to meet any action which clearly threatened Polish independence, and which the Polish Government accordingly considered it vital to resist with their national forces. Mr. Chamberlain would propose to make a declaration on the subject in the House of Commons the next day, 31st March. Mr. Beck informed Sir Howard that the Polish Government fully accepted the British Government's proposal." Beck said later that he had made up his mind on his reply "between two flicks of the ash off his cigarette."

Mussolini seized Albania a few days later, on Good Friday, 13th April, and Chamberlain, inspired by his new-found anger against the dictators, immediately countered by giving British guarantees to Greece and Rumania. As the Prime Minister was concluding his statement to Parliament on this new and further offer, there was an interjection, "What about Russia?" Chamberlain hastened to reply, "We are keeping in the closest touch with the representative of that country," which was untrue. He then added the proviso, "We have to consider not only what we wish, but what other people are willing to do." By this cryptic remark, he was referring to anti-Soviet feelings in Poland and Rumania.

Little did Chamberlain know of what was already astir in Germany and the Soviet Union. On 10th March, 1939—five days before Hitler seized Prague, three weeks before the guarantee to Poland and more than a month before the guarantees to Greece and Rumania—Stalin had addressed the Eighteenth Congress of the Soviet Communist Party. His speech was a highly skilful political manœuvre. In particular, he made two very significant points which went largely unnoticed in London and Paris, but not in Berlin. Stalin had first given his own analysis of the intentions of the Anti-Comintern Pact signatories—Germany, Italy and Japan—on the one hand and of the Western democracies on the other. The Anti-Comintern Pact, he said, was a cover for the aggressive designs of Germany, Italy and Japan upon British and French positions in Europe and upon British, French and American positions in the Far East. In this way he implied the idea that he did not consider the Pact as a bar to a Soviet-German agreement. Stalin then went on to state that Western appeasement of the aggressors did not stem from weakness. "The chief reason," he said, "is that the majority of the non-aggression countries, particularly Britain and France, have rejected the policy of collective security . . . and have taken up a position of non-intervention, a position of neutrality. The policy of non-intervention reveals an eagerness, a desire, not to hinder the aggressors in their nefarious work; not to hinder Japan, say, from embroiling herself in war with China or, better still, with the Soviet Union; not to hinder Germany, say, from embroiling herself in a war with the Soviet Union." The deepest of Stalin's fears—his belief that the Western Powers wished Hitler to attack Russia—was now out in the open for Chamberlain to see if he had so wished. Stalin continued with his definition of Franco-British policy as an implied warning to Hitler: "To allow the belligerents to sink deeply into the mire of war . . . to allow them to exhaust and weaken one another; and then when they have become weak enough, to appear on the scene with fresh strength, to appear, of course in the interests of peace and to dictate conditions to the enfeebled belligerents." Stalin had stated the nightmare with which he had lived since Hitler re-militarised the Rhineland in March, 1936.

What was Stalin's answer to Franco-British policy to be? He made his proposal very carefully. He wanted his words to be clear enough to be understood by Hitler—but not so clear that they would cause embarrassment at this stage. Accordingly, he defined the attitude of the Soviet Union to its immediate neighbours: "We stand for peaceful, close and friendly relations with all neighbouring countries which have common frontiers with the U.S.S.R.," he said. "That is our position; and we shall adhere to this position as long as these countries maintain like relations with the Soviet Union and as long as they make no attempt to trespass, directly or indirectly, on the integrity and inviolability of the frontiers of the Soviet State."

Stalin's overture to Hitler came at precisely the right time. There had already been some new thinking in military quarters on the German side where the Bismarck tradition and the threat of a war on two fronts ran deep.[1] But Hitler still had not made up his mind and his old inhibitions remained. As early as 25th January a German trade mission bound for Moscow had got as far as Warsaw, but was recalled by Hitler. Furthermore, Hitler was then —up to March, 1939—still thinking in terms of settling his Danzig and Polish Corridor claims by offering the Poles a share in a campaign against the Ukraine upon which he had his major designs. He had been making tentative approaches to Poland to this effect.

Yet here was Stalin with a tentative but discernible proposal for Hitler. True, it was not new; the Soviet Union had been making approaches of one kind or another to Nazi Germany for a long time. The days went by. Then came the British guarantees to Poland,

[1] Admiral Raeder declared at Nürnberg: " I have always advocated Bismarck's policy of an understanding with Russia." *Trial of the Major Criminals before the International Military Tribunal*, official English text vol. xiv, p. 220.

Greece and Rumania already described. For Hitler, the situation changed completely. He was at last face to face with the fact that his aims of expansion eastwards would lead to the danger of a war on two fronts. And the significance of the new situation was that Stalin had already offered him a way out of his difficulty by his speech on 10th March.

While Hitler was considering Stalin's offer throughout April, 1939, the exchanges between Moscow and the Western democracies were continuing in the old familiar pattern. Chamberlain's offer of guarantees to Greece and Rumania on 13th April was followed by meetings between Maisky and Halifax on 14th April and by Sir William Seeds, the new British Ambassador in Moscow, with Litvinov. Seeds proposed formal talks.

Meanwhile, Stalin's double game was continuing. Taking advantage of the opportunity created by Chamberlain's guarantees, he sent Merekalov, the Soviet Ambassador in Berlin, to call on the German State Secretary, Weizsäcker, for the first time since the Ambassador had arrived in Berlin the previous June. The ostensible reason for the conversation was the fulfilment of some arms orders placed by the Soviet Government with the Skoda works in Czechoslovakia. But Weizsäcker's note after the meeting says that after some verbal skirmishing, the Soviet Ambassador "asked me point-blank what I thought of German-Russian relations." Weizsäcker was non-committal in reply but kept the door open. "The Ambassador then spoke as follows," continues Weizsäcker. "Russian policy has always followed a straight course. Ideological differences of opinion have had very little effect upon relations between Russia and Italy and need not disturb those with Germany either. Russia had not exploited the present friction between Germany and the Western democracies against us, neither did she wish to do that. As far as Russia was concerned, there was no reason why she should not live on a normal footing with us, and out of normal relations could grow increasingly improved relations. With that remark, to which he had been steering the conversation, Merekalov ended the talk." Next day, 18th April, Maisky left London for consultations in Moscow. A day or so later, Merekalov also headed for Moscow. On 28th April, in a speech in the Reichstag, Hitler denounced the seven-month-old Munich Agreement, the Anglo-German naval treaty and the Polish-German non-aggression pact, without once mentioning the Soviet Union. It was a most significant omission.

Stalin now realised that Hitler also was reconsidering his attitude.

He, therefore, took his next important step. At 11.45 on the night of 3rd May, Moscow Radio announced that Litvinov had been relieved of his post "at his own request" and had been replaced by Molotov, who was to continue in his office of Prime Minister. The departure of the Jew, Litvinov, so long identified with the policy of collective security, "struck Hitler like a cannon ball." He later told his generals before the invasion of Poland: "The replacing of Litvinov was decisive." The German Foreign Ministry now reacted with speed. Schulenburg, the Ambassador in Moscow, who was in Teheran at the time for the wedding of the Crown Prince of Persia, was telegraphed to go at once to Munich, along with the Assistant Military Attaché in Moscow. In order to avoid attracting any attention they were requested to stay separately in Munich.

In London and Paris, the reaction to Litvinov's dismissal was appropriately leisurely and there was little or no appreciation in Government quarters of what it might mean. On 20th May Schulenburg had his first interview with Molotov, the new Commissar for Foreign Affairs. In the course of their talk, which ranged over proposed trade negotiations, Molotov indicated that negotiations should have "a political basis." Ten days later Schulenburg was told by Weizsäcker that Hitler had decided upon an approach to Russia, "contrary to the policy previously planned." But true to the pattern of his character, in order to secure the best possible terms from Hitler, Stalin continued with the sporadic Anglo-French talks begun by Seeds in April.

Meanwhile Chamberlain was under pressure to send a mission to Moscow from London and eventually decided to do so. The British Government nominated William Strang, then head of the Central Department in the Foreign Office, and he reached Moscow on 14th June. Together with Seeds and Naggiar, the French Ambassador, Strang saw Molotov next day.

Three years later, in August, 1942, in a discussion in the early hours of the morning after a Kremlin banquet, Stalin gave Churchill an account of how he had seen the situation in 1939. "We formed the impression," said Stalin, "that the British and French Governments were not resolved to go to war if Poland were attacked but that they hoped that the diplomatic line-up of Britain, France and Russia would deter Hitler. We were sure it would not." "How many divisions," Stalin had asked, "will France send against Germany on mobilisation?" The answer was: "About a hundred." He then asked: "How many will Britain send?" The answer was:

"Two and more later." "Ah, two and more later," Stalin had repeated. "Do you know," he said, "how many divisions we shall have to put on the Russian front if we go to war with Germany?" There was a pause. "More than three hundred."

The British and French Ambassadors and Strang made no progress. At times there were rumours that agreement was close—only for some new difficulty to arise. Then Zhdanov, Chairman of the Foreign Affairs Commission of the Supreme Soviet and a member of the Politbureau, gave a public warning to the Western Powers through an article in *Pravda* on 29th June. He said that he could not agree that the British and French were sincere. "Anglo-Soviet negotiations, in the direct sense of the word, that is, since 15th April . . . have been going on for seventy-five days. Of these, the Soviet Government took sixteen days preparing answers to the various British projects and proposals, while the fifty-nine days have been consumed by delays on the part of the British and the French."

By now the British were asking for Soviet guarantees for Holland and Switzerland as well as for Poland and the Baltic States, but Zhdanov pointed out that the U.S.S.R. had no diplomatic relations with Holland and Switzerland and did not know if the Baltic States wished for a guarantee. The Western Powers, therefore, dropped their request for guarantees to Holland and Switzerland but the obstacles on Poland, the Baltic States and a military convention continued. From the other side, Keith Feiling, Chamberlain's biographer, puts the British position thus: "The crux had come; while we accepted an obligation to defend Russia herself, we would neither compel the Baltic States to accept this Russian protection, nor coerce the Poles to admit Russian armies."

Back to Germany: in early July, Hitler appeared to withdraw slightly. He then took a decisive step forward on 26th July. That night Astakhov, the Soviet Chargé d'Affaires in Berlin, and Barbarin, the head of the Soviet Trade Delegation, were invited to dinner by Schnurre, an official of the German Economic Policy Department, at a Berlin restaurant. The dinner took place on German initiative and by order of the highest authority. The Russians ate and drank well and stayed until 12.30 a.m. The talk ranged wide. Schnurre, who had been briefed carefully, gave the outlines of a scheme for a Soviet-German rapprochement by stages. He told the Russians that there were no vital problems from the Baltic to the Black Sea or in the Far East that need stand between them. He felt that Germany and the Soviet Union had a common ideology in so far as they were

71

opposed to capitalist democracy. "It would appear to us to be quite paradoxical," said Schnurre, "if the Soviet Union as a Socialist State were to side with the Western Democracies." Astakhov agreed with great gusto and replied: "The way to an understanding with Germany is through that which corresponds with the vital interests of both countries." But the Russians considered it would have to be a gradual affair because of such obstacles as the Anti-Comintern Pact and the German assumption that the Baltic countries, Finland and Rumania, lay within the German sphere of interest.

Because of his brief, Schnurre was in much more of a hurry than his guests. "What in fact can Britain offer to Russia? At best a participation in a European war," adding: "Now is the right moment but it will not be so after the conclusion of a pact with London." In short, Schnurre had told Astakhov and Barbarin that Moscow had to choose.

The men at this strange and momentous dinner party went on to sketch out a possible partition of Eastern Europe. Astakhov concluded by asking the German whether his Government "would maintain similar opinions if a prominent Soviet representative were to discuss these questions with a prominent German representative." Schnurre replied his Government would. Nothing could have been plainer.

With his plans for invading Poland already far advanced and the summer coming to an end, it was now or never for Hitler. Weizsäcker telegraphed Schulenburg: "Before arranging further interviews please await further dispatch concerning information and language to be used now in the course of preparation." Weizsäcker's secret dispatch followed immediately: "If Molotov abandons the reserve he has so far maintained, you could go a step further in your exposition and put into a little more concrete form what is expressed in general terms in the memorandum. This applies particularly to the Polish question. We would be prepared however the Polish situation may develop . . . to safeguard all Soviet interests. . . . In the Baltic question too . . . the idea could be advanced of so adjusting our attitude . . . as to respect vital Soviet interests."

On 31st July, Weizsäcker followed this up with a cable to Schulenburg: "Please report by telegram the date and time of your next interview with Molotov." In Berlin, Ribbentrop saw Astakhov on 2nd August. The German Foreign Minister hinted at a joint settlement over Poland and at the possibility of ultimately settling

Russian-Japanese differences. He concluded by telling Astakhov that if the Russians were interested Molotov should take up the matter with Schulenburg.

On the next day—3rd August—a new sense of urgency was injected into the German attitude. Indeed, according to Benes, it was on this day that the Nazi leaders took the major decision to accept the Soviet demands—as distinct from initiating the exploratory talks. Also, according to Benes, negotiations had been conducted up to this point at a level at which the German position could have been repudiated without involving Hitler. "On the morning of 19th July," Benes wrote, "General Ingr and Colonel Frantisek Moravec brought me news from Germany of very active negotiations between Germany and the Soviet Union. Between 10th and 12th August, 1939, we got further important reports through the same channels. So far as Germany was concerned, the decisive moment in the Soviet-German negotiations was the night of 3rd-4th August. That night there was a meeting of Ribbentrop, Goering, Goebbels, Keitel, Jodl and others at the Foreign Office in Berlin. Hitler was in Berchtesgaden and took part in the conference by telephone, being permanently connected to the room in which the conference was taking place. . . . It emerged from these discussions that Berlin had not negotiated through its Ambassador in Moscow, Count Schulenburg, but had already sent a special negotiator to Moscow, Ingr Hilger [Commercial Attaché of the German Embassy, holding the rank of Counsellor]. . . . The discussions lasted until the early hours of 4th August and the German negotiator was able to take his answer back to Moscow by plane on the same morning [4th August]."

Benes's reference to Hilger's part in the negotiations raises a fascinating side issue. Were Hitler and Stalin really conducting negotiations at two different levels? And, if so, why? The British newspaper, the *News Chronicle*, published also an article by its political commentator, A. J. Cummings, giving an extraordinarily accurate forecast of the terms of the Molotov-Ribbentrop Pact on *11th July, 1939*—fifteen days before Schnurre had dinner with Astakhov. For this to have appeared in print indicates one of two possibilities. Either some Soviet-German soundings had taken place, as suggested by Benes, which the published documents have never disclosed and news of this reached Cummings by sources that cannot now be checked as Cummings himself is dead. Or Cummings had access to information from the Soviet side. As Cummings was a personal friend of Maisky, who in his turn was a sincere believer in a Soviet-British *entente*, this is a possible explanation. The tone of the *News Chronicle* story also indicates that it came from Soviet sources and the ideas of "the partition of Poland" and "freedom of action in Asia and the Far East" for Russia, were considerations that only existed at that time in Soviet policy thinking and were not fully disclosed to the Germans until much later, as the story will show.[1]

[1] *News Chronicle*, 11th July, 1939

Unofficially and indirectly Hitler has made the following proposals to Moscow:

(1) Freedom of action for Germany in Eastern Europe involving no threat against Russia or the Ukraine.
(2) Partition of Poland.
(3) Freedom of action for Russia, with full German support, in Asia and the Far East.
(4) Germany's withdrawal of co-operation with Japan—that is, dropping Japan from the Axis.
(5) Political Russo-German Alliance on these lines.

The proposals mark the third German attempt in the present year to buy off Russia. The two approaches in the early months of the year were curtly rejected. The latest effort signifies to the full Hitler's fear of the consequences of a close British-French-Russian line-up against aggression.

GOEBBELS AND STALIN

For months past there has been practically no anti-Russian propaganda in Germany.

If the new proposals hold out even a faint prospect of success Dr. Goebbels will organise mass-propaganda designed to transform German opinion about the Russian bugbear and to show that Stalin has "liquidated" Bolshevism and is now converting Russia into a National-Socialist State with which it will be quite proper for Germany to be on the friendliest terms.

THE ONE CERTAINTY

It should be in the power of the British Government to torpedo this alluring Nazi plan to-morrow. Yet there are Conservatives in high places who do not want the British Pact with Russia. The *Daily Express* says the Pact is like an egg which is addled.

If there is one certainty in an uncertain world it is that failure to come to agreement with Russia will make war almost as inevitable as death—war in circumstances of grave peril to the British Empire.

Author's Note: The files of the *News Chronicle* show that A. J. Cummings made no subsequent reference whatsoever, in circumstances that would have been natural and legitimate, to one of the most extraordinary "scoops" in newspaper history. Nor did he speak of his remarkable revelation to his surviving colleagues on the newspaper staff. All this supports the view that Maisky may

Schulenburg saw Molotov on 4th August, but as news of the high-level meeting in Berlin and its momentous decisions had not yet reached him, his talks covered the same ground as that between Schnurre and Astakhov. Schulenburg reported: "From Molotov's attitude it was evident that the Soviet Government was, in fact, prepared for an improvement in German-Soviet relations but the old mistrust of Germany remains. My over-all impression is that the Soviet Government is at present determined to sign with England and France if they fulfil all Soviet wishes. . . ."

Meanwhile, the Soviet talks with the Western Powers in Moscow were still going on. Stalin was determined not to give away all his cards to Hitler and the perfidious farce was essential to his plans. However, a little progress was being made. The difficulty about guarantees to the Baltic States and Poland had been overcome by agreeing to name the countries only in the protocol of the Pact. The relationship between the Pact and the proposed Military Convention had also been agreed. And Molotov had accepted military talks. The British and French Governments had also agreed to the suggestion that a military and naval mission should go to Moscow, and the names were announced on 21st July. The names and responsibilities of the respective delegations for the talks indicate the shrewdness of the Russians in impressing the Germans. The Soviet delegation was led by Marshal Voroshilov, the Commissar for Defence. It included Admiral Kuznetsev, Commissar for the Navy, General Shaposhnikov, Chief of Staff of the Red Army, General Loktianov, Chief of Staff of the Red Air Force, and General Smorodinov, Assistant Chief of Staff of the Red Army. It was the strongest delegation that Stalin could name without taking part himself. On the other hand, the composition of the British delegation indicated Chamberlain's approach. This delegation was led by Admiral Sir Reginald Plunkett-Ernle-Ernle-Drax, Principal A.D.C. to the King. The French delegation at least included a member of France's Supreme War Council, General Doumenc. As though they had all the time in the world,

---

have been instrumental in placing information which would have cost him his life if Stalin had ever known. Two other facts point in this direction. Maisky, himself, had returned to London after consultations in Moscow, where he would have learned of Stalin's plans. He may have thought that by using Cummings, who was a friend of his, he could bring pressure on the British Government to change its attitude. Secondly, as he stated subsequently, he was in the habit of using Cummings in this manner. See *Who Helped Hitler?* p. 35.

the Western missions decided to proceed by sea to Leningrad.

The first difficulty to arise was on the question of powers granted to the delegations. The Soviet delegation was authorised to sign military agreements for the protection of peace and against the aggressor. The British, however, had no formal written powers. Voroshilov thereupon expressed his astonishment and impatience. Next the Russians were contemptuous of the smallness of the British commitment to France. Finally, at the end of the session on the second day (13th August) Voroshilov asked what action was expected by Russia in the event of an attack by Germany on France, Britain, Rumania, Poland or Turkey. The French delegates replied in vague terms next morning (14th August). But Voroshilov insisted that he must know precisely; in particular whether Poland would allow the passage of Soviet troops through her territory. On 15th August Voroshilov refused to continue discussions until his questions had been answered. The talks were, therefore, suspended whilst the French delegation frantically telegraphed Paris, urging that one of its number should visit Warsaw to negotiate with the Poles.

Events were moving fast in the parallel negotiations with Germany that Stalin was conducting through Molotov—too fast for Stalin, who was nothing if not suspicious and cautious. But Hitler was now determined upon war. For him, every day counted. He wanted his Soviet Pact urgently.

Three days later, 15th August (the day upon which Voroshilov had refused to continue with the military talks until the issue of Soviet troops crossing Poland had been settled), Molotov heard in the evening from Schulenburg that Ribbentrop himself was offering to come to Moscow. Molotov "warmly welcomed the German intentions of improving relations with the Soviet Union" but stressed the need for adequate and detailed preparation. He could see that the Germans were desperate for time and he was ready to use their difficulty to strengthen the Soviet position.

Molotov asked Schulenburg three questions. First, was the German Government prepared to sign a non-aggression pact with the Soviet Union? Secondly, were the Germans prepared to bring pressure on Japan to improve the border situation in the Far East? Thirdly, would the Germans contemplate a possible joint guarantee to the Baltic States?

That day Voroshilov also asked the British and French delegations for a postponement of the Moscow military talks until 21st August. General Doumenc sent a representative to Warsaw to see the Polish leaders in person. When he arrived, Smigly Rydz is supposed to have told him: "With the Germans we risk losing our liberty: with the Russians, our soul."

By now Ribbentrop was very anxious. The hour of the German attack scheduled for the end of August was approaching. He was prepared to sign almost anything to ensure Soviet neutrality when the decisive moment came. He telegraphed Schulenburg agreeing to the trade agreement. He asked him to get Russian acceptance for an immediate visit by himself. Schulenburg saw Molotov twice on Saturday, 19th August.

On the afternoon of Wednesday, 16th August, Ribbentrop telegraphed German acceptance of all three points to Schulenburg, but stressed the need for speed. He also offered to come to Moscow at the end of the week or early in the following week. When Schulenburg arrived at the Kremlin next day to deliver Ribbentrop's telegram to Molotov, the Russian Foreign Minister handed the German Ambassador a note from the Soviet Government summarising the position. It said that if German policy was changing, "the Soviet Government could look upon such a change only with pleasure." The first step for improving relations, according to the Soviet note, was a trade agreement. Then the two countries could proceed to a non-aggression pact "with the simultaneous conclusion of a special protocol which would define the interests of the parties." This protocol was to be the hub of the pact. In short, Stalin had now decided to show his hand and ask openly for the division of Eastern Europe.

The Soviet-German trade agreement was duly signed that night and it was proclaimed next day. Molotov also agreed to the visit by Ribbentrop "as early as 26th or 27th August." But this was still not good enough for Hitler's time-table. Somehow or other he must get Ribbentrop to Moscow to secure the Soviet signature upon a political agreement, before the German armies marched into Poland. Hitler, therefore, telegraphed Stalin direct, asking him to receive Ribbentrop on 22nd August, or, at the latest, 23rd August.

Hitler's telegram went off in the afternoon of Sunday, 20th August. Hitler could not now contain himself in his anxiety and rang up Goering in the middle of the night to say how concerned he was at the time Stalin was taking to reply. On Monday morning he received the Soviet leader's answer:

To the Chancellor of the German Reich, A. Hitler
I thank you for your letter. I hope that the German-Soviet
Non-Aggression Pact will mark a decided turn for the better in
the political relations between our two countries. . . . The
Soviet Government has authorised me to inform you that it
agrees to Herr Von Ribbentrop's arriving in Moscow on 23rd
August.   *J. Stalin*

Hitler is said to have hammered on the wall when he got the
reply, "uttering inarticulate cries and finally exultantly 'I have the
world in my pocket!' " He need not have worried, for on the
evening of 19th August Stalin had already told the Politbureau
that he was going to sign the pact with Hitler.

Ribbentrop set off for Moscow early on 22nd August. On that
same fateful day, 22nd August, Voroshilov was playing hide-and-seek
with the Allied missions in Moscow who had got their answer
about Poland. Eventually, Doumenc managed to see Voroshilov
at 7 p.m. Voroshilov told him bluntly: "The question of military
collaboration with France has been in the air for several years but
it has never been settled. Last year, when Czechoslovakia was
perishing, we waited for a signal from France but none was given.
Our troops were ready. . . . The French and British Governments
have now dragged out the political and military discussions too
long. For that reason the possibility is not to be excluded that
certain political events may take place." Doumenc realised that
his mission had failed.

When Ribbentrop reached Moscow at midday on 23rd August
he went first to the German Embassy. He met Stalin in the Kremlin
at 3 p.m. Almost immediately, Stalin raised the vital question
that he wanted the Latvian ports of Windau and Libau on the
Baltic. The conference was adjourned whilst Ribbentrop telephoned for Hitler's agreement and he asked also for authority to
sign the secret protocol defining each country's sphere of influence.

When Hitler received Ribbentrop's message he was still at the
Berghof eagerly awaiting the news. He had an atlas brought to
him, and having looked at a map of the Baltic, replied, "Yes.
Agreed." This was at about 8 p.m.

Ribbentrop was having a hurried dinner at the German Embassy
when Hitler's reply came through. At once, he returned with it to
the Kremlin. The talks went on far into the night. They became

cordial and grew even more so as the champagne flowed. The Pact and a secret protocol were duly signed and dated 23rd August. Under the secret protocol, whose existence was not discovered until after the Second World War, Russia was assured of control of Finland, Estonia and Latvia; of Eastern Poland to a point appreciably to the west of the former "Curzon Line" and of Bessarabia. In his geniality "Herr Stalin spontaneously proposed a toast to the Führer: 'I do know how much the German nation loves its Führer; I should therefore like to drink his health.'" The news burst like a roll of Wagnerian thunder upon the whole world.

Next day the Soviet Government formally broke off the military talks with the Western Powers. The Western mission forlornly packed for home. For the record, Voroshilov stated the Soviet position in a Press interview: "The U.S.S.R. having no common frontier with the aggressor, could only extend aid to France, Great Britain and Poland through the passage of its troops through Polish territory. The French and British missions did not agree with the position of the Soviet Government and the Polish Government openly announced that they did not require and would not accept the military aid of the U.S.S.R. These circumstances made military collaboration with the U.S.S.R. and these countries impossible." The Soviet-German Pact had made war inevitable. Ribbentrop, still intoxicated by his visit to the Kremlin, told Hitler that he had "felt more as if he were among old Party comrades." On 1st September the Wehrmacht attacked Poland.

The arguments as to why and how the incredible had happened and who was responsible will remain in dispute amongst the historians. Yet the known facts must speak for themselves. A politically demoralised and virtually unarmed German nation had been so galvanised and equipped under Hitler that within six and a half years of his coming to power it was able to make a challenge for world domination. Britain and France had cast away positions of seemingly impregnable strength and world influence by irresolution and by mistaken policies. France was soon to be overrun and humiliated, as her national fibre crumpled. Britain was to face ruin before she emerged into a strange world, with new balances of power and a secondary role in it for Britain. She escaped France's fate for various reasons—the existence of twenty miles of sea between Calais and Dover; Hitler's subsequent mistakes; but her salvation was her national inability to grasp the peril in which she stood.

The truth was that when the world expected Britain to give up, she did not do so because such a prospect never occurred to the people.

As for the Soviet Union, the course upon which Stalin had embarked stemmed from his deep suspicions of others and his determination to safeguard the citadel of Communist revolution at all costs. His distrust of Western liberalism, his contempt for weakness, his respect for power, and his fascination by it, all made him take steps that were to lead directly to the great Armageddon on Soviet territory two years later. His people were to pay more dearly in terms of death and suffering than any other nation as a result. Yet, behind Stalin's attitude and motivating it, there was also the Marxist-Leninist doctrine of two worlds and the ultimate goal of Communist world revolution.

The true Soviet intention at the time of Munich must still remain an enigma. Voroshilov's later statement of 22nd August, 1939, in *Izvestia*, when he broke off the Soviet-Western military talks, made the excuse that the U.S.S.R. could not collaborate militarily with the Western Powers against Germany because of Polish opposition to Soviet troops on Polish territory. If Voroshilov's reasoning was valid in 1939, it was even more true in 1938, when Czechoslovakia was under pressure and, therefore, it must again cast doubt upon all the Soviet Union's intentions.

The Chamberlain Government has been accused many times of failing to take the appropriate steps to overcome Soviet suspicions. This charge has weight and the British record in the Soviet-Western negotiations, throughout the period that began with the first Czechoslovak crisis and which ended in war, makes appalling reading. One sees Chamberlain's deep suspicions of the Soviet Union coming to the front again and again. There was his complete misunderstanding of Hitler's character and appetites. He was also supported and surrounded by individuals in the British Conservative Party who felt themselves to be closer to Nazism than to Communism. For that was the British Tory Party of the 1930s—the same party that kept Churchill in the wilderness; and the majority of whose members of Parliament, in 1940, still preferred Chamberlain and defeat to the leadership of Churchill. (The actual figures in the historic division of 8th May, 1940, were: for the Chamberlain Government, 281; against, 200 [including only 32 Conservatives, 4 Independents and 4 National Liberals].)

At almost any time during these shaming years 1938 and 1939 Chamberlain could have accepted a Soviet proposal at its face value—and thereby tested its sincerity. He did not choose so to do and therefore the judgment of history upon this man may be merciless.

Nevertheless, certain charges against Chamberlain are untrue. It had been said frequently that a more senior official than Strang should have been sent to the 1939 Moscow talks, perhaps even a political leader? It has also been argued that Strang's rank at the time was regarded by the Soviet Government as an affront. The answer to this charge is that none of the preliminaries of the Molotov-Ribbentrop Pact either was negotiated at a high level. By the time Strang went to Moscow, Stalin had announced to the world on 10th March his long-standing aim of reaching accommodations with Hitler. Only one thing could have reversed Stalin's decision to come to terms with Hitler—if Britain and France had been able to offer more to the Soviet Union than Germany was able to offer, and that was impossible.

One can also see Chamberlain's political difficulty in dealing with Stalin, the Polish and Rumanian attitudes being what they were. He never found a way of overcoming the geographical obstacles. Finally, there was the Soviet Union's fundamental incompatibility as an ally for the Western democracies because of Communism's belief in world revolution, and Stalin's earlier decision to come to terms with Hitler if he could do so.

Stalin sent for Schulenburg, the German Ambassador in Moscow, at two o'clock in the morning of 17th September, 1939. Molotov and Voroshilov were also there when Schulenburg arrived in the Kremlin. Stalin announced that the Red Army would cross the Polish frontier at 6 a.m. and read a note that was to be handed immediately to the Polish Ambassador. Hitler was delighted when he heard the news. It had followed continuous pressure upon the Soviet Government to intervene in Poland in order to occupy the territory allotted to Russia under the secret protocol of the Nazi-Soviet Pact of 23rd August.

The event makes nonsense of the main Soviet justification for its action in Poland which has always been that it was undertaken to forestall the Germans and to defend Russia. On 3rd September, Ribbentrop had formally invited the Soviet Government to move its troops into Poland. Molotov replied on 4th September, saying that it was "still too early." Ribbentrop renewed his invitation on 9th September. Molotov again replied, "in a few days." When

Schulenburg, who was delivering Ribbentrop's message to the Soviet Government, pressed the point, Molotov referred to the Soviet need for political justification for such a step. Molotov then said: "The Soviet Government intended to take the occasion of the further advance of German troops to say that Poland was falling apart; and that it was necessary for the Soviet Union to come to the aid of the Ukrainians and the White Russians 'threatened' by Germany." From this, it was clear that Stalin meant to keep up his "neutrality" fiction. But even the hitherto accommodating Nazi Government thought that it was going too far to suggest a threat to Russia as the pretext for the Soviet Union implementing the very treaty that Molotov and Ribbentrop had only just signed, and the Germans protested most strongly.

For a few days there were differences between Moscow and Berlin, especially on the wording of a joint communiqué to be issued announcing the military occupation of Poland, once the Russian troops had marched. Stalin, for his part, rejected one draft. He said disarmingly, "It presented the facts all too frankly." Nevertheless, Stalin gave in, dropping all mention of the "threat" from the official communiqué. Instead, he used international Communist propaganda services[1] to provide the justification that he had been unable to write into the German-Russian communiqué —hence the subsequent Communist mythology, that the Russian move had been undertaken in self-defence and to forestall the Germans.

The plunge having been taken, the Germans and Russians now worked together in military harmony. But some political problems remained unresolved—especially the decision as to whether the

---

[1] For an illustration of the way in which Stalin deployed his case: *Daily Worker*, 18th September, 1939:

SOVIET COUNTERBLOW AGAINST NAZIS

RED ARMY TO STOP HITLER ENTERING UKRAINE

The Red Army is on the move. With the Polish State in dissolution and the Nazis already reaching out for domination of the peoples of the Ukraine and Byelo-Russia, west of the Soviet Border, the Soviet Government has acted swiftly and decisively.

In the early hours of yesterday morning, divisions of workers and peasants of the Red Army of Soviet Union began to move across the former Soviet-Polish frontier into the threatened areas of Ukraine and Byelo-Russia.

"The Red Army," said Molotov, ". . . will fulfil their duty with honour and glory."

former Polish State should continue to exist. Hitler was inclined
to support a small Polish State. But Stalin had other ideas. Accordingly, Molotov sent for Schulenburg on 19th September to tell him
that the Soviet Government wished to negotiate a final settlement
on the status of Poland. Unaware of what was going to happen,
Ribbentrop agreed on 22nd September to fly to Moscow on 27th
September. On 25th September, however, Stalin sent for Schulenburg at eight o'clock in the evening. Molotov was also present.
Stalin began by saying that in the final settlement of the Polish
question, anything that might create friction between Germany
and the Soviet Union must be avoided. With this thought as his
starting point, he considered it wrong to leave an independent
Polish State. He, therefore, proposed the following: from the
territory to the east of the demarcation line, all the province of
Lublin and that portion of the province of Warsaw which extends
to the Bug should be added to Germany's share. "In return,"
Stalin went on, "Germany should waive her claim to Lithuania."
Stalin offered this suggestion as a subject for the forthcoming
negotiations with Ribbentrop and added that, if Germany consented, the Soviet Union would immediately take up the solution
of the problem of the Baltic countries in accordance with the
protocol of 23rd August, and expected in this matter the unstinting
support of the German Government. Stalin expressly indicated
Estonia, Latvia and Lithuania, but did not mention Finland.

It was a bold, avaricious proposal. Stalin was offering a strip of
Poland that did not belong to him for Lithuania. If Germany
accepted, Stalin would now gain control of three Baltic states and
Lithuania would become Russian territory. He would also be
ridding himself of the exclusively Polish areas, thereby passing over
the notoriously intractable Polish problem to Germany.

Ribbentrop, on his arrival in Moscow on 27th September, was
given a splendid reception. Special flags, made in his honour,
adorned his route. They bore both the hammer and sickle and the
swastika—something which few could have foretold a few months
before. The German Foreign Minister was taken immediately to
the former Austrian Embassy. His first meeting with Stalin began
at 9 p.m. and it continued until nearly one o'clock in the morning.
Ribbentrop listened to Stalin's expanded proposal and he weighed
carefully the issues overnight, telegraphing Hitler for guidance at
the same time. Ribbentrop could see that Stalin had everything
to gain from his point of view, but he (and Hitler also, as it turned

out) was attracted by the prospect of rich provinces in the west of Poland and by the free hand that Germany was to be given in dealing with the Poles. Ribbentrop, in his heady confidence, considered that this last point would present little difficulty.

When the Nazi-Soviet conference resumed at three o'clock in the afternoon of 28th September, Ribbentrop, after hearing from Hitler, had decided to accept. The agreement was then signed. A Supplementary Secret Protocol was added on the morning of 29th September to the original Secret Protocol. A dinner was given in honour of Ribbentrop by Molotov, with Stalin, Kaganovich, Voroshilov, Beria and Mikoyan radiating bonhomie towards the Nazis. The German delegation thoroughly enjoyed itself. Some called it a memorable night. Forster, the Gauleiter of Danzig, who was present, summed up their feelings by, once again, calling the Russians "old comrades"—the term which most clearly expressed the state of Soviet-Nazi relations.

Ten days later, as a result of Stalin's initiative, Hitler instituted by decree the "Government General of Poland," a name that was to acquire a terrible significance in Polish history. Also, as a result of Stalin's initiative, Hitler was given a free hand to deal with the specifically Jewish areas of Poland, with consequences that are now known to the world.

Hitler, at this time, rated Stalin as one of "three great statesmen" living—the other two being Mussolini and himself. He was "only afraid that he [Stalin] might be replaced by an extremist." He sent a German trade mission, led by Schnurre, to Moscow which concluded an agreement leading to Soviet raw materials being exchanged for German manufactured goods. Hitler also launched a peace offensive against the Western Powers—following on the fall of Poland. Stalin, keeping in step, supported him with all the Soviet Communist Party's world-wide propaganda agencies.

In the meanwhile, Stalin's eyes had turned also to Finland. A Finnish representative was summoned to Moscow in October. The Finnish Government sent Paasikivi, who had signed the peace of 1921 with Russia. The Soviet demands which he met on arrival were sweeping. They included the moving back of the Finnish frontier on the Karelian Isthmus, so that it was out of artillery range of Leningrad, the cession of certain islands, the lease of Petsamo (Finland's only ice-free port in the Arctic) and, above all, the leasing of the port of Hango at the entrance to the Gulf of Finland, for a Russian naval and air base. The Finns were prepared to give way on almost every point, except the last.

Finnish-Soviet negotiations broke down on 13th November. The Finnish Government, in alarm, immediately strengthened its forces on the Karelian Isthmus. On 28th November Molotov denounced the Soviet-Finnish Non-Aggression Pact. And, on 30th November, the Red Army attacked Finland at eight different points along her thousand-mile frontier, bombing Helsinki at the same time.

The Russians made very little progress at first—to universal astonishment. Their main drive on the Karelian Isthmus ran into the "Mannerheim Line," so named after the Finnish Commander-in-Chief. The Soviet attacks in the waist of Finland proved disastrous to the invaders. The Finnish frontier posts withdrew down long roads between tall pine forests, followed by Russian columns. After the Soviet troops had penetrated about thirty miles, they were set upon from behind by the Finns and cut to pieces. The Finns also invented a new type of anti-tank hand-grenade which they gaily named "The Molotov Cocktail." Stalin had counted on a walk-over and was facing humiliation.

The astonishing Finnish resistance continued successfully for over two months through the winter of 1940. In the West, there was a great wave of sympathy for the small nation attacked by the larger one. The accumulation of anti-Soviet feeling, built up since the Nazi-Soviet Pact, suddenly burst. There was incessant talk in the British Government about sending aid. A recruiting bureau was opened in London in January, 1940. But typically—and, as subsequent events proved, fortunately—no significant steps were taken by Chamberlain's Government before the Red Army launched a major offensive on 1st February, 1940.

The plight of the Finns was soon desperate. The Mannerheim Line was breached after a fortnight's bitter fighting. The Daladier Government in France agreed as a last desperate measure, on 2nd March, to send fifty thousand French volunteers and a hundred bombers. But it was too late. Finland sued for peace on 7th March, and Stalin's hard terms were finally accepted on 12th March.

Through all this, the German Government had only reluctantly supported the Soviet action. Indeed, it had no alternative. With his plans for *Blitzkrieg* on the Western front almost ready for fruition, Hitler was in no position to do anything different. His own thoughts were elsewhere and on much larger targets.

85

Hitler's bid for world domination began when he launched his attack upon Norway in April, 1940. And with his facility for making the ill-judged utterance, Chamberlain spoke three days before, on 5th April, to the Central Council of the Conservative and Unionist Associations: "After seven months of war, I feel ten times as confident of victory as I did at the beginning. . . . I feel that during the seven months our relative position towards the enemy has become a great deal stronger. . . . One thing is certain: he [Hitler] missed the bus." Within three weeks of this speech by Chamberlain, Hitler was reaching out for control of both Norway and Denmark. In just over a month, it was Chamberlain himself who was driven from office by the British House of Commons. In less than three months, partly thanks to Stalin's connivance, nearly all Western Europe lay under Hitler's domination and Britain stood alone.

Soviet Russia's other contribution to Hitler's amazing military successes, apart from the major strategic results of the Nazi-Soviet Pact, was the mobilisation by Stalin of the Communist International against Britain and France. The Communist propaganda described the British and French war efforts as "an imperialist and capitalist crime against democracy." One of the secretaries of the Communist International, Walter Ulbricht (later to be leader of East Germany), launched an attack upon all socialists who fought with the Western democracies against Hitler. "The German Government," Ulbricht wrote obligingly about Hitler's régime, "announced its desire for friendly relations with the Soviet Union, whereas the Anglo-French warmongers wished to make war on her. It is in the interests of the Soviet people and the German workers to thwart Britain's plans." This type of Communist propaganda had little effect in Britain, where the Communists had only a derisory following, but in France it was a different and less savoury story. The Comintern's activities contributed markedly to the task of destroying French morale and to the debacle that followed. Yet another Russian contribution to the Nazi strength was economic aid to break the Western Powers' blockade. As a result, considerable quantities of raw material, principally oil, raw cotton, scrap and iron ore, were delivered by Soviet Russia.

The Battle of France ended with the signing of the Franco-German Armistice, and the Battle of Britain soon began. Before it did so, however, Hitler's preoccupation with the idea of reaching some compromise with Britain again came to the fore. It was a curious thought, showing how little he had understood the true character

86

of the British nation. Addressing the Reichstag on 19th July, in the full panoply of the greatest victory since Napoleon's day, Hitler praised the German-Soviet co-operation to which he owed so much. Then he turned to Churchill, warning him against any ideas that he might have of undermining it. He said: "In this hour I feel it is my duty before my own conscience to appeal once more to reason and common sense in Great Britain as much as elsewhere. . . . I see no reason why this war should go on." *Pravda*, in giving the Communist lead, said: "We now see how great a responsibility for rejecting Germany's peace proposals and for starting a new imperialist war in Europe rests on the shoulders of the Anglo-French imperialists."

The Battle of Britain began only when Churchill contemptuously rejected Hitler's offer. It raged for nearly eight weeks in the skies over the English Channel. As the weeks went by, it became clear to Hitler that his country's aim might be thwarted and the German Fuehrer now faced a dilemma. He still possessed, virtually intact, a huge and brilliantly efficient war machine. What was he to do with it, if the risk of invading Britain without air supremacy proved too strong? In June, 1940, the British operation known as *Sea Lion* had seemed easy to Hitler. Gradually, the German enthusiasm for a cross-channel assault began to wane and the invasion project soon looked difficult and treacherous.

Stalin, for his part, had been watching all the summer's developments from Moscow, partly in admiration and partly with apprehension. When the German Ambassador had gone to see Molotov to announce the German offensive in the West, Molotov had replied: "I understand that Germany has to protect herself against the Anglo-French attack." When France fell, Molotov summoned Schulenburg to his office on the evening of 18th June to express "The warmest congratulations of the Soviet Government on the splendid success of the German Armed Forces." But little did Stalin know what was going on in Hitler's mind.

Hitler first thought of "settling accounts" with Russia during the French campaign. He mentioned it at the time to General Jodl. He brought it up again at a conference at the Berghof, on 29th July, when General Jodl and Keitel were present. His reason was that he had been profoundly disturbed—and later very alarmed—by Russian actions, first in the Baltic, where wholesale Sovietisation was taking place, and later in the Balkans. As an illustration of Stalin's readiness to utilise Hitler's preoccupations in the West, a

Soviet ultimatum to Rumania demanding the cession of Bessarabia and the northern part of Bukovina had been delivered to the Rumanian Minister in Moscow at 10 p.m. on 26th June. Hitler, when he heard, knew he could not do anything about Bessarabia—this had been signed away on 23rd August, 1939, when he had been obsessed by the need not to fight a war on two fronts. But he now protested strongly over Northern Bukovina and he was all the more resentful when he discovered that there was little that he could do about this also.

Hitler's generals told him, after the Berghof revelation, that an attack upon Russia was out of the question for 1940. Accepting this, Hitler issued his first directives in August, 1940, to draw up the preliminary plans for the attack against the Soviet Union. Later that same month Goering told General Thomas, head of the Economic and Armaments branch of the German High Command, that deliveries to Russia (to pay for the incoming Soviet raw materials) should be made punctually up to the spring of 1941, but not later. Hitler still persisted with the aim of bringing Britain to her knees by siege. But, on the other hand, how could he allow the finely tempered German war machine to rust through idleness? It was another example of history's lesson that revolutionary movements on the march cannot stand still. Therefore, he decided to look east and took a preliminary step. Partly to regularise the situation in the Balkans that had arisen in June, and partly to forestall further encroachments by Stalin, the German and Italian representatives met at Vienna in late August, 1940. Under the Vienna Award—as it became known—of 30th August, 1940, Hitler and Mussolini compelled Rumania to cede a large part of Transylvania to Hungary and to return Southern Dobruja to Bulgaria. They decided to guarantee the new Rumanian frontiers—a guarantee that could only be directed against Russia—and with almost a tinge of Chamberlain about it!

Stalin, who was certainly not satisfied with Bessarabia alone, instructed Molotov to protest strongly at these German moves. Ribbentrop replied blandly on 9th September, 1940, that, so far as his Government was concerned, the zones of interest in the Balkans had been settled finally by the secret protocol of 23rd August, 1939, and by the Russian seizure of Bessarabia. Molotov angrily told Schulenburg that he did not share Ribbentrop's opinion. The record shows that the discussion became embittered—it was the crucial moment in Soviet-German relations. Ciano wrote later in his diary: "The dream of an understanding with Russia has vanished for ever in the room of the Belvedere in Vienna."

Nevertheless, it was still early days to think of a Russian-German war. Not even Hitler had decided finally. Ribbentrop made another effort to divert Russia south and east towards Persia and India in order to prevent any further friction in the Balkans. Part of his proposal was to associate the Soviet Union with the Three Power Pact between Germany, Italy and Japan, signed on 27th September, 1940, defining new zones of influence. Correspondence between Berlin and Moscow ensued, some of it direct with Stalin, in which Ribbentrop suggested both a visit by himself to Moscow and a visit by Molotov to Berlin. Eventually, Stalin agreed to send Molotov to Berlin in November. To show that some Germans still felt optimistic about relations with Russia, Ribbentrop asked Molotov to bring with him to Berlin a signed portrait of Stalin; and the Soviet Foreign Minister duly obliged.

Molotov reached Berlin on 12th November. He saw Ribbentrop first and Hitler later on that same day; and he saw Hitler again next day. There were three items for the agenda: Soviet adherence to the Three Power Pact, the definition of the various spheres of influence and the future of the Montreux Agreements, dealing with access to the Black Sea. Ribbentrop told Molotov: "The German-Soviet Pact has benefited both partners," and went on to ask whether "they could not continue to do good business together? By this, Ribbentrop envisaged the cutting up of the British Empire in Asia and Arabia. Hitler himself followed up this attractive idea and set out to dazzle Molotov. To his chagrin, Molotov agreed blandly with his ideas about "Great Asia" and then returned obstinately to Europe. Not all Hitler's talk of the imminent collapse of Britain—"a gigantic world-wide estate in bankruptcy," as Hitler put it—made any difference. Thus Molotov left Berlin ready to accept the German ideas in principle, but cautious on detail, refusing to commit himself, as he wished to know Stalin's views. And, as a result of Molotov's visit, Hitler's half-formulated thoughts of an attack upon Russia began to crystallise.

Ten days after Molotov had returned to Moscow, he sent for Schulenburg to give him Stalin's reply to the German proposals. The Soviet Union would accept the German proposals, he explained on certain well defined conditions. The area south of Batum and Baku in the general direction of the Persian Gulf was to be recognised as the centre of gravity of the aspirations of the Soviet Union.

The U.S.S.R. claimed the right to establish a land and naval base in the Dardanelles. Turkey was to be coerced. Japan was to renounce her rights in Northern Sakhalin. Bulgaria was to be "within the security zone of the Soviet frontiers."

Hitler was furious. His Government never answered these Russian proposals despite repeated Russian requests that the Germans should do so. The reason is now clear—he decided immediately to follow the course that had occurred first to him in the high summer and which—fostered by Molotov's grasping diplomacy—had since become his growing preoccupation.

Hitler issued his historic Directive No. 21 on 18th December, 1940.

OPERATION BARBAROSSA

The German Armed Forces must be prepared to crush Soviet Russia in a quick campaign even before the conclusion of the war against England. . . .

Hitler's anger with Stalin became merciless. The idea that Stalin was a "statesman" disappeared. "Stalin," he now said in a conference with his admirals in early January, 1941, "must be regarded as a cold-blooded blackmailer." His new objective, as he stated, was the so-called "A-A line," running from Archangel to Astrakhan. His provisional date for the great attack on Russia was 15th May, 1941.

Stalin's reaction—ever since he first saw it coming in 1936—had been to keep out of the war at all costs. He had always expected the war, when it came, to spread, involving both the United States and Japan. He realised that one day he might become involved too. But he hoped that, by delaying his decision for as long as possible, he would be in the best possible position to partake of any and all the spoils that might be going.

During the early months of 1941, there was a steady build-up of German forces in Eastern Europe, so much so that Molotov became anxious and sent for Schulenburg on 17th January. He began by expressing surprise that he had received no answer to his proposals of 25th November, and then asked what the troops were for—were they to occupy Greece and the Dardanelles? He also emphasised that Bulgaria was in the Soviet Union's security zone. Schulenburg referred these questions to Berlin. Ribbentrop answered reassuringly on 22nd January that the troops were to prevent the British landing in Greece; and that once the danger of this had passed, they would be withdrawn.

Three events upset Hitler's original 15th May time-table. Wavell's Middle East offensive, launched on 9th December, had come "like a thunderbolt" to the Italians, as Ciano put it. Therefore Hitler was hurriedly forced to take troops to form his Africa Korps in order to save the North African situation, and this meant a diversion of some German forces. Secondly, the Italians were also driven back in Greece, instead of advancing as expected. Finally, and most important of all, there was a *coup d'état* in Belgrade shortly after Yugoslavia decided to join the Three Power Pact on 25th March. The Yugoslav Regent, Prince Paul, was promptly expelled and Hitler decided, almost on the spur of the moment, to attack Yugoslavia and Greece—which he did on 6th April—in order to protect the right flank of "Barbarossa." The Greece and Yugoslav campaigns were over in a few days.

Stalin had been drawing his conclusions through all these events and he had been reading the dark omens. He had one last move available to improve his position before any storm broke. His opportunity was provided at the end of March by a visit to Moscow by Matsuoka, the Japanese Foreign Minister. The object of Matsuoka's trip was to sign a Soviet-Japanese Non-Aggression Pact and never was a man more unsuited for his task.[1] The Japanese Foreign Minister lectured Stalin for fifty-eight minutes out of a sixty-minute first interview on the connection between Japanese family life and Communism; but Stalin was not a man to be guided by personal irritations. So just when Matsuoka was preparing to return home empty-handed, the Japanese envoy was summoned to the Kremlin, and Stalin suggested a Soviet-Japanese Pact of neutrality and friendship, including a tentative division of spheres of influence— Manchuria to Japan, Outer Mongolia to Russia. Matsuoka was amazed and delighted. He signed the pact at once amidst much ingratiating talk from Stalin about them both being "Asiatics."

Stalin also decided upon a final gesture to Hitler. He went to the Moscow railway station to see off Matsuoka. After embracing his "fellow Asiatic," he looked around the large gathering of diplomats and newspapermen. Schulenburg tells the story: "He publicly asked for me and when he found me, he came up to me

[1] Within a few days Matsuoka had told the Pope that his country was fighting not the Chinese but Bolshevism, which was supported in Asia by the Anglo-Saxons.

and threw his arm around my shoulders. 'We must remain friends and you must now do everything to that end!' Somewhat later Stalin turned to the German military attaché, Colonel Krebs, first made sure that he was a German, and then said to him, 'We will remain friends with you in any event'. " It was his way of telling Hitler that he had called off the Balkan argument.

We now know that Stalin hoped somehow to postpone the great blow right up to the last moment. He received warnings, from Churchill, through the British Ambassador, Sir Stafford Cripps, from Eden via Maisky, and from his own intelligence service. And, paradoxically, only he, Molotov, and Schulenburg—brought up in the Bismarckian tradition and striving so long for Russian-German accord—really believed that war could be avoided. Cripps is reported by German Intelligence to have mentioned the actual date, 22nd June, but there is no other evidence to support the view that Cripps had shown such perspicacity: rather the contrary, for Cripps strongly and foolishly resisted having to deliver Churchill's warning message, originally dispatched on 3rd April. Sensing the situation, Stalin himself took over the post of formal head of the Soviet Government on 6th May, but he continued with the Soviet policy of economic collaboration right to the end. General Thomas stated later: "The Russians delivered their supplies on schedule right up to the start of the attack, and even during the last few days cargoes of rubber from the Far East were rushed through by express train."

Stalin was prepared to do almost anything to re-establish Nazi-Soviet harmony. His final effort reached the point of farce. On 13th June, just over a week before the critical day, he instructed *Tass* to put out a most unusual statement, denouncing Sir Stafford Cripps for spreading rumours of an impending German-Russian war and simultaneously Molotov sent for Schulenburg to give him a special copy of the *Tass* statement.

Two German documents tell what happened next:

Schulenburg to German Foreign Ministry
Moscow, 22nd June, 1941, 1.17 a.m.

Molotov summoned me to his office this evening at 9.30 p.m. After he had mentioned the alleged repeated border violations by German aircraft, with the remark that Dekhanosov [the Soviet Ambassador in Berlin] had been instructed to call on the Reich Foreign Minister in this matter, Molotov stated as follows: "There were a number of indications that the German

Government was dissatisfied with the Soviet Government. Rumours were even current that a war was impending between Germany and the Soviet Union. They found sustenance in the fact that there was no reaction whatsoever to the *Tass* report [denouncing Cripps] of 13th June: that it was not even published in Germany. The Soviet Government was unable to understand the reason for Germany's dissatisfaction. . . . He would appreciate it if I could tell him what had brought about the present situation in German relations."

I replied that I could not answer his question, as I lacked the pertinent information; that I would, however, transmit his communication to Berlin.

Ribbentrop to Schulenburg

Berlin, 21st June, 1941

1. Upon receipt of this telegram all of the cipher material still there is to be destroyed. The radio set is to be put out of commission.

2. Please inform Herr Molotov at once that you have an urgent communication to make to him and would therefore like to call on him immediately. Then please make the following declaration to him:

"The German Government of the Reich declares that the Soviet Government, contrary to the obligations it assumed,

   (i)   has not only continued, but even intensified, its attempts to undermine Germany and Europe;

  (ii)   has adopted a more and more anti-German foreign policy;

 (iii)   has concentrated all its forces in readiness at the German border.

Thereby the Soviet Government has broken its treaties with Germany and is about to attack Germany from the rear, in its struggle for life. The Führer has therefore ordered the German armed forces to oppose this threat with all the means at their disposal."

Please do not enter into any discussion of this communication. It is encumbent upon the Government of Soviet Russia to safeguard the security of the Embassy personnel.

Ribbentrop delivered a formal declaration of war to the Soviet Ambassador in Berlin at 4 a.m. on 22nd June. Schulenburg arrived at the Kremlin at dawn to see Molotov. The Soviet Foreign Minister listened in silence to Schulenburg as the German Ambassador read his statement. Molotov was very pale. "It is war. . . . Do you believe that we deserved this?" Molotov asked plaintively.

It was the last act of Schulenburg's diplomatic career. Late in 1943 his name was mentioned in a secret anti-Nazi conspiracy. After the attempt on Hitler's life on 20th July, 1944, Schulenburg was arrested by the Gestapo. He was executed on 10th November, 1944.

PART TWO

THE HINGE OF HISTORY

CHAPTER 5

THE SHOT-GUN MARRIAGE

If Hitler invaded Hell, I would make at least a favourable reference to the Devil in the House of Commons.   *Churchill*

Churchill drove down to Chequers on the evening of Friday, 20th June, 1941, knowing that the German attack was only a matter of hours. The news reached Colville, Churchill's Private Secretary, at 4 a.m. on the Sunday. But, as Churchill had given strict instructions that he was not to be awakened for anything except the invasion of Britain, Colville told him the news at 8 a.m. His only comment to Colville was, "Tell the B.B.C. I will broadcast at nine o'clock to-night."

Churchill's broadcast on 22nd June set out to answer clearly any thoughts that Stalin might have had that Britain would treat Russia as Russia herself had treated Britain. He said in the course of it: "Any man or state who fights against Nazidom will have our aid. . . . The Russian danger is therefore our danger, and the danger of the United States. . . ."

The American reaction to the news was much more circumspect than the British. Roosevelt allowed Sumner Welles, who was Acting Secretary of State, to tell the American Press on 23rd June: "In the opinion of this [American] Government, consequently, any defence against Hitlerism will therefore redound to the benefit of our own defence and security." Next day Roosevelt unfroze Soviet assets in the United States and made them available for arms purchases. But he remained very cautious. For example, he was asked at his next weekly Press conference, "Is the defence of Russia the defence of the United States?" Roosevelt countered by suggesting that the questioner should ask another kind of question such as "How old is Ann?"

In Moscow there was no formal response to Churchill's broadcast, although *Pravda* printed some extracts from it. Stalin personally remained silent. His position was understandable. His policy had collapsed completely. His expressed beliefs that the German threat had been only "an English plot" had been proved ridiculous. His armies had been surprised and were being cut to pieces. For some days he was a bewildered man.

Thus began the Grand Alliance. It was completed on 7th December, 1941, when Japanese aircraft bombed Pearl Harbour, bringing the United States of America into the war.

The German attack on Russia caught large numbers of Soviet aircraft on the ground. Tremendous initial disasters befell the Red Army. To that extent, and despite all the warnings that Stalin had received from various sources, the Germans achieved complete tactical surprise. Stalin admitted this shortly afterwards;[1] but in later years he was to justify the Red Army's appalling setbacks by claiming that it had been his grand design to allow the German forces to advance into Russia in order so to extend their lines of communications as to lead eventually to their destruction.

Churchill was quick to react to the new situation and characteristically impatient to take advantage of it. He received no response from Stalin personally, following his broadcast on 22nd June, so he asked Cripps to deliver a personal letter to Stalin on 7th July, assuring him of Britain's goodwill and determination. Stalin, who saw Cripps for one hour on 8th July—a welcome if temporary change from Cripps's point of view—proposed a Soviet-British agreement under two headings. First, Stalin suggested that there should be a mutual aid agreement, without specifying quantity or quality of materials. Secondly, he asked that both sides should agree never to conclude a separate peace and he added that without this form of agreement Russia would feel isolated. Churchill was telegraphed at once and he had a reply and draft agreement ready next day. This was amended slightly by the War Cabinet, to leave out a paragraph referring to ethnographical boundaries and self-determination, in the drawing up of post-war frontiers, as it was thought that it might prejudice Polish-Russian negotiations. The British draft was telegraphed to Moscow on the night of 9th-10th July and Cripps replied almost at once, saying that Stalin had accepted. The Anglo-Soviet agreement, broadly following Stalin's proposals, was duly signed in Moscow on 12th July. It had been

[1] In a conversation with Harry Hopkins, Roosevelt's special emissary.

quick work, considering the unpromising atmosphere before Churchill's letter was delivered on 8th July.

A week later, Maisky called on Churchill with the first direct communication from Stalin. It was a letter calling for a Second Front in the West—in fact, a request for two "second fronts," one in northern France and another in the Arctic. Stalin wrote optimistically that the French front "would be popular with the British Army, as well as with the whole population of Southern England." It was the first of the many demands for the Second Front that were to follow in the succeeding months and which became an essential part of the story of Soviet-Western relations.

What of the new military situation that had been created by the German drive east? The British Chiefs of Staff's assessment of the war position at the time was that Hitler's invasion of Russia would give Britain only a temporary—if very welcome—respite. They feared that the Russian campaign might be over quickly. The American War Department's estimate was similar, "a minimum of one month and a possible maximum of three months." German officers in the field said that they were astonished at the ease of the Wehrmacht's advance. Once the main Russian resistance at any point was overcome, the Red Army units usually surrendered in large and docile numbers. Many Russian officers also showed active anti-Communist feelings and were ready to collaborate. It was only later, as the Nazis' brutal methods of repression became widely known, that the Russian resistance took on its heroic form.

It was against this background of rapid German advance and pessimistic Western opinion, that Roosevelt threw caution aside and sent his personal representative, Harry L. Hopkins, to Moscow via Britain. On the lawn at Chequers, in the late evening of 27th July, Churchill explained to Hopkins the vital importance to the West of the Russian struggle and his own plans for sending British aircraft and other aid to Stalin. When Hopkins asked if he could repeat any of this to Stalin, Churchill replied excitedly, "Tell him! Tell him! Tell him that Britain has but one ambition to-day, but one desire—to crush Hitler. Tell him that he can depend on us. . . . Good-bye—God bless you, Harry." With this message and wearing a grey Homburg of Churchill's, with the initials W.S.C. inside, Hopkins flew in an R.A.F. Catalina flying-boat from Invergordon to Archangel. A Russian aircraft then took him to Moscow. After a brief rest and drive around Moscow, he reached the Kremlin at 6.30 p.m. on 31st July, where Stalin was awaiting him.

Hopkins went straight to the point. He told Stalin: "The President considered Hitler the enemy of mankind and that he therefore wished to aid the Soviet Union in its fight against Germany." Hopkins's report of the meeting goes on: "Describing Hitler and Germany, Mr. Stalin spoke of the necessity of there being a minimum moral standard amongst all nations and without such a minimum moral standard nations could not co-exist. He stated that the present leaders of Germany knew no such minimum moral standard and that, therefore, they represented an anti-social force in the present world. The Germans were a people, he said, who without a second's thought would sign a treaty to-day, break it to-morrow and sign a second one on the following day. . . ." Stalin's bitter reaction to what he considered to be German bad faith, after the Molotov-Ribbentrop Pact, was revealing and significant. Later, this feeling became part of general Soviet attitude towards Germany—a deep scar on the Russian national psychology, analogous in some ways to the effect Pearl Harbour was to have upon American defence strategy and thinking.

As soon as the Stalin-Hopkins talks turned to the practicalities of American aid to the Soviet Union, Hopkins was impressed by the nature of Stalin's requests. "Give us anti-aircraft guns and aluminium and we can fight for three to four years," declared Stalin. From this, Hopkins concluded that a man asking for aluminium was not thinking of immediate capitulation as the British and American military had feared. Stalin also attached great importance to Hopkins's visit and Hopkins wrote of him years later: "Not once did he repeat himself. He talked as he knew his troops were shooting—straight and hard. . . . There was no waste of word, gesture or mannerism. . . . Only once while we talked did his telephone ring. He apologised for the interruption, telling me he was making plans for his supper at 12.30 that night. Not once did a secretary enter with dispatches or memoranda. And when we said good-bye, he shook hands again with the same finality. He said good-bye once, just as only he said hallo. And that was that. No man could forget the picture of the dictator of Russia as he stood watching me leave—an austere, rugged, determined figure in boots that shone like mirrors, stout baggy trousers and snug-fitting blouse. . . ."

Hopkins was only in Moscow for a brief period. Complete with his report on Soviet needs, he flew from Moscow to Archangel on 1st August. The British Catalina left for Scapa Flow at once, where the battleship *Prince of Wales* was waiting to take Churchill to a conference with Roosevelt—the same conference at which the Atlantic Charter was signed. Hopkins arrived at Scapa Flow in a state of complete exhaustion. He was hauled into the Admiral's launch from the Catalina by a boat-hook and put to bed.

When they met in Argentia Bay, Roosevelt and Churchill decided to send an Anglo-American mission to Moscow, as soon as possible, to work out the long-term details of aid to Soviet Russia. A joint message from Roosevelt and Churchill, proposing such a conference in Moscow, was dispatched on 12th August. And without waiting for a reply, Britain and the United States also sent quantities of arms and other supplies to Russia, mainly by the northern sea route.

As another preliminary to the mission, Churchill wrote again to Stalin on 29th August, offering yet more fighter aircraft (amounting to 445 in all since 22nd June), to which Stalin replied on 4th September, thanking Churchill for his offer to *sell* the aircraft— a thought which had not been in the Prime Minister's mind. And Stalin asked once again for the Second Front. Maisky, delivering Stalin's note, underlined this latter demand by stressing the gravity of the situation on the Russian front. He asked Churchill: "If Soviet Russia is defeated, how can you expect to win the war?" Churchill—who had listened sympathetically at first—now lost his temper. He roared at the Soviet Ambassador: "Remember that only four months ago we in this island did not know whether you were not coming in against us on the German side. Indeed we thought it quite likely you would. Even then we felt sure that we would win in the end. . . . Whatever happens and whatever you do, you of all people have no right to make reproaches to us." The Prime Minister's reaction was such a shock to Maisky that he cried defensively, "More calm, please, my dear Mr. Churchill!"

Nevertheless, the demand for the Second Front by Stalin continued unabated. So lately indifferent to British survival, he was concerned as always only for his own interests. Thus he welcomed any steps in the West, however costly in human life, that might take the pressure off the crumbling and defeated Red Army before Moscow. Stalin also had the secret fear that influential circles in Britain preferred to let Soviet Russia and Nazi Germany exhaust each other in mortal combat, whilst Britain was reserving her position to collect the spoils of victory—much as Stalin had been ready to do after Hitler's Polish campaign.

On 4th September, Churchill telegraphed Stalin again, explaining once more why a second front was impossible and reviewing the aid that was coming. He sent another cable on 9th September saying that he was sending 5,000 tons of aluminium from Britain and 2,000 tons monthly thereafter. But this was not good enough for Stalin, who telegraphed in reply on 15th September, asking for 25-30 British divisions to be sent at once to Archangel or through Persia, which Stalin claimed could be done "without risk." Churchill was dismayed.

Meanwhile, the American half of the joint mission to Russia, led by Averill Harriman, had arrived in London. Churchill appointed Lord Beaverbrook, who had become the leading advocate of aid to Russia in the Cabinet, to be head of the British delegation. Both the American and British parties were equipped with friendly personal letters to Stalin, from Roosevelt and Churchill respectively. Alas, it availed them little on their arrival in Moscow on 28th September and their reception was bleak. Beaverbrook described their first meeting in the Kremlin in his own sharp, dramatic manner:[1] "There was Stalin. There was Molotov. Both were ice-cold and formal. I had asked for Litvinov to interpret, so that the Russians had every confidence. Nobody else was present. Litvinov was pleased as Punch, having been brought from some Moscow cellar, with his coat cuffs frayed and worn." At the first meeting, Stalin's hostility was apparent, and at the second meeting he became openly rude. He also ignored Churchill's reference, in his introductory letter, to General Ismay's presence in the British delegation, "who is my personal representative on the Chiefs of Staff Committee, and is thoroughly acquainted with the whole field of our military policy" and "is authorised to study with your commanders any plans for practical co-operation." Thus, astonishing as it may seem, Ismay never had any conversations with Stalin or the Russian commanders. Stalin also seemed to regard the help that was being offered as of little importance, and he imputed that Britain was allowing the Soviet Union to bear the whole brunt of the war. In view of all that had gone before, the British delegation in particular were disgusted. Stalin then raised with Beaverbrook the case of Rudolph Hess, who had flown to Britain in May, 1941, with the extraordinary notion that he could persuade Britain to cease hostilities against Hitler. Stalin asked of Beaverbrook, "Why don't you shoot him, if you don't really want to make a separate

[1] In a conversation with the author.

peace?" Beaverbrook had to explain patiently that such a course would not be possible in a democracy. To support the case for British good faith, he produced the transcript of a long talk with Hess which he had wisely brought to Moscow in case of such an eventuality. He now handed the transcript to Stalin, to the latter's great interest and surprise.

At the third meeting with Stalin and Molotov, there was a complete change of mood. The Russians gave up trying to extract the impossible and an agreement settling the arrangement for supplies from Britain and the United States was reached at once. Litvinov bounded out of his chair, saying, "Now we shall win the war!" A great reception in honour of the visitors was held that night in the Kremlin as the German guns drew closer to Moscow. Beaverbrook's recollections of the scene were vivid: "There was chatter, chatter, chatter. Everywhere people were talking and drinking under the bright chandeliers. Suddenly there was silence. Stalin appeared at the head of the stairs. Slowly he came down, in a grey uniform and long grey boots. All eyes were on him. You could feel the machine-guns in the shadows."

The Soviet-Western cordiality did not last. Within a few days Molotov was complaining to Cripps that he had received no answer to the Soviet request for 25-30 divisions. Cripps told him that he thought the answer that Britain could not send 25-30 divisions anywhere at that time had been made clear. Churchill confirmed this in a message describing this Russian suggestion as "a physical absurdity." The wrangle continued until Churchill in London suddenly realised that Ismay had taken no part in any strategic conversations in Moscow. Therefore he telegraphed Stalin offering to send Generals Wavell and Paget to Moscow. In response to Churchill's warm letter, Stalin's reply, delivered on 11th November, referred sarcastically to the proposed visit of the Generals. Instead, he said that the lack of clarity in Anglo-Soviet relations was due to two circumstances: "(a) There is no definite understanding between our countries on war aims and on plans for the post-war organisation of peace; (b) There is no agreement between the U.S.S.R. and Great Britain on mutual military assistance against Hitler in Europe."

For good measure, Stalin also raised the question of Britain declaring war upon Finland (which had now come in upon the German side) and upon Hungary and Rumania. Churchill did not reply and he hoped that "the silence was expressive." The

Russians realised that Stalin had gone too far and, after nine days, Maisky asked to see Eden at the Foreign Office. Maisky told Eden: "It had certainly not been M. Stalin's intention to cause any offence to any members of the Government, and least of all to the Prime Minister. . . . 'My Fatherland,' said Stalin [according to Maisky], 'finds itself in a humiliating position'."

Churchill responded at once, offering to send Eden to Moscow to explain the full situation. He also offered to declare war on Finland, if the Finns did not stop fighting within a fortnight. Nevertheless, Eden realised the difficulty of his Moscow mission and he wisely decided, before leaving, to send Stalin a memorandum and a draft of a proposed declaration of policy. The Foreign Secretary took as his two starting points: A joint declaration not to make a separate Anglo-American peace; and secondly—for the peace settlement—the Atlantic Charter, together with a speech by Stalin on 6th November, 1941, stating that the U.S.S.R. had no war aims for "the conquest of foreign territory, and the enslaving of other nations." Eden had reached Invergordon, on his way to Moscow, when Pearl Harbour was bombed by the Japanese.

Eden, who travelled by sea, reached Moscow in just over a week. The battle for Moscow was raging a few miles outside the city. Morale in the city was low. Rioting had been reported in some districts. There were also stories of Communists tearing up their Party cards so as not to be found with them when the Germans entered. But Stalin had remained behind in the Kremlin to direct the great and desperate battle, although the Soviet Government itself had been evacuated to Kuibyshev.

It is against this background that we have to consider Stalin's talks with Eden. Stalin began by saying that he wanted an agreement, not a declaration. He said a declaration was "algebra," whereas an agreement was "practical arithmetic." He coolly produced a draft agreement providing: first, for military assistance during the war; and secondly, for post-war reconstruction arrangements and for the contents of the peace treaties. He then suggested a secret protocol under which East Prussia was to be given to Poland; and Tilsit and the German territory north of the River Niemen added to Lithuania, by now part of the U.S.S.R. The Rhineland, according to Stalin, should be detached from Prussia; and Austria and Bavaria might become separate states. Stalin stated that he wanted the Russian frontiers in Finland and the

Baltic area restored to the position of June, 1941, and he suggested that the Curzon Line (with some amendments) might serve as the Russian-Polish frontier. Finally, he wanted to take back Bessarabia and Northern Bukovina from Rumania and Petsamo from Finland.

In return for these sweeping Soviet demands, Stalin suggested that Britain should receive concessions in Western Europe. If France did not emerge from the war as a major power, he thought that Britain should be granted military bases at such places as Boulogne and Dunkirk—also bases with garrisons in Belgium and Holland. He added that he would not object to British bases in Norway and Sweden.

Considering the military situation outside Moscow, Stalin's long-term views and his confidence in achieving them were remarkable. Eden had expected that Stalin might propose some form of secret protocol and just before he left England he had also been warned against accepting any such arrangement in a hurried message from Cordell Hull, the American Secretary of State. After listening to Stalin, the Foreign Secretary asked for time to study the proposals. His second meeting with Stalin took place at midnight on 17th-18th December—an indication of the strange hours at which the Soviet leader conducted his business. He now explained to Stalin that it was out of the question for him to sign such a protocol without consulting his colleagues. But Stalin pressed his claim and, with Molotov's aid, he argued at length that the future Russian frontier and the swallowing-up of the Baltic States should all be settled on his lines. Eden plodded on doggedly in reply, whilst leaving the door open for future arrangements and explaining again and again to Stalin that he could not possibly sign anything before his return to London.

British thinking at this time is interesting. Churchill was reluctant to discuss any of Stalin's demands with Roosevelt because he thought that they would only alarm the Americans. He was right, because when Eden loaned his notes to Winant, the American Ambassador, to pass on information to Roosevelt, the American reaction was angry. Thus Stalin's demands had to wait for an answer, the British feeling being that if it had to be a final choice between Russia and the United States, they would naturally choose the United States. However, Churchill also thought there should be a determined attempt to harmonise the position amongst the three, even if it meant agreeing to some Soviet bases in the Baltic and Black Sea regions after the war; with the fate of the Baltic States and other issues to be left to a peace conference. Halifax, by now British Ambassador in Washington, was instructed to approach the U.S. Government on these lines. When he did so, he was coldly informed by Sumner Welles that Roosevelt intended to take up the matter direct with Stalin through Litvinov, who had just been appointed Soviet Ambassador in Washington.

For all that, Stalin kept up the pressure on Churchill. Maisky was instructed to follow up the proposals Stalin had made to Eden. Churchill, therefore, sent a message to Roosevelt asking for American acquiescence to an Anglo-Soviet treaty. But the President remained obdurate and told Litvinov that he could not agree to any treaty—secret or open—about frontiers until the end of the war. Thus, Churchill had to make his own decision in isolation. He took it bravely by opening negotiations for a treaty with the Soviet Union including implicit recognition of the Soviet claim to their 1940 frontiers, but leaving aside the whole issue of Poland. Also the questions of the future relationship of the Baltic States with the U.S.S.R., Finland and Bessarabia, were to be left to a peace conference.

There were three reasons for the British initiative, which was received very coldly in Washington. First, British feeling was that the Soviet Union could always revert to the kind of neutrality it had pursued between 1939 and 1941, and this had to be avoided. Secondly, there was a genuine British desire for collaboration with Stalin after the war, despite all the misgivings and disappointments since 22nd June, 1941. Finally, it was a matter of realism: the Russians would anyway have to reconquer the territories in question, and to recognise the 1940 frontiers might be the best way of accepting gracefully a *fait accompli*. Indeed, no one could see the Russians giving up the ground they had won. Eden explained the British decision to Maisky and suggested that the negotiations for the treaty should take place in London.

In the meanwhile, Roosevelt had been attempting to persuade Stalin to send Molotov to Washington first, implying that it might be possible to discuss a second front in 1942. But Stalin had other views and Molotov's first stop turned out to be London. Stalin told Churchill on 23rd April of his intention to send Molotov, but the Soviet Foreign Minister did not, in fact, reach Britain until 20th May. Molotov and his small party began by adopting the original Russian position and the negotiations moved steadily towards a deadlock. To break it, Eden therefore introduced a new proposal, for a twenty-year treaty of mutual assistance. He explained to Molotov that although it did not deal with frontiers, if there was to be friendship between the two countries, it was clearly the British wish that Russia should remain strong and secure. On 26th May the treaty was signed, after its text had been referred to Stalin. The treaty fell into two parts: a repetition of former agreements for mutual aid; and, secondly, a promise to collaborate after the war. Once the negotiations started, the American attitude changed almost overnight, and Sumner Welles generously described the treaty to Halifax as "a miracle."

An interesting sidelight on the suspicions of the Soviet delegation was disclosed when Churchill offered Chequers to Molotov and his party, after the Russians had requested that they should be allowed to sleep in the country because of the aerial bombing on London. The Soviet party insisted upon the most elaborate security precautions. Molotov's room was given a thorough search for any possible bombs. The Russians demanded keys for all their bedrooms. Finally, all the beds had to be re-made in order to enable the occupants to jump out in the middle of the night, in case they were attacked by the Chequers' staff. To complete their military precautions, Molotov and his party had revolvers laid out each evening, along with their night clothes.

The incessant Soviet refrain for a second front, started by Stalin, was reiterated by Molotov immediately on his arrival in London. Molotov emphasised to Churchill, whom he saw several times in the course of his stay, that the Second Front was more important than the treaty.

Churchill was guarded and indefinite to Molotov on the Second Front issue when the latter was in London. But Molotov found Roosevelt in a much more expansive mood when he reached Washington.[1] He, therefore, put the question bluntly to the American President and his advisers in the White House. Hopkins's note states: "Mr. Molotov realised that the British would have to bear the brunt of the action but he was also cognisant of the role the United States plays and what influence this country exerts in questions of major strategy. Without in any way minimising the risks entailed by a second front action this summer, Mr. Molotov

[1] In fairness to Roosevelt, the Hopkins-Marshall mission to London in April, 1941, had come away with the impression that the British would agree to a second front in 1943 and possibly 1942.

declared his Government wanted to know in frank terms what position we take on the question of a second front, and whether we were prepared to establish one. He requested a straight answer. . . ."

Hopkins's minute goes on: "The President then put to General Marshall the query whether developments were clear enough so that we could say to Mr. Stalin that we were preparing a second front. 'Yes,' replied the General. *The President then authorised Mr. Molotov to inform Mr. Stalin that we were expecting the formation of a second front this year. . . .*"

This was a very important statement. The American promise to the Soviet Union was definite. Whatever may have been the growing difference of assessment between London and Washington, the Roosevelt promise "of a second front this year" went much further than anything that had been agreed between them in military talks. Unfortunately Roosevelt's words had been spoken. They could not be recalled. But Churchill tried very hard to recall them.

When Molotov returned to London on his hazardous flight home, Churchill personally handed him the following *aide-mémoire* in the presence of his colleagues in the Cabinet Room at Downing Street:

AIDE-MÉMOIRE

We are making preparations for a landing on the Continent in August or September, 1942. As already explained, the limiting factor to the size of the landing is the availability of special landing-craft. Clearly it would not further either the Russian cause or that of the Allies as a whole if, for the sake of action at any price, we embarked on some operation which ended in glorification at our discomfiture. It is impossible to say in advance whether the situation will be such as to make this operation feasible when the time comes. *We can therefore give no promise in the matter*, but provided that it appears sound and sensible we shall not hesitate to put our plans into effect.

At the same time, Churchill accepted an unpublished communiqué worked out between Molotov and Roosevelt containing the following sentence: "In the course of the conversations full understanding was reached with regard to the urgent tasks of creating a second front in Europe in 1942." This last announcement was immediately publicised in the Soviet Union and accepted by the Russians as a firm promise, which it was most certainly not.

The Prime Minister was by now thoroughly alarmed. He decided that he must travel to Washington himself to reconcile the divergent attitudes. He telegraphed Roosevelt saying that he was sending Admiral Mountbatten to explain British views about action in 1942. Churchill with only a small party including Brooke and Ismay, flew to Washington on the evening of 17th June.

In the discussions that now took place Churchill overwhelmed the Americans by the sheer force of his eloquence. He painted graphic pictures of the consequences of failure. At one point, he described the English Channel as "a river of blood" and recalled the carnage of Passchendaele and the Somme in the First World War. With dramatic effect he described his feelings as he had often stood in the House of Commons and looked around at "the faces that are not there," the missing generation of the earlier conflict. At the end of a very emotional day on 21st June, it was decided to go ahead—until 1st September—as far as possible with the planning for the 1943 Second Front. On 1st September the situation would be reviewed once more by the Allies. Any thought of an earlier landing, either to divert attention from the Eastern Front or to take advantage of a new situation, was to be postponed, which is not how Molotov had understood the situation when he was in Washington.

The Anglo-American argument over the Second Front and Roosevelt's promise to Molotov was not yet over. Churchill was determined to bury "Sledgehammer"—the tentative plan for a more limited bridgehead in 1942. On his return to London he telegraphed Roosevelt: "No responsible General, Admiral, or Air Marshal is prepared to recommend 'Sledgehammer' as a practicable operation in 1942." Next he introduced his earlier preference: "I am sure that French North Africa is by far the best chance of effecting relief to the Russian front in 1942. This has all along been in harmony with your ideas." (Churchill admitted afterwards that he had made a careful study of the President's mind whilst he had been in Washington and that he had detected that Roosevelt was attracted to a North African proposal.) "In fact, it is in your commanding idea," continued Churchill shrewdly. "Here is the true second front for 1942.".

The Prime Minister had won the day and there was to be no second European front in 1942. Nevertheless, the fact remained: the Russians had been misled. The blame lay broadly with Roosevelt in his over-eagerness to please. The problem now was to tell Stalin that there would be no second front in 1942, and possibly not even in 1943. The British and American ambassadors in Moscow were reporting that the Russians regarded the words in the 11th June communiqué as a firm promise, and had ignored Churchill's *aide-mémoire* to Molotov. The position was worsened by the growing losses, inflicted by the Germans, on the Arctic convoys carrying the sinews of war to the Soviet Union. The latest July convoy had actually lost twenty-three ships out of thirty-four bound for Archangel, thereby forcing Churchill to suspend further convoys until the long summer nights were over.

All this had to be put into a message to Stalin, to which Stalin sent the angry answers, refusing to accept the situation which led the new British Ambassador in Moscow, Sir Archibald Clark Kerr (Cripps having returned to London a hero to the British public despite his lack of success), to cable the Foreign Office with the suggestion that Churchill, in person, should come to Moscow to explain to Stalin why it was not possible to open a second front in Europe in 1942. Churchill promptly decided to accept this unpleasant assignment and—after a visit to Cairo, where he reorganised the Desert Command, replaced Auchinleck by Alexander and appointed Montgomery to the 8th Army—he flew to Moscow.

Because of mountains, the Prime Minister's aircraft had to fly at 12,000 feet, and the party were soon sucking oxygen tubes. Churchill's private thoughts at that time are fascinating: "I pondered on my mission to this sullen, sinister Bolshevik State I had once tried so hard to strangle at birth, and which, until Hitler appeared, I had regarded as the mortal foe of civilised freedom. It was like carrying a large lump of ice to the North Pole."

When the aircraft had landed at Moscow, Churchill made a short speech to Molotov and the assembly of generals, diplomats and a magnificent guard of honour that had been drawn up for him. He then drove into Moscow in Molotov's car. On the way he was surprised, on lowering the window to get some fresh air, to find that the glass was over two inches thick. "The Minister says it is more prudent," explained the obliging interpreter to Churchill.

That evening, 12th August, he went to the Kremlin for the first meeting with Stalin. In the belief that it was better to get the worst over, Churchill began with the Second Front. He reminded Stalin of the carefully worded *aide-mémoire* to Molotov in May, and he explained that it would be impossible to mount the operation in 1942. He went on to outline the build-up for 1943. The scene was grim. Stalin looked more and more despondent as Churchill unfolded his case, and he became very restless indeed when Churchill said at one point that war was not folly. Stalin, when he spoke, said he took a different view: "A man who is not prepared to take risks cannot win a war. Why are the Western allies so afraid of the Germans? If you do not blood your troops, you have no idea what their value is," he retorted. Churchill, keeping his temper with difficulty, said that Hitler had not crossed the Channel at the height of his power when Britain was virtually defenceless—and the reason was obvious.

Churchill has described the impasse: "There was an oppressive silence. Stalin at length said that if we could not make a landing in France this year he was not entitled to demand it or to insist upon it, but he was bound to say that he did not agree with my arguments."

Very skilfully, Churchill now turned the conversation towards the North African invasion. He first discussed what was meant by a second front. Then he talked about the Allied bombing of Germany. This broke the tension and Stalin became exuberantly anxious that people's homes should be bombed as well as military objectives. The Prime Minister felt that the moment had come to explain the African venture and he set it out graphically, concluding by his famous drawing of a crocodile, explaining to Stalin that it was as well to strike its soft under-belly (the Mediterranean) as an addition to hitting the snout (Northern France). To Churchill's enormous relief, Stalin grasped at once the strategic implications and summarised the advantages with brilliance and enthusiasm. The party got up from the table and gathered round a large globe where Churchill held the floor, explaining the desirability of clearing the Germans right out of the Mediterranean. The meeting lasted four hours, and Churchill went to bed feeling satisfied with a good day's work.

The next day's discussion, therefore, came as all the greater surprise. The meeting started at 11 p.m. and Stalin began it by coldly handing Churchill and Harriman copies of a memorandum re-opening the Second Front issue. Stalin appeared to have no further interest in the North African operation. Instead he accused the Allies of a breach of faith and—for good measure—he indicted the British for cowardice. Point by point and without bitter words, Churchill refuted Stalin. Stalin ended the argument by saying stiffly that they could carry the discussions no further. Instead, rather gruffly, he asked Churchill to dinner the next evening. The

Prime Minister accepted and added that he would be leaving Moscow in the early hours of the morning immediately after the dinner. When this news was translated, Stalin was taken aback. The Soviet leader asked, somewhat hesitantly, if the Prime Minister could not stay longer. Churchill was by now extremely angry and could control himself no longer. He could stay, he explained, if it were of any use, but, having come so far to establish a working relationship, he had found no ring of comradeship in Stalin's attitude. Before the Prime Minister's remarks could be translated, Stalin threw back his head and laughed, saying, "I do not understand your words but I like your spirit." These extraordinary and fluctuating discussions now took yet another turn. Stalin, anxious to atone and to please Churchill, explained his own war plans in detail, and asked for Churchill's comments, which the Prime Minister was delighted to give, and the meeting ended on a most amiable note after all.

Next morning, feeling that at least he was achieving results, Churchill postponed his departure another day, until dawn on 6th August. On the night of 15th August, when Churchill had said his farewells at the Kremlin to Stalin, the Russian leader suggested a drink in his private flat. Churchill accepted with alacrity and found a pleasant apartment of four rooms—a room for working, a bedroom, a dining-room and a large bathroom.

The last talk had ranged far over the war and the past, including Churchill's part in the Intervention and Stalin's recollection of the great collectivisation drive of the 1930s. At one point in the late-night conversation, Churchill asked Stalin whether the stresses and strains of war had been as bad personally for him as the carrying through of the Collective Farm policy. "Oh, no," he cried, "the Collective Farm policy was a terrible struggle." It had been an exciting evening, and Churchill slept soundly as his plane droned southwards towards Teheran.

It is inconceivable that Stalin by now did not appreciate the reasons for the abandonment of the Second Front in 1942. Indeed, he may have realised the true position all along. But this realisation —if it existed—did not prevent the Soviet Government from persisting with its campaign for the "Second Front Now," especially when the Battle for Stalingrad was at its height in September and October. Nor did it stop periodic Soviet outbursts of recrimination on the subject. Thus it would be wrong to imply that Churchill's visit to Moscow in August, 1942, had any lasting effect upon Russian attitudes towards Soviet-Western relations. These relations worsened again when Stalin learned shortly afterwards that the shipping demands of the North African operation had caused the suspension of the Arctic convoys.

The winter of 1942-3 was the turning point of the war. The advance of the 8th Army from El Alamein and the successful American and British landings struck decisive blows upon the German position in the Mediterranean. In late October, Hitler made his great blunder at Stalingrad. From the skies over Europe, grievous blows were also inflicted upon the Germans.

The American staffs, occupied with the problems of pressing forward the plans for North Africa, began at last to see the practical difficulties of a second front in 1943. They now slowed down the arrangements for the Second Front. By late November, paradoxically it was Churchill who was thoroughly alarmed and telegraphed Roosevelt. The President replied, still supporting the idea of a second front in Europe, but somewhat surprisingly he implied that it might not be possible in 1943. He also suggested a military conference between the United States, Britain and the Soviet Union. In Churchill's view this did not meet the needs. As an alternative, he suggested a meeting of the three leaders. Stalin had also expressed a desire in the conversations in Moscow to meet Roosevelt and, therefore, Roosevelt now sent a formal invitation to a meeting in North Africa. Stalin's reply, when it came, said that he could not leave the Soviet Union at the time, and he proposed a discussion by correspondence on the best ways of attacking Germany—and he returned to the inevitable topic, asking about the possibility of a second front for the spring of 1943.

Without Stalin—whom they agreed to keep informed—Roosevelt and Churchill arranged to meet as quickly as possible. Casablanca was named as the place and mid-January the time.

As far as Soviet-Western relations were concerned, the significance of the Casablanca Conference was set out in a joint message from Roosevelt and Churchill to Stalin, on 26th January. It summarised Anglo-American plans for the elimination of the German forces in North Africa, and for plans in the Far East to wage the war against Japan. The message went on: "We shall concentrate in the United Kingdom a strong American land and air force. These combined with the British forces will prepare themselves to re-enter the continent of Europe as soon as practicable."

This message was duly delivered to Stalin and Molotov in the Kremlin by the U.S. Ambassador and the British Chargé d'Affaires. When Stalin had heard the American Ambassador's statement, he passed the Russian text to Molotov and asked him something. Molotov "uttered two short, sharp exclamations." It turned out that Stalin was asking urgently whether he was getting a definite promise on the Second Front and Molotov was saying, "No—not yet, not yet."

In the spring of 1943, Churchill and Roosevelt decided to proceed with a plan to invade Italy, instead of a cross-Channel attack, which would have to be postponed until 1944. The news was conveyed to Stalin in a joint message which Roosevelt and Churchill had great difficulty in drafting. Stalin's reaction was only natural. He telegraphed Roosevelt that the postponement would cause "quite exceptional difficulties for the Soviet Union" and that it would create a "painful impression upon the Russian people and army." The Soviet leader concluded: "As far as the Soviet Government is concerned, it cannot join in this decision, which may have grave consequences for the further course of the war, and which, moreover, was taken without its participation, and without any attempt to consider together the questions of such tremendous importance."

Clark Kerr, the British Ambassador in Moscow, followed up Stalin's message with a telegram to the Foreign Office, warning that it would be unwise to disregard Stalin's last sentence and that the Russian feeling of resentment and lack of faith in Western intentions was very real. Recognising that there were genuine grounds for Stalin not being able to be present at conferences, and at the same time no Russian of sufficient power being able to take his place, Clark Kerr added: "Thus we find ourselves in the unhappy position of being in fact unable to consult him and at the same time of provoking his anger because we have failed to admit him to our counsels." Therefore, the British Ambassador thought that it was imperative to fix a meeting between Churchill, Roosevelt and Stalin as soon as possible.

Churchill, in reply to Clark Kerr, said that he was sending Stalin "a soft answer," but he also felt that there was no reason to apologise to him. The Russians themselves had "destroyed the second front in 1939 and 1940 and stood by watching with complete indifference what looked like our total obliteration as a nation."

The summer of 1943 saw major Russian victories following

Stalingrad. The German forces in North Africa were liquidated. Sicily was invaded on 9th July. Mussolini's twenty-one years of rule came to an end on 25th July when he was arrested and bundled into an ambulance after an audience with the King of Italy. Italy sued for peace and, in an olive grove near Syracuse, the Italian armistice was signed on 3rd September. Victory had begun to loom.

In the midst of these momentous events, Churchill journeyed to Quebec to meet Roosevelt once more. From Quebec, on 7th August, Churchill telegraphed Stalin suggesting a meeting of the three Heads of Government. Stalin replied saying he could not leave the front "even for one week" and suggested a preliminary meeting of "responsible representatives" to decide upon a date, place and agenda of a meeting of the Heads of Government. After a wrangle as to place, it was agreed that the Foreign Ministers should meet in Moscow in mid-October. Then came news that Stalin was prepared to go as far as Persia to meet Roosevelt and Churchill.

It appeared that at long last the Grand Alliance was beginning to function in harmony. The Moscow Foreign Ministers' Conference, which opened on 19th October, and the Teheran Conference of the Heads of Government that followed, were the high tides of Soviet-Western accord during the war.

The discussions at the Moscow Foreign Ministers' Conference, attended by Molotov, Cordell Hull and Eden, fell under four main headings. First, Molotov raised the second front issue to inquire whether the undertakings given by Roosevelt and Churchill for a second front in the spring of 1944 remained valid. Next day Hull and Eden both confirmed this. Ismay, who had accompanied Eden, explained also—so that there could be no more misunderstanding— that the operation would only become practicable if there was a substantial reduction in the German fighter force in North-West Europe and if German mobile land forces in northern France did not amount to more than twelve divisions at the time of landing and could not be increased to more than about fifteen divisions within two months. As Molotov attached great importance to these Anglo-American undertakings it was embodied in a "Most Secret Protocol" of the conference.

Eden now had to deal once more with the vexed question of the convoys which Molotov had asked to be resumed; and which Churchill, personally, was anxious to facilitate. In a long telegram on 1st October, Churchill had told Stalin that he proposed to restart the convoys, but pointed out British grievances about the Russian suspicion and hostility towards the British personnel arriving in the Soviet ports. As the Prime Minister received no answer to this message for several days, he telegraphed Clark Kerr on 12th October pressing for a reply, in order that the first convoy could leave on 12th November. Next day he got his answer from Stalin. It was angry and insulting. It accused the British personnel of spying, amongst other things.

Churchill was furious and he promptly returned Stalin's message to the Soviet Ambassador, explaining that he declined to accept it. Instead he telegraphed Eden in Moscow asking him to take up the matter on the spot. The British Foreign Secretary saw Stalin and Molotov as a result and went over the ground. After some plain speaking by Eden, it was agreed that the Foreign Secretary should meet Molotov again next day to see if the Soviet Union could meet the list of British requirements. Thus it came about that the convoys were re-started.

Cordell Hull, to whom the Moscow Conference had been a considerable adventure (it was the first time that the elderly American Secretary of State had ever flown in an aircraft), made a proposal on behalf of the U.S.A. that there should be a joint pledge by the Three Powers to continue their collaboration after the war and to recognise the need for setting up an international organisation for the maintenance of peace and security—the forerunner of the United Nations. This was accepted by Eden and Molotov. The Foreign Ministers also agreed to a suggestion by Eden that a European Advisory Commission should be established in London to study and to make plans for all the multitudinous problems that would arise in the liberated and occupied countries. At last the Alliance was getting down to the practicalities of what to do with Germany. The one major discordant note was when Eden and Molotov clashed over an idea of Eden's that the three powers should affirm that all peoples should be free to choose their own forms of government and be free also to associate themselves with other States.

The Alliance moved into a new phase at Teheran. For all the acrimony it had aroused at times, the "Second Front Now!" issue was to prove of relative unimportance as compared with the disagreement about the fate of Poland that was to come to a head at Potsdam; the Soviet Union's post-war policies in Europe which was soon to alarm Churchill and to be so misunderstood by Roosevelt; and the ultimate division of Germany, marking the clash of struggle for world domination.

In the meanwhile, the various aircraft carrying Churchill, Roosevelt and Stalin and their advisers to their rendezvous at Teheran on 28th November droned across the dry landscapes of the Middle East.

CHAPTER 6

FROM TEHERAN TO YALTA

Your heroes are the soldiers whose only weapons against tanks, planes and guns were revolvers and bottles filled with petrol. Your heroes are the women who tended the wounded and carried messages under fire, who cooked in bombed and mined cellars to feed children and adults, and who soothed and comforted the dying. Your heroes are the children who went on playing quietly among the smouldering ruins. These are the people of Warsaw.

A broadcast from Warsaw, received in London

The Teheran Conference between Roosevelt, Stalin and Churchill, from 28th November to 1st December, 1943, took place in a heady mood of optimism. After perilous years of struggle, in which total defeat had been close, the leaders of the Grand Alliance met to settle their plans to end Hitler's attempt at world domination. Much hard fighting remained, including the hazardous Anglo-American crossing of the English Channel. But victory was now certain. At Teheran there was another apparent gain: Roosevelt felt that, at long last, he was establishing the personal relationship with Stalin to which he attached so much importance in the planning of the peace.[1]

In these circumstances it is not surprising, therefore, that few people had foresight of the events to come. Yet the central issues of dissension that led rapidly to the outbreak of the Cold War had already appeared—Poland, the mounting prospect of Communist domination of Eastern Europe, the fate of Germany and the arguments about the establishment of the United Nations. It was a strange irony.

---

[1] Frances Perkins, *The Roosevelt I Knew*, pp. 70-1: "For the first three days, I made absolutely no progress. I couldn't get any connection with Stalin. . . . I began to tease Churchill about his Britishness, about John Bull, about his cigars, about his habits. It began to register with Stalin. Winston got red and scowled, and the more he did so the more Stalin smiled. Finally, Stalin broke out in a deep, hearty guffaw. . . . It was then that I called him 'Uncle Joe'. . . . The ice was broken and we talked like men and brothers."

Teheran, as seen in retrospect, was an impossible choice of place for such a meeting. The conditions in the city itself limited the length of the conference and thereby contributed to leaving the most difficult issues unresolved. Roosevelt and Churchill had canvassed various alternative meeting-places, but Stalin had been determined on Teheran. His real reason was that a large Soviet Embassy existed at Teheran in which he could stay and where—taking as general practice the Soviet policy of installing microphones for purposes of listening in—he felt sure that there could be no Western advantage. To make matters worse, Molotov, who had reached Teheran twenty-four hours in advance, claimed that the Soviet Intelligence Service had discovered a plot to kill one of the three leaders. As he put it, apparently without humour, "If anything like that were to happen, it could produce a most unfortunate impression." The result was that Molotov, with Churchill's full support, successfully persuaded Roosevelt to move into the Soviet Embassy. A combined force of Allied troops sealed off the area that included adjacent Russian and British headquarters.

The small incident of the Prime Minister's support for Molotov's proposition indicated his magnanimity because American policy towards her Russian and British allies had been undergoing a significant change that was causing Churchill considerable concern. Up to mid-1943, Britain had played an almost equal part in the Western partnership that helped to make up the Grand Alliance. The relatively inexperienced Americans had only been learning the realities of waging a war and they had been ready, despite some open disagreements, generally to accept British policies. Now, as American military strength was mobilised to a point at which it outweighed Britain's power, Roosevelt began in mid-1943 to assert his own policies, regardless of British wishes. He and his advisers also began to show that the United States, with its anti-colonial tradition, had serious reservations about Britain's post-war position; and he firmly believed that American policy might have a greater sense of affinity with Soviet aspirations. After all—so the American thinking ran—Britain was the repository of imperialism; but the United States and Soviet Russia were both created by revolution and dedicated to the emancipation of man. Roosevelt, in making this clear and in showing his trust in the Soviet Union, hoped thereby to win Stalin's support for his own post-war policies, and also to secure early Soviet participation in the war against Japan.

The first independent American move was made in midsummer, 1943. Roosevelt asked Harriman to fly to London to tell Churchill he was proposing to meet Stalin alone, in advance of any full-scale meeting of the three Heads of Government. Alaska was canvassed as the likely place for this Roosevelt-Stalin meeting. Churchill's immediate reaction was alarm but, fortunately for him also, Stalin was most unwilling to oblige Roosevelt, for reasons of his own.

The American and British delegations flew in to Teheran on 27th November, 1943. Roosevelt agreed to move next day into the Soviet Embassy, arriving at his new quarters at three o'clock in the afternoon. Fifteen minutes later, Stalin called. It was an historic moment. The two men were alone except for their interpreters.[1] The President began characteristically, "I am glad to see you. I have tried for a long time to bring this about." He put himself out to be friendly and jokingly cautioned Stalin against raising the issue of India with Churchill. Stalin chuckled as they made their way to the conference.

The first plenary session of the Teheran conference was held immediately after this brief Stalin-Roosevelt talk, at 4 p.m. on Sunday, 28th November. The large round table in the spacious and impressive Soviet Embassy was surrounded by the three delegations. Churchill had already arrived before Stalin and Roosevelt, bringing Eden, Dill and Ismay. Unfortunately for the President, Marshall and Arnold had mistaken the time of the meeting and had gone off sight-seeing, so Roosevelt began without them, bringing only Hopkins and Admirals King and Leahy. Stalin was alone, except for his two faithfuls, Voroshilov and Molotov. On the joint proposal of Stalin and Churchill—arranged by staff work beforehand—Roosevelt was elected to the chair for the first meeting.

The President began by welcoming the Russians as the "new members of the family circle." The first session lasted over three hours and it gave the three parties a chance to hear Roosevelt's assessment of the American commitment in the Far East, before turning to the Second Front in Europe and to an Anglo-American plan for a landing in southern France to support it. The President also made references to Turkey's position and to a possible drive north-eastwards into Rumania, to link up with the Red Army. This latter, however, did not meet with Stalin's approval. The

[1] The American interpreter was Charles E. Bohlen, who was later to become one of the shrewdest and most influential State Department officials in all matters of Soviet-Western relations.

Soviet leader, although welcoming the idea of bringing Turkey into the war, was particularly anxious that there should be no weakening of the Second Front assault force, as (so he pointed out) "the Balkans were far from the heart of Germany." There was another reason, too, at the back of Russian thinking—Stalin wanted Soviet forces to end the war as far west as possible unhampered by Anglo-American excursions into the Balkans.

That night, Roosevelt acted as host for a dinner party of about a dozen. The meal was a triumph for his Filipino cook, who had been given very little time to establish himself in the Soviet Embassy compound, and it contributed much to the prevailing Soviet-American harmony. In the course of the general discussion at dinner and afterwards two significant aspects of Stalin's thinking emerged. First, the Soviet leader was clearly determined to prevent the emergence, after the war, of a rearmed Germany. Secondly, he wanted to draw Poland's frontier lines in advance and he appeared pleased when Churchill demonstrated on the sofa after dinner, with the aid of three matches, how the new Poland could be moved westwards.

The next day Churchill received a sharp rebuff from Roosevelt. The Prime Minister suggested that he and the President should lunch together, as Stalin had already had a private talk with the President. But Roosevelt refused, partly because he felt himself surrounded by the Soviet Secret Police, who would report everything to Stalin, but really because he believed that the gesture itself might arouse Stalin's suspicions. Indeed, it was a bad day altogether for the Prime Minister, redeemed only briefly, when he presented to Stalin on behalf of King George VI the "Sword of Honour" to commemorate the Russian defence of Stalingrad. For this impressive, yet simple, ceremony the large outer hall of the Soviet Embassy was crowded with Russian officers and soldiers standing stiffly to attention. Churchill was at his best. His few glowing sentences of explanation moved everyone present. Roosevelt sat silently in his wheel-chair watching. Stalin kissed the scabbard, and handed the sword to Voroshilov, who promptly dropped it.

But to return to the conference, the plenary session of that day was again devoted to the European war. Stalin fired the crucial question: "Who will command Overlord [the Second Front]?" Roosevelt hesitated and said that this had not been decided; although Stalin pressed his point without getting satisfaction. The truth was Roosevelt would have liked to have named Marshall but did not want to lose him, and had not yet got general agreement from all concerned for Eisenhower. Churchill now returned to his theme of the wider Mediterranean strategy, to the obvious irritation of the Americans and the Russians. He used all his oratorical art to parade "the gleaming opportunities" but to no avail. The Russian suspicions about British intentions towards the Second Front grew as the Prime Minister went on. The session ended with Stalin looking across the table and saying coldly: "I wish to pose a very direct question to the Prime Minister about Overlord. Do the Prime Minister and the British Staff really believe in Overlord?" Churchill, somewhat taken aback, replied that provided certain considerations were fulfilled, they did. Realising the doubts he had created, he followed this up by seeing Stalin next day to explain in greater detail the Anglo-American plans.

That same evening of Churchill's bad day, 29th November, there was an angry scene at the dinner table at which Stalin was host. Churchill was not feeling too well. Roosevelt added to his bad humour by making some fun at his expense. Then the Soviet dictator began mercilessly goading Churchill. He went on and on about the subject of Germany. At one point, Stalin suggested that the best way of dealing with the German problem was to shoot 50,000 German officers and technicians in cold blood. Churchill flushed and declared that the British Parliament and public would never tolerate such mass executions. Stalin insisted that this was the only course if the world was to avoid the resurgence of German militarism. "I would rather," Churchill retorted, now very angry, "be taken out into the garden here and be shot myself than sully my own and my country's honour by such infamy." Roosevelt, realising that things had gone too far, tried to make a joke of it. Eden attempted to come to the rescue by frantic signs to his leader to calm down. But the last straw for the irate Prime Minister was a speech supporting Stalin from Elliott Roosevelt, the President's son, who had only just walked into the room. The Prime Minister jumped up from his place and walked out of the party, pursued by Stalin and Molotov, both eager to atone and to explain that it had only been a joke. With their assurance, Churchill returned and everyone present made attempts to restore an atmosphere of good humour.

Fortunately, the next day turned out to be quite different. First, there was the satisfactory interview between Churchill and Stalin (already mentioned), aimed at showing Britain's support for the Second Front. The plenary session also formally decided upon the Second Front being launched in May, 1944; and, at this, the clouds of Soviet doubts appeared to be cleared immediately. Churchill wisely said little about his Mediterranean strategy, thereby contributing to the general harmony. In the evening, as it was his sixty-ninth birthday, Churchill claimed the right to be host at a grand dinner party, at which many kind things about the Prime Minister were said. The Teheran Conference drew to its close next day, the principal decision of the Second Front having been made.

Issues dealing with Poland and the future of Germany and Europe, however, came to the fore in the informal discussions at Teheran; and it becomes necessary to place the Polish issue in perspective as it is the first major watershed of disagreement that led directly to the Cold War. A Polish Government-in-exile had been set up in France in 1939. When France collapsed in 1940, the Government-in-exile had been transferred to Britain. On 23rd June, 1941, following upon the German invasion of Russia, and after consultation with Churchill and Eden, General Sikorski, the Prime Minister of the Polish Government-in-exile, announced on the British radio that he desired reconciliation with Russia. He added: "We are entitled to assume that Russia will cancel the [Nazi-Soviet] Pact of 1939 and bring us back to the Treaty of Riga of March, 1921."

Maisky told Eden a few days later that the Soviet Government was prepared to deal with Sikorski as the head of the Government of Poland. This was an important step forward. Stalin was also ready to grant facilities for the establishment of a Polish National Committee in Russia and to provide arms for a Polish force fighting on Russian soil. The Soviet Ambassador explained to Eden that Stalin had changed his mind about the previous arrangement with Ribbentrop and that his view was now in favour of an independent Polish state with frontiers "corresponding to ethnographical Poland." This last point meant that Stalin was not prepared to agree to return those parts of Poland that had been annexed from the Soviet Union at the end of the Russian-Polish war of 1920 and which he had re-taken in the 1939 Soviet advance.

For justification of Stalin's position, all Soviet spokesmen were later to claim that these areas were not inhabited, in the majority, by Poles. Secondly, they argued that Britain had already supported, in July, 1920, the so-called Curzon Line, which amounted to the same thing.[1] Finally, as they always pointed out that Stalin had said—by implication, in his first war-time message to Churchill on 18th July, 1941—Poland's fate was a matter of Russian security. Stalin's actual words had been: "The position of the German forces would have been many times more favourable had the Soviet troops had to face the attack of the German forces not in the regions of Kishinev, Lwow, Brest, Kaunas and Viborg, but in the regions of Odessa, Kamenets Podolski, Minsk and the environs of Leningrad." In this sentence of Stalin's, telegraphed at the very beginning of the Grand Alliance, is embodied the crux of Soviet thinking towards Eastern Europe, upon which so much was to depend in years to come.

To return to the London negotiations, the first meeting between Maisky and Sikorski was "frigid." Nevertheless, by ignoring the post-war frontier issues, it was possible to sign a Soviet-Polish agreement, promising mutual aid and support for the war against Germany. Largely under British pressure, Stalin agreed also to release a number of Poles who had been taken by the Russians after 1939 Soviet invasion; and many of these were now allowed to leave Russia via Persia.

The evidence of the Poles, who were released, raised a very ugly query. Whilst the Soviet authorities vehemently maintained that all Polish prisoners had been freed, several thousand remained unaccounted for. There emerged also a new cause of Polish hatred for the Russians—thousands of the released Poles told of how they had suffered appalling privations and humiliations at Soviet hands.

With this unfortunate situation as the background, Sikorski travelled to Moscow to see Stalin in December, 1941. Somewhat surprisingly, however, the talks went well. In an atmosphere of apparent cordiality the two men signed the Russian-Polish Declaration of Friendship and Mutual Aid. Furthermore, Stalin promised Sikorski that all Polish citizens would be released—thereby implying that many were still there—and he appeared to agree to take

[1] The "Curzon Line" was put forward by Lord Curzon, the British Foreign Secretary, as the line to which Polish forces should retire when they were being driven westwards in July, 1920. The northern point of the line divided the former Suvalki province between Lithuania and Poland. The line then ran south, bulging westwards from Grodno to the Bug at Brest-Litovsk, with both towns left to Russia but leaving Bialystock to Poland, and following the Bug to the Galician border near Sokal; and on to the Carpathians, just east of Przemysl. The Nazi-Soviet frontier of 1939 was slightly to the west of the Curzon Line.

steps to see that the instances of ill-treatment would be investigated and appropriate action would be taken. In the course of the Moscow talks, Stalin asked Sikorski about post-war frontiers. Sikorski replied that he could not discuss the matter. It was to prove an historic answer for Poland.

Polish disillusionment was quickly to follow the Stalin-Sikorski agreement. By a piece of prevarication—to great Polish anger —he claimed as Russian citizens all people who, on 1st-2nd November, 1939, were on Polish territory annexed by the Soviet Union.

In early 1943—to leap more than a year—the Red Army began to advance from Stalingrad. Shortly afterwards a new and much more serious development took place. Sikorski came to lunch with Churchill at Downing Street in early April, 1943. He said to the Prime Minister that he had proof that the Soviet authorities had murdered 15,000 Polish officers and other prisoners—the same people who had not been accounted for in the earlier exchanges— and had buried them in mass graves in the forests around Katyn, near Smolensk. The Polish leader's charge was soon supported by a German radio statement, on April 13th, accusing the Russians of the murder of 14,500 Poles in three camps and proposing an international inquiry. Without informing the British Government, the Polish Government-in-exile issued a communiqué stating that the International Red Cross in Switzerland was being asked to send a delegation to Katyn to investigate on the spot. Three days later, the Polish Ambassador in Moscow presented himself at the Kremlin and asked the Soviet Government for its observations.[1] Stalin replied to Sikorski's action by sending Churchill a note through Maisky announcing the "interruption" of Russian-Polish relations. The Soviet leader remained adamant throughout the next few days, although Churchill telegraphed pleading for magnanimity. Moscow radio formally announced the Soviet-Polish break on 26th April, 1943.

To make the Soviet-Polish prospect worse, Sikorski, who was a man of common sense, and who had admitted privately that the statement announcing the appeal to the International Red Cross had been a mistake, was killed in an air crash on 4th July, 1943.

[1] The Soviet authorities later undertook an inquiry after the recapture of Smolensk, in September, 1943. The Soviet report issued in January, 1944, states that the three Katyn camps had fallen into German hands and their occupants were all slaughtered by them.

Stanislaw Mikolajczyk, leader of the Polish Peasant Party and also a responsible moderate, became his successor, but unfortunately the new Polish Prime Minister lacked Sikorski's commanding influence—a serious difficulty when it came to persuading the Government-in-exile along responsible courses.

In the meanwhile, the Polish issue was becoming yet more urgent because the Red Army was approaching Polish territory. The specific problem was the Polish underground army—known as the Home Army—which maintained close contact with the Government-in-exile. In view of the situation there was a real possibility that the Polish Home Army might now resist Soviet occupation of Polish territory.

At Teheran, the Polish issue was first raised informally. Stalin, when asked by Churchill casually, said he thought that Poland's western frontier should be moved to the Oder and that he favoured a Polish advance at the expense of the Germans. Churchill, seeing the difficulties of dealing with the Poles, did not want to be associated with any exact formula. He suggested instead an agreement to the effect that "it was thought in principle (by the three Heads of Government) that the home of the Polish state and nation should be between the so-called Curzon Line and the line of the Oder, including for Poland East Prussia and Oppeln, but the actual line required careful study and possibly the disentanglement of population at certain points."[1] Stalin accepted the proposal of the Curzon Line, apart from demanding for the Soviet Union the German city of Königsberg. Stalin also remarked at Teheran that he would be ready to renew relations with the Government-in-exile if the Polish Home Army would give up "killing partisans" and fight the Germans.

On 5th January, 1944, the Red Army crossed the frontier of Poland. The moment had come. The Polish Government-in-exile issued a statement stating its position as "the sole and legal steward of the Polish nation," and demanding "the earliest re-establishment of Polish sovereign administration in the liberated territories of the Republic." The Polish statement said also that the Home Army

[1] The American position on the Polish issue had varied prior to this. At first Roosevelt had been against *any* frontier agreement in advance of a peace conference. But by Teheran he had approached close to the British attitude. Gradually he came to accept the Curzon Line. At Teheran, the differences between him and Churchill really amounted to whether the city of Lwow should be in Russian hands (Churchill's view) or whether the city, and at least a portion of the nearby oilfields, should be Polish territory (Roosevelt's views).

had been ordered to continue fighting the Germans, avoid conflict with the Red Army and to co-operate with Soviet commanders in the event of the resumption of Russian-Polish relations.

But the real problem was still to be faced. From January, 1944, to midsummer, whilst the Red Army and the Wehrmacht fought each other west of the former Polish frontier, but east of the Curzon Line, the diplomatic wrangle between Stalin and the Polish Government-in-exile continued. Stalin saw Clark Kerr and laid down two conditions for a resumption of relations—definite acceptance of the Curzon Line and a reconstructed government-in-exile. He said that he was extremely angry about the Polish Home Army and the way it was being directed, but he promised that if it co-operated with the Russians, he would see that it was given help. Stalin was more friendly when he spoke about the future. Poland should be free and independent, in his view. He promised that the government-in-exile could return and the Soviet Union would not interfere with Poland's Government. This was reassuring. Thus there were now hopes, at least in British Government circles, that a Russian-Polish agreement might be possible despite a great deal of mistrust of Soviet intentions in the part of Mikolajczyk and his colleagues.

Churchill sent Stalin a message, only after much discussion with the Poles, saying that the Polish Government-in-exile, with British participation, was now prepared to discuss, as part of a general settlement, a new Polish-Soviet frontier. At the same time, he explained to Stalin that as the territorial compensations that Poland would receive in the west and in East Prussia from Germany could not be published, for their part the Poles could not publicly declare their willingness to cede the territory east of the Curzon Line. Things appeared to be moving at last.

Stalin's answer was a dismaying rebuff. When Clark Kerr delivered Churchill's message, according to the Ambassador, he dismissed the Polish Government in London "with a snigger." He flatly refused to believe that they even wanted a settlement and he would not accept that the Poles could not agree to the Curzon Line and the reconstruction of the Government, immediately and publicly. All the advances had come to nothing. The situation was deadlocked. Then, suddenly, in May, 1944—as it has been so often the case throughout this story of Soviet-Western relations—Soviet rigidity appeared briefly to thaw. Lebedev, the Soviet Minister to the Allied Governments in London, had two secret meetings with

Grabski, the President of the Polish National Council in London—on 23rd and 31st May. It appeared from these talks and from a message that Benes, the Czechoslovak President, was asked to pass on to Mikolajczyk, the Russians now genuinely wanted an agreement. Lebedev saw Mikolajczyk again, on 20th June, after the latter had returned from a brief visit to Washington. The Soviet Minister appeared to raise no objection to the resumption of diplomatic relations and the adoption of a common plan for military action.

But only three days later there was a change of policy, as swift as the previous change. Lebedev now told Mikolajczyk that his Government rejected all possibility of resuming diplomatic relations with Poland until and unless the Government-in-exile had been reconstructed, certain members dismissed, certain "democratic" Poles included and the new Government had recanted for its predecessor's error over the Katyn affair. On that same significant day, 23rd June, the Union of Polish Patriots, a body formed on Russian soil in 1943, and under Soviet control, denounced the Polish Government in London as "illegal" and declared that the true representatives of the Polish people were the "Polish National Council of the Homeland," which was clearly preparing the way for the establishment of a rival Polish Government.

Mikolajczyk was desperate. He thought his last hope of rapprochement lay in a visit by him to Moscow. He approached Eden, and both the British and American Governments agreed to intercede on his behalf with the Soviet Government, and eventually Stalin agreed to see him. The Polish Prime Minister left for Moscow on 26th July, accompanied by two trusted colleagues. The party flew to Moscow via Teheran. The dates are important in view of what happened. They first saw Stalin and Molotov on the night of 3rd August. To the intense surprise of the Poles, Stalin behaved in a friendly manner; although they said afterwards that they thought him badly informed about the Polish Home Army. At the interview, Stalin was determined to discuss frontiers and to place the Soviet frontier west of the towns of Vilna and Lwow. He claimed to see the Polish problem and he offered as compensation to the Poles the towns of Breslau and Stettin and a new frontier down the River Oder.

Mikolajczyk, under strong pressure from Stalin, also met a fresh body, the Polish "Committee of Liberation" that had been set up in Lublin by the "National Council of the Homeland." It was his first meeting with a strange, new figure, Boleslaw Beirut, appearing as the Chairman of the National Council. Beirut was completely unknown to Mikolajczyk and his two colleagues. A small, dark man, he faintly resembled Hitler in appearance with his cropped moustache, but his manner was soft and suave. When asked for his real name, Beirut declined to give it, although it was discovered subsequently that it was Krasnodewski.[1]

Beirut was nothing if not bold. He promptly asked Mikolajczyk for a new Polish Government of eighteen ministers, fourteen from the Russian-based Committee of Liberation and four, including Mikolajczyk and Grabski from London. Mikolajczyk, who explained that his authority was limited, promised to consult his Polish colleagues in Britain. After this, the Polish Premier had another meeting with Stalin on 9th August, before returning to London. At this second meeting, Stalin told Mikolajczyk that he had no intention of "communising" Poland, and, possibly by way of assurance, he added that "Communism was no more fit for Germany than a saddle for a cow."

Whilst these talks—containing some goodwill on the surface—had been going on, a shattering event was taking place in Warsaw. It was to leave an indelible imprint upon the Soviet-Western conflict over Poland. The people of Warsaw, led by the Polish Home Army, had risen against the Germans. General Bor-Komorowski, the Polish Commander of the underground Home Army in Poland, had been authorised by Mikolajczyk's Government to proclaim a general insurrection against the Germans whenever the Russian advance into Poland made it appropriate. In the last days of July, as Mikolajczyk was flying to Moscow, the prospects for the uprising had grown rapidly more propitious. On 22nd July, the Germans ordered a general withdrawal to the western bank of the Vistula, and the Poles in Warsaw intercepted orders to this effect. Russian patrols crossed the river the same day. Bor-Komorowski had 40,000 armed men and supplies and ammunition for about ten days' fighting. He could hear the Russian guns. In this same week, Russian forces reached the edge of the Praga district, a suburb of Warsaw on the east bank of the Vistula. Bor hastened his preparations.

---

[1] Whilst serving a prison sentence in a Polish jail in 1927 as a Soviet agent, Krasnodewski was once exchanged for an imprisoned Polish agent, in an arrangement with the Soviet authorities. Later, Krasnodewski was reported as serving with the N.K.V.D. and he was said also to have taken part in the Spanish Civil War.

On 29th July, three days before the uprising was due to begin, the Polish Committee of National Liberation broadcast an appeal over Moscow radio saying that liberation was at hand and that all Poles should join battle with the Germans, as in 1939. "For Warsaw, which did not yield but fought on, the hour of action has already arrived." The Moscow broadcast called for "direct active struggle in the streets and houses of Warsaw" to hasten liberation and to save "the lives of our Soviet brethren." Soviet tanks broke into the German defences east of the city on 31st July. Bor ordered his general insurrection for 5 p.m. on 1st August. "At exactly five o'clock thousands of windows flashed as they were flung open. From all sides a hail of bullets struck passing Germans, riddling their buildings and their marching formations. The battle for the city was on."

The news reached the Polish authorities by radio in London on 2nd August. At once they appealed to Britain for an air-drop of supplies. Churchill telegraphed Stalin informing him of the new situation and of the British intention to send aircraft carrying some sixty tons of equipment and ammunition. Stalin's chilling rejoinder described the information about the general insurrection as "greatly exaggerated." Mikolajczyk, now in Moscow, was asked to intercede with Stalin. The Soviet leader appeared good-humoured in response to Mikolajczyk but made no definite promise at the first meeting between the two men on 5th August.

In the meanwhile, the battle raged on in Warsaw, British aircraft based in Italy, some flown by Polish volunteers serving with the Royal Air Force, together with British and Commonwealth crews, made attempts to get through, with little success. Two aircraft reached Warsaw on 4th August and three on 12th August. Some of the crews reported that they were fired on by Russian anti-aircraft guns on their run into Warsaw from the east and they suffered casualties at Russian hands. Churchill cabled Stalin on 12th August, quoting a report from Bor and appealing again for help.

Stalin's answer was given in a *Tass* statement broadcast by Moscow radio on 14th August. It was heard by Bor in Warsaw.

"Information from Polish sources on the rising in Warsaw on 1st August by order of the Polisk émigrés in London has recently appeared in various newspapers abroad. The Polish Press and radio of the émigré Government in London have asserted that the Warsaw insurrectionists were in contact with the Soviet High

Command and that this Command has sent them no help. The announcement is either a misunderstanding or a libel against the Soviet High Command.

"*Tass* is in possession of the information which shows that the Polish circles in London responsible for the Warsaw rising made no attempt to co-ordinate this action with the Soviet High Command. In these circumstances, the only people responsible for the results of the events in Warsaw are the Polish émigré circles in London." Bor stated: "The effect of this announcement, in Warsaw, was stupefication."

The Americans now took a hand. That same day, 14th August, Harriman in Moscow asked the Soviet Government for permission for a force of American four-engined aircraft, with fighter escort, to undertake a daylight shuttle operation on 15th August, weather and operational conditions permitting. The aircraft were to drop supplies in Warsaw and to attack German airfields in the vicinity of the Soviet troops, before landing on Soviet-controlled territory, where they were to refuel.

The Soviet Government immediately refused permission. Vyshinsky, who acted as Soviet spokesman because Molotov was out of Moscow for the day, referred to the Warsaw uprising as "the work of adventurers." On 16th August, explaining that he wanted to avoid misunderstanding, Vyshinsky sent for Harriman and read him an amazing statement: "The Soviet Government cannot of course object to British and American aircraft dropping arms in the region of Warsaw, since this is an American and British affair. But they decidedly objected to American or British aircraft, after dropping arms in the region of Warsaw, landing on Soviet territory since the Soviet Government did not wish to associate themselves directly or indirectly with the adventure in Warsaw."

To add to the confusion, that same day, 16th August, Stalin cabled Churchill telling the Prime Minister that after his last talk with Mikolajczyk on 9th August—at which Stalin appears to have promised the Poles aid to Warsaw—he had now ordered the Red Army Command "to drop arms intensively in the Warsaw sector. A parachutist liaison officer was also dropped who, according to the report of the command, did not reach his objective because he was killed by the Germans." Stalin said that he was "convinced that the Warsaw action represented a reckless and terrible adventure" and that the Soviet Command "must dissociate itself." Mikolajczyk later denied Stalin's statement to Churchill. He claimed that two Russian officers reached Bor's headquarters. A Soviet colonel had also been there for some days and had been appealing constantly to the Red Army Command for help.

On Churchill's suggestion, a joint telegram by Roosevelt and Churchill was sent to Stalin on 20th August. It was brief. It began gravely: "We are thinking of world opinion if the anti-Nazis in Warsaw are in effect abandoned." It asked for a Soviet air drop; or, alternatively, for permission for British and American aircraft to undertake the operation.

Stalin answered on 22nd August: "Sooner or later the truth about the group of criminals who have embarked upon the Warsaw adventure in order to seize power will become known to everybody. . . . From the military point of view, the situation which has arisen by increasingly directing the attention of the Germans to Warsaw, is just as profitable for the Red Army as for the Poles. Meanwhile, the Soviet troops which have recently encountered new and notable efforts by the Germans to go over to the counter-attacks of the Hitlerites. . . ." In fairness to Stalin, it is true that the German forces were launching attacks on the Red Army positions and claimed to have annihilated a Soviet armoured force. But the main problem for the Germans was the battle inside the city and German pressure was certainly no answer to the Anglo-American request for landing facilities on Soviet territory for a shuttle service.

Inside Warsaw, there was taking place one of the most bitter and ruthless struggles of the war. Whole districts were being razed to the ground and the inhabitants shot. Part of the battle was fought literally underground, as the Polish Home Army was only able to communicate between the various sectors it held through the sewers. The Germans threw grenades and gas bombs down manholes. Fighting took place in black darkness as men, waste deep in excrement, killed each other in hand-to-hand fighting. Often they drowned each other in the filthy waters, lacking any other means of destruction. Above ground, the great city was burning and a huge pall of smoke drifted across the Vistula to where the Red Army lay.

Russian aircraft flew over Warsaw dropping leaflets, telling the inhabitants that the city would soon be liberated and that the leaders of the uprising would be punished. Eden impatiently proposed that British and American aircraft should "gate-crash" Soviet territory and drafted a joint message telling Stalin of this intention, for Churchill and Roosevelt to sign. Roosevelt would not agree. In a message to Churchill on 26th August he said: "I do not consider it would prove advantageous to the long-range general war prospect for me to join with you in the proposed message to Stalin, but I have no objection to your sending such a message if you consider it advisable to do so." It was one of the less honourable decisions that the President ever took.

Mikolajczyk, back from Moscow, went to see Churchill on 1st September. He told him that in view of the tragic situation, the Polish Government-in-exile had agreed to accept Beirut's Moscow terms, for fourteen seats for the Lublin Committee in a reconstructed Polish Government. He added that this request had been debated and accepted by the Home Army Command in a cellar in Warsaw as the battle was taking place.

The Prime Minister tells in his memoirs of the scene at a cabinet meeting on 4th September. Because of the flying-bomb danger, the meeting was held in its underground room. Churchill himself had risen from a sick bed to be present because of the important issue. "I do not remember any occasion when such deep anger was shown by all our members, Tory, Labour, Liberal alike," he said. The Cabinet were so enraged that they would have liked to have stopped the Arctic convoys there and then, unless Stalin agreed to let British aircraft land in his territory. Slowly, calmer councils prevailed.

A very different atmosphere existed in Washington. Out of it Roosevelt cabled Churchill next day: "I am informed by my Office of Military Intelligence that the fighting Poles have departed from Warsaw and that the Germans are now in full control. The problem of relief for the Poles in Warsaw has, therefore, unfortunately been solved by delay and by German action, and there now appears to be nothing we can do to assist them." He added: "I have long been distressed. . . . I hope that we may together still be able to help Poland to be among the victors."

The Russians changed their tactics, as if to add to the torment of the Poles. From 14th September onwards, the Soviet Air Force dropped supplies, although very few of the parachutes opened and the arms were damaged beyond use. On 15th September the Red Army occupied the Praga district and stared across the flat scene of the Vistula and the burning city on the opposite bank, where the struggle was continuing into its eighth week. Three days later, on 18th September, the Russians relented about the use of Soviet landing grounds. Over a hundred American heavy bombers made the long flight to drop supplies in Warsaw and flew on to refuel in Soviet territory. It was the only shuttle flight permitted during the uprising.

On 3rd October, with the Red Army occupying the opposite bank, General Bor-Komorowski was compelled to surrender after sixty-three days' fighting against overwhelming German forces. He had started with only ten days' supplies.

Figures speak for themselves. Out of Bor's command of 40,000 men and women of the Polish Home Army, 15,000 were dead. Out of the city's population of about a million, nearly 200,000 were killed. The Germans lost 10,000 killed, 7,000 missing (mainly in the terrible silent struggles in the sewers) and 9,000 wounded. The Red Army sat on in the Praga district for three more months and the Nazi commander systematically destroyed nearly everything that remained standing. In January, 1945, the Soviet troops crossed the Vistula.

What motivated Stalin to be the instigator of the mass martyrdom of Warsaw—because it cannot be forgotten that he gave the order authorising the Poles in Warsaw to attack? The only official Soviet answers are to be found in his repeated charges against "the adventurers" which appear in his messages to Churchill and Roosevelt. In an interview with Harriman and Clark Kerr on the evening of 17th August, Molotov spoke repeatedly of "bankrupt Polish adventurers." He claimed that the Polish Government and radio in London were being used to slander the Soviet Union. He also admitted a change of Soviet policy after Stalin's promise to Mikolajczyk on 9th August. This was due, according to Molotov, to the fact that the Soviet Government had discovered "the true nature of the uprising."

But the truth about the Soviet attitude to the Warsaw uprising is different. The clue was to be found in the words of Stalin's telegram to Roosevelt and Churchill of 22nd August: "criminals who have embarked upon the Warsaw adventure *in order to seize power.* . . ." Stalin always believed that the nature of Poland's postwar government was vital to Soviet interests. He was not prepared to countenance any anti-Soviet elements in it. Equally, he was acutely aware of Polish hostility towards Russia—whatever may have been the reasons for this hostility. Therefore, Stalin was determined to destroy all elements within Poland that might uphold a Polish Government possessed of its own national spirit. With these thoughts in mind, he promoted, first, the Lublin Committee as the alternative Communist Government to the Polish Government in London. With true opportunism, he then took full advantage of the Warsaw uprising to destroy the Home Army and to discredit Mikolajczyk's administration. His own plans for the Poland of the future were based upon Beirut and his fellow puppets; that was the only Poland he cared about. As he sat inside the ancient fortress walls of the Kremlin, Stalin's actions were governed throughout by calculations and not by emotions. The feelings of honour, humanity, decent commonplace good faith, did not enter into his reasoning. In short, he believed that the Warsaw uprising manifestly threatened to reinstate upon Polish soil Mikolajczyk's Government-in-exile, thus displacing his own Lublin Committee. He was prepared to make Poland pay the price of two hundred thousand lives and the almost total destruction of her capital city to prevent such a rebuff to his aims. He could wait. It cost him nothing.

The Warsaw uprising of August, 1944, was the most dramatic example of an already developing situation in which as the Red Army advanced westwards across Russia's former frontiers, Soviet interests and Western policies were coming increasingly into conflict with each other.

Meanwhile the war situation was changing fast. The Red Army was sweeping forward all along the eastern front. In the north it reached the Vistula before pausing outside Warsaw, in early August. Farther south, on 23rd August, the young King Michael of Rumania overthrew the pro-German Government of General Antonescu in a dramatic coup, several days in advance of any Soviet troops reaching Bucharest, thereby transforming the whole military situation in the Balkans.

Bulgaria was overwhelmed by the Red Army in early September, and Soviet forces now drove up the Danube towards Budapest, with their left flank on the Yugoslav frontier, at last making common cause with Tito's partisans.

In the far north, Finland, accepting the inevitable, asked for terms on 25th August.

They were great days for the Allied armies in the field. On the western fronts, Rome fell on 4th June. The Second Front in France was successfully established from 6th June onwards. After much heavy fighting the American and British forces forced their way out of their Normandy bridgehead at the end of July. By 17th August they reached Chartres; and, on 20th August, American forces under Patton crossed the Seine. Paris was taken from within after a magnificent uprising of the French underground movement on 24th August. American forces had also landed in southern France on 15th August and were soon driving north against little opposition to link up with the Normandy armies.

Immediately after the fall of Paris, the German forces in Western Europe were in very grave disarray. They were only able to reconstitute themselves and to hold a coherent line later because Eisenhower, who was in command of the Anglo-American forces, overruled a plan by Montgomery to make a concentrated thrust for the Ruhr. Instead, Eisenhower preferred an attack upon a much wider front, thus giving the German armies their chance to recover.[1]

Whilst Europe was in turmoil, Roosevelt became increasingly preoccupied by his own fourth election campaign for the Presidency, due to take place in November. In these circumstances, Churchill sensed the developing political danger arising from the Soviet advance westwards and the opportunity being missed by the Allies in Europe. The British leader believed that he could no longer afford to wait for the President, nor for the American electoral timetable. At the same time he was in a difficulty—British post-war policy remained based upon Anglo-Soviet co-operation. Thus the question before Churchill was: after allowing for Roosevelt's preoccupations and unwillingness to grasp the implications of Soviet policy as shown first in Poland and as it was now unfolding in Eastern Europe, how best could he avoid the great clash between Stalin's ambitions for a cordon of puppet states around the Soviet Union and the Western aims of self-determination as laid down in the Atlantic Charter? Churchill characteristically decided in September, 1944, to fly to Moscow, taking Eden with him.

Churchill and his party arrived in Moscow on the afternoon of 9th October. After a welcome rest and dinner alone, Churchill and Eden went to the Kremlin at 10 p.m. to see Stalin and Molotov. At this historic meeting, apart from the two interpreters, Major Birse and Pavlov, no one else was present, but the story is well known. The Prime Minister instinctively felt that the time was

---

[1] The definitive work upon this period is *The Struggle for Europe* by Chester Wilmot, one of the most penetrating books to emerge from the Second World War and remarkable for the time at which it appeared. Wilmot was killed in an air crash in 1954.

opportune to do business, so he said to Stalin: "Let us settle our affairs in the Balkans. Your armies are in Rumania and Bulgaria. We have interests, missions and agents there. Don't let us get at cross-purposes in small ways. So far as Britain and Russia are concerned, how would it do for you to have ninety per cent pre-dominance in Rumania, for us to have ninety per cent of the say in Greece, and go fifty-fifty in Yugoslavia?"

While this was being translated, Churchill wrote out his rough proposals on a sheet of paper.

Stalin had understood, from the translation, what was being pro-posed. He stared at Churchill's piece of paper. Taking a blue pencil, he made a large tick upon it and passed it back. There was a long silence. The paper lay on the table.

Churchill said later that he was sure Stalin understood perfectly well that the proposal he had made referred only to immediate war-time arrangements and that all the larger issues would remain for the peace conference. The Russians, for their part, despite Stalin's acceptance, immediately sought to change the percentage figures on the next day, in order to strengthen their hand. Molotov saw Eden for this purpose; and a lengthy bargaining session began in which Eden explained again and again to the Soviet Foreign Minister that the British were not so concerned about actual per-centages, but they certainly wanted more say than they were getting up to that point in the direction of affairs in Rumania.

At their first meeting on 9th October, Churchill had also gained Stalin's agreement to sending for Mikolajczyk, Grabski and Romer from London to make yet another attempt to settle the Polish issue. He telegraphed for Mikolajczyk to come at once. The London Polish representatives, therefore, left London on the night of 10th October. And, as they were on the way, Churchill tackled the grim issue of the Russian attitude to the Warsaw uprising. It pro-duced nothing. Stalin was adamant that the Russian failure to relieve Warsaw was due entirely to military reasons and the Prime Minister was forced to drop the matter unresolved.

The first Polish-Russian-British meeting took place at five o'clock on 13th October—"All Poles Day," as Churchill called it. It was depressing and inconclusive. Stalin demanded that the London Poles must begin by accepting the Curzon Line. Mikolajczyk, in answer, repeated all the old arguments against immediate accept-ance. Churchill said that the British Government supported *de facto* acceptance of the Curzon Line. When no progress was being made he asked Mikolajczyk and his colleagues to ponder the gravity of their refusals overnight.

At ten o'clock that same night the British and Russians met the Lublin Poles, who now made the worst of impressions upon Churchill. As the days went by, the Polish issues narrowed down to three points: (1) Whether the Poles should accept publicly the Curzon Line in advance of the publication of their territorial compensation from Germany. (Mikolajczyk was willing to accept "The Curzon Line as a line of demarcation between Russia and Poland" but Stalin insisted upon the additional words, "as a basis of frontier between Russia and Poland.") (2) Lwow: Mikolajczyk insisted, at first, upon Lwow being upon the Polish side of the line. (Here, Churchill was able to help and persuaded Mikolajczyk to withdraw this claim.) (3) A bitter dispute about the composition of the new Polish Government. (Beirut although accepting Mikolajczyk as Premier, wanted three-quarters of the places. Mikolajczyk, in reply, proposed that each of the five Polish parties should be represented, and also promised Stalin that he would conduct a government "thoroughly friendly to the Russians." To underline his point, Mikolajczyk warned Churchill that the Ministry of the Interior would become vital, as soon as the N.K.V.D. entered Poland. Stalin, for his part, insisted upon a majority for the Lublin Poles, until Churchill pointed out to him that a Prime Minister must have a majority in his own cabinet.

Churchill struggled manfully with his invidious task. He felt bitterly that Poland's fate was being sealed as Mikolajczyk and his colleagues were procrastinating. On the other hand, he had no stomach for the task of browbeating them. In the end, no agreement was reached because neither side was prepared to give way on what it considered to be a vital interest. Churchill advised Mikolajczyk strongly to secure the support of his colleagues in London and to set up a government on Polish soil as soon as possible. But Mikolajczyk, upon reaching London, met with even greater difficulties from his colleagues than he had expected. Even his own limited concessions to Stalin had gone too far for the London Poles and he was compelled to resign.

The paradox of the 1944 Moscow Conference was that the two delegations all felt that they had gained considerably as a result of Churchill's visit. The Prime Minister believed that he had gained most of all because of his personal talks with Stalin. The two men had eaten most of their meals together and had often sat up late into the night drinking. In fact, only Stalin, keeping his own counsel, had real reason to be satisfied with the bargains that had been struck when the conference is reviewed in the hindsight of history. Yet even he had formed an exaggerated assessment of Churchill's capacity for scheming as is shown by his description of the Prime Minister to Djilas. "Churchill? Churchill is the kind of man who will pick your pocket of a kopeck if you don't watch him. Yes, pick your pocket of a kopeck! By God, pick your pocket of a kopeck!" he kept repeating. "And Roosevelt? Roosevelt is not like that. He dips in his hand only for bigger coins. But Churchill? Churchill—will do it for a kopeck."[1]

After Moscow, the storm continued to gather and its focal points soon included the future of Germany and the plan for a United Nations Organisation. The starting point of the United Nations Organisation had been the Atlantic Charter, proposed by Roosevelt and first drafted by Churchill at Argentia Bay in August, 1941. It had been received by the Soviet Government with a certain amount of uneasiness. The earliest co-ordinated views for a working arrangement to implement Allied post-war policy were set out in a memorandum drawn up in the British Foreign Office in autumn, 1942, by H. M. G. Jebb.[2]

Jebb's long memorandum, which was to undergo many changes, was called "The Four-Power Plan." It envisaged the setting up of a World Organisation under the direction of the United States, the Soviet Union, Britain and China. The inclusion of China, in Jebb's memorandum, was only in deference to Roosevelt's wishes because Britain did not then regard China as a Great Power; nor was she. France was left out, again because of American pressure. But the British internal view was that she should certainly be brought in at the appropriate time.

Behind the scenes, and before Teheran, there also had been a great deal of Anglo-American discussion about post-war plans for international security. Eden, for instance, had produced a draft plan on 25th May, 1943, for the negotiation and execution of an armistice. He had advocated that Germany should be "totally occupied" and, for this purpose, divided into three zones of

---

[1] Milovan Djilas, *Conversations with Stalin*, p. 70. This particular conversation, it must be noted, took place in the spring of 1944, before the Moscow Conference. But it gives a fascinating insight into Stalin's private opinion of the Prime Minister and the President.

[2] Rt. Hon. Lord Gladwyn, G.C.M.G., G.C.V.O., C.B.

British Russian and American troops under inter-Allied command.

When Eden and Hull went to Moscow for the Foreign Ministers' Conference of October, 1943, they had found the Russians pre-occupied with the need for a second front. In these circumstances, they had met with no difficulty in getting Soviet agreement for both Hull's Four-Power Declaration and for a plan by Eden to set up a European Advisory Commission to sit in London to consider and to make recommendations upon European problems that would arise at the end of the war. It is fascinating now to look back upon the respective positions about the future of Germany taken up by the Foreign Ministers at the Moscow Conference. First, Eden secured general agreement to the proposition for a free and independent Austria. He said also that Britain favoured the dismemberment of Germany and support by the Allies for German separatist movements. Hull, less emphatic, thought that American opinion was generally in favour of dismemberment of a defeated Germany. Molotov went to some lengths to apologise to his own colleagues that Russian thinking on post-war Germany was somewhat backward, as Soviet leaders had been preoccupied with waging the war itself. However, his view was broadly the same as that of Eden, he added.

Just over a month later, at Teheran on 1st December, 1943, Roosevelt and Stalin both said firmly that Germany should be broken up. The President's view supported a division into five parts: (i) Prussia, (ii) Hanover and the north-western area, (iii) Saxony and Leipzig area, (iv) Hesse-Damstadt, Hesse-Cassel and the area west of the Rhine, (v) Bavaria, Baden and Württemberg. The Kiel Canal and the city of Kiel, Hamburg and the Ruhr and the Saar areas were to be under the control of the United Nations. Churchill reacted in astonishment to this, telling Roosevelt: "Mr. President. You have said a mouthful!" In the Prime Minister's more cautious opinion the units, as proposed by the President, were too small for independent existence. Therefore, his own plan was to detach Prussia as the most belligerent element in the German state and to try to "work in" south Germany with a Danubian Confederation.

With all three leaders favouring, in one form or another, the partition of post-war Germany, the matter was referred by the three Heads of State at Teheran to a special committee to be set up under the European Advisory Commission. A difficulty now arose. The Advisory Commission was slow to start work on the subject. In

January, 1944, the Soviet representative asked for adjournment on the grounds of the insufficiency of his staff. Even by June, 1944, little had happened; and therefore the British decided to initiate discussion on their own.

Some weeks later, on 9th September, 1944, the British Chiefs of Staff produced a remarkably far-sighted document. They said that they favoured, on balance, the partitioning of Germany under military occupation for a period. Their reasons were: (1) It would prevent any renewal of German aggression; (2) It would insure against the possibility of post-war Soviet hostility and the danger of a Russian-German rapprochement. The Chiefs of Staff pointed out that, in the event of Soviet-Western hostility after the war, the West would need German help. They considered that the Soviet Union would be most unlikely to agree to the rearmament of a united Germany unless she could dominate it. Therefore, the Chiefs of Staff did not believe that help for the Western Powers would be forthcoming from a united Germany. In short, they favoured a form of dismemberment, with the retention of north-west and possibly southern Germany within the orbit of the West European group. It was a highly political and forward-looking argument that was hurriedly buried in the archives where its grim and accurate prophecy has lain these many years.

Meanwhile, on the other side of the Atlantic, Henry J. Morgenthau, Jr., the U.S. Secretary of the Treasury, initiated an even more startling proposal in another direction. Morgenthau believed strongly in the most severe treatment of Germany. Personally he wanted to "put Germany back as an agricultural country," harshly restricting her industry. Morgenthau wanted to dismember, uproot and oppress. He thought also that severe inflation, with its consequent distress, would teach the Germans a salutary lesson. What is more, Roosevelt was now persuaded to accept his plan, and at the Quebec Conference in September, 1944, Churchill too allowed himself to be won over. However, when the plan became public, American opinion quickly forced Roosevelt to give up all thoughts of following Morgenthau's ideas.

Parallel with the Allied discussions about Germany there had been the developing plans (of which the Jebb memorandum had been one of the forerunners) for the World Organisation. In the course of his Washington visit of May, 1942, Churchill had spoken of a possible World Council. He had envisaged under it that there would be three regional Councils—Europe, the American hemisphere and the Pacific. He had talked, too, of "A form of United States of Europe." But—as in 1918—the mainspring of the movement for the idealist concept of a World Order came from the United States. The American Senate passed a resolution on 5th November, 1943, recognising the necessity of establishing "at the earliest practicable date a general international organisation based on the principle of sovereign equality of all peace-loving States, and open to membership of all such States, large and small, for the maintenance of international peace and security."

In addition to these ideas, Paul-Henri Spaak, the Foreign Minister of the Belgian Government-in-exile, had formulated in early 1944 a plan for a Western bloc, extending from Norway to the Iberian Peninsula and *including* Britain. This was to be the forerunner of the Common Market. When Eden pointed out to him that this would be looked upon unfavourably by the Soviet Union—and that in any case the Western bloc might be dominated by Germany—Spaak retorted that the Russians were already organising a bloc in Eastern Europe. Spaak's plan had the support of the Belgian, Dutch and Norwegian governments-in-exile, all of whom realised the vulnerability of small nations.

The Americans became even more anxious to proceed quickly to a World Order as the war entered its final year. Underlying the strong American feeling was also a sense of guilt at their nation's record in repudiating Wilson's League of Nations. As with the British over Munich, there was a deep desire to atone for past failures.

The British had been forthcoming in response to the American proposals but the Russians were lukewarm about the idea of a World Order. Such idealism made little appeal to Communist realism. Following Hull's mission to Moscow, Roosevelt raised the matter with Stalin at Teheran. After several more discussions at official level, the Americans persuaded Stalin to send a strong delegation to a conference at Dumbarton Oaks, which met from 22nd August to 28th September, 1944, and which became the forerunner of the United Nations Organisation.

There were three issues of major substance between the Soviet Union and the Western Powers at the conference, none of which was resolved at this stage, despite much Anglo-American pressure. First, Gromyko, who was leading the Soviet delegation, astonished the conference by demanding individual representation in any future international organisation for all sixteen units of the Union of Soviet Socialist Republics. There was deadlock for several days, and the conference resolved it only by leaving over the Soviet demands to be settled at a later date. Secondly, when it came to the composition of the Security Council—the body that was going to function as the main executive committee of the organisation and in whom the principal powers of decision and action would be vested—there was an acrimonious dispute about membership. All agreed that the United States, the Soviet Union and Britain should be permanent members. After more discussion, and under British pressure, it was also decided to keep a place open for France, despite American hostility to the proposal. Then there was prolonged argument on the American desire to include China. Eventually, the American view prevailed upon this issue and China became a permanent member of the Security Council. It was a decision about which the world was to hear more in later years.

Finally, there was the issue of a veto. The original American position, before the Dumbarton Oaks Conference, was that the permanent members of the Security Council should have the right of veto on its decisions. The Russian position was similar to the American, Stalin at Teheran having placed much emphasis upon the need for unanimity amongst the Great Powers. However, the British persuaded the Americans to change their policy. Cadogan, who was heading the British delegation, reported to the British Government that the Americans had come round to the British view that all parties to a dispute, whether they happened to be permanent members of the Security Council or not, should vote upon it. Gromyko, on behalf of the Soviet Union, objected strongly. Despite the successive interventions of Stettinius, Cadogan, Hull and finally Roosevelt, he "remained immovable" in his insistence upon the unanimity of the permanent members. The Americans had had enough and they were anxious to bring the Dumbarton Oaks Conference to a conclusion. Therefore it was agreed to allow the outstanding matters to remain for discussion at a major United Nations Conference. This was to take place at San Francisco, in the following spring.

The broader story has now been brought up to the point at which Churchill and Eden were returning from their October mission to Moscow. It was clear, for those who wished to see into the future, that Poland was going to be the major obstacle to Soviet-Western co-operation. The fate of the other East European countries, despite—and partly because of—Churchill's "percentage arrangement" with Stalin, was in jeopardy. The establishment of the United Nations Organisation was going to raise serious problems in the near future. Above all, the policy of the Grand Alliance towards Germany remained unsettled. The clouds of the Cold War were gathering but few people observed them or heard the distant thunder.

CHAPTER 7

STALIN'S HOUR

Stalin's greatest victory.   *Chester Wilmot*

An ugly situation was developing in Greece in the early autumn of
1944. It was precisely the sort of problem that Churchill had in
mind when proposing his "percentage agreement" with Stalin. The
German garrison started to evacuate Athens on 2nd October. Hard
on their heels came a British force of parachutists. They were
followed by British infantry and naval units, and all were received
rapturously by the Greek population. The Greek Government-in-
exile—broadened to include Communists of E.A.M. (The National
Liberation Front)—arrived with the liberating British forces. But
it soon became apparent that the departing Germans had left chaos
in their wake. The new Greek Government was unequal to the
task, and units of E.L.A.S. (The People's National Army of Liberation), which was Communist-dominated like E.A.M., threatened
to take over the country. The only chance of averting civil war was
to disarm the E.L.A.S. guerrillas—a course which was naturally
opposed by the Communist members of the Greek Government.
The matter came to a head on 1st December. Six E.A.M. Ministers
in the Greek Government resigned. The situation developed fast.
On 2nd December, a supporting general strike was proclaimed by
the Communists in Athens. Next day, 3rd December, fighting broke
out when Communist demonstrators came into conflict with Greek
police and E.L.A.S. retaliated by attempting to seize the capital
city by force.

Churchill, in London, decided to intervene personally. He and
Eden sat up late into the night of 4th December and sent a telegram
in the early hours of 5th December, ordering General Scobie, the
British Commander in Athens, to open fire on "any male in Athens
who assails the British authority or Greek authority with which we
are working. . . . We have to hold and dominate Athens. It would

be a great thing for you to succeed in this without bloodshed if possible, but also with bloodshed if necessary." Churchill was vehemently attacked, both in the House of Commons and in the American Press for his action.

Churchill and Eden decided to fly to Athens to settle matters on the spot when the fighting continued for three more weeks. They reached Athens on Christmas Day. After a three-hour conference in their aircraft at the airfield, surrounded by an armed British escort, they made their way to the cruiser *Ajax* lying off the shore in apparent safety. An important figure in the situation was Archbishop Damaskinos, who had been suggested earlier as a possible Regent of Greece by the British Ambassador in Athens—pending a decision about the monarchy—and rejected by both King George of the Hellenes and Churchill himself. Churchill decided, at the airport, to send for Damaskinos to come to the cruiser *Ajax*. Churchill agreed in the discussions with the Archbishop that a conference was to be convened next day, to be attended by representatives of E.L.A.S. When the conference met, the Prime Minister listened to all sides in the dispute. He then departed, allowing the Greek parties to talk amongst themselves for a whole day. Finally, Churchill decided to reverse his previous decision about Damaskinos and to appoint him Regent. Churchill and Eden flew back to London on 29th December, resolved to ask King George of Greece to make him Regent "unless a plebiscite of his people call for his return"—a strange appointment which Churchill eventually obtained from the most reluctant King at half past four on the morning of 30th December. It had been an arduous four days, fraught with personal danger and political crisis for the Prime Minister. But, in his eyes, it was the triumphant vindication of his Moscow "percentages agreement." Stalin had loyally stood by, agreeing to Britain having "90 per cent of the say."

Nevertheless, the Greek episode had left bad feelings in the American administration. It had confirmed the suspicions of Britain's post-war policies that had been forming since Churchill's Moscow visit. It was to form part of the background of distrust towards the British that was soon to manifest itself at Yalta.

The war was now reaching its climax. In the West, the American and British armies had advanced to the borders of Germany. In the East, the Red Army had crossed the Danube. And in Poland it was massing for its break-out across the Vistula.

Whilst Churchill had been dealing with the situation in Greece, Roosevelt had been conducting an unprofitable correspondence with Stalin on Poland. Roosevelt, whilst attempting to see Stalin's difficulties, warned him of the consequences of precipitate recognition of the Lublin Committee. Unfortunately, it was too late and indeed Stalin had no intention of being diverted. The machinery of Soviet recognition of the Lublin Poles had been set in motion. Stalin disclosed in another cable to Roosevelt on 1st January, 1945: "The position is that as early as 27th December the Praesidium of the Supreme Soviet of the U.S.S.R. informed the Poles in reply to an inquiry on the subject that it is proposed to recognise the Provisional Government of Poles as soon as the latter was formed. The circumstances make it impossible for me to fulfil your wish."

Thus the Polish story had started yet another chapter and there was now nothing more that could be done by the Western Powers in advance of the next Three-Power meeting, envisaged from the moment Churchill had proposed his personal trip to Moscow in the previous autumn and when the President had secured his election for his fourth term. The original thought in Roosevelt's mind had been for a meeting in late November, perhaps in the Black Sea. This went by in the pressure of events. Stalin remained adamant that he could not leave Russia and chose Yalta in the Crimea. Roosevelt's inauguration ceremony, fixed for 20th January, imposed another limitation upon the date for the Three-Power meeting.

The President's Inaugural Address, over which he took a great deal of trouble, gave an interesting indication of his state of mind as he set off for Yalta. It was very brief, only five minutes, partly because Roosevelt insisted on standing, despite his infirmity, and partly because he was determined only to wear a lightweight suit with no waistcoat, hat or overcoat in the bitter cold. His words rang out bravely: "We have learned to be citizens of the world, members of the human community. We have learned the simple truth, as Emerson said, that 'the only way to have a friend is to be one'." But, although Roosevelt's words were brave, many people there were shocked by his physical deterioration.

For reasons of health, the President had decided to go by sea to Malta, where he was to link up with Churchill's party. They were all to fly from there on to Saki in the Crimea, the nearest suitable airfield to Yalta. Churchill, as was his custom and inclination, immediately suggested preliminary Anglo-American military talks in Malta to be followed by a meeting of the three Foreign Ministers,

Eden, Molotov and Stettinius, in Egypt. Roosevelt promptly rejected the first suggestion (apart from a short staff meeting) as he had done before Teheran. He said brusquely also that Stettinius could not be spared for a Foreign Ministers' meeting.

An unpleasant shock awaited the British delegation when it met the American party at Malta. Despite Churchill's gay phrases that he had cabled beforehand to Roosevelt, "No more let us falter! From Malta to Yalta! Let nobody alter!"[1] the Americans arrived in the most suspicious frame of mind towards the British—the legacy of Moscow and Greece. The President and his entourage obviously now believed that Russia, unlike Britain, was not an imperialist power. This distinction between her allies was shortly to influence American attitudes towards the unresolved United Nations Constitution, including the veto; and also towards Russian terms for entry into the Japanese war and Russian policies in Poland.

However, on the surface at Malta, cordiality was manifest. An escort of British Spitfires, massed bands and the booming of guns welcomed the U.S.S. *Quincy*, as she steamed into Valetta Harbour with Roosevelt on board, on 2nd February. The President gave a dinner party on board for Churchill and Eden before the two delegations, numbering seven hundred persons, took to the air on the fourteen hundred miles' flight to the Crimea.

The Germans had been driven out of Yalta some ten months before and the debris of occupation and war lay around. But the Soviet authorities had gone to enormous trouble to ensure the comfort of their guests, although accommodation was so limited that even the senior members of the American and British delegations were sometimes sleeping six in a room.[2] The American delegation was centred at the sumptuous Livadia Palace where, in order to save Roosevelt inconvenience, all the plenary sessions of the conference were held. Nearby were the Soviet headquarters in the Yusupov Palace. Churchill and the British delegation were some

---

[1] The Prime Minister had elaborated this for private use:
    "No more let us alter or falter or palter
    From Malta to Yalta, and Yalta to Malta."
He did not send it to Roosevelt!

[2] On one occasion Portal, the British Chief of Air Staff, remarked on a glass tank in the British headquarters and said that it contained no fish. Two days later it was full of goldfish. At another stage a remark was passed that the cocktails contained no lemon peel. The next day a whole lemon tree was growing in the hall, imported by air.

miles away in the Vorontzov Palace, a strange, half Gothic, half Moorish architectural fantasy, basking in the Black Sea sunshine, with the snow-capped Crimean mountains in the background.

After the usual preliminary courtesies, the first plenary session at Yalta opened at 4.15 p.m. on 5th February around a large round table in the Livadia Palace. There were about twenty people present.

The purpose and task of the conference differed in the minds of the various delegations. On the Russian side, Stalin wanted to settle his terms for entry into the Pacific war in such a way as to achieve the maximum Soviet domination over Northern China. By entering the Pacific conflict, he also hoped to gain American gratitude—and thereby even to consolidate his political position in Europe. Churchill took a cooler view. He was determined to find out what use the Soviet Union intended to make of its new military power after the war, and how far she meant to collaborate with the Western Powers. He was by now acutely aware of the potential dangers of the European situation and the threat of Communist expansion in Western Europe and in the Mediterranean. As for the Americans—Roosevelt, whilst appreciating that there was some danger from Soviet expansionism, was prepared to be much more easily satisfied by Stalin's assurances. His main concern at this stage was the Far East war and the help he could expect from Stalin. The American attitude to Soviet-Western relations is best summed up by Hopkins in a memorandum he wrote later: "We know or believe that Russia's interests, so far as we can anticipate them, do not afford an opportunity for a major difference with us in foreign affairs. We believe we are mutually dependent upon each other for economic reasons. We find the Russians as individuals easy to deal with. The Russians undoubtedly like the American people. They like the United States. They trust the United States more than they trust any power in the world."

The Conference opened with a discussion on the dismemberment of Germany. Stalin began it, pointing out that the three Powers had accepted the idea of dismemberment in principle, but had not yet decided how or what was to be done. Churchill returned to his earlier declaration that Roosevelt's proposal on dismemberment at Teheran for "Five Germanies" was impractical. He still preferred "Two Germanies"—Prussia and Austria-Bavaria, with the Ruhr and Westphalia under international control. He also protested that the issue was much too complicated to be settled in the five or six days at Yalta; it called for a searching examination of the historical, ethnographical and economic facts.

Roosevelt, however, wanted the decision to be taken in principle at Yalta. As at Teheran, he showed irritation at the length of Churchill's speeches. The President had also made arrangements to see a number of people after the Yalta Conference, including Haile Selassie, Ibn Saud and Farouk. Indeed, by the end, Stalin and Churchill had difficulty in persuading him to stay to finish the business.

In the first plenary session, Roosevelt caused a major stir by stating that, whilst the United States was prepared to take all reasonable steps to preserve peace, she would not be prepared to do so at the expense of keeping troops in Europe indefinitely, three thousand miles away from home. He declared that the American occupation in Germany would be limited to two years. Shortly before Roosevelt made this statement there had been a discussion about a zone of occupation for France. Churchill had pressed strongly for this and he now redoubled his efforts, alarmed lest the alternative might be for Britain to undertake the occupation of the whole of Western Germany—a task far beyond his country's strength.

Stalin did not want French troops in Germany or French representatives in the German Control Commission. He remarked disparagingly that France had "opened the gates to the enemy" and added that the Control Commission should consist only of those powers that had stood firm against Germany—a curious comment to come from the leader of the government that had signed the Nazi-Soviet Alliance. Somewhat to Churchill's chagrin, Roosevelt supported Stalin on the issue of the French being excluded from membership of the Control Commission.

The Yalta Conference then discussed the proposed United Nations Organisation and the unresolved argument at Dumbarton Oaks on the Security Council's proposed procedure. To retrace the story: in December, 1944, after Dumbarton Oaks, Roosevelt had produced a new and somewhat complicated scheme. Each member of the Security Council was to have a vote. But on all major issues, all the permanent members of the Security Council were to be in agreement. In short, on key matters no action was to be taken by the United Nations unless the so-called "Big Four"—U.S.A., U.S.S.R., Britain and China—were all agreed. This, then, was the

veto in a compromise form. Stettinius expounded the scheme to
the Yalta Conference, and when Stalin seemed puzzled Churchill
explained it to him in his own colourful way. Stalin then admitted
that he had not had time to study the issue, and Molotov returned
next day to accept the Roosevelt plan.

Next, there was a debate upon the wider membership of the
United Nations. Molotov had demanded earlier with some
persistence that the various Soviet Republics should be entitled to
United Nations membership if the British Dominions and Latin
American countries were also to belong in their own right. He was
now more reasonable. He agreed that the Soviet Union would be
satisfied if three, or at any rate two, of the republics were represented. He named the Ukraine, Byelo-Russia and Lithuania.
Absurd though the proposition still was, it came as a great relief
to Roosevelt, who was quick to congratulate the Soviet delegation.
A long and, at times, difficult discussion took place in the earlier
plenary sessions upon the issue of reparations. Maisky began it at
the first session by explaining, at Stalin's request, a Soviet scheme
which fell into two sections: (1) The complete removal of German
plant, machinery, tools and other capital assets to the extent of
about 80 per cent of Germany's industrial wealth, and (2) Ten
annual payments in kind. He said that the Russian claim was for
10,000 million dollars. He suggested a Reparations Commission to
sit in Moscow and to work out the details. It was an extraordinary
and impractical demand. Churchill reacted sharply, by pointing
to the grim lessons of the period following the First World War.
He asked, "What will happen if Germany is reduced to starvation?"
And he added, "If you want a horse to pull your wagon, you must
give him some hay."

At Churchill's suggestion, the three Foreign Ministers were asked
to draw up a draft directive for a Reparations Commission. The
Foreign Ministers began work upon this on 7th February, and
Molotov produced a document stating that the reparations should
amount to 20,000 million dollars over ten years. Of this, the Soviet
Union should receive 10,000 million dollars. Eden rejected these
figures and, at a further meeting, Stettinius supported him. The
British position was that the figures were unrealistic, partly because
any system of valuation was impossible and partly because the
Soviets wanted too much. In the British view, no figures should be
mentioned. At another plenary session Stalin sought once more to
get the figures inserted. Again Churchill refused. Finally, Stalin

said that he wanted to settle the principle that Germany would pay reparations in kind and that the Commission could decide the amount. As for the Soviet Union, it would put in the same figures to the Reparations Commission when it came to be set up and the other countries could submit their own claims. On hearing Stalin's statement, the conference agreed upon a secret protocol to this effect. It was the nearest they were likely to reach in compromise.

With this issue at least temporarily out of the way at Yalta, the conference accepted a suggestion of Roosevelt's to refer the decision on Germany's dismemberment to a meeting of Foreign Ministers to report in thirty days. The British now got their way on France. An invitation was to be sent to De Gaulle, for France's participation in the Control Commission and to take up a French zone of occupation; the zone to be agreed by the European Advisory Commission. Nevertheless, Stalin persisted in his hostility towards De Gaulle. He described him contemptuously as "an unrealistic figure."

Stettinius now raised an American proposal for a "Declaration on Liberated Europe." Stettinius's draft began: "The Premier of the Union of Soviet Socialist Republics, the Prime Minister of the United Kingdom and the President of the United States of America . . . jointly declare their mutual agreement to concert during the temporary period of instability in Liberated Europe the policies of their three governments in assisting the peoples liberated . . . to solve by democratic means their pressing political and economic problems." The declaration went on to promise that the three governments would assist the governments in liberated Europe: "(a) to establish conditions of internal peace; (b) to carry out emergency measures for the relief of distressed peoples; (c) to form interim governmental authorities broadly representative of all democratic elements in the population and pledged to the earliest possible establishment through free elections of governments responsive to the will of the people; and (d) to facilitate where necessary the holding of such elections."

Stettinius's proposed Declaration was accepted without much debate, although Molotov inserted a qualification on its implementation, pledging the Three Powers "to consult together on the measures necessary." Even so, the earlier clauses remained mandatory and any government failing to carry them out could be held to have violated its obligations—an important point of view of what was to come later.

The famous discussions on Russia's entry into the Far East war took place in very great secrecy. Roosevelt and Stalin acted as principals. Sometimes there were meetings between certain chosen members of the two delegations. But the gatherings were highly selective. Even Stettinius was kept out, although he was Secretary of State, on the pretext that these were military talks and were *not* political. Stalin indicated to Roosevelt his willingness to declare war on Japan within two to three months after the ending of the war in Europe on certain conditions. He demanded the preservation of the *status quo* in Outer Mongolia—which he considered was an area of Soviet influence. He insisted on the restoration of the former rights of Russia "violated by the treacherous attacks of Japan in 1904," an interesting attachment to Tsarist positions. Here, he claimed: (1) The southern part of Sakhalin, as well as all the islands adjacent to it, shall be returned to the Soviet Union. (2) The commercial port of Dairen shall be internationalised, the pre-eminent interests of the Soviet Union in this port being safe-guarded and the lease of Port Arthur as a naval base of the U.S.S.R. restored. (3) The Chinese-Eastern Railroad and the South Man-churian Railroad, which provides an outlet to Dairen, shall be jointly operated by a Soviet-Chinese company, it being understood that the pre-eminent interests of the Soviet Union shall be safe-guarded and that China shall retain full sovereignty in Manchuria, and (4) the Kuril Islands shall be handed over to the Soviet Union.

It was a formidable set of terms. Amazing though it is, Roosevelt accepted them. The President also undertook to secure Chiang Kai-shek's concurrence to these terms, though the Chinese leader had not been consulted about them—in itself, an extraordinary procedure.

When the agreement was presented to the British delegation, Eden urged Churchill very strongly not to sign it, especially as he had played no part in formulating it. Churchill decided reluctantly to reject his Foreign Secretary's advice. In his memoirs he evaded the whole affair. He merely stated: "In the United States there have been many reproaches about the concessions made to Soviet Russia. The responsibility rests with their own representatives. To us the problem was remote and secondary." The bleakness of his words speak for his feelings at the time.

The remaining major issue of the Yalta Conference was Poland. It was the crunch, naturally, and it had been the Polish issue, in the first place, which had been the principal reason for calling the conference. It dominated the discussions—the transcript record of the Yalta meeting shows nearly 20,000 words of talk on Poland amongst the three leaders, to say nothing of innumerable meetings amongst the Foreign Ministers. At the beginning of the conference the situation was that whilst the Soviet Union had recognised the Lublin Committee as the Government of Poland, the U.S.A. and Britain still recognised the London Government-in-exile. Reports of mass arrests and deportations had been coming out of Poland following upon an announcement by the Lublin Government that it intended to try as traitors all members of the Polish Home Army. Roosevelt began the discussion on Poland at the second plenary session by saying that on the whole he was in favour of the Curzon Line, but he considered that the Poles should have Lwow. Churchill was more ready to permit Lwow to go to the Soviet Union, but he was less interested in boundaries than in a strong, free and independent Poland, living in amity with the Soviet Union. Stalin was adamant about the Lublin Government and the issue of Lwow. He complained sharply that the Polish Home Army had killed over 200 Red Army soldiers. He again demanded the Western Neisse as the future Polish-German frontier. In one of the sessions the argument became so heated that when Roosevelt suggested an adjournment Churchill insisted that he and Stalin had received different accounts of what was happening in Poland. According to his information, the Prime Minister continued, the Lublin Government did not command the support of more than one-third of the Polish people. Roosevelt was now very anxious to end the discussion for the day. "Poland," he said impatiently, "has been a source of trouble for over five hundred years." "All the more," retorted Churchill, "must we do what we can to put an end to all these troubles."

The conference went over the familiar Polish ground, again and again. Churchill declared eloquently on one side: "Britain declared war on Germany so that Poland should be free and sovereign. Everyone knows what a terrible risk we took and how it nearly cost us our life in the world. . . . Our interest in Poland is one of honour. Having drawn the sword on behalf of Poland against Hitler's brutal attack, we could never be content with any solution that did not leave Poland a free and independent state."

Stalin answered equally warmly: "For the Russian people, the question of Poland is not only a question of honour but also a question of security. Throughout history, Poland has been the corridor through which the enemy has passed to Russia. Twice in the last thirty years our enemies, the Germans, have passed through this corridor. It is in Russia's interest that Poland should be strong and powerful, in a position to shut the door of this corridor by her own force. . . . Therefore, it is not only a question of honour but of life and death for the Soviet State."

From this, it was apparent that Stalin would not give way upon the question of the Lublin Committee. The Red Army was also in possession of the country. Stalin surprised the Western leaders on the subject of the time table. "How soon will it be possible to hold the elections?" asked Roosevelt. "Within a month, unless there is some catastrophe on the front, which is improbable," answered Stalin. This answer by Stalin went a long way to reducing the tension. The Soviet leader also agreed that the Lublin Government "should be recognised on a wider democratic basis with the inclusion of democratic leaders from Poland itself and also from Poles living abroad. This new government shall be called the Polish Provisional Government of National Unity." This government was to be "pledged to the holding of free and unfettered elections as soon as possible on the basis of universal suffrage and secret ballot. In these elections, all democratic and anti-Nazi parties shall have the right to take part and to put forward candidates." It was decided that Molotov, Harriman and Clark Kerr would meet in Moscow to work out, with the Poles of both sides, the details of the arrangements for the broadening of the Polish Government and the holding of the elections. The Curzon Line, with digressions from it of "5 to 8 kilometres in favour of Poland," was accepted, and "the final delimitation of the western frontier should thereafter await the Peace Conference."

The Yalta Conference concluded with a sense of relief amongst the British delegation—leaving the Far East issue aside. It had feared the worst on Poland, and it now hoped that Stalin meant to keep his word about Polish elections in "a month's time." The Americans, too, were very optimistic, to the point of delight. In their view, Stalin had committed himself to the Far Eastern war and they entertained great hopes for the future of the United Nations.

And Stalin? He was well satisfied. It had been his outstanding success. The Soviet leader now held nearly all the significant cards for the Peace Conference to come; and the initiative in Europe was his for the taking. His military victories in Europe combined with the misguided Western military strategy had given him the ultimate political power in Eastern Europe over all the areas in which Churchill had foreseen it might hold sway. Only Greece remained completely outside his sphere of influence. It is true that he had been forced to sign a document relating to liberated Europe that contained obligations, but his opinion was that this was an affair largely of words to please the Americans. The Reparations Commission was to meet in Moscow, where it would be under his gaze. The Commission to deal with Poland again was to meet in Moscow, where the Soviet Government would dominate it. The significant fact from Stalin's point of view was that he had conceded nothing at Yalta that could not be ignored or circumnavigated when the appropriate time came.

The Poles in London did not see Yalta in the way that Roosevelt and Churchill did on their return. With their embittered experience, they realised where the power now really lay. The London Polish Government issued a despairing statement describing it as "the fifth partition of Poland, this time by her allies."

The most interesting question to ask, in retrospect, is what lay behind the American attitude? In subsequent years, Roosevelt's actions at Yalta have been explained away, by his illness or by his fatigue. But this cannot be the excuse for one of the main decisions at Yalta—the secret agreement on the Far East. This was planned beforehand. Even at Teheran, Roosevelt had gone some way towards preparing Stalin for the arrangement. He had received nearly two months of prior warning from Stalin of the sort of terms he would demand. Stettinius stated later that the American position had been carefully worked out in advance of Yalta. The Far East agreement was all the more illogical in view of earlier American hostility to any possibility of Churchill negotiating zones of influence.

On the other hand, Roosevelt at Yalta was a man who was operating at the limits of his strength and no longer in control of his powers of argument. As the conference continued he rapidly became more tired. He behaved, too, in a curiously secretive manner. Again, this was understandable to a degree, in view of the commitment he had shouldered regarding China and the charges of bad faith that he knew would certainly be made against him. But his preoccupation with secrecy does not explain his locking up the secret agreement in his White House safe on his return to America —which he did—and not even letting the State Department know the details. The story was told later, by Byrnes, when he became

Secretary of State in July, 1945. Although Byrnes had been at Yalta he first learned of the agreement through a newspaper story originating in Moscow.

The truth is that three factors motivated Roosevelt's thinking at the time of Yalta. First, he was concerned with saving American lives in the forthcoming assault upon Japan. It has to be recalled that the atomic bomb was still only a prospect of the future, with no certainty of its operation as an effective weapon. The American Chiefs of Staff who, together with Roosevelt, were determined to prevent further major British participation in the Far Eastern war, had at last understood the practical difficulties of foregoing British support. They advised Roosevelt that in the absence of Russian intervention, as the alternative to British help, the Japanese war might cost an additional million American lives. Now to the crux of American thinking—Roosevelt and his Chiefs of Staff had decided to limit the British stake in the Far East really because they feared deeply that Churchill might use this fact to insist that Britain shared, by ownership or trusteeship, in the dismemberment of the Japanese Empire. To illustrate this American thought: at an earlier point in the war, following the 1944 Quebec Conference, Churchill had made the offer of sending a large part of R.A.F. Bomber Command to the Far East after the European victory and Roosevelt had accepted. But not so the American Chiefs of Staff. When they heard "All hell broke loose," according to General Arnold, and Admiral King "hotly refused to have anything to do with it." To these old-fashioned Americans, British imperialism still remained the danger to be kept in check after the war. But, in their eyes, the Soviet leaders and Communist system held out no such danger. They could not see it in any other way. When Mikolajczyk visited Washington in 1944, Roosevelt told him: "Stalin is a realist and we mustn't forget, when we judge Russian actions, that the Soviet régime has had only two years of experience in international relations. But of one thing I am certain, Stalin is not an imperialist." Stettinius also tells the story of how Roosevelt once said to Churchill: "Winston . . . you have four hundred years of acquisitive instinct in your blood, and you just don't understand how a country might not want to acquire land somewhere if they can get it. A new period has opened in the world's history and you will just have to adjust yourself to it."

The third factor in Roosevelt's thinking was his belief that the origins of much of Stalin's suspicious behaviour and Russia's apparently expansionist policies lay in a defensive psychology bred by the hostility of the Western world ever since the 1917 Revolution. Roosevelt really believed that this situation could be overcome by American trust. Accordingly, he was determined to see the best in Soviet Russia's foreign policies. And he expected the best in return. Yalta was Roosevelt's supreme opportunity to put his personal idealism to the test. It failed tragically.

As for Churchill, his position at that time was different. All along he had understood more clearly than any other Western leader the broad nature of the post-war Communist danger. He had tried to come to terms with Stalin personally; and to some extent he had succeeded in so far as that was possible. He had saved Greece from Communism, for the time being. He had started with few expectations in Eastern Europe or illusions about Russian policy, but he was determined to battle for Poland. Throughout the Polish wrangle he had been handicapped by what he considered to be the intransigence of the Polish Government-in-exile. He found its members an exasperating liability. Therefore, when the Prime Minister heard Stalin at Yalta agree to elections in "a month's time" he understood that the Moscow Commission would only be dealing with an arrangement that would last for a very short time. He was anxious to settle for the Yalta arrangement on Poland for the additional reason that British and American recognition of the new Polish Government would enable Western Ambassadors accurately to report back on what was actually happening within Poland —information that he could not get from the Poles in London.

The period from Teheran to Yalta represents the watershed of Soviet-Western clash. The struggle, as it developed later in Germany and Eastern Europe, has its origins in the period bounded by these two great international conferences. The British attempt at bargaining with Stalin over Poland failed because Churchill could not negotiate either from military strength or from geography— Greece remaining the solitary exception. The American attempt to play the good neighbour failed for the same reason as did Neville Chamberlain's policy of being the good neighbour to Hitler and Mussolini. Dictatorships are never appeased.

CHAPTER 8

VICTORY?

Like to the apples on the Dead Sea's shore,
All ashes to the taste.   *Byron*

The Yalta Conference ended on 11th February, 1945. Within a fortnight a Soviet-inspired *coup d'état* in Rumania, which must have been planned whilst the conference was in progress, indicated clearly the way in which Stalin intended to interpret the Yalta decisions on liberated Europe and to use his Soviet power in the areas where it could not be challenged.

The Radescu coalition government set up by King Michael had turned out to be most ineffective.[1] It was an easy target for Communist agitation, carried on with the connivance of the Soviet authorities. An ugly situation developed quickly. Shooting broke out on 24th February between the Radescu Government forces and local Communists. That same evening Radescu, speaking on Bucharest radio, stated that a handful of Communists was trying to terrorise the nation.

The American and British members of the Control Commission for Rumania immediately asked for a meeting to deal with the crisis. The Soviet chairman refused. On that same day, Harriman in Moscow was instructed to inform the Soviet Government that the Americans wanted to see an orderly development of the Rumanian situation under the Allied Control Commission. Clark Kerr was instructed to do likewise. Both Ambassadors dispatched letters of protest to the Soviet Government.

By the time the Western protests had reached the Kremlin, Vishynsky, the Soviet Deputy Foreign Minister, was already on his

[1] General Radescu had formed an administration early in December, 1944. He had succeeded General Satanescu, who had resigned largely because of Communist attacks, and at the time of his appointment Radescu had appeared acceptable to the Soviet authorities.

way to Bucharest. On his arrival in the Rumanian capital, Vishynsky went straight to the Palace and read out to King Michael a long list of charges against the Radescu administration, including the charge that it was incapable of maintaining order. He ended by demanding Radescu's instant dismissal. Early on the following evening, Vishynsky appeared again at the Palace and demanded whether the King had acted upon the previous day's interview. King Michael explained that he was consulting party leaders. When Visoianu, the Rumanian Foreign Minister, who had been present at both meetings, pointed out that the King, being a constitutional monarch, had to follow constitutional practice, Vishynsky turned on him angrily and shouted, "Shut up!" Vishynsky then looked at his watch. It was five minutes to six. Dramatically, he gave the King just two hours and five minutes—until eight o'clock to announce the name of the new Prime Minister. The Soviet Deputy Foreign Minister left the room banging the door behind him with great violence.

King Michael, who was in no position to argue with the Red Army in occupation of his country, capitulated. He announced that he had dismissed Radescu and that he was asking Prince Stirbey to form a government. This was no better because the Communists refused to serve under Stirbey. Another day went by. At the end of it, Vishynsky sent word to the Palace that the Soviet choice was Petro Groza, a man who had been associated with the Rumanian Communists. The King, after some discussion, again gave in and asked Groza to submit the names of an administration. However, the first list of ministers produced by Groza was so unrepresentative that the wrangle dragged on for a few more days. Again the King largely gave in to Groza's demands. On the evening of 6th March handbills were passed around the streets of Bucharest announcing the new administration, of which thirteen belonged to extreme left-wing or Communist groups and only four to the Peasant and Liberal parties—the two main parties in Rumania.

It was only at this point, after a prolonged delay, that Molotov agreed to answer the growing pile of Western protests—mainly American. He blandly told Harriman: "I presume that the question raised in your letter has lost its keenness inasmuch as the Government crisis brought about by the terrorist policy of Radescu which was incompatible with the principles of democracy has been overcome by the formation of the new Government." The Americans were very angry and, to add to their feeling of frustration, they felt also that the British let them down by not protesting more strongly at the way in which the Soviet authorities had established the rule of a Communist minority by force and misrepresentation. The documents show that there is substance in this charge against the British, who were inhibited by Churchill's agreement to give the Soviet Union 90 per cent of the influence in Rumania and by the British action in Greece. Thus whilst the American reaction was justified, the question which history will ask and which only the judgment of political practicality can answer is: Would stronger Western representations have changed the outcome of the Rumanian crisis?[1]

Poland, once more, was to provide the answer to this question. The first meeting between Molotov, Harriman and Clark Kerr, acting as the Commission on Poland, took place on 23rd February, 1945 —less than a fortnight after the conclusion of the Yalta Conference. There was an immediate clash. When the two Western Ambassadors proposed Mikolajczyk, Grabski and Romer as suitable Poles from outside Poland to be invited to the Moscow consultations, Molotov objected on the ground that he felt that the Lublin Poles might reject Mikolajczyk—as if they were in any position to reject Soviet advice. The Soviet Foreign Minister suggested that the Lublin Poles should be asked for their opinion in the first instance. Molotov insisted when Harriman and Clark Kerr demurred.

To make matters worse, the Commission soon received an impertinent reply from the Lublin Poles, ruling out Mikolajczyk and Romer as being hostile to the Yalta decisions. At the Commission's second meeting, on 27th February, Molotov suddenly announced to Harriman and Clark Kerr that, as neither the American nor British Governments had information on the situation in Poland, they might care to send observers themselves to Moscow. Clark Kerr promptly welcomed this idea as a constructive proposal which he would be prepared to recommend to his government provided it did not imply recognition of the Lublin Poles. Churchill, when he heard of Molotov's proposal, was delighted. He cabled Clark Kerr immediately, saying that it was of the greatest importance to establish direct sources of information from inside Poland and that he should accept the "friendly offer." Unfortunately the

[1] In fairness to Churchill it must be noted also that, in considering the case of Rumania, the general Western view was that she was a country that had aided and abetted the Germans. Therefore, feelings towards Rumania were in a different category at that time to those towards Poland.

Prime Minister's hopes were soon dashed. Molotov was so disconcerted at this prompt—and for him unexpected—acceptance that he retracted and explained that he would have to secure the "clearance of the Lublin Poles first." He then withdrew the whole proposal within a week, on the new grounds that Eden had made unfavourable remarks about Beirut's administration in the House of Commons[1], and also because the Western Powers had refused to invite the Lublin Poles to Moscow.

It was now the turn of the Americans to show inhibitions in pressing Western protests at Soviet policy. Eden sought American agreement at a joint Anglo-American message to the Soviet Government pointing out that the Yalta Agreement had been to secure conditions in which free elections could be held speedily and also refusing the Russian demand that the Lublin Poles should come to Moscow in advance of the others. But, when the State Department would not go as far as Eden wished, Molotov had no hesitation in rejecting the isolated British viewpoint. Churchill—by now very disturbed indeed—intervened again with a telegram to Roosevelt enclosing a draft message which he wanted to send Stalin warning that, unless certain conditions were fulfilled immediately, the Prime Minister would have to make a statement to Parliament announcing the failure of the Yalta Conference. The President said in his reply to the Prime Minister, dated 11th March, that whilst the object of the British and American Governments "was identical" there was a difference of view on tactics. Whereas Churchill wanted to place his demands squarely before Stalin, the Americans thought they stood a better chance of success by asking for "a political truce" amongst the various parties in Poland.

When he had read the message, Churchill reluctantly agreed to defer sending his own telegram to Stalin. Instead, he sent Roosevelt another cable couched in most urgent terms. It shows more clearly than any other document of this particular time the Prime Minister's disillusioned state of mind, so soon after his brief optimism over Poland after Yalta.

Prime Minister to President Roosevelt   *13th March, 1945*
At Yalta also we agreed to take the Russian view of the frontier line. Poland has lost her frontier. Is she now to lose her freedom? That is the question which will undoubtedly have to be fought out in Parliament and in public here. I do not wish to

[1] Eden had said frankly that he "disliked" the Lublin administration.

reveal a divergence between the British and United States Governments, but it would certainly be necessary for me to make clear that we are in the presence of a great failure and an utter breakdown of what was settled at Yalta, but that we British have not the necessary strength to carry the matter further and the limits of our capacity to act have been reached. The moment that Molotov sees that he has beaten us away from the whole process of consultations among Poles to form a new government he will know that we will put up with anything. On the other hand, I believe that combined dogged pressure and persistence along the lines on which we have been working and of my proposed draft message to Stalin would very likely succeed.

The American answer on 16th March (signed by Roosevelt but not written by him because of his state of health) was carefully argued. It showed deep concern on the American side. "I do not understand what you mean by a divergence between our two Governments. . . . We have been merely discussing the most effective tactics, and I cannot agree that we are confronted with a breakdown of the Yalta Agreement until we have made the effort to overcome the obstacles incurred in the negotiations at Moscow. . . ." The President said he accepted the first and third points of Churchill's draft—Molotov's conflicting translation of the Yalta Agreement and the idea that the Poles should discuss among themselves the composition of their future government. However, the Americans did not believe that the Russians would accept the proposal that "any Pole could be invited [to the consultations] unless all three members of the Commission object." Roosevelt was also willing to include the fifth suggestion—that Western observers should go to Poland—in his instructions to Harriman. When it came to the issue of the proposed order to Beirut's administration not to take any steps affecting the political and constitutional conditions in Poland, pending the outcome of the Moscow meeting, Roosevelt again pressed for "a political truce."

This last divergence illustrates the fundamental gulf between the British position and the American assessment, from their ordered society 3,000 miles away, of the realities of the situation in war-torn Poland, with hatreds, murderous feuds and the naked struggle for power waged by a small group of political gangsters.

The ailing Roosevelt was wearily considering the exchange of telegrams with Churchill in London and what to do about the Polish Communists in Moscow, when he received word that Stalin did not propose to send Molotov to the United Nations Conference at San Francisco, due to open on 25th April. Stalin's reason for this decision was that the Americans had not accepted the Lublin Poles to the United Nations Conference as the only accredited representatives of Poland. It was a sad blow to the President's hopes.

Also, the internal situation in Poland was worsening fast. Information reaching London indicated that the Lublin Poles had only a small minority of support in the country. The feeling in Poland was so explosive that even a national uprising appeared in prospect.

Certain conclusions about these events may be drawn in retrospect. The situation in Eastern Europe showed that Stalin himself intended to continue the struggle between the Communist and Western worlds—naturally in a new form—once the German war had ended. He also expected the Western Powers to do likewise. As for Roosevelt's amiable overtures and the President's careful attempts to place the United States in the role of the mediator— in Stalin's eyes these moves had been irrelevant, almost frivolous, in their naïvety and it is possible that he may even have thought that they had a hidden meaning. The record bears out the assessment. The *coup d'état* in Rumania and the implacable Russian determination to dominate Poland with a Communist puppet government had become clear. Similar Soviet plans, at varying stages of development and rates of progress, were also beginning to emerge in the other East European countries. In Bulgaria a coalition "Fatherland Front" government had been established, with the real power resting in Communist hands. Western attempts to organise "free elections" in Bulgaria were making little progress. In Hungary and Czechoslovakia, the political situation had yet to develop. The provisional coalition Hungarian Government under Miklos, with a Communist element in it, was being accepted by the Russians, for the time being. The position in Czechoslovakia was somewhat different, partly because of that country's Munich experience and also because of Benes's own prestige as head of the Government-in-exile. Benes himself had travelled to Moscow during the second half of March, 1945. During this visit a new Czechoslovak Government had been formed, in which seven posts out of twenty-five in the administration went to Communists. The new Prime Minister was Zdenek Fierlinger, the Czech Ambassador in Moscow, who was working closely with the Russians, even at that time, and who was later to play a significant part in the betrayal of his country in 1948. In a series of cordial exchanges between Stalin and Benes during this visit, the Soviet leader also reassured the Czech President that he had no intention of "Communising" Czechoslovakia. "You were justified in sharing this opinion in the past," Stalin said soothingly, but it was no longer Soviet policy. Only three years were to pass before those words became meaningless.

Thus, as the armies of the Grand Alliance converged upon Berlin, Poland remained the central political issue. However, Eisenhower, in Germany, had been warned by his Intelligence staff that Hitler and his most fanatical followers might entrench themselves in the mountainous Alpine area of Southern Bavaria and Western Austria known as "The National Redoubt." There, with munition factories built into the mountains and with new secret weapons that were being developed, it was feared that Hitler might be able to carry on a prolonged resistance—maybe for years. As it turned out, "The National Redoubt" was merely a crazy fantasy which did not exist. But Eisenhower did not know this and he decided to ignore the objective of Berlin and, after neutralising the Ruhr, to concentrate his forces for a drive southwards towards supposedly "The National Redoubt" under General Bradley, aiming to link up with the Red Army in the Dresden-Leipzig area. At the same time Eisenhower intended to leave Montgomery commanding the forces in the north, to protect Bradley's left flank. When Eisenhower had made his plans, he cabled the outlines on 28th March to Washington, London and Moscow, marking the last cable, "Personal to Marshal Stalin." This cable to Stalin was sent by Eisenhower without his informing either Air Chief Marshal Tedder, his Deputy, or the Combined Chiefs of Staff. Eisenhower's reasoning was that he was communicating upon a military matter with Stalin as Commander-in-Chief of the Red Army, as he had been authorised so to do at Yalta, although in the United States he reported to General Marshall—not the President. Churchill was so outraged when he was informed of Eisenhower's indiscretion on 29th March that he telephoned Eisenhower immediately. The Prime Minister was yet more angry when he had heard that Stalin had agreed blandly that "Berlin has lost its strategic importance" at the very moment the Red Army was pressing forward to capture it.

Churchill did not challenge the American view that the greatest potential of German resistance lay in the south; to him this was irrelevant, as the war was won. What mattered to him now in the light of unfolding Soviet policy, was the post-war balance of power. By this time he had come to regard the Soviet Union as a mortal danger in Europe. He considered Berlin to be the prime objective and he wanted the new front with Russia as far east as possible. In Churchill's opinion there were also other urgent considerations —American entry into Prague and Allied participation in the occupation of Vienna on an equal basis were vital. There was also a developing situation in the Adriatic, in which Tito was showing aggressive intentions towards Italy.

Whilst the puzzled Eisenhower was defending his plan to ignore Berlin, and to attack "The National Redoubt," the Allied advance eastwards was still under way. Armoured units reached the Elbe near Magdeburg on the evening of 11th April. They found the river crossing lightly defended. To the north-east lay the prize of Berlin, now only 53 miles away. As the Russians had not yet crossed the River Oder, Berlin was almost midway between the two armies. It was still possible that the American and British forces could have seized the German capital, and this was admitted later by General Bradley, although Bradley warned that there may have been heavy casualties in the course of the operation.

On Thursday, 12th April, Roosevelt had a stroke whilst he was having his portrait painted in Warm Springs, Georgia. He never recovered consciousness. He was sixty-three. The U.S. forces journal *Yank* in its next issue showed how many Americans felt at the time: "He was the Commander-in-Chief, not only of our armed forces but of our generation." Roosevelt, for all his limitations— despite the parochialism apparent to British people, whose recent past had led them to think on a much bigger political scale—had pursued a foreign policy that had been far ahead of his country. During the 1930s he had led America slowly but steadily away from isolation. In the early days of the war he had been a good friend of Britain, and, therefore, of freedom—for there was a period when the two were synonymous. He had been gravely mistaken in his attitude towards the Soviet Union, but his faults were the faults of his own warm, human generosity. The pages of world history will bear his name always.

Truman was catapulted to power by Roosevelt's sudden death. His background had been machine politics in the Democratic Party. He had made a considerable reputation in the Senate and Roosevelt had accepted him as Vice-President because he was effective in Congress. Truman's horizons were limited when he came to office, and the responsibility that was thrust upon him was stupendous. Yet he was a man of sterling character, as time was to show. Brave and decisive, the history of the United States will eventually dignify him as one of the greatest Presidents, although many years will pass before his countrymen will make a detached judgment of this controversial man.

The first effect of Roosevelt's death, in terms of policy, was to enable Eisenhower to continue with his original military plans of preparing to attack Hitler's non-existent "National Redoubt," leaving Berlin to the Russians. Events were moving fast in Germany. Truman was too new, and without sufficient knowledge of what had gone before, to think of overruling his Commander-in-Chief in Europe, in the midst of the final battle. On 14th April, 1945, Eisenhower cabled the Combined Chiefs of Staff: "The essence of my plan is to stop on the Elbe and clean up my flanks." On 21st April Eisenhower told the Russians, after having got Truman's permission, that he intended to halt his armies on the Elbe, at its tributary the Mulde, and on the mountainous frontier of Czechoslovakia. Thus free to concentrate upon "The National Redoubt," he launched his drive on 22nd April against what he believed to be Hitler's final defences. Alas, he was charging a phantom and the Germans had made no plans beyond romantic talk for prolonged resistance in the area.

The war was now in its final throes. The German forces in Italy surrendered on 29th April. The Red Army reached Berlin in this same week and Hitler committed suicide on 30th April with the Russian tanks less than half a mile from his bunker. Vienna fell also to the Red Army. The Russians overran Berlin on 2nd May, the same day as the German armies in Italy stopped fighting.

Paradoxically, only Prague—which had been so betrayed in 1938—remained still in German hands. Eisenhower's forces could have taken it with ease but the American Commander-in-Chief had handicapped himself out of the hunt, by promising Stalin to remain on the frontier. Eventually, as he had substantial forces lying idle, Eisenhower advised General Antonov, the Red Army Chief of Staff, that he would advance to Prague "if the situation required." Antonov reacted by protesting violently and insisted that the Americans should not advance beyond the line, Karlsbad-Pilsen-Bundejovice. More difficulties were to follow from Eisenhower's promise. On 5th May, when the Americans crossed the border with the instructions not to go beyond this line, the Czech underground movement rose in the capital and broadcast an appeal for Allied aid. To the shame of the Western Powers, General Bradley's hands were tied and American forces were compelled to remain outside the city. To conclude the Prague story, it was only with the general capitulation of the German Army at midnight on 8th-9th May that Red Army units entered Prague. Thus it came about that all the great capitals of Central Europe—Berlin, Vienna, Prague, Warsaw, Budapest, Bucharest, Sofia and Belgrade—were in the hands of the Red Army when the fighting ended. Stalin had achieved one of the most formidable negotiating positions in recorded history.

As all this was happening, three main issues remained still to be dealt with, some of them of extreme urgency. First, there were the arrangements for the occupation of Germany and her allies; and a decision by the Grand Alliance upon whether Germany was to be left as a whole or to be cut into several pieces. Secondly—and looming large in American thinking—was the San Francisco Conference to found the United Nations, that had started on 25th April. Finally, there was the unresolved struggle over Poland and Eastern Europe, of which so much has already been heard.

The policies of all the Allies on dismemberment had been undergoing a change, ever since the shock created by the Morgenthau Plan. Whereas Stalin and Roosevelt had begun by being strongly in favour of the break-up into several pieces of the lands of the Third Reich, Churchill had supported a more limited dismemberment and was against the creation of a large number of small units on practical economic grounds. The pace of military advance and the decision of the Yalta Conference to set up a committee to study the partitioning of Germany, made it impossible for the issue to be avoided any longer. Each country, therefore, had to formulate its policy.

A paper drawn up in the British Treasury and submitted to the War Cabinet on 7th March, 1945, had a decisive effect upon Churchill's policy. The Treasury paper laid down a number of conditions essential to British interests. Some of the principal points in this paper were also relevant from the standpoints of the Soviet and American Governments. The British Treasury pointed out that if the occupying Powers placed themselves in a position whereby they were paying for imports into Germany, whilst the Germans were paying reparations, the Allies would, in fact, be paying for the German reparations. Secondly, the Treasury went on to show, from the experience gained in Italy, that if Germany were stripped of her capital resources, large sums would also be required for working capital; and Germany's impoverishment would lead to the impoverishment of Europe as a whole, with possible civil disorders which would represent the occupying Powers in a most unfavourable light. The British Treasury paper added another thought which supplemented the view expressed earlier, in September, 1944, by the British Chiefs of Staff. The Treasury pointed out that if the Soviet Union were to develop a governmental and administrative system, amenable to Soviet policy in the Russian zone of occupation, Britain, America and France should at least consider whether it was desirable that there should be a unified, separate German State that could be fitted into the general economy of the Western European countries.

Whilst the Treasury paper was being discussed in Britain, Russian policy on dismemberment also changed abruptly. The reason was that thinking inside the Kremlin had now turned to wider aims, and dismemberment would have placed a limitation upon Stalin's hopes of securing all Germany. The Soviet Government, therefore, informed its allies on 26th March that they understood that the decision of the Yalta Conference was "not an obligatory plan, but as a possibility of exerting pressure on Germany with the object of rendering her harmless in the event of other means proving inadequate." As dismemberment ceased to be an issue, the arrangements for the occupation of Germany became more important. Churchill telegraphed to Truman on 6th May urging that the Western Powers "should hold firmly to the existing position obtained by our armies in Yugoslavia, in Austria, in Czechoslovakia, on the main central United States front, and on the British front reaching up to Lubeck, including Denmark. . . . Thereafter I feel that we must most earnestly consider our attitude towards the Soviets and show them how much we have to offer or withhold. . . ." Churchill's contention was that there should be a meeting of the three Heads of Governments as soon as possible. Truman's view was somewhat contrary. He expressed it in a reply on 9th May, saying that he would prefer that the request for such a Three-Power meeting should come, in the first instance, from Stalin himself.

Realising only too well that Stalin was most unlikely to ask for such a meeting, Churchill cabled back to Truman warning him: "Mr. President, in these next two months, the gravest matters in the world will be decided." The Prime Minister followed it by a further cable to the President on 12th May. In his memoirs, Churchill has written: "Of all the public documents I have written on this issue I would rather be judged by this." His telegram sets out with stark clarity the grave issues as he saw them. It is indeed a bitter document to appear from the British Prime Minister amidst the victory cheers and celebrations of the nation that had faced complete ruin and disaster five years before.

Prime Minister to President Truman:

TOP SECRET *London, 12th May, 1945*
I am profoundly concerned about the European situation. I learn that half the American Air Force in Europe has already begun to move to the Pacific Theatre. The newspapers are full of the great movements of the American armies out of Europe. Our armies also are under previous arrangements likely to undergo a marked reduction. The Canadian Army will certainly leave. The French are weak and difficult to deal with. Anyone can see that in a very short space of time our armed power on the Continent will have vanished except for the moderate forces to hold down Germany.

2. Meanwhile, what is to happen about Russia? I have always worked for friendship with Russia, but like you, I feel deep anxiety because of their misinterpretation of the Yalta decisions, their attitude towards Poland, their overwhelming influence in the Balkans excepting Greece, the difficulties they make about Vienna, the combination of Russian power and territories under their control or occupied, coupled with the Communist technique in so many other countries, and above all their power to maintain very large armies in the field for a long time. What will be the position in a year or so, when the British and American armies have melted and the French has not yet been formed on any major scale, when we may have a handful of divisions mostly French, and when Russia may choose to keep two or three hundred on active service?

3. An iron curtain is drawn down upon their front. We do not know what is going on behind. There seems little doubt that the whole of the regions east of the line Lubeck-Trieste-

Corfu will soon be completely in their hands. To this must be added the further enormous area conquered by the American armies and the Elbe, which will I suppose in a few weeks be occupied, when the Americans retreat, by Russian power. All kinds of arrangements will have to be made by General Eisenhower to prevent another immense flight of the German population westward as this enormous Muscovite advance into the centre of Europe takes place. And then the curtain will descend again to a very large extent, if not entirely Thus a broad band of many hundreds of miles of Russian-occupied territory will isolate us from Poland.

4. Meanwhile the attention of our peoples will be occupied in inflicting severities upon Germany, which is ruined and prostrate, and it would be open to the Russians in a very short time to advance if they chose to the waters of the North Sea and the Atlantic.

5. Surely it is vital now to come to an understanding with Russia or see where we are with her, before we weaken our armies mortally or retire to the zones of occupation. This can only be done by a personal meeting. I shall be most grateful of your opinion and advice. Of course we may take the view that Russia will behave impeccably and no doubt that offers the most convenient solution. To sum up, this issue of a settlement with Russia before our strength has gone seems to me to dwarf all others.

The Prime Minister's cable was out of tune with the new President's thinking. This is not to say that Truman was blind to the potential Soviet menace in Europe. Truman's famous interview with Molotov, on Poland, in which he had rebuked the Soviet Foreign Minister, had also taken place three weeks before Churchill's message of 12th May. The truth was that Truman, still new to his awesome responsibility and as yet uninformed on all that had gone before, was leaning heavily upon some of Roosevelt's old advisers.

Truman, therefore, turned aside Churchill's warnings and advice. On 11th May—the same day as the Prime Minister had drafted his massive full-scale argument—Truman telegraphed of the dangers of any suspicion of "our ganging-up" and urged the need for Churchill and himself to proceed separately to any meeting that might be arranged between the heads of government. In reply to Churchill's major argument Truman was very non-committal. On

14th May he cabled in perfunctory response to Churchill's iron curtain warning: "From the present point of view it is impossible to make a conjecture as to what the Soviet may do when Germany is under the small forces of occupation and the great part of such armies as we can maintain are fighting in the Orient against Japan." The answer showed how little the new President grasped as yet the great issue that had been posed by Churchill.

The Polish disagreement had become worse by this time. An ugly event had actually taken place much earlier, with repercussions to come. On 3rd March an officer of the Red Army, Colonel Pinienov, acting on behalf of General Ivanov, the Soviet Commander in Poland, had written to Jankowski, the Vice-Premier of the Polish Government-in-exile, in London, inviting its representatives to Poland for talks. Pinienov's letter had stated: "I give you my absolute word of honour that from the moment of your arrival amongst us I shall be responsible for everything that happens to you and that your personal safety is completely assured." After consultations with the Foreign Office and the State Department, a delegation led by Jankowski left for Poland. After meetings with the Russians on 27th March, at Pruszkow, these non-Communist representatives (numbering fifteen Poles in all) suddenly disappeared. Clark Kerr in Moscow was instructed to ask Molotov about their safety. Molotov wrote a letter to Clark Kerr saying that the Soviet authorities were "overburdened with urgent work" and could not answer inquiries about "these or those Poles."

Meanwhile, there was a slight rise in Western hopes on Poland— optimism was never far from the surface. When Harriman called to see Stalin shortly after Roosevelt's death, the Soviet leader asked what expression of goodwill he could make to the new President. Harriman promptly suggested that he should send Molotov to San Francisco. To Harriman's surprise, Stalin agreed.

Molotov arrived in Washington on 22nd April and had a cordial first meeting late in the evening with Truman, who was living at this time in Blair House. Unfortunately this was as far as the Soviet-Western cordiality got. Next day Stettinius and Eden found Molotov as obdurate as ever on the same old issue of the status of the Lublin Poles and Polish representation at the forthcoming San Francisco Conference. Truman saw Molotov again that same evening determined to speak "in words of one syllable." He spoke so sharply to the Soviet Foreign Minister about the Soviet implementation of the Yalta agreement that Truman records in his memoirs that Molotov said: "I have never been talked to like that in my life."

Churchill made one more appeal to Stalin in a long message dispatched on the night of 28th-29th April. In this he referrd to the missing Poles and he reiterated the British view that there was no intention of creating a Poland hostile to Soviet interests—in fact, the contrary. The Prime Minister's message concluded with some moving words: "There is not much comfort in looking into a future where you and the countries you dominate, plus the Communist parties in many other states, are all drawn up on one side, and those who rally to the English-speaking nations and their associates or dominions are on the other. It is quite obvious that their quarrel would tear the world to pieces and that all of us leading men on either side who had anything to do with that would be shamed before history. . . ."

The San Francisco Conference began in the worst of atmospheres. First, there was a dispute about the chairmanship, Molotov objecting to Eden's proposal that Stettinius should hold the position. This particular argument was resolved when it was agreed that each of the sponsoring powers should take the chair in turn. Next, Molotov made yet another attempt to secure an invitation for the Lublin Poles. On 3rd May Molotov suddenly admitted to Eden and Stettinius at dinner that the Red Army had arrested sixteen Poles on the charge of anti-Soviet activities. These included the Poles who had gone from London in response to Colonel Pinienov's invitation and guarantee of safe conduct. Eden and Stettinius coldly informed Molotov that they must discontinue the discussions on Poland. In his report of the meeting, Eden stated that he had never seen Molotov "look so uncomfortable."[1]

But the most serious dispute at San Francisco was yet to come. It was over the interpretation of the Yalta formula regarding the rules of the Security Council of the United Nations. The Soviet Union maintained that the "veto" agreed at Yalta applied not only to action stemming from decisions by the Security Council

[1] The Poles were tried and sentenced on 21st June. All the accused "confessed" with the exception of General Okulicki, formerly acting Commander-in-Chief of the Polish Home Army, who was sentenced to ten years' imprisonment. Three were acquitted. There was one sentence of eight years and another of five years. During the trial, the prosecution acknowledged by implication that the accused had been given a safe conduct. It was learned later that the Polish prisoners had been taken to Moscow by air, thinking they were going to London, and that all had been placed in solitary confinement in the Lubianka prison.

but also to the subjects to be discussed in the Security Council. In Molotov's contention, the agenda itself had far-reaching political implications leading to action and it was no mere procedural matter. Stettinius said plainly that the United States could not sign a charter in these circumstances. Molotov thereupon returned to Moscow, leaving the leadership of the Soviet delegation to Gromyko.

Again it was deadlock. The post-war prospect was bleak in the hour of victory. In the face of the situation—Stalin's implacable determination on Poland and the United Nations constitution and Churchill's growing alarm in London over Soviet intentions—Truman decided upon a new initiative. He asked Harry Hopkins, despite the fact that he had become increasingly ill since Yalta, to undertake one more mission to see Stalin in the hope of breaking the Soviet-Western deadlock. Simultaneously, he sent Joseph E. Davies, the former American Ambassador to Moscow, to London to see Churchill in order, so the President thought, to allay the Prime Minister's fears of Soviet policies and to acquaint him of the President's views.

The Davies mission turned out to be a most unfortunate episode. Churchill saw the American envoy at Chequers late on the evening of 26th May. The interview started at eleven o'clock and continued until 4.30 in the morning. Davies began by telling Churchill of the new President's concern at "the serious deterioration of relations of the Soviets with both Britain and the United States." He went on to refer to "fears, distrusts and suspicions on both sides" and for this reason he (Davies) had been sent to London and Hopkins to Moscow "for similar discussions." Davies then sprang a surprise. He informed Churchill that Truman considered himself at a disadvantage because he did not know Stalin. "The President, therefore, desired an opportunity to meet the Marshal immediately before the scheduled forthcoming meeting." Churchill rejected this idea vehemently and he said later: "I was indeed astonished. . . . I would not agree in any circumstances to what would be an affront, however unintentional, to our country after its faithful service in the cause of freedom."

Davies now asked pompously for permission to state his personal views. In his report he said he actually told Churchill: "I had been shocked beyond words to find so violent and bitter an attitude, and to find what appeared to me so violent a change in his attitude towards the Soviets. Its significance was appalling. . . . I had

wondered whether he, the Prime Minister, was now willing to
declare to the world that he and Britain had made a mistake in
not supporting Hitler." The effect on Churchill of this extraordinary accusation was to leave the Prime Minister almost speech-
less with anger, which was fortunate as it turned out. Davies then
went on to lecture Churchill, quite oblivious of the situation as it
would have appeared to any outsider. In his opinion "We could
rely upon the good faith of the Soviet leaders: (1) to work for a
practical Peace Structure; (2) to co-operate with Western Europe
as good neighbours and not seek to proselytise Europe to the degree
that was consistent with her security as against possible implacable
religious, economic, or political hostility of Western neighbours."
Churchill had recovered himself by now. He restrained himself so
successfully that the insensitive Davies paid tribute to his "cordiality
and fine hospitality." Churchill even told him how much he had
appreciated the American's frankness and the discussions with
someone who was "so familiar with European problems during
these years." But underneath the Prime Minister was seething. He
so distrusted Davies's understanding of what he believed was at stake
in Europe that he proposed next day sending the American back
with an *aide-mémoire*. Tartly, the Prime Minister remarked to
Eden, when he gave the Foreign Secretary a draft of the document:
"If he [Davies] desires to carry it back to Washington himself, as
a great honour he may be allowed to do so. I have not formed the
best opinion of the man." After his anger had subsided further,
Churchill toned down the original draft but the *aide-mémoire* still
contained a pointed rejection of the proposal for separate talks
between Truman and Stalin: "The Prime Minister received with
some surprise the suggestion conveyed by Mr. Davies that a meeting should take place at some agreed point, and that the representatives of His Majesty's Government should be invited to join
a few days later. It must be understood that the representatives
of His Majesty's Government would not be able to attend any
meeting except as equal partners from its opening. This would be
undoubtedly regrettable. The Prime Minister does not see that
there is any need to raise an issue so wounding to Britain, to the
British Empire and Commonwealth of Nations. . . ." At the same
time Churchill accepted Truman's desire to get to know Stalin
better and went on to explain that there were ample opportunities
for private meetings on all sides immediately before and during
international conferences. In its final form, the *aide-mémoire*

became a direct message to Truman, to which Churchill thought the President replied on 29th May: "I am now making a study of a possible date for our three-party meeting and hope to have further information on the subject in the most distant future." Churchill in his own memoirs stated that he took this to mean that the idea of the separate Soviet-American meeting had been abandoned.

Yet such is the human fallibility of envoys that there had never been any such proposal in Truman's mind of a separate Soviet-American meeting as put forward by Davies. Nor did Churchill ever send the *aide-mémoire*, either through Davies or direct to Truman, although he clearly thought he had done so. As to Truman's message of 29th May, this was not in reply to any *aide-mémoire* as Churchill imagined. It referred, in fact, to the Three-Power meeting that had already been advocated by Churchill, and which the Americans—without telling the British—had come round to accepting, Hopkins having been instructed before he left for Moscow to raise it with Stalin, without awaiting Soviet initiative.

The truth behind the extraordinary misunderstanding was that Davies began it by exceeding his instructions. He also took it upon himself to send a personal cable direct to Molotov suggesting a Two-Power meeting. Copies of this Molotov-Davies correspondence have never been found but we know of its existence because Molotov referred to Davies's initiative in a letter to Harriman, after the first meeting between Stalin and the Hopkins mission that took place on 26th May—the same day as Davies's first meeting with Churchill. In his letter, Molotov corrects a remark by Stalin to Hopkins "that he had already replied to President Truman concerning the place of meeting [of the three heads of government] and he suggested Berlin." Molotov states: "For the purpose of accuracy I must tell you now that mention was made of this area for a meeting not in the above-mentioned message but in my answering telegram to Mr. Joseph Davies who, referring to his conversation with the President, recently raised the question of a meeting of the two heads of government and also a place of this meeting."

Churchill, in a message to Stalin on the same day—26th May—regarding the disposition of the German Fleet, said that this question "should form part of the general discussions which ought to take place between us and President Truman at the earliest possible date." Therefore, it was not surprising that when the Hopkins talks opened that night at eight o'clock in the Kremlin—with Hopkins raising the issue of a meeting "to discuss all of the problems arising out of the war in Europe," Stalin should assume that Churchill's message was part of the pattern of joint Anglo-American initiative which he fully accepted. Accordingly, Stalin cabled back to Churchill on 27th May: "Mr. Hopkins, who has arrived in Moscow, on behalf of the President has suggested a meeting between the three of us in the immediate future. I think that a meeting is called for and that the most convenient place would be the vicinity of Berlin. That would probably be right politically as well. Have you any objection?"

The Prime Minister was pleased when he received this message. It arrived simultaneously with a message from Truman saying he was accepting Berlin as a meeting-place in his instructions to Hopkins. Churchill saw his hopes of an early conference being met. He cabled back to Stalin on 29th May, sending a copy of the message to Truman. "I shall be very glad to meet you and President Truman in what is left of Berlin in the very near future. I hope this might take place about the middle of June. . . ." Next came Truman's message on 29th May, which Churchill states in his memoirs as being in reply to his *aide-mémoire* which had never been sent. Finally, the story of the Davies misunderstanding is closed by a telegram from Churchill to Truman on 31st May which left the President bewildered. It stated: "I had agreeable talks with Mr. Davies which he will report to you when he returns. I may say, however, at once that I should not be prepared to attend a meeting which was a continuation of a conference between you and Marshal Stalin. I consider that at this victory meeting, at which subjects of the gravest consequences are to be discussed, we three should meet simultaneously and on equal terms. . . . I am also hoping to have the pleasure of meeting you for the first time."

Very wisely, Truman did not answer until Davies had returned home to report personally on 5th June. When the President had heard how Davies had made his proposal he realised what had happened. He states, "I had no such idea in mind." He cabled Churchill: "Your position as to the simultaneous character of the first meeting as reported by Mr. Davies I can readily understand and gladly concur with it." In his blundering way, Davies had started the administrative process that led to the Potsdam Conference. Without realising it, he had contributed to breaking the self-imposed deadlock as to who was to initiate the conference by making Stalin believe that Truman had proposed the meeting; and by making Truman and Hopkins believe, in part, that Stalin had proposed the meeting and had been ready with Berlin as the rendezvous. Unfortunately, it was a success that he never fully appreciated.

The parallel American mission to Moscow, in the experienced hands of Hopkins, with the shrewd and capable Harriman at his elbow, was a different story. According to the full record of the meetings made by Bohlen, who acted as interpreter on the American side, Hopkins told Stalin: "Two months ago there had been over-whelming sympathy among the American people for the Soviet Union and complete support for President Roosevelt's policies which the Marshal knew so well. This sympathy and support came primarily because of the brilliant achievement of the Soviet Union in the war and partly from President Roosevelt's leadership. . . ." But now things were different and Hopkins said he wished "to assure the Marshal with all the earnestness at his command that this body of American public opinion who had been the constant support of Roosevelt's policies were seriously disturbed about their relations with Russia." In the course of what was, in effect, his main opening speech, Hopkins admitted that it was not easy "to put a finger" on the causes of the deterioration of relations and he raised the failure to implement the Yalta decisions on Poland.

Stalin retorted that the reason for the failure was whilst Russia wanted a friendly Poland, Britain wanted to revive the old policy of the *cordon sanitaire*. Hopkins assured him that the United States had no such intention. In the course of this first meeting, on 26th May, Stalin asked about the Peace Conference. "The question was ripe and, so to speak, knocking at the door," he remarked. It was at this point he told Hopkins that he had already sent a message to Truman suggesting Berlin as a preliminary meeting-place—infor-mation that Molotov corrected in the note later that night to Harriman, as being sent to Davies regarding a Two-Power con-ference, but which Stalin mistakenly still thought of as referring to a three-power conference in his cable to Churchill next day, 27th May, because he could not conceive a Two-Power conference.

The Hopkins-Stalin talks continued for five more sessions, including a private meeting between Stalin and Hopkins over dinner on 1st June. In the course of these conversations various subjects were discussed. Stalin gave Hopkins to understand that the Red Army would be properly deployed in Manchuria by 8th August. However, there still remained the difficult question of telling the Chinese about Roosevelt's agreement at Yalta on the price demanded by Stalin. Stalin, according to Hopkins's cabled report to Truman, "made [the] categorical statement that he would do everything he could to promote [the] unification of China under the leadership of Chiang Kai-shek," although Bohlen's notes of the meeting are not so specific on the question of Chiang Kai-shek personally. On the method of telling the Chinese of what had been decided at Yalta, Hopkins and Stalin agreed that the American Ambassador in Chungking would tackle Chiang in early July simultaneously with the arrival in Moscow of T. V. Soong, Chiang Kai-shek's brother-in-law and Foreign Minister, who was due to pay a visit to the Soviet Union. There was also agreement between Stalin and Hopkins on the date for the Three-Power Conference in the region of Berlin. Churchill had been adamant for an early conference, before the American withdrawals to the zones of occupation had taken place and the forces of the Western Powers had been diverted to the Pacific war. In several messages to Truman he stressed his point. "Time is on his side if he digs while we melt away," was one phrase used by the Prime Minister in order to awaken the President to the danger. Churchill, although faced with a General Election, emphasised that he was quite ready to leave the election campaign in the middle for more important matters at an early Three-Power meeting. Finally, Hopkins secured Stalin's acceptance for 15th July, a date proposed by Truman. He also persuaded Stalin to invite to Moscow the Polish representatives, both from Poland and from without, to consult on the formation of a broader Polish Government. These were important decisions but the most important outcome of Hopkins's talks was Stalin's acceptance of the American position on the procedure for the United Nations agenda—the issue that had left the San Francisco Conference in a state of complete deadlock. The following is an extract from Bohlen's notes of the sixth and last meeting:

Mr. Hopkins said he would like to raise an entirely separate question with Marshal Stalin and that relates to the impasse which had come about at the San Francisco Conference in regard to voting procedure in the Security Council. He said he had received an urgent message from President Truman to take this matter up with Marshal Stalin and to indicate the seriousness of this matter. He said it referred to the Soviet insistence that nothing could be discussed by the Security Council without the unanimous vote of the permanent members

179

exclusive of those involved in a particular situation. He said that the United States Government had agreed with the Marshal that there must be unanimity among the members in regard to all questions involving enforcement action in any of its aspects, but that in the consideration of methods for the peaceful settlement of disputes, parties to the dispute, whether permanent members or not, would abstain from voting. He added that the United States thought the Yalta formula, as agreed on, safeguarded the freedom of discussion and the right of any member to bring before the council any situation for discussion. And that this right, which was rightly a question of the agenda, should therefore be decided by the council by simple majority without any power having the right to veto it. He said he earnestly hoped the Marshal would see eye to eye with us (the Americans) and the other sponsoring powers and France who were agreed on this question.

Mr. Molotov said that the Soviet position was based squarely on the Crimea decision and that in matters involving peaceful settlement parties to (the) dispute would not vote and that the full unanimity applied only to enforcement action. The Soviet position was that the same formula for peaceful settlement should apply in deciding whether or not the council should take up and discuss any given question. (Ensued a conversation in Russian between Mr. Molotov and Marshal Stalin from which it was clear that the Marshal had not understood the issues and had not had them explained to him. During this conversation (with Molotov) Marshal Stalin remarked that it was an insignificant matter and that they should accept the American position.)

Marshal Stalin then stated that he was prepared to accept the American position on the point at issue at San Francisco in regard to voting procedure.

The San Francisco Conference had been saved! This was the issue that mattered more, in those days, to the Americans than the mere date of a Berlin Conference, or even the circumstances preceding the retirement of Western forces to their allotted zones of occupation. Hopkins returned home, a nationally popular figure for the first time in his life.

As for Churchill, he has told how it was with a heavy heart and a sense of deep foreboding that he lived through these days. His description of the 1945 General Election which followed the break up of the British Coalition Government at the ending of the war conveys it: "All the while I felt that much we had fought for in our long struggle in Europe was slipping away and that the hopes for an early and lasting peace were receding. The days were passed amid a clamour of multitudes and when at night, tired out, I got back to my headquarters train where a considerable staff and all the incoming telegrams awaited me I had to toil for many hours. The incongruity of party excitement and clatter with the sombre background which filled my mind was in itself an affront to reality and proportion." The extraordinary accuracy of his understanding of what was then happening—and what lay in the future—is shown in a message by him to Eden in San Francisco on 4th May even before the war had ended: "I fear terrible things have happened during the Russian advance through Germany to the Elbe. The proposed withdrawal of the United States Army to the occupational lines which were arranged with the Russians and the Americans in Quebec[1] and which were marked in yellow on the maps we studied there, would mean the tide of Russian domination sweeping forward 120 miles on a front of 300 or 400 miles. . . . This constitutes an event in the history of Europe to which there has been no parallel, and which has not been faced by the Allies in their long and hazardous struggle. The Russian demands on Germany alone for reparations alone will be such as to enable her to prolong the occupation almost indefinitely, at any rate for many years during which time Poland will sink with many other states into the vast zone of Russian-controlled Europe, not necessarily economically Sovietised but police-governed." Such was the British Prime Minister's forecast of the Cold War as it would develop, and the story will show how close he came to foreseeing the future.

On 12th June Truman told Churchill that the tripartite agreement about the occupation of Germany made it impossible for him to delay the withdrawal of American troops from the Soviet zone in order to press for the settlement of other problems. Truman stated he had been advised that failure to undertake this step would harm relations with the Soviet Union.

On 1st July the American and British Armies began their with-

[1] The Soviet representatives were not present at Quebec. The British and American delegations discussed zones of occupation and the actual agreement amongst the Three Powers was signed in London on 14th November, 1944.

drawal to their zones of occupation. The roads were crowded once more with refugees. It marked the consummation of the diplomatic victory that Stalin had won at Yalta. In fairness to Truman it must be emphasised again he was new in his immense task and felt bound by Roosevelt's policy. He had been excluded by the operation of the American constitution from being privy to the formulation of high policy and the multitudinous array of secret and confidential reports upon which it was based until the actual moment at which he succeeded to the Presidency. Furthermore, the weight of advice that Truman was still receiving, both from within his own circle, from the State Department and from Eisenhower in Germany, conclusively pointed to withdrawal. Eisenhower himself at that time took a clear and simple view of the Soviet Union and its people. He believed that the Russians bore "a marked similarity to what we call an average American." He considered that an especial affinity existed between the two countries and that "both were free from the stigma of colonial empire building by force."

The Moscow meeting of the various Poles, decided upon by Stalin and Hopkins during their May talks, assembled in mid-June. Following the treacherous arrest of the Polish underground leaders, there was great difficulty in getting such Poles as Mikolajczyk to make the journey. Mikolajczyk also considered, at first, that it would be wrong for him personally to be in Moscow negotiating with the Russians and the Lublin Poles in the Kremlin, whilst his betrayed compatriots languished in prison a few hundred yards away. But Churchill was adamant—he persuaded Mikolajczyk to change his mind, principally on the grounds that the Pole's duty directed that he should go to Moscow to take this last chance of moulding the future pattern of Poland. Adding snorts and threats to pleas and entreaties, Churchill told Mikolajczyk: "If you back out now, I will wash my hands of the whole Polish case."

Thus, at long last the conference amongst Poles was to take place. Even then the Soviet Government soon made its preferences clear, although the invitations were issued in the name of the Three-Power Commission. Whilst the Poles from within Poland that were unconnected with the Lublin Committee and Mikolajczyk's own party made a forlorn and unheralded arrival at Moscow Airport, Beirut and his group were treated as if they were visiting heads of state. Waiting on the Moscow tarmac for Beirut on 13th June were Molotov, Vishynsky and Bulganin backed by a splendid

guard of honour. Next, on 19th June, whilst the talks were proceeding, the Russian newspapers announced the opening of the
trial of the sixteen arrested Poles as a reminder to Mikolajczyk and
the others of the realities of power. The Moscow talks largely took
place amongst the Poles themselves. To the surprise of many
people in the West, an agreement was reached, which all three
parties of Poles announced to the Commission on the night of 21st
June. One of twenty Cabinet posts in the new Polish Government,
six were to go to Poles independent of the Lublin Committee.
Beirut was to be President of the National Council, Osubka-
Morawski became Prime Minister and Wladislaw Gomulka—of
whom more was to be heard many years later—First Deputy
Prime Minister. Mikolajczyk was only a Second Deputy Prime
Minister and Minister of Agriculture. The Communists had
claimed far more than their due, but Mikolajczyk and his independent colleagues hoped that they would exercise influence within
the new administration far exceeding their actual numbers. The
new Polish Government was promptly taken by Russian aircraft
to Warsaw on 28th June. The inevitable happened. Mikolajczyk
was given a huge and spontaneously popular demonstration by
people of the capital, whereas the unknown Beirut and his supporters slunk away ignored.

Whilst the Polish negotiations had been taking place in Moscow,
arrangements had been going forward for the great Three-Power
Conference, to open at Potsdam on 15th July—"Terminal" as
Churchill called it. The Anglo-American withdrawal to the
occupation zones agreed by the European Advisory Commission
had been proceeding satisfactorily, but a major difficulty had
arisen about the joint occupation of Berlin, a hundred miles inside
the Russian zones. By an incredible omission, there was no arrangements for access to the agreed occupation areas.[1] The truth was

[1] The Allied military commanders had met briefly in Berlin on 5th June, 1945,
formally to sign the documents relating to the defeat of Germany that had been
prepared for them by the European Advisory Commission. There were three
documents:
(1) The Declaration regarding the Defeat of Germany and Assumption of
Supreme Authority with respect to Germany by the Governments of the U.K.,
U.S.A. and the U.S.S.R. and the Provisional Government of the French Republic.
(This document deposed the national and vested all authority in the hands of
the four Allied Commanders-in-Chief.)
(2) Statement by the Governments of the U.K., U.S.A., the U.S.S.R. and the
Provisional Government. (The statement vested authority within each zone

that the Western military authorities had always regarded the problem merely as a practical question of transporting and supplying occupation troops. They had never considered the larger political issues of operating across Soviet-occupied territory.

A conference of military representatives was hurriedly arranged. The Allied representatives went to Zhukov's headquarters on 29th June. The Americans were represented by General Lucius D. Clay and by his political adviser, Robert D. Murphy, and the British spokesmen were Lieutenant-General Sir Ronald Weeks and his political adviser, Sir William Strang—the same Strang who had negotiated with the Soviet authorities in the fateful period in 1939 before the signing of the Nazi-Soviet Pact.[1] The Western commanders had assumed unrestricted access. They wanted to move into Berlin, using two autobahns, three railway lines and free use of the air. They were in for quick disillusionment. Zhukov said flatly that he was not prepared to agree to this—his point being that access was a privilege, not a right, nor could he agree that it was necessary. The British and American representatives were dismayed but there was little they could do. After much wrangling, they accepted reluctantly the joint use by both Western Powers of only one autobahn, running from Helmstadt to Berlin; a single railway line to Berlin via Magdeburg and one main airline from Berlin to Magdeburg with two branch air lanes, Magdeburg-Frankfurt and Magdeburg-Hanover. Clay, in his memoirs, implies that he did not realise at the time the long-term implications of

---

in its Commander-in-Chief subject only to the overriding authority of the four Commanders-in-Chief acting unanimously. In brief, it was a form of veto.)

(3) Statement by the Governments of the U.K., U.S.A., the U.S.S.R. and the Provisional Government of the French Republic on Zones of Occupation in Germany. (This laid down the four occupation zones and the four occupation sectors within Greater Berlin.)

In view of the events in Germany as they developed later, these documents are of great importance. The case of the Western Powers regarding their rights in West Berlin stems specifically from the signing that took place at the Red Army headquarters at Karlshorst on 5th June. The signatories were Montgomery (U.K.), Eisenhower (U.S.A.), Zhukov (U.S.S.R.) and de Lattre de Tassigny (Provisional Government of the French Republic). (See *Official Gazette of the Control Council, Berlin*, Supplement, 1945, p. 7, and also *Documents on the Status of Berlin 1944-1959*, selected and edited by O. M. Von Der Gablentz, R. Oldenbourg Verlag, Munich, 1959.)

[1] There was no French representative at this meeting as the arrangements for the French sector had not been finally decided.

what was being agreed. He also admits that he rejected the advice of Major-General Parks, head of the American advance party, who was urging him to insist upon the more direct autobahn from the American zone, running via Halle. To make matters even worse, Clay and Weeks came away from Zhukov without a formal written agreement. In retrospect, it can be argued that Clay and Weeks should have adopted a different attitude to Zhukov but, in fact, they had no alternative following upon the major decisions made by the United States over the previous few months—Eisenhower's decision to ignore the strategic importance of Berlin and then to reject Churchill's policy of ending the war with Western troops as far east as possible.[1] Finally, there was Truman's own decision, in the face of Churchill's warnings, to withdraw Western forces to the zones of occupation, in advance of a Three-Power meeting.

[1] An interesting and important account of American policy at this time was given by Robert Murphy, *Diplomat Among Warriors*. In this Murphy places a great deal of the blame for failing to secure proper access to Berlin upon Winant and the European Advisory Commission.

CHAPTER 9

BERLIN AT LAST

Now I see
Peace to corrupt no less than war to waste.
                                    Milton

Truman set out for Potsdam on the evening of 6th July. Although he used a long sea journey on the cruiser *Augusta* to prepare himself for the conference, Truman felt irritated at the prospect. He regarded the expedition as both an interruption of his routine of work and a diversion from his pressing internal problems.

Churchill arrived at Potsdam exhausted and full of foreboding. He had just been embroiled in the British General Election. Polling had taken place on 5th July but the counting of the votes had been postponed for three weeks until 26th July, in order to allow time for the postal votes of servicemen who were overseas to arrive. The general view in Britain—even amongst the Labour leaders—was that Churchill had been returned to power. Nevertheless, to cover eventualities, Churchill took the unusual step of inviting Attlee, as Leader of the Labour Party, to come with him to Potsdam in order to preserve continuity of policy should the election go against him. After a few days' holiday in the Basque sunshine, near Hendaye, Churchill flew from Bordeaux to Berlin on 15th July—the same day as Truman arrived in Berlin. Churchill said contemptuously he did not need briefing for the conference—it was all in his head.

As for Stalin, he reached Berlin late for the conference on 17th July. He had suffered a slight heart attack a few days before, but when he called to see Truman he gave as his excuse that he had been delayed by negotiations with the Chinese (T. V. Soong had been visiting Moscow) and also that "his doctors had forbidden him to fly because of the condition of his lungs."

The Potsdam Conference arrangements included the usual lavish Soviet hospitality. The American headquarters were at no. 2

Kaiser Strasse in Babelsberg, a suburb of Berlin about twelve miles south-west of the city. It was a large three-story yellow-painted stucco house, belonging once to a prominent figure in German cinema circles who, so the Russians explained laconically, was "with a labour battalion, somewhere in Russia." The British party were only two blocks away at No. 23 Ruigstrasse, which the Americans felt with slight envy was a little better furnished for the Prime Minister. Stalin was housed much nearer the Cecilienhof Palace in Potsdam, where the conference was to be held. Cecilienhof itself was formerly the Potsdam home of the German Crown Prince. It was a very large brown stone mansion, built in the form of four wings making a quadrangle, which the Soviet authorities had carpeted with a twenty-four-foot red star of geraniums, pink roses and hydrangeas. The building had been a hospital during the war, used by both the Germans and the Russians. Each delegation had its suite of offices and the plenary sessions met in the sixty-foot long great hall, with a gallery at one end.

There were the usual pre-conference exchanges of courtesy calls, during which Churchill and Truman appeared to take an instant liking to each other. Both the President and the Prime Minister made tours of Berlin before Stalin arrived. For Churchill, it was a macabre moment when he clambered down into Hitler's bunker and stared around the room where Hitler and his mistress, Eva Braun, had died.

The Potsdam Conference first met in plenary session at ten minutes past five on the afternoon of 17th July. The participants might have been excused for thinking that it marked the end of one period in history and was the beginning of a new one. In fact, only Truman really appeared to have any such ideas. Immediately he was pressing for quick decisions in the fashion that is so typical of Americans. "I don't want just to discuss," the President remarked in irritation towards the end of the first session, "I want to decide." "You want something in the bag each day?" queried Churchill, somewhat amused. Stalin and Churchill began the conference by proposing and seconding that Truman should take the chair. The President put forward a number of items for the agenda, beginning with a proposal that the Allies should establish a Council of Foreign Ministers. This was to be a standing committee to prepare the way for the fuller Peace Conference that would have to take place in due course. This Council's membership was to be made up by the five permanent members of the United Nations Security Council—

187

Britain, U.S.S.R., China, France and the United States. The British delegation had decided already to support the American idea and Stalin raised no objections. It was a first decision made quickly in the manner that encouraged Truman. Unfortunately, it was to be almost the only easy agreement of the conference.

From there on and throughout the conference the discussion flowed from one subject to another and back again, largely because the many issues—for example, the future control of Germany, the fixing of Germany's new frontiers including the Polish frontier, and arrangements for free elections in Poland—all had interrelated implications. Truman read a lengthy paper on Germany. It envisaged the administration of Germany as a single economic unit. On Churchill's proposal, this plan was referred to a meeting of the three Foreign Ministers present at Potsdam—a pattern similar to the procedure adopted at Yalta.

A curious wrangle took place on the inclusion of China in the Council of Foreign Ministers which had already been agreed in part. It kept re-emerging in the discussion and showed again the American emotional fixation with China. The record taken at Cecilienhof reads: "Stalin . . . said he was not clear about the inclusion of China in the Council [of Foreign Ministers]. He said he supposed that it was contemplated that the Council would discuss European problems . . . they [the Soviet delegation] wished to question the inclusion of China. . . . The President pointed out that China was one of the permanent members of the Security Council which [it] had been agreed at San Francisco to set up. . . . Churchill thought it was a complication, even though it might look like a simplification, to bring in China. . . . He questioned the advisability of bringing in from the other part of the world a country which had contributed little to the defeat of the enemy in Europe. It was easy to get up bodies that look well on paper but which do little in practice. Could not the future of Germany be decided without China? . . . China was far away and did not see questions the way they did. . . . He did not see that China could give us good advice on handling the Rhineland question. . . ." Reluctantly, Truman gave in, agreeing that China would not be allowed to vote on European questions. Later, a similar limitation was placed upon France in issues relating to countries with whom she had not signed an armistice.

The Potsdam Conference included thirteen plenary sessions of the conference and eleven formal meetings of the Foreign Ministers.

There were countless other meetings and intense activity at all levels. There was a break of two days in the middle—from late on 25th July to 28th July—during which Churchill, Eden and Attlee returned to England for the counting of the votes in the British General Election; and on 28th July Attlee and Ernest Bevin, the new British Foreign Secretary, flew back to Potsdam to take over where Churchill had left off. In the interregnum Sir Alexander Cadogan, the Permanent Under-Secretary of State at the Foreign Office, deputised for the missing British Foreign Secretary.[1]

The central issue at Potsdam soon emerged. It was Poland again. The long discussions and wrangles of Yalta were repeated at Potsdam but the issue itself loomed over the conference to an even greater extent than at Yalta. The decisions on whether Poland was to be an independent state with its own representative government or become a puppet régime of the Soviet Union, and where the new Polish boundary was to be in the west, were now immediate.

The Western Powers' principal difficulty at Potsdam stemmed from the lack of Anglo-American bargaining positions. The British Foreign Office had drawn up in advance a series of points upon which Soviet Russia might be seeking Western concessions or accord. These included credits from the United States for post-war rehabilitation, Russia's share in the German fleet and merchant navy, most of which was in British hands at the end of the war, and a revision of the Montreux Convention for access to the Mediterranean and arrangements for Soviet access to the Baltic and a Soviet share in the control of the Kiel Canal. It was pitifully clear that these did not weigh satisfactorily in the scales against Russian vital interest in Poland.

Stalin, at Potsdam, asked again about the position of the Polish émigré government. He now sought also the transfer of all Polish assets abroad to the new Warsaw Provisional Government. This brought forth a torrent of oratory from Churchill. "The burden of the matter," he declared, "rests on Britain. We received the Poles when they were driven out by the Germans." Churchill went on to explain the problem: "We must deal with the transfer of forces which have fought with us against the Germans. Some of

[1] The 1945 British General Election result in which Labour was returned to power with a majority of 200 seats in the House of Commons appeared to have caused the most profound shock to the Russians. Years later, at the 1954 conference of Foreign Ministers in Berlin, Molotov remarked to Eden in a private discussion on possible free elections in East Germany: "The trouble with free elections is that you can't be sure of the outcome!"

them came from France when France fell. . . . We built up five divisions of 50,000 escaped Poles. . . . These men have fought with great bravery. . . . I must make it perfectly clear that this involves the honour of His Majesty's Government. . . ." "Of course," said Stalin soothingly. Seeing how he had stung Churchill, the Soviet leader agreed promptly to give Churchill time to deal with the Polish issue insofar as it affected British commitments of honour. But the Prime Minister still had a parting shot for Stalin when Truman proposed that the Polish issue should go back to the Foreign Ministers for incorporation in the agenda at the appropriate time. Churchill cried, "We ask for trust and confidence in making Poland a place which will attract them [the Poles abroad]." Stalin appeared not to notice.

The second day's plenary session on 18th July opened with an amusing incident. Churchill asked at once that something should be done about the Press who were waiting outside in angry frustration. "When we were at Teheran, there were no journalists," he said. "At Yalta there were few. Here they are all about. They carry powerful weapons. They are making a great outcry." The conference was aghast, particularly the Russians. "Where are they?" demanded Molotov, looking around the room as if expecting them to be in the gallery. "Who let them in?" exclaimed Stalin, who considered that he knew how to deal with newspapermen. "They are not in the compound," exclaimed Churchill reassuringly. He offered to go out and have a word with them "as an old newspaperman." The impish suggestion did not commend itself. The meeting passed to the agenda drawn up by the Foreign Ministers and very soon the conference was back to Poland, with long and somewhat repetitious speeches by Churchill throughout the next four sessions.

Stalin sought continually to get the Polish-German frontier settled along the line of the Western Neisse and the River Oder as it ran out to the sea west of Swinemünde. He wanted the great Baltic port of Stettin to be in Poland.

The major Polish clash came in the fifth plenary session on 21st July with the Americans forced to take sides at last. Stalin adroitly proposed that the conference should express its agreement to the frontiers he was suggesting, leaving the final question to the future Peace Conference by which time it would be too late to alter the situation. He said that the Germans had all fled from the lands in dispute. Truman retorted: "I wanted the administration in the four zones to be as we have agreed. We cannot agree on reparations if parts of Germany are given away." It was a hint that he might be adopting the British view about the Oder-Neisse territories.

"We are concerned about reparations but we will take the risk," answered Stalin rather gruffly. The Soviet leader went on: "Our practice is as follows. An army is fighting when a war is on. Its efforts are concerned in war. To advance, it must have a quiet rear. . . . It needs the quiet and, if possible, a sympathetic rear. Even if the Germans had not fled, it would be difficult to use the Germans, as the majority in the area are Polish. Imagine a situation where the Germans shrink or flee and the Polish population receives us. It is natural in those circumstances to set up a sympathetic administration. There was no other way out. But that does not mean that we determined ourselves a frontier. If you do not agree, the matter can be arranged later."

There was substance in the Soviet leader's argument but to his listeners it was clear that Stalin was explaining the *fait accompli* which the British had always feared would take place if there was delay. Churchill intervened to point out: "Poland is now claiming vastly more territory than she gave up. I cannot concede that such an extravagant movement of populations should occur. If the Germans have run out, they should be encouraged to return." He stressed that the areas in question were amongst the most important agricultural areas in Germany. "The Poles have no right to create a catastrophe in the feeding of Germany," declared the Prime Minister. He then warned grimly: "Take your population of the Ruhr. If enough food is not found we may be confronted with conditions like those in the German concentration camps, even on a vaster scale." It was a grizzly reminder of the recent terrible scenes of the piles of dead and living skeletons that had been discovered by the liberating armies at such places as Auschwitz, Belsen and Buchenwald. In the face of it, Stalin remained unmoved and adamant.

The leaders carried on next day where they had left off. Stalin argued with even greater vigour. He appeared convinced that Churchill and Truman were only seeking to make life easier for the Germans who had, after all, the real responsibility for the situation. Churchill, on the other hand, was equally certain that Stalin's real goal was Soviet domination of Poland. As for Truman, who had come to Potsdam to make decisions—he was extremely angry and frustrated. In his exasperation he was coming round to

191

the opinion that it might be better to leave the difficult Polish issue for decision at a later date, provided the conference could get on with the easier decisions. In an effort to break the impasse, the Provisional Polish Government was asked by Truman on behalf of the conference to send two or three representatives to Potsdam by 24th July.

The Poles lost no time in coming. They appointed three official delegates: the new Polish Prime Minister, Osukba-Morawski, Rzymowski, the Foreign Minister, and Mikolajczyk. For good measure five more Poles, including Beirut himself, boarded the Russian aircraft flying to Potsdam. Upon arrival the Poles then proceeded to lobby the various delegations with intrepid and tireless determination, backed strongly by the Russians.

Two major issues became even clearer as the hours went by. First, there was the original boundary dispute upon which Beirut refused to give way and in which he was supported by Mikolajczyk, the principal non-Communist Pole in the party. Secondly, there were the free elections which should have taken place long before, according to Stalin's promise. Beirut in various interviews with almost anyone he could accost began by promising that these elections would take place in a proper manner and fairly soon. He told Eden that if the Allies carried their interest too far they would be encroaching upon Polish sovereignty. However, Beirut saw that this would not be good enough for Churchill, who was by now extremely hostile. So Beirut blandly promised the Prime Minister on 25th July that the Polish elections would be even more democratic than the recent British elections—a view that he did not venture to repeat to Bevin after the British results had become known. Whilst Beirut's stormy interview with Churchill was taking place, Eden and Clark Kerr were talking simultaneously to Mikolajczyk in another room where the non-Communist Pole was telling them that Beirut's talk of free elections was "nonsense." The picture Mikolajczyk was painting was most alarming. According to him the situation in Poland was deteriorating fast. He pleaded that the only hope of Polish independence now rested upon free elections being held without delay and, in their turn, the freedom of these elections depended entirely upon the withdrawal of the Red Army and the settlement of the Western Neisse frontier which Mikolajczyk was supporting. He had faced the British negotiators with an awkward dilemma. It was at this point that the plenary sessions were suspended because the British delegation had to leave for

Britain for the counting of election votes. Before he left, Churchill told the other leaders that he and Attlee would be back and added, after a pause and a long look at Attlee sitting hunched up, "In such order as the British electorate may so determine." "Mr. Attlee doesn't look very eager," joked Stalin, who did not believe that Churchill could possibly be defeated or, maybe, allow himself to be defeated.

During Churchill's period at Potsdam, an event of very profound importance took place. The first atomic bomb had been tested. In 1943, both Roosevelt and Churchill had initialled an *aide-mémoire* pledging full collaboration between the United States and Britain in the development of the atomic bomb. For reasons of convenience and because of their invulnerability to German bombing, it was agreed that the research and development work would be undertaken exclusively in American laboratories. The British contribution involved both personnel and making available to the Americans all their previous research. The long and very secret work was nearing completion when the German war ended, but there still remained the war against Japan. Truman heard the first news of the successful test at Alamogordo, New Mexico, from Stimson, the American Secretary for War, when he returned from his drive around Berlin before the conference opened, on the afternoon of 16th July. A very brief telegram to Stimson had come from George L. Harrison, Acting Chairman of the Interim Committee on S-1, the code name for the project. The actual words of the historic message when decoded were: "Operated on this morning. Diagnosis not yet complete but results seem satisfactory and already exceed expectations. Local Press release necessary as interest extends great distance. Dr. Groves[1] pleased. He returns to-morrow. I will keep you posted." Then came the fuller reports. Stimson's diary for 21st July states: ". . . At eleven thirty-five General Groves's special report was received by special courier. It was an immensely powerful document, clearly and well written and with supporting evidence of the highest importance. It gave a pretty full and eloquent report of the tremendous success of the test and revealed far greater destructive power than we expected in S-1. . . ." The Americans informed the British. Churchill, having read the Groves report, which was shown to him by Stimson, exclaimed: "Stimson, what was gunpowder? Trivial. What was

[1] Leslie R. Groves, Commanding General, Manhattan District project.

electricity? Meaningless. This atomic bomb is the Second Coming in Wrath." They were apocryphal words indeed.

Groves's account began: "0530, 16 July, 1945, in a remote section of the Alamogordo Air Base, New Mexico, the first full-scale test was made of the implosion type atomic fission bomb. For the first time in history there was an explosion. And what an explosion! . . ." Churchill states in his memoirs that there was never any question in Anglo-American circles as to whether or not to use the atomic bomb on Japan, if it were developed. He writes: "We seemed suddenly to have become possessed of a merciful abridgement of the slaughter in the East and of a far happier prospect in Europe. . . . There was unanimous, automatic, unquestioned agreement around our table; nor did I ever hear the slightest suggestion that we should do otherwise." The only issue was what and how to tell Stalin. The Combined (U.S.-British) Policy Committee meeting in Washington on 4th July had already given formal British sanction to the Americans to use the bomb at their discretion, if the test proved successful but they had left open for the politicians the question of telling the Russians. Stimson in a memorandum written at Potsdam and dated 19th July, which considered the whole question of Soviet-American relations, shows American thinking at the time. Recognising the fundamental gulf between East and West he wrote: "With the best of efforts we cannot understand each other." Stimson attached great importance to the Soviet Constitution of 5th December, 1936, which made him believe that Stalin was leading the Russian people towards "free speech, free assembly, free Press and other essential elements of our Bill of Rights. . . ." However, there remained "Russia's Secret Police State" and Stimson wondered whether the American lead in atomic research and Russian desire to participate, amongst other things, could not be used in some way to break down the prevailing barriers and to encourage a more free society in the Soviet Union. Truman took a different view. He came quickly to the conclusion that Stalin ought to be told. In this, he was supported by Churchill, who felt that if this were not done, the Soviet leader would be able to reproach them all on the grounds that vital military information had been kept from him. Therefore it was decided by the President and Prime Minister that the news would be imparted by Truman himself in the most casual fashion possible, after one of the plenary sessions.

Truman took the agreed step on 24th July, at the end of the

day's session, when the various members of the conference were waiting for their cars. It was half past seven in the evening. The President walked around the table to where Stalin and Pavlov, the Soviet interpreter, were standing and mentioned casually that the Americans had a new bomb, more powerful than anything that had ever gone before. Churchill describes the scene in his memoirs: "I saw the President go up to Stalin . . . I was perhaps five yards away and I watched with the closest attention the momentous talk. I knew what the President was going to do. What was vital to measure was its effects upon Stalin. I can see it all as if it were yesterday. He seemed delighted. A new bomb! Of extraordinary power! Probably decisive on the whole Japanese war! What a bit of luck. . . . I was sure that he had no idea of the significance of what he was being told. . . . As we were waiting for our cars I found myself near Truman. 'How did it go?' I asked. 'He never asked a question,' he replied." The account given later by Truman himself and also the account by Byrnes and Admiral Leahy, who were also present, corroborate Churchill's description completely.[1]

The arrival at Potsdam of Attlee as Prime Minister and Bevin as Foreign Secretary introduced two new British figures into the international scene. As already mentioned, Attlee had been present throughout, on Churchill's invitation, although in a minor role. His method of work and attitude of mind were very different from Churchill's. Yet, during most of the war he had acted as deputy Prime Minister to Churchill with selfless loyalty. He had been leader of the British Labour Party since it had rejected its pacifist leader, George Lansbury, in 1935. Attlee came from a most respectable middle-class background and he had been drawn into the Socialist movement only through his experiences in social work in the East End of London. It has been the custom to write him off as a colourless and indecisive man. This mistake continued to be made until he retired from public life, when it was realised suddenly by his countrymen that he was a skilful man of extreme toughness and deep principle. One illustration serves to show it: Attlee led a major British political party for a longer period than any other man since the days of Pitt—longer even than Disraeli, Gladstone and Baldwin to name a few of his predecessors.

Ernest Bevin was again a very different and much rougher per-

[1] This is not the view of some historians who appear to consider that Stalin's apparent lack of interest was due to the fact that he already knew of the project through his own Secret Service. This is largely speculation.

sonality than Eden. He was Attlee's staunch friend and supporter. He had already played the major part in the incident that drove out Lansbury in 1935 and made Attlee leader of the British Labour Party. Bevin came from the humblest of backgrounds and he had no known father.[1] His home had been broken up when his mother died and he was only eight, and he had forced his way up in the world through his unique self-reliance. Bevin's socialism owed more to Methodism than Marxism. This burly, self-reliant man had become a national figure in Britain by his championship of the dockers after the 1918 war. After this he had forged and built the million strong British Transport and General Workers' Union in the 1920s. In the 1930s he had taken his place on the intellectual committees of the Fabian Society and had played a decisive part in creating the *Daily Herald* as the British Labour Party's daily newspaper with a mass circulation. Bevin had been in the act of retiring when war had come and Churchill had sent for him. In Churchill's war cabinet he had been Minister of Labour, responsible for mobilising Britain's man-power, and he had shown himself as one of the few men capable of standing up to Churchill. Now Bevin was Foreign Secretary. According to Byrnes, his aggressive demeanour on arrival startled the Americans at Potsdam. Later they came to appreciate his qualities, as the story will show.

Attlee and Bevin assumed the leadership of the British delegation at that moment which happens in most international conferences, when the log jam of deadlock begins suddenly to break. On 29th July Bevin launched an intensive attack on the Polish problem, culminating in a ruthless cross-examination by him of Beirut and his delegation on 31st July. He told Beirut that he wanted short and direct answers. When Beirut protested that he had already answered the British Government's questions, the new British Foreign Secretary retorted even more sharply, "Your answers have been evasive and indefinite." When Beirut said that the policy of the Polish Government was to hold elections as soon as possible but that its attitude could not be considered as a concession to the point of view of another government, Bevin cut in to tell the Polish Communist to be frank. The new British Foreign Secretary wanted to to know if, subject to the withdrawal of Russian troops and the speeding up of repatriation of Poles abroad, the Polish Provisional

---

[1] For a full account of Ernest Bevin's career, the reader should study *Ernest Bevin, Portrait of a Trade Union Leader*, by Alan Bullock (Heinemann). It is a fascinating and great biography.

Government would make every effort to hold elections in 1946. Bevin eyed his man intently. Beirut hesitated, but Bevin pressed him again. With obvious reluctance Beirut then agreed to give an assurance that the Polish elections would be held not later than the first part of 1946. The Polish leader agreed even more reluctantly to Bevin's demand that the foreign correspondents should be allowed into Poland. It was an impressive interview, but it can be seen in retrospect that Bevin might have saved himself the effort because the realities of the situation in Poland created by Russian armed power there would always enable Beirut to withdraw from any commitments as and when the time became appropriate.

Of the other major deadlocks that remained at this stage of the conference, the most critical was the future administration of Germany and the extensive Soviet claims for reparations. The American and British Governments had started at Potsdam with the understanding that the administration of Germany would be considered as a whole, although for the time being no central German Government would be established. The original Anglo-American view was that each of the zones of occupation, including the Greater Berlin area, would draw its supplies from the regions of Germany that had provided them before the war. The Russians thought differently, as the Western Powers soon discovered. The Soviet delegation refused to accept a reparations settlement until the Potsdam Conference had decided first upon the frontiers of the new Germany. Their object was clear. They wished to exclude from any arrangements related to the German occupation consideration of the Oder-Neisse territories that Stalin was determined to hand over to Poland, and which contained valuable capital equipment suitable for reparations. Molotov returned also to the earlier Soviet demand, originally made at Yalta, for total reparations for the Allies amounting to 20,000 million dollars, of which 10,000 million dollars was to go to the Soviet Union. On 27th July, Byrnes pointed out in vain that this figure was meaningless. He stressed that it had been agreed at Yalta only as a basis of discussion. Then Byrnes added a new suggestion involving a concession. He suggested the Russians should collect their reparations from out of the Soviet zone of occupation, whilst the Americans, British and French would do the same thing in their own zones and agree also to meet the further claims of Belgium, Holland and other countries from the Western zones. Molotov remained adamant. He excluded the question of reparations from Silesia. He would not accept

Byrnes's plan unless the Soviet Union still received some 2,000 to 3,000 million dollars' worth of reparations from the Ruhr, now in the British zone.

Next, there was the issue of what to do about Italy, on which the Americans had come to Potsdam with certain ideas. Truman had put forward a suggestion, at the first plenary sessions, despite British objections, to admit Italy to the United Nations. Churchill and Molotov both asked at different times for a period in which to study the proposal, to which they were very lukewarm.

With Attlee and Bevin in Potsdam, Byrnes made the suggestion formally on 30th July that three issues—Poland's western frontiers, German reparations and the entry of Italy into the United Nations —should all be made the subject of "a package deal." His plan, in essence, was that the Western Powers should accept Polish administration over the former German territories up to the Western Neisse pending the German peace treaty. He demanded a more realistic view of reparations and the admission of Italy into the United Nations. When Byrnes's package deal was put before plenary session on 31st July, Stalin objected to the Secretary of State's tactics. He insisted that the Russians would vote separately on each proposal. However, it was clear he had got what he wanted on Poland. A flurry of unreal bargaining over figures ensued in which Stalin began by demanding a huge increase in reparations, and Bevin talked as if he were conducting a wage negotiation on behalf of his trade union. Stalin finally accepted a figure of 15 per cent of capital equipment to be removed from the Western zones in return for raw materials such as food and coal which he promised would be supplied from the Soviet zone. In addition, he was to receive further reparations, amounting to 10 per cent of the non-essential capital equipment for which he would not have to deliver supplies. The Polish right to administer the German lands up to the Western Neisse came up next. Byrnes asked for Soviet and British agreement without his having to read out the American proposal as it had been circulated. But Bevin was not satisfied. "I think the document should be read," he demanded. Byrnes was forced to comply, and Bevin thereupon pressed Truman to make clear to all that the disputed territories were only to be administered by the Poles and their ultimate future was subject to the Peace Treaty. After the President had done so Bevin succeeded in getting Stalin to agree to withdraw all Soviet troops from Poland, excepting those that were needed for communication purposes.

Finally, the conference turned to the third part of the American "package deal"—the admission of Italy to the United Nations. The Italian problem was considered along with the anomalous positions of Bulgaria, Hungary, Finland and Rumania. The tension had gone out of the conference. There was little discussion. Italy's entry, subject to the conclusion of a peace treaty, was accepted quickly. A string of lesser problems remained, including the fate of the German Fleet, and proposed War Crimes trials. Rapidly, these were disposed of one after the other, or postponed to another day, as Truman's eagerness to get away became more manifest. The final act took place at 10.30 p.m. on 1st August. Truman remarked, "I hope the next meeting will be in Washington." Stalin answered surprisingly, "God willing!"

In retrospect, it can be seen that Potsdam was still an extension of Roosevelt's attempt to come to terms with the Russians and to do nothing that would justify Stalin's suspicions of Western good faith. The underlying American policy was the real cause of Byrnes's capitulation to Soviet pressure on the Polish issue and his acceptance of Stalin's demands for reparations for Russia from the Western occupation zones. Nor did Truman and Byrnes ever seem to grasp that once they had given way upon the subject of Polish administration of the territories up to the Western Neisse, there was no practical prospect of the issue being re-opened at a peace conference.

The Russians for their part considered that the Italian arrangement was a small price to pay for the Polish reparation concessions by the Western Powers. The British delegation, whether it was led by Churchill and/or Attlee and Bevin, profoundly disagreed with the Americans on Poland. But Attlee and Bevin—on whom must rest the ultimate responsibility for accepting Byrnes's terms—knew that they were in no position to break on the issue. The two British Labour leaders realised what their followers in Britain never understood fully, that the newly elected British Labour Party's hopes for the Welfare State to which they were committed were dependent upon American goodwill. Nor would their Labour supporters at that time of public goodwill in Britain for Russia have understood an open breach with the Soviet Union. Stalin and Molotov had reason to be as satisfied with their labours at Potsdam as they had been after Yalta.

CHAPTER 10

THE END OF THE GRAND ALLIANCE

As one shouts into the wood, so the echo replies.   *Russian proverb*

An American B.29 aircraft over Hiroshima, named the *Enola Gray* and piloted by Colonel Paul W. Tibbets, began its run in to its target at 8.11 on the morning of 6th August. Many of the people of Hiroshima, thinking that the lone aircraft was on a reconnaissance mission, were ignoring the air-raid warning and were walking nonchalantly about the streets.

The war against Japan had been reaching its climax even before the successful atomic test at Alamogordo. The Allies had come a long way from Pearl Harbour and the fall of Singapore. Burma had been liberated in May, 1945, after a remarkable military campaign. In the Pacific, the Americans had succeeded in capturing Okinawa in the face of suicidal Japanese resistance. Paradoxically, by the time the Potsdam Conference had met, in July, 1945, the United States Government had become disinterested in the same Soviet participation in the war against Japan that Roosevelt had striven so hard to secure at Yalta, only six months before.

Stalin, whatever may have been his reactions at Truman's original recounting of the Alamogordo test, realised upon hearing the news about Hiroshima that he must move quickly if he was to be in any position to participate in the Far Eastern peace settlement. Every hour counted for him. The Red Army, which he had been building up steadily on the borders of Manchuria and Korea ever since the end of the European war, was alerted. Two days went by as the final Soviet preparations went forward with frenzied haste. Then, at five o'clock in the afternoon of 8th August Molotov sent for the Japanese Ambassador in Moscow to inform him curtly that the Soviet Union would consider itself at war with Japan in seven hours' time—at one minute past midnight.

To return to the event at Hiroshima: there was terror followed by indecision in Tokyo as the reports of it came in. Whilst the Japanese leaders hesitated, at eleven o'clock on the morning of 9th August the people of Nagasaki suffered the same fate as the citizens of Hiroshima. The Japanese Supreme War Direction Council was meeting at the time in the Imperial Palace in Tokyo to consider the Soviet declaration of war when it received the news from Nagasaki. The men who had assembled now realised—if they had any doubts before—that there was no hope or escape from total destruction except through Japan's capitulation. Even then, the Japanese leaders hesitated. A long and wretched argument went on all that day of 9th August as to whether the Supreme War Direction Council and the Japanese Cabinet could accept the Potsdam demand for unconditional surrender, if this meant the actual suppression of the Imperial family who were the focal point of Japanese society. Eventually, in the early hours of 10th August, the Japanese Prime Minister, Suzuki, cleared his throat and asked the Emperor himself to take the fateful decision. The Emperor, speaking softly, ruled that the Japanese Government would accept the terms laid down at Potsdam "with the understanding that the said [Potsdam] declaration does not compromise any demand which prejudices the prerogatives of His Majesty as sovereign ruler."

The Second World War was now over. Each citizen of the Western Powers has his own memories of that particular day, whether he was engaged in bringing succour to imprisoned starvelings in the Orient, walking ruined avenues of rubble in Europe, struggling desperately to repatriate himself or waiting anxiously at home for the news bulletins. A great wave of pent-up emotion swept parts of the world, leaving untouched those to whom defeat had brought desperate problems of survival amidst the ruins of their own countries and their ambitions.

The immediate effect upon the minds of the men in power in Washington and London was so to free them from Far East issues that they were able to address themselves more fully to the gigantic problems that stemmed from the ending of the European war. To them, Europe was the main cockpit of decision. But Stalin, always consistent in his determination to look after every possible interest in every part of his activity, still had wider horizons. As for the European peoples of the Grand Alliance, in each country the dams of self-restraint broke. Immediately they were obsessed with the internal problems of peace—the cherished hope that the distant one would now return and that the ravages and shortages of war would disappear as if by magic.

To survey the scene amongst the so-called victors, the United States had come off best by far. She had escaped any destruction at home by the good fortune of geography. Nor had she suffered the same pangs of famine that were now grimly threatening exhausted Europe. To say this is not to belittle the generosity of the American people, nor the prodigious American war effort. Yet alone of the countries of the Grand Alliance she was still in a position to give, and she had emerged from the war in a position of world influence and power such as the United States of America had never possessed before in her history.

Russia, too, had ended the war, by virtue of the feats of the Red Army and because of Stalin's far-sighted and rapacious political sagacity, as a great new world power. Nevertheless, the toll had been appalling. It is estimated that over sixteen million had been killed and an unknown number of millions had been wounded. Over thirty thousand Soviet factories had been razed and about a quarter of the Soviet Union's capital equipment had been destroyed or expended. Her coal production had fallen from 166 million tons to 113 million tons. Soviet steel production had fallen from 18.3 million tons to 11.2 million tons and great areas of her richest agricultural territory had been laid waste.

Finally, there was Britain which had stood alone in 1940 when heaven itself was falling. From being a great imperial centre in 1939, with a far-flung empire, she was now a bankrupt and crowded island, with stupendous commitments abroad and no real means of meeting them. To make matters more difficult for her chances of revival, she was a democracy, unlike Soviet Russia, led by a newly elected Labour Government pledged to creating quickly a British Welfare State. Her people were, as yet, a long way from understanding and accepting Britain's new position in the world, nor had they been told the truth about her perilous economic situation and the inevitably conflicting demands between more welfare, more consumer goods, the urgent necessity to refurnish her industry after six years of war, and Britain's overseas military and moral commitments.

The understanding amongst the Allies had always been that the generous war-time American Lend-Lease system would continue until the end of the Japanese war, and this had been expected to continue for at least a year after the European war. Thus the sudden collapse of Japan created a new political and economic situation. Truman found himself faced with a major decision—should Lend-Lease continue for the expected period to allow his Allies time for transition to peace production? He faced the additional problem that Congress had specifically limited the use of funds for Lend-Lease to the duration of the war. Congress had also forbidden the extension of funds allocated to Lend-Lease to cover post-war schemes of rehabilitation and relief beyond the end of the Japanese war. In fairness to him, even if Truman had wanted to do so, it is doubtful whether he could have extended the system by which the United States was still sustaining, in August, 1945, the main burden of Europe. However, he did not wish to extend Lend-Lease and this was partly because he had not grasped fully the extent of Britain's dependence upon American help and the consequences to America that flowed from it. Secondly, his personal thinking had been so recently concerned with internal American problems had not yet been extended to the point of being able to see the larger interests of the Western Powers.

On 21st August, Truman directed that Lend-Lease should be ended. It was a dramatic, peremptory decision and, as a small concession, he agreed that the United States Government would still deliver on credit the goods on order in the actual Lend-Lease "pipeline." In fact, he could scarcely do less without creating industrial disruption inside the United States. The sense of shock at Truman's decision on Lend-Lease was felt particularly in Britain because, more than any other country, she had placed her economy in pawn to American goodwill in the interests of waging war. And to be fair to them, the British Government had never envisaged such a situation. Attlee in announcing Truman's decision to the House of Commons stated that he was sending immediately a high-level mission to Washington to discuss the situation. Churchill, now Leader of the Conservative Opposition, replied sombrely that it was "very grave, disquieting news" which Attlee had just given to the British Parliament.[1]

The Truman Administration, in August, 1945, was determined to return to what it considered was a peace-time normalcy.

[1] The British financial mission led by Lord Halifax and Lord Keynes at once launched into talks in Washington. Their negotiations led later to the so-called American Loan to Britain of 3,750 million dollars in 1946 and part of a pattern of shift in American policy.

Naturally, it was prepared to fulfil its obligations in maintaining its army of occupation in Germany. But it saw this occupation force as operating solely for the purposes of administering Germany and unrelated to any tasks of maintaining the balances of power in Europe. Truman had great popular support for this view. To the American public, the President could not move fast enough. The American troops themselves held this same feeling with even greater intensity because they wanted to get home—the natural reaction to the situation after years abroad. To placate the mood, Truman issued a statement in mid-September saying the American forces were now being demobilised at the rate of 650 an hour and that the speed of demobilisation was to increase. The British Government also faced similar pressures for quick demobilisation from its public opinion and was having to act accordingly. Demands for quicker demobilisation of the forces were raised daily in the House of Commons by Labour and Conservative members alike. Britain also had the added spur to demobilisation from the ending of Lend-Lease, which had now posed such a serious economic challenge that the newly elected Labour Government's survival depended on how quickly it was able to convert British industry and manpower from war to peace-time production.

The mood of public opinion proceeded to make itself felt. In both Western countries it remained unaware of the strategic implications of over-rapid demobilisation. It did not know, nor was it prepared to recognise that if the withdrawal of the major part of the American and British forces in Europe were not accompanied by a corresponding withdrawal by the Red Army, the whole of continental Europe would be at Stalin's mercy should he decide to move westwards. This sombre thought was still confined at the time to only a few people, nearly all in Britain—Churchill, who had already warned against the danger, the British Defence Chiefs, and Clement Attlee and Ernest Bevin in the British Cabinet.

The first major diplomatic conference to be held after Potsdam and the fall of Japan began in London on 11th September, less than a month from "V.J. Day." It was the meeting of the full Council of Foreign Ministers set up at Potsdam on Truman's initiative. One by one, they arrived to join Bevin: Molotov, Byrnes, Georges Bidault of France—then a new spirit from the French Resistance Movement—and Wang Shih-chieh of China, a shadowy figure from Chiang Kai-shek's *ancien régime*. Byrnes took the lead immediately and said that the object of the meeting was to draft the European peace treaties. Furthermore, Byrnes was under pressure that the sooner he could secure these peace treaties (with Italy, Bulgaria, Rumania, Hungary and Finland) the easier would become the major American withdrawal from Europe. Molotov came to London with very different views. He began by demanding that the Council should discuss the arrangements for the occupation of Japan—part of Stalin's return for the Yalta bargain. Byrnes was taken aback. Neither he nor his Government had yet formulated its policy towards the Japanese occupation. He knew he was not in a position to negotiate, so he offered informal talks on Japan as a holding operation. To Byrnes's chagrin, however, Molotov remained adamant. It was two days, therefore, before the London Conference got down to considering the Italian Peace Treaty, taking as a basis a draft submitted by Bevin. Molotov immediately raised the question of the Soviet Union's right to a share in the Italian colonies. Soviet expansionism was apparent. He also demanded that the whole of Trieste should be handed over to Yugoslavia. This was also something that Byrnes and Bevin—whose British interests were now even more directly affected—had not expected. There were several more days of argument during which it emerged that Molotov was accusing the Western Powers of a breach of faith on the disposal of the Italian colonies. His case rested on the fact that Stettinius, Byrnes's predecessor, had—in discussing colonial territories in general terms at San Francisco—agreed with Molotov that the Soviet Union was "eligible" to receive the administration of a colony for trusteeship. Molotov had taken this to mean that the United States would actively support Russia's claim to colonial territory.[1] Byrnes explained defensively: "In the United States any citizen is eligible to become President but that does not mean every citizen is going to be President." Unfortunately for him Molotov was not interested in such analogies.

There was a bitter clash over Rumania. Molotov accused the two Western Powers of being hostile to the Groza Government because it was friendly to the Soviet Union. The Western position was made all the more difficult because King Michael in Bucharest

[1] A similar instance of Russian interpretation of Western intentions and of Western failure to anticipate Russian thinking occurred when Eisenhower agreed (at the Camp David talks of August, 1959) with Krushchev that the situation in Berlin was "not normal." Krushchev immediately took it that Eisenhower would support proposals to make it "normal."

was overtly seeking to get rid of Groza; and on 21st August he had appealed to the Allies for help, thereby hoping to invoke the Yalta declaration on Liberated Europe, allowing freedom to peoples.

On the morning of 22nd September there was a dramatic development. Molotov suddenly sent word to the other Foreign Ministers that he would not be present at the morning session due to begin at eleven o'clock. Instead he asked if Byrnes would come to see him at 11.30. He also asked Bevin for twelve o'clock. The Soviet Foreign Minister told Byrnes on arrival that the Soviet Government wanted to conclude a treaty to prevent the resurgence of Japanese militarism. Byrnes again explained that he would take up the Japanese question upon his return to Washington and that he would discuss it later with Molotov. However, when Bevin walked in whilst they were discussing this—having arrived too early—it became clear that the Japanese issue was only an opening gambit. Molotov explained that he wished to say something more to Byrnes alone and asked Bevin to leave the room. He now came to his major point. He considered that they had all made an error in breach of the Potsdam Agreement by allowing the presence of China and France in discussions that did not concern them. He said that China had no business to be discussing European affairs and that France should be excluded from all but the German and Italian talks. Therefore, Molotov demanded, Bidault and Wang should be told to withdraw from the conference when subjects were under discussion that came outside the terms of their specific interests as laid down at Potsdam. Byrnes did not feel able to tackle this new challenge on his own, and Bevin was asked to rejoin the talks. Bevin now lumbered in from a nearby ante-room. He insisted immediately that the Potsdam understanding was that whilst France and China had no voting rights on issues affecting other countries with which they had not signed armistice terms, they could certainly take part in the discussions. Bevin also pointed out very sharply the adverse effect on the atmosphere of the conference if Molotov informed the other two delegations of his objections; they would feel humiliated. Molotov remained unmoved. These were his instructions and he meant to adhere to them. Later that same day, when the full Council met, he reiterated his demands to the whole assembly. It was all that Byrnes and Bevin could do to prevent Bidault walking out immediately to the Press to make a public attack upon Molotov.

The conference was now in jeopardy, and Byrnes made several desperate attempts at a formula for compromise, but he failed each time. By 2nd October, it was clear that there was complete deadlock. So great was the bitterness Molotov had injected into the discussions that the conference broke up without even being able to agree a communiqué. All recognised it as being a complete failure. For his part, Molotov appeared surprised that the Western Powers had not been able to give way on the major points as they had done at Yalta and Potsdam. This was a new experience for the Soviet Foreign Minister.

Molotov had some right on his side in each of the issues he had sought to raise. There was also a fundamental contradiction in the terms of which Byrnes and Bevin were seeking to achieve in Eastern Europe. The two Western Foreign Ministers were insisting that whilst they wanted to see in these countries only governments that were friendly to the Soviet Union, this aim was just not compatible with the reality of any free election. Byrnes and Bevin would not recognise what Molotov and Stalin clearly understood—that even if any other circumstances of anti-Communism had not existed, the experience of being overrun by the Red Army was the most effective way of making all Eastern Europe anti-Communist!

There was a brief and resounding silence after the London Conference. The peacemakers had met. They had realised suddenly the extent of the gulf which separated the outlooks of the Soviet Union and the Western Powers in the Grand Alliance. After some days, Byrnes decided to try again. He saw himself as a latter-day liberal in the Wilson tradition and he conceived it his duty to make the next move. Therefore he initiated a series of minor conciliatory gestures, which were undertaken in collaboration with Bevin. First, Britain and America recognised the provisional governments in Austria and Hungary in return for Soviet promises that free elections would be held. And Molotov saw to it that these elections were duly and promptly held—in Hungary on 4th November, and Austria on 25th November. Whilst there was a great deal of intimidation, the Communists in each case still received only a minority of votes, showing that the elections were as genuine as could be in the conditions.

Byrnes then sent a special representative with known liberal views, Mark Etheridge, the publisher of the *Louisville Courier-Journal*, to Bulgaria and Rumania. Etheridge's mission was to make sure that Byrnes's criticisms of Russian methods in these Balkan countries, voiced at the London Conference, were not based on prejudiced or wrong information from the local American missions.[1]

Finally, Byrnes drafted a cordial letter to Stalin for Truman to sign, which Harriman delivered on 25th October. This direct appeal in Truman's name to Stalin stressed the genuine desire of the United States to conclude the European peace treaties. Stalin, on reading it, pointed out angrily to Harriman that it still contained no mention of Japan. He also told the embarrassed Harriman that his representative at General MacArthur's headquarters in Tokyo was being pushed around "like a piece of furniture."

It is important to understand American simplicity. Byrnes claimed later that he was very surprised by Stalin's reaction. He appears, up to this point, to have been under the impression that Molotov had been raising the Japanese issue only to extract other concessions in Europe. He had been conditioned by the climate of opinion in Washington that had always regarded the Far Eastern war as a largely American affair in which even Britain should be allowed only a minor interest. There were also the circumstances in which the Japanese war had been ended by the act of two American aircraft dropping atomic bombs.

Truman and Byrnes realised they could no longer ignore the issue as they had sought to do. They were also, by now, under pressure from the British Government, which was increasingly concerned at the apparent disregard of political control being shown by General MacArthur, the Supreme Allied Commander based upon Japan. This is not surprising as MacArthur himself was already a legend and a policy-maker on his own initiative. He had retired from the U.S. Army and had been recalled in 1941. Everything he did always had a sense of dramatic value and he had reversed early defeats at Japanese hands into great victories before the discovery of the atomic bomb.[2] It was said that "he travelled as if draped in the American flag." Yet he possessed many far-sighted and determined ideas—some of which did not commend themselves to the Allies of the United States.

Faced with these circumstances of Soviet intransigence and by British pressure, the United States Government accepted belatedly

---

[1] Byrnes even went so far as to stop Etheridge from seeing State Department telegrams about the situation in the Balkans so that Etheridge undertook his trip with a completely open mind.

[2] MacArthur was nothing if not dramatic: he was engaged to be married eight times!

that a larger share in the political control of the occupation of Japan must be granted to the Allied Governments. The way was thus opened for Byrnes to propose a new meeting with the Soviet Union. This time he limited it to the Foreign Ministers of the three Potsdam Powers in order to avoid the earlier invidious experience regarding France and China. Realising that the Secretary of State had something to impart, Molotov promptly accepted, and Bevin's attendance was taken as a matter of course as he was already aware of some of Byrnes's intentions.

The meeting-place decided upon for the new conference was Moscow, and Byrnes and Bevin set out to confront Molotov in the heavily furnished, overheated Spridinovka building with the streets outside deep in the snows of the Russian winter. It was an achievement that the first meeting of the Moscow Foreign Ministers' Conference took place on 16th December, less than three months after the London breakdown. Byrnes proposed courteously that Molotov should be made chairman and that there should be a very wide agenda. Unfortunately this friendly opening made no difference. The first few days of the conference were occupied by Soviet objections to the American plans for the Peace Conference. Then Molotov was suddenly called to the telephone in the middle of one of the sessions. He returned to tell Byrnes and Bevin that his caller had been Stalin, to say that Molotov was now authorised to accept the American plans. Thankful for the respite, the three Ministers also agreed upon Paris as the most suitable place for the Peace Conference—subject to the absent French Government's agreement— the date to be not later than 1st May, 1946.

In return for this Soviet acceptance of the American proposals, Byrnes and Bevin now agreed to Molotov's demands, voiced in the early discussions, that the preliminary considerations of the peace treaty terms should be confined to the signatories of the armistices, thereby excluding from the process of treaty drafting most of the countries who were to attend the conference. The news of this compromise was announced to the world on Christmas Day—as Byrnes put it in his memoirs, "Five months of negotiations had at last brought agreement on the holding of a conference to help to restore 'peace on earth'."

Byrnes now accepted Russian and British pressure regarding Japan. The conference agreed upon two bodies: (1) A Far Eastern Commission to sit in Washington (2) An Allied Council for Japan to be based in Tokyo. Byrnes, in fact, had given away little in this arrangement because the new agreements did not encroach seriously upon American authority.

Another agreement reached in the new mood was that the Rumanian Provisional Government was to be remodelled and, in return, it was recognised subsequently by the Western Powers. In Korea, the two zones of occupation by Soviet and American troops, arising from the circumstances in which the war had ended, remained in practice, but Byrnes, Molotov and Bevin reached a limited agreement for a conference of zonal commanders to negotiate local difficulties. It was a small step forward. For good measure, Molotov accepted the idea of a United Nations Atomic Energy Commission, indicating to Byrnes that he did not consider it an important issue. Finally, and regrettably, the Persian issue arising from the fact that Soviet troops were still stationed in Azerbaijan (although a promise had been made regarding their withdrawal) had to be dropped from the discussion because of Molotov's vehement intransigence.

Byrnes was very pleased with his own labour. He spoke as if the Moscow Conference had broken the impasse. Bevin was more cautious. He told a Press conference: "The conference achieved what was humanly possible under present circumstances. Its actual significance depends on the implementation of the agreements reached."

Byrnes's hopes were soon to be brought up against the reality of East-West differences that were still emerging. He returned to Washington, still in his optimistic state, to find that Truman was extremely angry with him for not having kept the President fully informed of the progress of the talks in Moscow. With surprising realism, Truman was also sceptical about the achievement of the conference. Truman sent for Byrnes again on 5th January, 1946, and read him a very sharp letter which drew attention, in particular, to the conference's failure to deal with the Persian issue. "I am tired of babying the Soviets," concluded Truman in this extraordinary communication to his Secretary of State.

The President was soon proved right about Persia, when the General Assembly of the United Nations, meeting for the first time in the large auditorium of Westminster Hall, London, on 10th January, 1946, had as its first major issue a formal complaint by Persia to the Security Council against the Soviet Union for not withdrawing her Russian troops. The world was at last having to face the true situation, and there were other and even more ominous indications of mounting tension and the break-up of the Grand Alliance.

Molotov had already warned on 6th November, 1945, in a little-noticed speech, "Our vigilance in regard to *possible new violators of peace*[1] should not slacken, and concern for the strengthening of co-operation between the peace-loving powers will continue to be our most important duty." It was a very clear hint. Then on 9th February, 1946, Stalin made the possibility of East-West conflict even more explicit to those who cared to study the situation. "The capitalist system of world economy conceals in itself the elements of general crisis and military classes," he said in one of his rare public speeches, delivered in a dull monotone that misled some of the Western journalists present.

People in the Western countries still cherished, even then, many of their illusions about co-operation with the Soviet Union, and so public opinion was most rudely affronted by another speech, comparatively moderate when read in retrospect, which was delivered nearly a month later on 5th March, 1946. It caused a world-wide sensation. Churchill, speaking as a private citizen, in front of Truman, delivered himself publicly of the views he had been expressing privately since Yalta. Churchill's central plea at Fulton was for the continuance of the Anglo-American partnership with increasing intimacy. He stated specifically, "We aim at nothing but mutual assistance and collaboration with Soviet Russia." Then he went on to warn grimly: "Nobody knows what Soviet Russia and its Communist international organisation intends to do in the immediate future, or what are the limits, if any, to their expansive and proselytising tendencies. . . . From Stettin in the Baltic to Trieste in the Adriatic an iron curtain has descended across the continent of Europe." (This was his first public use of the iron curtain phrase he used so often in correspondence to Truman and others.) "The Communist parties, which were very small in all these eastern states of Europe, have been raised to pre-eminence and power far beyond their numbers and are seeking everywhere to obtain totalitarian control. . . . Whatever conclusions may be drawn from these facts—and facts they are—this is certainly not the liberated Europe we fought to build up. Nor is it one that contains the essentials of permanent peace. . . ."

Churchill balanced his grave warning by going on: "On the other hand, ladies and gentlemen, I repulse the idea that a new

[1] Author's italics.

war is inevitable; still more that it is imminent. . . . I do not believe that Soviet Russia desires war. What they desire is the fruits of war and the indefinite expansion of their power and doctrines. . . . From what I have seen of our Russian friends and allies during the war, I am convinced that there is nothing they admire so much as strength, and there is nothing for which they have less respect than for weakness, especially military weakness. . . . If the Western democracies stand together in strict adherence to the principles of the United Nations Charter, their influence for furthering these principles will be immense and no one is likely to molest them. If, however, they become divided or falter . . . then indeed catastrophe may overwhelm us all."

Truman, who had travelled (to use Churchill's words) "a thousand miles to dignify and magnify the occasion," let it be known that he was very embarrassed by Churchill's words. The President declined to comment upon Churchill's speech in public, yet the truth was that Truman knew perfectly well what Churchill was going to say. He had seen the British war leader in advance of the speech, and whilst he still did not go as far as Churchill, his opinions were now beginning to differ markedly from the last days of the Roosevelt era. Naturally there was an outcry on the left in Britain. One hundred and five Labour M.P.s foolishly tabled a motion in the House of Commons condemning it as "inimical to the cause of world peace." Bevin and Attlee, who agreed with much of it in their hearts, were as cautious as Truman. Stalin alone of the heads of the Grand Alliance commented publicly. He took the unusual course of replying to Churchill in an interview in *Pravda*: "To all intents and purposes, Mr. Churchill now takes his stand among the warmongers. . . . A point to be noted is that in this respect Mr. Churchill and his friends bear a striking resemblance to Hitler and his friends."[1] Stalin continued: "Hitler began his work by unleashing war by proclaiming a race theory [a reference to Churchill's advocacy of the Anglo-American partnership]. . . . Mr. Churchill begins to set war loose also by a racial theory, maintaining that only nations speaking the English language are fully fledged and called upon to decide the destinies of the entire world." He concluded defiantly: "I do not know whether Mr. Churchill and his friends will succeed in organising a new armed camp against Eastern Europe after the Second World War; but if they

[1] These words of Stalin's also bore a striking resemblance to Joseph E. Davies's indictment of Churchill at Chequers in May, 1945.

do succeed—which is not very probable, because millions of plain people stand guard over the cause of peace—it may be confidently said they will be thrashed, just as they were thrashed once before, twenty-six years ago" [during "The Intervention"].

Even then words were one thing—the Persian-Russian dispute was reality. Some action had to be taken. The dispute had been referred by the Security Council to the two powers for bilateral negotiations. The date of 2nd March, on which it had been agreed earlier that the Russian troops would leave, came and went without a move. Then, after a further appeal by Persia to the Security Council and indications of growing American belligerence, the Soviet Government suddenly gave way. On 24th March agreement was reached for the Soviet troops to leave Persia by 6th May. And the Russians quite properly fulfilled the agreement, leaving behind them a ramshackle puppet Communist state of Azerbaijan.[1]

The Western Powers were extremely relieved and somewhat optimistic. The Council of Foreign Ministers met again in Paris on 25th April to consider the drafting of the peace treaties, a date which was considerably behind the schedule agreed in Moscow. Unfortunately for them, their optimism vanished overnight again, as Molotov began to switch his attack from the British to the Americans as the principal opponents of Soviet policy. It is significant that this is the first major occasion upon which the Soviet Union departed from the beliefs it had expressed ever since the Russian revolution that Britain—not America—was the citadel of imperialism and, therefore, the main threat to the Soviet system and aspirations. In the Russian mind also, the Cold War was taking on a much clearer shape.

The 1946 Paris Foreign Ministers' meeting had two phases. Until mid-May there was little progress. The conference then adjourned for a month and reassembled on 15th June. By 27th June it was apparent that Molotov was going to give way on a number of detailed points of the individual peace treaties and it became clear that the main issue that stood between the Ministers' continuing dialogue and the Peace Conference was a Russian demand for 100 million dollars' worth of reparations from Italy. Byrnes and Bevin, pretending that they were not going "to buy" the Peace Conference, in effect conceded this demand. Thus the Foreign Ministers' Council concluded its Paris meeting on 12th July after prodigious

[1] The Azerbaijan régime collapsed abjectly, later in 1946, when the central Persian Government troops marched northwards to assert their authority.

effort and with many sighs of relief. The Grand Alliance was obviously at an end but the chasm was no wider.

The Paris Peace Conference, held from 29th July to 15th October, 1946, was, on the whole, a surprising success. The decisive period was at the beginning when the delegates argued the procedure by which the conference would be conducted. Molotov wanted a two-thirds majority for all recommendations to be recorded but he was outnumbered and defeated. Two categories of recommendations by the conference were decided upon instead: those that had a two-thirds majority and those that were carried by a simple majority. Byrnes, manœuvring adroitly, also gained considerable support from the smaller countries by agreeing to accept in advance any "two-thirds recommendation" regardless of the American position on any specific issue. As the days went by, the five delegates from the Communist bloc, Ukraine, Byelo-Russia, Yugoslavia, Poland and the Soviet Union, along with Czechoslovakia, which had a government containing Communists, regularly voted together, revoking a counter-reaction amongst the other countries. It was the emergent pattern of many conferences to come. For the record, fifty-three recommendations at the Paris Peace Conference were passed by a two-thirds majority and forty-one by a simple majority.

Under the agreed rules of procedure, the Council of Foreign Ministers now had to meet again to consider the recommendations of the Peace Conference. They did so in New York by rotation on 4th November, 1946. Again it became apparent that Molotov was not going to accept any recommendation of the Paris Peace Conference that was not in accord with the Soviet Union's attitude as expressed in Paris. After nearly four weeks of wrangling, Byrnes told Molotov in exasperation that there was no point in continuing with the meeting. It was a dangerous card to play but it succeeded. Molotov knew quite well that the Soviet Union had a great deal to lose if there were no peace treaties in Eastern Europe, and in the Mediterranean. In Eastern Europe, the peace treaties would have the overall effect of consolidating Communist positions. In the Mediterranean, any Anglo-American withdrawal from Italy would open up new possibilities for the Communists. Thus Molotov retreated hastily from his previous positions—agreeing with astonishing speed to many disputed issues.

The final texts of the peace treaties for Italy, Hungary, Bulgaria, Rumania and Finland were agreed on 6th December at long last. The travelling circus of Foreign Ministers in search of five peace treaties had represented a feat of patience and determination by all sides. Future historians will be amazed by the repetitions and seemingly endless arguments that went on in four different capitals. Yet to Stalin and Molotov, it all had a purpose. They had now secured the Russian hold on Eastern Europe. In the case of almost every country east of the Elbe—with the exception of Italy, Finland and Bulgaria but including Poland—they could now use the argument that they had to maintain permanently their Red Army units to safeguard essential communications to the Russian occupation forces in Germany and Austria. Therefore, to the Soviet leadership, the peace treaties were the consummation of Yalta.

Stalin was now looking for the larger objective: prostrate before him was the greatest industrial, technological and political prize in Europe, if not in the whole world—Germany. He thought of Marx's dictum: "He who holds Germany, holds the key to Europe." Power over the bewildered, defenceless German nation in 1946 and 1947 also meant the probable conquest of all Europe as far westward as the English Channel. The situation for the Western Powers was now critical—in some ways as critical as it had been in 1940 and 1941.

PART THREE

YEARS OF PERIL

CHAPTER 11

AMERICA TURNS

America, thou half brother of the world.   *Philip James Bailey*

Germany was now to be the crux. The Soviet delegation that
journeyed to Potsdam in 1945 (along with nearly every leading
Red Army commander who had advanced into Germany in the
course of battle) had been dazzled by the extent of German industrialisation. For many of them, it was their first glimpse of the
relatively well furnished Western societies. It was only understandable when they saw, in a policy of uprooting and carrying off
back to Russia these German factories, their easiest and quickest
way to repair the damage that Russia had suffered. To them it was
also the shortest cut to the massive Soviet industrialisation upon
which Stalin had determined long before the war had ended and
which he announced finally in February, 1946, with the new Soviet
Five-Year Plan.

They did not realise at the time that the mass seizure of factories
was a misconceived policy because, as they discovered later, there
was a great deal more to an efficient industrial plant than its buildings and machinery. They had forgotten the need for the people to
operate these factories and the special skills, raw material supplies
and transport systems which all played equally important parts in
industrial production. Seemingly endless trainloads of machine
tools and plant travelled daily towards the east from Germany for
a period after the war.

The Western Powers, on the other hand, had approached the
German question from a different standpoint. America and even
more so Britain—were concerned lest Germany should turn out to
be a major economic liability to the occupying Powers. Thus they
had been determined all along since the abandonment of the
Morgenthau Plan on the need to limit the extent of Soviet reparations, as well as America and Britain being ready to hold back on

their own claims to reparations. To feed the Western zones of occupation, they had sought to exchange some of the inevitable reparations to be taken from these zones to Russia for food from the Soviet zone itself and from the rich agricultural lands in the vicinity of the rivers Oder and Neisse now being administered by Poland.

At the end of the war, both East and West had also possessed deep fears regarding the resurgence of Germany. These fears were shown to be particularly acute amongst the Russians and the French. To meet them, Byrnes had proposed at the September, 1945, meeting of the Council of Foreign Ministers in London, that they should all conclude a treaty providing for the demilitarisation of Germany. At that time Molotov had expressed interest. Later, at the Moscow meeting in December, 1945, Byrnes also formed the impression that Stalin personally was favourably inclined to the idea. The Americans, therefore, went ahead in the preparation of such a treaty. Proudly, Byrnes submitted a draft to the other Powers in early 1946. The new treaty was to provide for an effective inspection system to make sure that German rearmament could never again take place. The Four Powers were to bind themselves to intervene at once with military force if the German Government of the day ever broke the provisions of the treaty. The treaty was to last for twenty-five years, with the possibility of extension.

It was a bold and radical proposal. To Byrnes's astonishment, Molotov turned it down in April, 1946, despite the fact that both Britain and France had accepted it subject to the right to secure some amendments. Molotov, when challenged, varied his objections in such a manner that the only assumption that can be made in retrospect is that Soviet policy had changed between December, 1945, and April, 1946, and he did not now want an agreement on Germany. According to Molotov, "he wanted instead the Potsdam agreements on German disarmament and demilitarisation to be implemented and the treaty extended to forty years." When Byrnes explained that there was a clause in the American draft treaty specifically saying that "nothing shall prevent or delay completion of the [Potsdam] process" and agreed to extend the term to forty years, Molotov immediately produced other objections. These objections ended in a complaint that the draft treaty contained no mention of the reparations figure. Reparations were indeed the significant factor, and relations over them had gone from bad to worse in the Allied Control Council. The Soviet representatives had refused consistently to account for the amount that had been taken, thereby making it impossible for the Western Commanders to decide how much more was necessary from their zone. Clay, the American Commander, states in his memoirs: "Reports verified by photographs reaching our intelligence agencies in Germany showed that almost every siding in East Germany, and many in Russia, contained railway cars filled with valuable machine tools rusting into ruin." Thus a head-on conflict between the Soviet Union and the Western Powers was soon in sight. It came when Clay announced on 3rd May, 1946, to the Allied Council that the Americans were stopping the delivery of further reparations from their occupation zone until the Russians adopted a different attitude and they also made trade possible with the Soviet zone.

This was the first major East-West breach on Germany although there had been several earlier, lesser divergences of view. It was to have far-reaching effects because it was clear from Molotov's rejection of the draft demilitarisation treaty—and now from Clay's sudden action—that there was not going to be any common policy towards Germany. When the Council of Foreign Ministers met for the second time in Paris in July, 1946, Molotov launched his major attack on the Americans. After denouncing Clay's action, on 9th July, he accused the Western Powers of failing to eliminate "German war and military-economic potential." Molotov then completely switched his attack, accusing the Western Powers of wanting unduly to limit Germany's right to trade and to expand her production. Molotov's second speech was aimed at securing public support in Germany, especially as it went on to advocate German political unity. The struggle for all Germany had now become apparent.

The Americans immediately took up the challenge. As a counter to this new form of Soviet "electioneering" for German support, Byrnes travelled to Stuttgart on 6th September to make a most unusual public speech to a selected audience of Germans and Allied officials. The Americans carefully arranged the advance publicity. They stage-managed a ceremonial drive for Byrnes and his party through the city to the meeting hall. The Secretary of State was then accompanied on to the platform by Senators Connally and Vandenberg—senior members of Congress. Byrnes's task was to offer a more attractive policy to the Germans than Molotov had done. He began by being firm about the Potsdam agreement and did not mince words about Germany working her passage back into the circle of nations. He claimed that Molotov's continuing demands for reparations went too far—a point that appealed to the Germans. He stressed that Germany must be self-supporting and he went on: "It is the view of the American Government that the German people throughout Germany, under proper safeguards, should now be given the primary responsibility for the running of their own affairs. . . . The United States favours the early establishment of a provisional Government for Germany." This went far beyond anything that Molotov had offered. The Secretary of State's popular appeal increased even more when he continued: "The time has come to define the boundaries of the new Germany." Whilst agreeing that Königsberg must go to the Russians and the Saar to France, Byrnes specifically said that the Polish-German frontier would have to be settled at the German Peace Conference. He was thus bringing into question again the Oder-Neisse line— an issue upon which many Germans who had fled from this particular area to the Western zones still felt bitterly. Byrnes made one other point of great significance: dealing with the possibility of an American withdrawal from Europe, and rumours of growing isolationism, Byrnes said bluntly, "We will not shirk our duty. We are not withdrawing. We are staying here. As long as there is an occupation army in Germany, American forces will be part of that army." Byrnes's historic speech at Stuttgart was not only an American bid for German support in defiance of Molotov's challenge. In retrospect it has to be seen as more—it was part of the pattern of shift in American thinking that went on throughout 1946.

An earlier and even more striking indication was the major American loan to Britain, already mentioned briefly. The Halifax-Keynes mission, which had set out in August, 1945, to discuss the effects of the ending of Lend-Lease, had begun by proposing that the United States should assist Britain to a viable peace-time economy by "financial aid that approximated to a grant." Lord Keynes, the celebrated economist, who conducted the negotiations on behalf of Britain, had approached the talks, as he explained later in the House of Lords, with an explanation to the Americans of Britain's gigantic contributions to the war effort, especially in days when America's own part had been relatively small. He had been proposing, in fact, an extension of Lend-Lease. Keynes had soon discovered that this approach did not commend itself to American thinking, which was much more concerned with the future than the past. As the American negotiators held all the cards, they had then been able to impose virtually their own terms because any break-down of the talks would have been quite disastrous for the British Labour Government.

The amount of the American loan—the Anglo-American Financial and Trade Agreement—was 3,750 million dollars and far less than Keynes had hoped for. It represented what he considered to be a bare minimum to cover the anticipated British trade deficits for the succeeding five years. Keynes had also been forced to agree to an abolition of the system of financial controls by which the British Government could prevent the conversion of sterling into other currencies, including the U.S. dollar. There was a further provision in the agreement that amounted to Britain having to reconsider her system of Empire tariff preference. For all this, the terms of the loan itself were extremely favourable. Repayment was to be in fifty annual instalments and was not to begin until 1951. Interest was fixed at two per cent. And whenever the British trade balance fell below the 1936-8 levels, interest would be waived temporarily and written off. Thus, in effect, Keynes secured what amounted to an interest-free loan when times were bad. The American Loan Agreement had been announced on 6th December, 1945, and ratified by the House of Commons a week later by 345 votes to 98—the official Conservative Opposition abstaining and the votes against the agreement being drawn largely from Conservatives supported by a handful of extreme left-wing Labour M.P.s.[1]

There now began the great debate in Congress upon the Bill to implement the Loan. The measure did not reach the floor of the Senate until 17th April, 1946. A decisive factor in securing its passage was a sudden change of mind by Senator Arthur Vandenberg, a senior Republican Senator who was about to attend the April Foreign Ministers' Conference in Paris as "a special adviser" to Byrnes but whose presence was, in fact, necessary to preserve the bi-partisan nature of American foreign policy. Vandenberg—a wise, courageous and open-minded man—who was to play an important part later in securing Congressional support for some of Truman's international measures, stated suddenly that the Loan Agreement was a matter of "intelligent American self-interest." His announce-

---

[1] There is an interesting comparison between the voting pattern on the American Loan and the main sections of opposition to Britain's entry into the Common Market. As in 1962-3, Lord Beaverbrook's newspapers led the vocal campaign and were supported by a coalition of the extreme left and extreme right.

ment broke up the opposition to the agreement because he gave expression to a feeling that was already growing in the United States. Another Senator who supported him said in the course of the national debate: "The only reason I can find for making the loan is to bolster the British sufficiently to head off Communism in Europe. If that's the theory, we'll have to go on making loans to them." Largely because of this changing mood the Bill passed the Senate on 10th May, 1946, by 46 votes to 30, and the House of Representatives on 13th July, 1946, by 219 votes to 155.

The American debate on the loan to Britain has been compared to the great debate on isolationism versus intervention in the years 1939-41. Certainly it marked a turning point in post-war Anglo-American relations because it restored the special relationship between the two countries, that appeared in danger of being broken in August, 1945, by the circumstances surrounding the ending of the war. But, even more so, it forced Americans to face the implications of their earlier actions and begin to formulate a coherent policy towards the post-war world consistent with America's self-interest and her recent emergence as a world power. The Loan Agreement was a specific, concrete issue within the comprehension of the American man in the street and it was debated fiercely for many months. After ratification, British fears of an American return to isolationism, which had been anticipated by Bevin in particular from August, 1945, onwards, began to recede.

One other major expression of East-West difference in the immediate post-war period must be stated briefly. It was the manner in which the leaders of the Western Powers sought—or professed to seek—to impose international control of the atomic tiger that they had been riding ever since Hiroshima and Nagasaki. In Roosevelt's day and during the early months of the Truman administration there had been a school of thought led by Stimson and supported by some of the scientists to share American nuclear secrets with Russia. This was gradually defeated, partly by Byrnes and partly by the impact of Soviet policy. Thus it was that Truman, Attlee and Mackenzie King, the Prime Minister of Canada, met in Washington on 10th November, 1945, to formulate a policy. The specific object of their meeting, which is said in retrospect to have had a significant influence upon Truman personally in his attitude towards the Soviet Union, was to consider how the peaceful applications of atomic energy could be furthered and its military uses prevented.

These three heads of government issued a statement on 15th November, 1945, which began: "We recognise that the application of recent scientific discoveries to the methods and practices of war has placed at the disposal of mankind means of destruction hitherto unknown against which there can be no adequate military defence and in the employment of which no single nation can, in fact, have a monopoly." The three Western leaders proposed that a Commission should be set up under the United Nations at the earliest practicable date to bring about nuclear disarmament and control and to promote the peaceful uses for the fabulous and terrible discovery.

Byrnes, as we have seen, had also raised the matter at the Moscow Conference of Foreign Ministers in December, 1945. Molotov had then indicated to him that although he did not consider the matter of high importance, the Soviet Union would not object. Thus the United Nations Atomic Energy Commission was duly set up on 24th January, 1946, during the London session of the General Assembly. The first meeting was not held until June, during which interval each country formulated its policy.

In the meanwhile, the practice by which the United States and Britain exchanged secret information that had been agreed between Roosevelt and Churchill at Quebec was discontinued. As with their attitudes over Lend-Lease, Truman and his administration showed themselves less interested in previous American commitments and how they had arisen—in this case because the British Government had unreservedly made over the products of all its research over many years—than with the future.[1] A movement also grew up in

[1] There was always considerable confusion in American thinking about the Roosevelt-Churchill arrangement made on 18th or 19th September, 1944. Stimson, the U.S. Secretary of Defence, even claimed no knowledge of its existence during the Potsdam conference, so Churchill sent him a photostat copy. About its meaning there can be no doubt and it reads in full:

TOP SECRET

TUBE ALLOYS

Aide-Mémoire of Conversation between President and the Prime Minister at Hyde Park, 18th September, 1944

1. The suggestion that the world should be informed regarding Tube Alloys (the code name for the atomic project) with a view to an international agreement regarding its control and use is not accepted. The matter should continue to be regarded as of the utmost secrecy; but when a "bomb" is finally available, it might perhaps after mature consideration be used against the Japanese, who will be warned that this bombardment will be repeated until they surrender.

the United States Congress to prohibit by law any exchange of atomic secrets with any other country. Its leader, Senator McMahon of Connecticut, was completely unaware of the previous Anglo-American agreement, and Truman evaded his duty by withholding from McMahon knowledge of the secret arrangement, when McMahon promoted a Bill to give expression to his views.

Between the setting up of the U.N. Commission in January and its first meeting on 14th June, 1946, the United States Government devoted considerable time to the formulation of its own policy to be presented before the United Nations. A distinguished committee was set up under Dean Acheson, later to be Secretary of State in the Truman Administration. Acheson, an eminent lawyer, was to play an important part in world affairs—tall, distinguished-looking in the manner of an English aristocrat and with a crisp, analytical mind; he set to work with a will. He secured the services of a Board of Consultants which included David Lilienthal, the Chairman of the Tennessee Valley Authority, and Dr. Robert Oppenheimer, the leader of the team that had made the bomb at Alamogordo. The subsequent report by these consultants—principally the work of Oppenheimer—was published and became known as the Acheson-Lilienthal report. Despite its revolutionary nature, it also became the basis of the official United States policy that was put forward at the Commission by Mr. Bernard Baruch, the American delegate.

Baruch's dramatic opening words to the assembled United Nations gathering on 14th June, 1946, have become part of history: "We are here to make a choice between the quick and the dead. That is our business. Behind the black portent of the new atomic age lies a hope which, seized upon with faith, can work our salvation. If we fail then we have damned every man to be the slave of fear. Let us not deceive ourselves. We must elect world peace or world destruction."

The essence of the so-called Baruch Plan—in fact, largely Oppenheimer's plan—was an International Atomic Development Authority which would have managerial control over all atomic work with military potentialities. The power to license and inspect all other

---

2. Full collaboration between the United States and British Government in developing Tube Alloys for military and commercial purposes should continue after the defeat of Japan unless and until terminated by joint agreement.

F.D.R.   W.S.R.

activities in the atomic energy field was to be vested in the Commission. Baruch explained that there must be no question of a veto if the plan were to be accepted: "There must be no veto to protect those who violate their solemn agreements not to develop atomic energy for destructive purposes." American atomic bombs were to be placed at the disposal of the International Atomic Authority, and Baruch made it clear that the United States Government would cease manufacturing them as soon as adequate control machinery was in operation. It was the great blueprint for nuclear disarmament.

Unfortunately, it was opposed by the Soviet Union. Gromyko, the Russian delegate, put forward counter-proposals. He demanded the banning and destruction of all atom bombs as a first step before setting up any machinery of control—which merely meant unilateral disarmament by the United States in advance of any agreement. He then went on to propose two international committees, the first to supervise the exchange of atomic information and the second to prevent the use of atomic energy to the detriment of mankind. As the weeks went by and the end of 1946 drew near, it became clear also that the Soviet Union would not accept the abolition of the veto which the Americans regarded as crucial. Nor was Stalin prepared to accept the principle of inspection within Russia's borders. In the meanwhile, the McMahon Act became law on 1st August, 1946, prohibiting the exchange of American secrets until international control became a known fact. Thus, Britain was forced to embark upon her own atomic development if she was to become a nuclear power.

What is the explanation of Stalin's unwillingness to reach agreement when an agreement was quite possible? There were two factors already discernible. The traditional Russian xenophobia would have ruled out the Baruch inspection proposals in any case. But even more important—whilst going to great lengths to minimise the effect of nuclear weapons—Stalin was already developing his own atomic bomb aided by secret information from the West that was being supplied to the Soviet Union by a few dedicated Communists working within the orbit of atomic projects.[1] Therefore,

[1] It is interesting also to note the distinction between Stalin's propaganda policy at this time, when he used the "Peace" movements in the West to prey upon Western inhibitions for Soviet ends, and the Chinese "Paper Tiger" policy of the late 1950s and 1960s. See Henry Kissinger: *Nuclear Weapons and Foreign Policy*.

Stalin was not interested in international control of atomic energy. It would have inhibited him enormously in his plan for building up yet further Soviet power and extending Soviet influence. He saw Baruch's proposals and American idealism as a pitfall that must be avoided. A great moment and historic opportunity thus passed.

The end of Byrnes's stewardship at the State Department was in sight by December, 1946. His relations with Truman had never been easy, partly because of their previous rivalry for nomination as Vice-Presidential candidate in Roosevelt's last term. Byrnes had been considerably senior to Truman during nearly all of Roosevelt's administration—he had such power that he had been called "The Assistant President"—and Truman felt that he had tended to take too much authority upon himself as a result, despite the fact that it was Truman who was now President. After the bitter exchange between Truman and Byrnes in January, 1946, Byrnes had been meticulous in keeping the President fully informed, but, nevertheless, Truman had been considering his replacement. In April, 1946, Byrnes had written out his resignation "on the advice of a physician" and handed it to Truman, but it had been agreed by the two men that Byrnes would remain until the completion of the first batch of peace treaties.

Truman had already decided whom he wanted for the job. It was General George C. Marshall, the war-time army chief who had retired from the army shortly before and who was at that moment on his ill-fated mission to China, seeking to redress Chiang Kai-shek's crumbling position, the story of which appears later. Truman sent word to Marshall through General Eisenhower, who had succeeded Marshall as Chief of the Army Staff and who was going on an inspection tour of American Forces in the Far East. "Tell him," said Truman, "that I want a new Secretary of State. My present Secretary of State has stomach pains. And I would like to know if he would take the job." In due course the answer came back from Marshall, "Yes."

CHAPTER 12

THE CRITICAL YEAR

A victorious line of march had been prolonged above a thousand miles from the rock of Gibraltar to the banks of the Loire; the repetition of an equal space would have carried the Saracens to the confines of Poland and the Highlands of Scotland; the Rhine is no more impassable than the Nile or the Euphrates, and the Arabian fleet might have sailed without a naval combat into the mouth of the Thames. Perhaps the interpretation of the Koran would now be taught in the schools of Oxford, and her pulpits might demonstrate to a circumcised people the sanctity and truth of the revelation of Mahomet.   *Gibbon*

Marshall took office on 10th January. He brought to his new task his own immense war-time prestige and thereby he strengthened the Truman administration considerably. His appointment made for better relations between the White House and the State Department generally and it gave Truman a new confidence. Marshall, dry, austere, humourless, always brief, soon showed himself to be meticulous in the manner in which he managed his department in the formulation of its policy, and he was quickly to bring a new sense of purpose to American foreign policy in the hour in which it was to be most needed. Paradoxically, he did this not by imposing his own views—for he was not himself a man of wide imagination— but by establishing a system, whereby policies were properly formulated after thorough discussion. "Gentlemen, don't fight the problem. Solve it," was one of Marshall's most common exhortations. The new Secretary of State also owed much to Acheson, his Under-Secretary, who has been mentioned briefly in connection with his work in creating American Atomic Energy policy, for Acheson made the essential complement to Marshall. Whilst Marshall remained as he had been in the war, the Commander-in-Chief responsible to the President, his army training led him to establish the chain of command inside the State Department through Acheson. Thus, thanks to Marshall, Acheson's own remarkable potentialities had free rein at last in the manner that was never possible in Byrnes's day.

A word more about Acheson is essential. Acheson, in military language, soon showed himself to be an admirable Chief of Staff—but he was more. He was also a potential commander-in-chief in the manner that is not always given to good staff officers. He had developed a personal relationship with Truman which to Marshall's lasting credit the senior man fostered.[1] In some ways, the Acheson-Truman relationship was to become analogous to the Bevin-Attlee friendship that existed in Britain because there were the attractions of opposites—one man with the traditional upper-class university background, the other man with the tough, decisive character with his roots amongst the common people. The extraordinary mutual confidence in each other of these Americans—Truman, Marshall and Acheson—made possible much that followed.

It is essential to grasp the sudden transformation that took place in Washington in early 1947. It began a new phase in American history. By remarkable coincidence also Marshall's arrival at the American State Department coincided with the beginning of the most crucial years of the Cold War—the period that was to last until after Stalin's death in 1953.

There were three interrelated factors which now forced the United States to change all its traditional attitudes to the external

[1] Acheson and Truman have both spoken to me of this remarkable relationship. Acheson told me that it began comparatively late, after the Democratic Party defeat in the 1946 mid-term Congressional elections. I record Acheson's account, as I recollect it. "When the Presidential train came back from the campaign, I went down to the station to meet the President as a matter of duty. I expected the whole cabinet to be there, simply to fly our banners higher and play the bands louder because we had lost. To my astonishment, there was only a top-hatted stationmaster, a Press photographer and a lot of red carpet. The President got out. He looked up and down the empty platform and held out his hand. 'Dean, put it right there,' he said. After that I was always there. . . ." Later, "when I was Secretary of State . . . I suppose the closest person in the world to me was my daughter Mary (Mrs. McGeorge Bundy) and she was seriously ill. Whenever I was out of the country in Paris, London or wherever it was, the telephone would ring. It would be the President, he'd say: 'The news is better this morning' or 'worse' if that was the case. He never failed to call me during those years of E.D.C. and the Korean War. For a man like that you'd do anything!"

Truman's response, when I questioned him about Acheson, was equally warm. "Dean?" he said with his quick, sunny smile. Then his face changed. With measured deliberation he added: "He's the greatest Secretary of State since John Quincy Adams."

affairs. First, there was the sudden stripping bare, in the early months of 1947, of the full extent of Britain's economic weakness stemming from the Second World War. Secondly, there was the realisation by the American Administration of the mistakes of Roosevelt's days—a feeling that had been growing but not acted upon. Finally, there was the perilous military power vacuum opened up in 1947 by Britain's imperial withdrawals, accompanied by Russia's increasing expansionism.

The first event marking the new phase was a relatively minor internal episode in Britain. That country faced almost overnight, during a period of extreme winter cold, a fuel crisis. At a Cabinet meeting on 7th February the Minister of Fuel and Power suddenly disclosed the true situation to an astonished gathering. Electric power would have to be shut off from many areas of the country that week-end, he said. Unemployment in Britain, which had been 397,000, rose quickly in the following fortnight to a peak of 2,300,000. The result inside Britain was the first really heavy blow to the confidence of the British Labour Government. Abroad, it exposed the vulnerability of the British national economy and alerted the Americans to the dangers.

At about the same time, an internal debate was taking place in Whitehall between Bevin and Hugh Dalton, the Labour Chancellor of the Exchequer, the latter encouraged by the whole British Treasury which, by tradition, had always considered itself the arbiter of all British policies. On 21st February Dalton published a White Paper, the *Economic Survey for 1947*, which *The Times* described as "the most disturbing statement ever published by a British Government." This *Economic Survey for 1947* showed how Britain was obliged to buy 42 per cent of her food in dollar areas, whereas she sold only 14 per cent of her exports in these same areas. Simultaneously, Britain was then selling far more than she bought in the Eastern Hemisphere, but she was unable to use her Eastern surpluses as the countries concerned possessed no dollars or gold. The British dilemma was made all the more acute as she felt that she had obligations to the Eastern countries that she could not abrogate. Finally, by the terms of the 1946 American Loan, Britain was bound to start making her sterling currency freely convertible to dollars by 15th July, 1947—an increasingly alarming prospect.

It was in the context of this situation of increasing British economic weakness that Stalin decided to press in 1947 the Communist challenge in Greece and Turkey. He knew well that Britain was still carrying the main post-war burden in Greece from Churchill's earlier settlement in 1944-5. He recalled also the way in which the Americans had been most critical of the Churchill initiative to secure Greece against Communist expansion from the Balkans, because they had always regarded the move as an attempt to perpetuate British control of the Mediterranean and the sea routes to the Orient and he hoped that this atmosphere lingered in Washington. As to Turkey—Communist control of Greece would make this country ripe for the taking. Stalin's objectives in the area were clear. He was reviving the Soviet expansionist aims—in the Near and Middle East—that Molotov had expressed much earlier to Ribbentrop and Hitler in 1940 and which had alarmed the Germans. Since those days, Stalin had been developing these aims. At Teheran, in 1943, he had pressed strongly for a revision of the Montreux Convention governing access to the Mediterranean through the Black Sea Straits. Later, he had gone further and demanded secession of the eastern Turkish provinces, Kars and Ardhan, and the establishment of Soviet garrisons in the Bosphorus area. For their part, the Western Powers had been ready always to agree to a revision of the Montreux Convention in Russia's favour,[1] but these further demands upon Turkey had been resisted strongly by all concerned for they would have reduced Turkey to a status similar to that of Finland. Unfortunately for him, Stalin reckoned without the impact upon American official opinion of the Azerbaijan dispute of 1946.

The Soviet agitation and threats against Turkey had gone on ever since 1945. In early 1947 these tensions increased yet further. At the same time, diplomatic reports to London and Washington coming out of Greece in early 1947 indicated that without British aid, the Greek Government had little chance of surviving the spring against Communist guerrillas whose activity had been growing since the autumn of 1946. These reports said that panic in Greece was mounting. They warned that the Greek Government's fate could be settled in a matter of weeks, when the snows melted and

[1] Roosevelt and Churchill had been sympathetic to Stalin's first request (somewhat to Stalin's surprise) at Teheran and Yalta. Truman, at Potsdam, had also proposed the internationalisation of various key European waterways, including the Danube, the Rhine and the Kiel Canal—something that Stalin did not want at all because it meant merging his own control of nearly the whole length of the Danube.

the Communist E.L.A.S. mountain bands came down to the plains. The American Ambassador in Athens also reported rumours to Washington that there were ominous signs of a pending British withdrawal—the rumours of the Bevin-Dalton clash in London had leaked out as far as a small circle of top diplomats.

The decisive step by Britain was taken in the midst of Britain's fuel crisis. Bevin went to see Dalton at the Treasury. A large, heavy man, the Foreign Secretary was very much out of breath as he had been forced to walk up two flights of steps because the electric power for the elevator had been cut off. Bevin asked Dalton to come around to the Foreign Office to see the alarming reports that the British Ambassador in Athens was sending to London, but Dalton refused. Instead the British Chancellor of the Exchequer asked that "firm instructions" should be sent at once to the British Ambassador in Athens that Britain could not contribute any more aid to Greece after 31st March. Dalton added: "If the Greeks want an army they must pay for it themselves." Bevin demurred. He appreciated only too well the weakness of the British economic position, but he recognised the importance of sustaining Greece. He then had the flash of inspiration that comes sometimes to a great trade union leader, skilled in negotiation. He insisted to Dalton that he should be allowed to approach the Americans before going further. Dalton, who was interested in his internal difficulties, agreed readily enough but pressed for urgency.

Thus it was that on 21st February, a cold, grey Friday afternoon in Washington, the telephone rang in the American State Department. It was Lord Inverchapel's[1] secretary asking for an urgent appointment with Marshall to deliver two notes from Bevin. Most of the staff were packing to go. Marshall himself had left already for the week-end and—as he was going shortly to Moscow for another Foreign Ministers' Conference—Acheson did not want to recall him. Instead, the Under-Secretary of State asked for advance copies of the note to be sent round immediately and arranged for any preliminary work that was necessary to be done over the week-end, pending Inverchapel's formal delivery of the notes to Marshall on Monday, 24th February. The notes arrived about forty-five minutes later and referred to Greece and Turkey.[2]

[1] Rt. Hon. Lord Inverchapel, British Ambassador in Washington and formerly Sir Archibald Clarke-Kerr.

[2] For much of what follows I am indebted to the Hon. Dean Acheson and to Joseph M. Jones, *The Fifteen Weeks*.

The first note on Greece explained the perilous military situation in that country and recalled how Britain had borne the main burden of military aid since the Germans had been driven out two years before, whilst the United States had been contributing economic aid. This note estimated that about £40 million would be needed for relief and to bolster up the Greek Government. It said that military operations against E.L.A.S. and re-equipment for the Greek Government forces would require a further £20-£22 million. Then came the blow—the British Government could not hope to do any more after 31st March because of its financial situation. The other note on Turkey also stressed the grave situation there. It warned that the Turkish Government could not carry the economic and military expenses that would be needed to meet the Soviet pressure, nor could Britain help any more. Bevin's notes concluded that the Greek and Turkish obligations would, therefore, have to be met by the International Bank. The serious military implications, in his view, should be considered at once by the Combined Chiefs of Staff. Very shrewdly, the British Foreign Secretary added that the obligations *might* be carried by the United States Government.

The State Department official, Loy Henderson, who had received the envoy from the British Embassy, read the notes "with mounting excitement." He telephoned a colleague and together they went downstairs to Acheson. All three men realised "that Great Britain had within the hour handed the job of world leadership, with all its burdens and all its glory, to the United States." Acheson telephoned Truman and Marshall at once and set in motion a study of all the implications.

By the time Marshall returned to his office on Monday morning to receive Inverchapel, an attitude of mind was developing within the State Department. With extraordinary unanimity, from Acheson down, the view was taking shape that the United States must take up the challenge at once and agree to take over the British commitments in Greece and Turkey. On Monday morning the men in the State Department discovered also that Marshall and Truman were in complete agreement with them—the very thing for which Bevin had hoped in his daring calculation and for which Stalin, in his expansionist drive, had not prepared.

Two main problems confronted the American Administration in the week beginning 24th February. First, there was the practical issue of what was to be done, the extent of financial burden to be assumed and the physical action that would have to be taken.

Secondly, there was the task of securing the support from the American public and the essential congressional sanction. Acheson's study group dealing with the first problem went forward at an astonishing pace under the impulsion of the Under-Secretary of State's personality. The second task—achieving public and congressional agreement for the revolutionary change—appeared in some ways more difficult. There was still little sign of general American awareness of the grim world situation, as it had developed since V.J. Day. To make matters worse for the administration, the Democratic Party had just lost its majority in Congress for the first time since Roosevelt came to power. With the administration in the hands of the Democrats and Congress controlled by the Republicans, themselves isolationist in temperament and conservative by tradition, the prospects looked almost impossible. Bevin had thrown a challenge to America at what he had considered to be the psychological time, but it looked as though he had taken an enormous and irresponsible risk, despite the brave and magnanimous response that he had evoked in the Truman Administration. On 27th February—only six days after the advance copies of the British note had been delivered—Truman sent for a selected group of Congressional leaders. The most important man present was Arthur Vandenberg, Republican Chairman of the Senate Foreign Relations Committee, who had moved himself from early isolationism to the point where he had rendered decisive assistance to the Administration in securing support for the American Loan to Britain in 1946. Marshall explained the situation. His dry, cold manner failed to carry the meeting. He gave the impression that the aid to Greece was necessary because of American loyalty to the Greeks and the aid to Turkey was in order to bolster up Britain's crumbling position in the Near East. No two arguments could have commended themselves less to the quizzical and partly hostile group from Capitol Hill. As Marshall was floundering under a barrage of questions, Acheson leaned across to Truman and asked quietly, "Is this a private fight or can anyone get into it?" Marshall overheard the remark and immediately asked the President if Acheson could say a word. Acheson, who had lived with the problem for nearly a week, transformed the atmosphere. He invested Marshall's case with warmth and urgency. He explained how there had been, for some months past, every indication that Stalin was determined upon the domination of Germany as well as Eastern Europe. If the Soviet leader's drive were to be accompanied by a break-through into the Mediterranean, the situation would be critical. He told in graphic terms of Britain's declining power and the power vacuums she was leaving behind her as she was forced to withdraw from different commitments—including her fabulous Indian Empire. Acheson then went on to deal with the Soviet Union's tactics of infiltration and intimidation that had become manifest as the months had gone by. He concluded: "Only two great powers remain in the world: the United States and the Soviet Union. There has never been a situation like this since ancient times when Rome and Carthage held sway. The two great powers are divided by an ideological chasm. For us, democracy and individual liberty are basic. For the Soviet Union, there must be dictatorship and absolute conformity."

The Congressional leaders boggled. Vandenberg was the first to speak. He had been deeply impressed and so had the others. Yet the gulf between their feelings before they had entered the meeting and the facts as presented to them by Acheson was too great for them to make commitments. They filed out with Vandenberg giving the impression that, provided Truman spoke to the American public with the same frankness and in the same broad sweep as Acheson had done, he would support whatever measures that were necessary to save Greece and Turkey.

Truman and Acheson—for Marshall had left Washington on 5th March on his way to Moscow for the Foreign Ministers' Conference that opened on 10th March—decided to ask Congress for money for Greece and Turkey alone, and to set their request in the wide context of the world situation. The President called a special joint meeting of both Houses of Congress. The man who actually undertook the basic work of drafting Truman's statement was Joseph M. Jones, a State Department official, although many people played important parts under Acheson's guidance. Other Government departments, including the U.S. Treasury, were brought in at an early stage and accepted Acheson's general guiding policy.

The collective agreement inside the Administration made it possible for Truman to enter the House of Representatives at 1 p.m. on 12th March, just nineteen days after Bevin's messages had reached Washington. The President was carrying a large black folder under his arm. He acknowledged the applause with a friendly grin, and, opening the folder, he began to read the statement that has become known as the Truman Doctrine.

Truman's speech, which had a world-wide impact, began: "The gravity of the situation which confronts the world to-day necessitates my appearance before a joint session of the Congress. The foreign policy, and the national security of this country are involved." He explained the Greek and Turkish situations. Whilst admitting that their régimes were not perfect, Truman said that every nation was having to make a choice, adding, "The choice is too often not a free one.

"I believe that it must be the policy of the United States," the President continued, "to support free peoples who are resisting attempted subjugation by armed minorities or by outside pressure. I believe that we must assist free peoples to work out their own destinies in their own way. I believe that our help should be primarily through economic and financial aid which is essential to economic stability and orderly political progress." Truman asked Congress for authority to provide aid to Greece and Turkey amounting to 400 million dollars for the period ending 30th June, 1948. Concluding, he said: "The free peoples of the world look to us for support in maintaining their freedoms. If we falter in our leadership, we may endanger the peace of the world—we shall surely endanger the welfare of our own nation. Great responsibilities have been placed upon us by the swift movement of events."

The significance of the Truman Doctrine was that it marked the public abandonment of many of the hopes upon which the United States had sought to build its post-war foreign policy. It was the first time the United States recognised the limitations of working exclusively through the United Nations. It showed that the Americans now accepted the need to build a coalition of states within the United Nations, if possible—but outside it, if necessary. The earlier American criticisms and carping against Churchill and Britain for seeking to prevent Greece from falling under Communist domination were forgotten, and some of Acheson's testimony to Congress made strange reading in view of earlier policy statements. Indeed, the attitude within the Truman Administration was now most critical of Britain for not keeping her forces in Greece, rather than for these forces being there at all, as had been the case in December, 1944. Marshall, particularly, felt strongly on this score, complaining that Britain could have sustained her commitment in Greece if she had been prepared to withdraw her other large forces in the Far East. He quite forgot the running debate between Churchill and himself, which had taken place during the last eighteen months of war, in which Churchill had sought to prevent the specific situation arising in the Eastern Mediterranean which the United States was now seeking to redress. But the most remarkable aspect of Truman's speech was the speed and resolution of the American Administration's reaction to Bevin's note. Even Bevin, who had hoped so much and who had brilliantly anticipated the course of events, was astonished by the rapidity of what had happened.[1]

Away in Moscow, Marshall was facing Molotov at the Council of Foreign Ministers when Truman spoke in Washington. The object of the conference was to press forward with the Peace Treaties—this time with Germany and Austria. Its agenda went wider than this and included the report of the Allied Control Council for Germany, which had run into its major disagreements over reparations and was to deal with the manner in which the various zones were being administered.

With surprising speed the Foreign Ministers' Conference agreed to a suggestion of Bevin's to abolish the Prussian state—often regarded by outsiders as the core of German military expansionism. Unfortunately this was almost the only agreement of the conference. The differing standpoints of the delegations showed the gulf still separating them. Molotov was determined to exact the reparations that he had been demanding for so long. He accused Bevin of retaining in being, in the British zone, German military formations. Bevin answered back angrily that these were non-military squads for repairing roads and removing mines. Bidault, of France, was concerned about the need to step up German coal exports to supply industry in the various European countries, in particular France. Because his country feared German resurgence, he was cautious about proposals put forward by Marshall and Bevin to administer Germany as a single economic unit and to adopt a system of federal government to be run by the Germans. Marshall and Bevin, who had co-ordinated many of their views, were prepared to agree to some reparations out of German production, but, as before, they could not accept the quantities that Molotov was still demanding. Molotov then claimed that Germany's eastern frontier, on the Oder and Western Neisse, had been fixed "irrevocably" at Potsdam. This led to heated exchanges. Bevin and Marshall maintained rightly that the Potsdam settlement had only been an agreement to allow the Poles provisional administration up

---

[1] The Greek Civil War dragged on for many weary months, although the outcome was no longer in doubt. Tito's rift with the Cominform in 1948 also contributed to its end.

to this line pending a final peace settlement. Bidault put forward a scheme for economic integration of the Saar into France and for the internationalisation of the Ruhr. Stage by stage, as the discussions dragged on from 10th March until 24th April, the positions of the various countries became clearer. Marshall said later, "The critical difficulties . . . stand clearly defined." Bevin seemed to think that some progress had been made.

In fact, little was achieved in Moscow except enough understanding to prepare the way for the next conference which it was agreed would be in London or New York. Surprisingly for those in the West who have always believed that a tough Western policy evokes a tough Soviet reaction, the Truman Doctrine played little part in the conference.

Back in Washington, Acheson was maintaining his momentum. "Bevin had thrown me the ball and I had run with it. I now decided to throw it in the air!" he said later. He recognised that the Truman Doctrine was only the first essential stage in the vast world-wide responsibility that had been shouldered suddenly by the United States. Even before Truman had delivered his historic speech, Acheson had met Patterson and Forrestal, the U.S. Secretaries for War and Navy respectively. Confirming his agreement with them, he wrote to both on 5th March saying that he was asking the Committee that co-ordinated American foreign and military policies to address itself, along with the U.S. Treasury, to the larger problems arising out of Britain's declining power and the changing international political situation. This move by Acheson led to a Special Committee that worked feverishly on the task. It set up several sub-committees dealing with specific subjects such as economic aid or military requirements. The economic aid sub-committee soon took the view that Europe should be treated as a whole, including the Communist satellites. Its reasoning was that the European countries were so interdependent economically that it was impossible to separate their problems.

On 7th April Truman sent for Acheson and told him that he was in a personal difficulty. He had agreed some time before to address the Delta Council, at Cleveland, Mississippi, a gathering composed largely of farmers and small business men who lived in the Mississippi Valley. For the Delta Council, it was to be a historic visit by the President. Unfortunately for both, a local situation had arisen whereby it would be most embarrassing for Truman to appear because a violent controversy was raging around the Senator for Mississippi, Senator Bilbo. Truman explained to Acheson that it would be extremely difficult for the reigning head of the Democratic Party to set foot in Mississippi without being involved in the quarrel. At the same time he was under an obligation to the Delta Council.

"Have you any ideas you'd like to get off your chest, Dean?" the President asked cheerfully, "and would you like to deputise for me?" "As a matter of fact, there are some balls I would like to throw in the air, Mr. President," replied Acheson, thinking of the next stage from the Truman Doctrine and of the work going on in the special committee and study groups. "But I would like you to have a look at my speech." Thus it came about that Acheson took his next step. With the aid of the State Department he carefully prepared a speech dealing with the humanitarian aspects of the great problems of poverty and industrial collapse facing many areas of the world.

Truman saw the speech. Marshall arrived back from Moscow only just before Acheson delivered what he called "a preliminary canter" of his Delta Council speech to a lunch of the League of Women Voters on 1st May. The Secretary of State generously supported Acheson's wide views, although he had little time to assimilate them. On 7th May, 1947, Acheson flew down to Cleveland, Mississippi, in an American Army aircraft and addressed the Delta Council next day. Acheson's words at first had more impact abroad than in the United States. He began by gracefully praising his audience: "You who live and work in this rich agricultural region, whose daily lives are concerned with the growth and marketing of cotton and corn and other agricultural products, must derive a certain satisfaction from the fact that the greatest affairs of State never get very far from the soil." Acheson went on to develop this theme, explaining what a disparity existed between the affluence of American life and the abundance of her food supplies and the grim realities of life in war-suffering Europe and Asia. He told his somewhat puzzled audience that America would have to import more "in order that the financial gap between the world's needs and what it can pay for can be narrowed. There is no charity involved in this. It is simple common sense and good business." He warned them that the United States would have "to undertake further emergency financing of foreign purchases" and that they "must push ahead with the reconstruction of those two great workshops of

Europe and Asia—Germany and Japan—upon which the ultimate recovery of the two continents so largely depends.

"It is wheat and coal and steel that are urgently required to stave off economic collapse, not just dollar credits," continued Acheson. He ended: "Not only do human beings and nations exist on narrow economic margins, but also human dignity, human freedom and democratic institutions. It is one of the principal aims of our foreign policy to-day to use our economic and financial resources to widen these margins. It is necessary if we are to preserve our own freedoms and our own democratic institutions. It is necessary for our national security. And it is our duty and our privilege as human beings." This was a new concept of American foreign policy that went far beyond the Greek and Turkish commitments. The way was now cleared for the next and biggest step —the formal declaration of American policy and the plan for action. Marshall, when he read Acheson's speech, intended to do this himself. Characteristically, the Secretary of State did it in a very brief speech that he, Acheson and all associated with them worked upon carefully; and which Marshall, who was still not fully satisfied, amended in the aircraft as he flew up to Boston, Massachusetts, where he was going to take an honorary degree at Harvard on 3rd June.

There was no advance publicity, either for Acheson's speech at Cleveland, Mississippi, or for Marshall's at Harvard. But, on 4th June, Acheson invited three British journalists—Leonard Miall of the British Broadcasting Commission, Malcolm Muggeridge and Stewart McCall—to warn them of the momentous speech that Marshall was going to make at Harvard. He asked them to telephone the full text to their offices in London and have it rushed round to Ernest Bevin at the Foreign Office. The Under-Secretary of State was playing Bevin at his own game.

Marshall's Harvard speech was divided into three sections. He sketched graphically the dispirited scene in Europe in the aftermath of war: "Raw materials and fuel are in short supply. Machinery is lacking or worn out. The farmer or peasant cannot find the foods for sale which he desires to purchase. So the sale of his farm produce for money which he cannot use seems to him an unprofitable transaction. He, therefore, has withdrawn many fields of crop cultivation. . . ." Then came Marshall's analysis: "The remedy lies in breaking the vicious circle and restoring the confidence of the European people in the economic future of their countries and of

Europe as a whole." Finally, Marshall made his offer. "Our policy is directed not against any country or doctrine but against hunger, poverty, desperation and chaos." This was a different motive from the Truman Doctrine. "It is already evident that, before the United States Government can proceed much farther in its efforts to alleviate the situation and help start the European world on its way to recovery, there must be some agreement among the countries of Europe as to the requirement of the situation and the part those countries themselves will take in order to give proper effect to whatever might be undertaken by this Government. . . . The initiative, I think, must come from Europe. . . . The programme should be a joint one, agreed to by a number, if not all European nations. . . ." Marshall's dry, brittle voice crackled as he spoke.

The last word on the American side in these memorable weeks should go to Acheson—to him, to his courage, his vision and his extraordinary energy belongs the glory. Speaking at Middletown, Connecticut, ten days later—there is almost something symbolic in the name—he said: "We . . . can and should help within the limits of our capacity those who wish to help themselves. . . ."

Ernest Bevin in London read the reports from the newspaper offices on Marshall's Harvard speech. It was late at night, London time. In his own words, "I seized the offer with both hands." When he called a conference at the Foreign Office, one official suggested that the British Chargé d'Affaires in Washington should be asked to see Marshall in order to find out if he had really meant what he had seemed to mean. "No," snorted Bevin, "I don't want to take any chances."

Bevin now knew that his daring strategy, first imposed upon him partly by his own country's economic difficulties, was in sight of the larger success. He had been conducting Britain's foreign policy for two years from positions of weakness and in the shadow of massive Soviet military forces which, though stationed behind the Elbe, were only a few hours motorised advance from the English Channel. He had also been deeply concerned for months past by the fragmented nature of American policy. In a message to Marshall some days before the Secretary of State's Harvard speech, Bevin had actually pointed out that unless the United States Government ceased to deal piecemeal with Europe and framed a comprehensive policy, they would soon find it would be too late. Bevin's own private view at the time was that because of the debilitated state of affairs in most West European countries the Soviet Union was about to attempt to promote civil war on a large scale, acting initially through strikes. This was not idle speculation—it was the Labour leader, with his ear close to the European trade union situation, who was speaking. Mounting industrial strife in Italy and France at the time supported his view. Therefore, to Bevin, Marshall's words at Harvard delivered to him in London, first on paper from the newspaper offices and shortly afterwards in the form of a tape recording taken by Leonard Miall, sounded like the echo of much that he had been saying in London in his own blunt and colourful way. Like George Canning a hundred and twenty-one years before, Bevin had called in the New World to redress the balance of the Old. His resolve so to do, in 1947, was one of the great decisions in the history of the British foreign policy.[1]

Bevin quickly learned that Marshall's Harvard speech had evoked a most friendly reaction in Paris. Bidault cabled the French Ambassador in Washington on 7th June asking him to inform the American Secretary of State that the French Government accepted his views. Bevin and Bidault now set about the task of carrying the Marshall proposals a stage further. Bevin travelled to Paris on 16th June for talks that took up most of the next two days. Under Bidault's insistence—for the French Government was most concerned about the internal political situation in France and did not wish to provoke the large French Communist Party—they decided to invite Molotov to a preliminary conference to be held the following week. The intention was to follow this quickly by a full-scale conference, which was to include every European country except Spain.

The Russian reaction to Marshall's speech was slow. Nothing appeared in the Soviet Press whilst Stalin considered the issue. *Pravda* on 16th July made the first suspicious, hostile comment: "Mr. Marshall's Plan . . . notwithstanding its apparent novelty, is only a repetition of the Truman Plan for political pressure with the help of dollars, a plan for interference in the domestic affairs of other countries." Nonetheless, Molotov accepted the Bevin-Bidault invitation for a Three-Power meeting in Paris to open on 27th June. The news of Molotov's acceptance brought cheers in the British House of Commons when Bevin made the announcement.

As soon as the preliminary conference of the three Foreign

[1] Years later I was lunching with the Earl of Avon, formerly Anthony Eden. "What was your personal view of Ernie?" I asked. "Well," said Lord Avon thoughtfully, "he took the *big* decision."

Ministers met, it became apparent that Molotov's views on the way to respond to Marshall's offer were very different from those of the other two. Molotov's proposal was to suggest a form of clearing house for European requests for aid without the comprehensive approach to the European economic problem that Marshall, Acheson and Bevin envisaged. Needless to say, this would never have met the basic American condition as stated by Marshall. On the other hand, Bevin and Bidault were ready to propose a survey of European needs to be followed by an over-all European economic plan which would be submitted in due course to the United States for help and guidance. From this Anglo-French view stemmed the next of Molotov's objections. Molotov pointed out that the concept of the comprehensive European plan inevitably implied the inclusion of Germany and he objected strongly to the idea that ex-enemy nations should receive help before the needs of the Allies had been met. Molotov also insisted that the European countries should ask the Americans to state in figures just how much aid they were prepared to make available—an impossible political step for the Truman Administration to take in advance of a comprehensive statement of the problem.

Molotov in Paris realised that he was in a very embarrassing situation. The magnanimity of the Marshall offer had been welcomed by Czechoslovakia, whose coalition government included Communists and, to a lesser extent, also by Poland, which was under complete Communist control. He sensed the danger that Marshall's proposal could mean inroads into the East European Communist bloc, and he fought a delaying action as best he could. Finally, he withdrew from the Paris talks when it became clear that Bevin and Bidault were meaning to go ahead with the larger European conference anyway.

On 2nd July the preliminary conference broke up. On 4th July the invitations for the European conference were duly sent out despite Molotov's protests. The opening date was set for 12th July. To the Soviet Foreign Minister's chagrin, Czechoslovakia promptly accepted, though she was quickly forced to withdraw under Russian pressure, not before damage had been done to the Russian political position. The Czechoslovak authorities had sought the guidance of the Soviet Embassy in Prague. Upon being told by the Russian Chargé d'Affaires that no view had been formulated in Moscow, the Czech Cabinet accepted unanimously. Later upon Soviet instructions, telephoned by Gottwald from Moscow, they reversed their decision—also unanimously. Soviet policy had been interesting. It had been to try and stop Marshall's initiative ever taking effect. But if Stalin had been more subtle in his tactics he may well have achieved his objective. He should have joined in the European plan because it is very doubtful whether Truman could have got Congress to vote the vast sums involved in those circumstances. Thus Molotov's withdrawal from the Paris conference must be considered one of the major Soviet mistakes of the Cold War.

CHAPTER 13

BEVIN'S INITIATIVE

I called the New World into existence to redress the balance of the Old.
George Canning, 12th December, 1826

Stalin now decided to bind the East European countries even more closely to Russia. He found it possible to do so because the Russian hold on Eastern Europe had been strengthened in 1947 to the point of virtual domination in every country, except Czechoslovakia— the one country that had also shown independence in response to the Marshall offer. The pattern in most East European countries was broadly the same. First, there had been a coalition government in which the Communists had held certain key posts, notably the Ministry of the Interior, which meant control of the police and apparatus of state security. Next the non-Communists in the government were replaced by Communist sympathisers. Finally, the Communists took over completely. These three stages—the genuine coalition, the bogus coalition and the Communist dictatorship— came to be described by Rakosi, the Hungarian Communist leader, as the famous "salami tactics"—taking over a country slice by slice.

The situation in Poland since Potsdam—to give the most striking example—had gone from bad to worse. The free elections that had been promised in "a few weeks" by Stalin at Yalta and which had been the subject of so much bitter Western pressure, were held finally on 19th January, 1947. The elections were preceded by a campaign of murder, repression and intimidation. They were accompanied by gross abuses of procedure. Over 50,000 people had been deported to Siberia before the elections. Freedom of speech was suppressed long before. In March, 1946, when a Peasant Co-operative Congress was held in Warsaw, 1,200 out of 2,000 delegates were arrested on their way to the Congress; and again, in November, 1946, over 300 Polish Socialists were arrested on charges of co-operation with post-war underground organisations. The catalogue of tyranny was a very long one.

During the actual elections in January, 246 Polish Peasant Party candidates—Mikolajczyk's party—were disqualified, 149 were arrested and eighteen were murdered. Over a million voters were struck off the electoral register on various pretexts. "In Cracow, which was the only constituency where a joint peasants' and workers' list was passed by the returning officers, Zulawski [the Socialist leader] was not allowed to publish one single electoral appeal or manifesto. On polling day on 19th January all factory and office employees were ordered to assemble, and with appointed leaders were marched to the polling stations and forced to vote openly for the 'Democratic Bloc.' Twelve thousand people were arrested on that same day."

In these appalling circumstances of intimidation, it was not surprising that Beirut's Communists secured complete control in Poland. A similar pattern of Communist domination had developed—or was in the course of developing—in Bulgaria, Rumania, Hungary and Yugoslavia. Only in Czechoslovakia and Finland, of the countries that contained Soviet forces, were there semblances of democratic procedures.

As the Paris Conference on Marshall's Harvard proposals got under way, a succession of East European leaders travelled to Moscow. Then came the Soviet alternative plan. At a Communist conference at Wiliza Gora, in Silesia, on 22nd and 23rd September, 1947, the Communist parties of nine countries—Soviet Russia, Yugoslavia, Poland, Czechoslovakia, Hungary, Roumania, Bulgaria, France and Italy—resolved to set up the Cominform, the Communist Information Bureau to direct and to co-ordinate the activities of the Communist parties in Europe. Unlike the earlier Comintern, this was a gathering of men who were in power or who were backed by very large Communist parties which might soon be in power, as in Italy and France.

The issue of the Marshall Plan became the parting of the ways for almost every European country. Simultaneously on the Communist side, Stalin took the decision to found the Cominform in September, 1947. Zhadanov's speech to it represented an all-out declaration of ideological war. Military alliances—such as the Brussels Treaty, the North Atlantic Treaty Alliance and the Warsaw Pact—came later, but from mid-1947 onwards, the alignment of most nations was decided irrevocably for the next generation. Thus 1947 became the vital year of decision in this respect.

The March meeting of the Council of Foreign Ministers in Moscow had been followed by an interval during which the diplomatic efforts of both sides were occupied in the Marshall Plan and Cominform discussions. The Foreign Ministers were now to meet again in London to discuss Germany. Bevin, who had felt that some progress had been made in Moscow in making clear the issues of disagreement, went so far as to say in the House of Commons on 15th May, 1947: "The London conference, now that the issues are perfectly clear before us, is the most vital in the world's history." But much of his enthusiasm had evaporated by the time the conference met on 25th November.

The London Foreign Ministers' Conference lasted until 15th December, 1947. Molotov had obviously arrived with instructions to be more belligerent than he had been in Moscow, and delivered a vehement attack upon the imperialist aims of the Western Powers. This was how the Russians now saw the thinking behind the Marshall Plan and other Western policies. The issue then turned again to Russian claims for reparations. Although the Soviet Union had taken out reparations already from Germany to the value of several thousand million U.S. dollars—estimates varied from 3,000 million to 8,000 million dollars—Molotov's claim for 10,000 million dollars never varied. Nor was he prepared to grant the Western Powers an account of what had been taken already. At one point Bevin burst out angrily: "Every time we ask for information we get insults, insinuations or accusations. . . . Although we have no means of checking it we are told that the Soviet Union has taken material to the value of at least 7,000 million dollars out of Germany since the war ended." The conference was brought to a conclusion by a vitriolic attack by Molotov upon the Americans and British on 12th December. Marshall was so angry that there were no meetings for three days. Thereupon the conference was ended formally on 15th December.

Therefore, the London Conference—coming after the Marshall Plan—was another decisive event of 1947. Molotov's behaviour made Bidault and his government realise finally that France's position as an intermediary between the Powers was untenable— a view that the French had begun to accept at the time of the Marshall Plan Conference in Paris. Molotov's angry bitterness in London had also astonished and alarmed the British and American delegations. It drew the Western countries much closer together and it increased the feeling that Bevin's strategy of bringing the Americans back into European affairs was showing itself to be vital for the survival of the West.

Now Bevin's strategy had to be taken a stage further. As Bevin saw it, he had secured what amounted to comprehensive American commitments in Greece and Turkey. He had seen the Americans adopting a broad European economic policy, with great practicality and generosity. The next stage, in his view, was to obtain major American military commitments in Europe. But American opinion was not yet ready for such a proposal. Not even Acheson, with his forward-looking views, was in a position to move Marshall to the point of such a decision as 1947 drew to its close.

Bevin, therefore, decided upon a three-stage manœuvre, and to his relief he was able to secure Bidault's support in the French Government's new state of mind. In a talk on 23rd December with Field-Marshal Montgomery, by this time Chief of the Imperial General Staff, Bevin explained his intentions. He said that he had just secured Bidault's agreement to "a Federation or Union in Western Europe" and that it was his intention to associate the United States with it. He told Montgomery that he considered the Russian attitude was so serious that he wanted military staff talks, first with France and then with America. Thus, whilst Montgomery set to work on the military issues, Bevin pressed ahead with his wider aims. First, he proposed to secure a Western Union Alliance incorporating Britain, France and the Benelux countries. Secondly he hoped to bring in other non-Communist European states, notably Italy and the Scandinavian countries, excepting Sweden. Having got this far, he felt that he might be able to persuade the Truman Administration to reconsider its attitude to the military commitment in Europe because he knew always that it was sympathetic to the idea of European unity. It was a bold and daunting strategy but he knew that the greatest difficulties had been surmounted already by the announcements of the Truman Doctrine and the Marshall Plan.

It must be noted that the political climate in Europe in late 1947 had changed considerably, and this was a great help to Bevin. People were now beginning to ask openly if there would be war. Bevin, therefore, had the stage already set for himself when he launched his plan for Western European union in a tense, crowded House of Commons on 22nd January, 1948. The Russian answer, given in *Pravda*, was at its most sharp: "His [Bevin's] plans can be expressed in two words—split Europe. The project of a Western bloc is not new. Churchill has been busy with it. Bevin . . . reproduces the essence of the American plans for the creation in Europe of a military bloc of Western countries financed by the United States, based on the rebirth of Germany's war potential and directed against the Soviet Union and the countries of the new democracy."

The West European reaction to Bevin was most favourable. Spaak, Prime Minister and Foreign Minister of Belgium, a country which had been one of Europe's traditional neutrals for over a century, spoke for them all when he said to the Association of Socialist Journalists in Brussels: "The hour of choice has arrived. We must choose our friends and allies not in a spirit of hostility towards anyone but to preserve peace and liberty." Talks at diplomatic level went forward at once to put into practical effect the Bevin proposals.

The Marshall Plan, followed by the failure of the London Conference, had also posed anew for the Western Powers the issue of Germany. Up to this point they had been most unwilling to take steps that might make it appear that they were responsible for dividing Germany. However, they could not put off indefinitely a decision about West Germany's relationship to the Marshall aid, nor could they postpone permanently steps towards West German self-government.

In the absence of a united German Government, Marshall and Bevin felt that they had now to move towards the setting up of a West German State, and they were helped in this aim by France's recent more amenable attitude. To Marshall's and Bevin's relief, France decided to merge her zone with the British and American zones, and Bidault agreed also to Three-Power discussions that might lead to a separate West German Government.

Thus, on 20th January, two days before Bevin's Western union speech in Parliament, as a part of his grand design of bringing Western Europe together, invitations to the three occupying Powers and to the Benelux countries were sent out for a conference to meet in London on 23rd February to discuss the future of Germany. Not surprisingly, the Western move drew another strongly worded Soviet protest on 13th February before the conference opened.

Events in Europe moved yet faster. As the London Conference on Germany was assembling, a political crisis developed in Czecho-

slovakia, the only country in the Russian orbit that was not yet
under full Communist control. The origins of the Czech crisis lay
in the fact that Czech elections were approaching. The earlier
elections held in 1946 had been genuinely free and the Communists
had emerged with nearly 40 per cent of the votes. Now it was clear
that they had lost much of their popularity and a crude public
opinion poll taken by the Communists themselves showed that in
the forthcoming election there would be a different result.

The Czechoslovak Communists, led by Klement Gottwald, the
Prime Minister, were very alarmed. They had to face electoral
defeat or to prepare for physical action. In this situation, Nosek,
the Minister of the Interior—and inevitably a Communist—proceeded to replace key non-Communist police officials with Communist appointments. The intention was obvious. This preposterous policy was brought to a head when Nosek dismissed eight
non-Communist police officers in Prague itself and replaced them
by Communists. There were angry protests in the Czechoslovak
Cabinet from the non-Communist ministers. By a majority vote,
taken in dramatic circumstances on 13th February, the Cabinet
overruled Nosek and ordered him to replace the dismissed officers.
With great effrontery, Nosek refused. He was blandly supported by
Gottwald, the Communist Prime Minister, and the other Communist ministers who knew their political futures were at stake.

In the deadlock that followed, twelve non-Communist members
of the Czech Cabinet tendered their resignations to Benes, the
President, on 20th February, thereby hoping to precipitate a crisis
which would make Benes bring forward the national elections.
Unfortunately the Social Democrats hesitated and then decided to
remain in the Government, thereby giving Gottwald a semblance
of authority and a majority in the Czech Parliament. A sinister
part in all this appears to have been played by Fierlinger, nominally
a Social Democrat but, in fact, a man who had been working
secretly for the Communists ever since he had served as Czech
Ambassador in Moscow during the war.

Nosek at once proceeded to bring Communist-controlled police
units into the Czech capital. He struck in the course of the night
of 22nd February. Certain people who opposed the Communists
were dragged from their beds by hammering on their doors. They
were then arrested, hustled in police vans and flung into prison
upon charges that they were hatching a plot against the state in
association with the United States of America. The non-Communist

newspapers were suppressed next day. The offices of non-Communist parties were also occupied by Communist lackeys. The very ruthlessness of the Communists' actions took their opponents by surprise. In a few hours they rallied, but some anti-Communist riots on 23rd and 24th February were put down so forcibly that the resistance now crumbled. Benes, never a strong man, thereupon gave way and accepted the resignations of the non-Communist ministers with the exception of the Social Democrats, who did not offer to resign.

The sad truth was that the non-Communist ministers in the Czech Cabinet had miscalculated appallingly. They had reckoned without the foolishness or perfidy of the Social Democrats—call it what you will. They had also misjudged the wisdom and fibre of Benes. The Czech President had always believed that he could manœuvre successfully in his relations with Russia—his greatest mistake—and by the time of the Prague coup he was also a failing man who was to die before the year was out.

Yet there was no doubt also that the coup had been planned most skilfully and it had been pressed home with great resolution. An important factor in Benes's final surrender, which took place on 25th February, was a mass general strike organised by Gottwald on 24th February, which was followed by the surrounding of Prague by armed Communist activists who camped in the woods outside the city, waiting for the order to march on the capital, in the manner of Mussolini's forces marching on Rome many years before. It all created an atmosphere of political hysteria.

Another important and significant aspect of the coup was the presence in Prague of Zorin, a deputy Foreign Minister of the Soviet Union and a former Soviet Ambassador in Prague, throughout the vital days. Zorin's sinister presence was explained to the public as a desire to attend to some deliveries of Russian wheat—a most extraordinary function for a man in his position. His interest in the wheat also apparently led him to maintain close contact throughout the crisis period with the commander of the Red Army units in the area and with Gottwald.

The Czechoslovak coup created great consternation and alarm in the West. There was much talk of Munich again, although the analogy did not apply. But the most dramatic event of the whole affair was yet to come: the body of Jan Masaryk, the Social Democrat Foreign Minister in the new Gottwald administration, was discovered in the courtyard of his Foreign Ministry on 10th March.

The circumstances of his death have never been cleared up. The official Communist claim was that he committed suicide. Others still believe that he was murdered. The news of Masaryk's death caused a particular shock in Western political circles for he was not only the son of the founder of the Czechoslovak state, Thomas Masaryk, but he was also well known abroad in his own right from the Czechoslovak Government's war-time period in exile and by his activities at the United Nations.

As far as the Czech coup is concerned, it remains to be recorded that Benes himself resigned office on 7th June. He was succeeded by Gottwald and he died three months later. Benes's extraordinarily sad career had been marked by two great political tragedies for himself and for his country. His beliefs, following the Munich betrayal in 1938 and because of Stalin's later bland assurances that the Soviet Union would always act as democratic Czechoslovakia's friend without seeking to impose upon her the Communist system, had led him to orientate his country's policies towards Russia. His grizzled legacy embodied a lesson that the West took to heart immediately, because the Czech coup became the greatest single event to raise the alarm to the perils of Communist expansionism.

As a consequence of the train of events, Bevin now had no difficulty in securing his West European Union Treaty. Discussions in Brussels were actually being concluded when the news of Masaryk's death reached the conference. The agreement was initialled on 13th March and the Treaty was signed formally on 17th March. The London talks on Germany also went forward at a redoubled pace. The first communiqué of this conference was published on 8th March and it expressed the view that, whilst a Four-Power agreement on Germany was still possible and to be sought, there were "urgent political and economic problems" to be settled arising out of the need to effect the economic reconstruction of Europe. The implications of this were obvious to the Russians— a Western German state was about to be set up and incorporated into the Marshall Plan.

The Soviet reaction was most hostile. A protest had been delivered already to the Western Powers on 6th March, saying any agreements at the London Conference were "incapable of having legality and international authority." At the next meeting of the Allied Control Council in Berlin on 20th March, Marshal Sokolovsky, the Soviet representative, suddenly demanded to be told about all agreements on West Germany reached at the London Conference, and then read a violently worded protest. As the British representative was starting to reply, Sokolovsky and the whole Soviet delegation stood up as one man as if by prearrangement. Sokolovsky, whose turn it was to be in the chair, then said sharply, "I see no sense in continuing this meeting and I declare it adjourned."

Sokolovsky's walk out in Berlin was the beginning of a new stage in the German struggle. For the discerning student, a clear warning of Soviet intentions had already been given. A leading article in *Tägliche Rundschau*, the official Red Army newspaper in Berlin, had stated on 19th December, 1947: "It was decided at Yalta that Berlin must remain the German capital. . . . This means that as long as there is a quadripartite administration of Germany and the control council functions, Berlin will have a quadripartite administration. The situation changes if quadripartite administration becomes fictional. . . . If a West German Government was set up it would affect Berlin."

Berlin was now to be the issue.

CHAPTER 14

IS IT WAR THEN?

Is it war then? Will ye perish as dry wood in the fire?   *William Morris*

General Lucius D. Clay, the United States Military Governor, had a foreboding as to what might happen in or around Berlin if the Western Allies pressed their plans for a West German State. He dispatched a telegram to the U.S. Army Director of Intelligence on 5th March, 1948, shortly after the Communist coup in Prague and fifteen days before Marshal Sokolovsky walked out of the Allied Control Council meeting in Berlin:

> For many months, based on logical analysis, I have felt and held that war was unlikely for at least ten years. Within the last few weeks, I have felt a subtle change in the Soviet attitude which I cannot define but which now gives me a feeling that it may come with dramatic suddenness. I cannot support this change in my own thinking with any data or outward evidence in relationships other than to describe it as a feeling of a new tenseness in every Soviet individual with whom we have official relations. I am unable to submit any official report in the absence of supporting data, but my feeling is real. You may advise the Chief-of-Staff of this for whatever it may be worth if you feel it advisable.

The first indication of Soviet intentions was given on 30th March when the Russians published new regulations for rail and road traffic between Berlin and the Western zones. All Western military trains were to be subjected to a search as from the following day. This proposal was rejected as unacceptable by the Western Powers. Instead they decided to supply the small numbers of occupation forces in Berlin by air. A shadowing Soviet M.I.G. fighter flew too close to a British Viking aircraft in one of the recognised air-lanes on 5th April and collided with it, both machines crashing near

Gatow airport. Following the incident, there was widespread indignation in Britain, and Bevin demanded compensation for the relatives of the victims, whilst the Soviet Government counter-claimed for the pilot of the M.I.G. On 22nd April the Russians cancelled the Nord Express to Berlin and attempted to insist that all night and bad-weather flights to Berlin should be cancelled. "Berlin these days is no place for a nervous person," remarked Clay ominously.

In the meanwhile, the London Conference on the future of Germany had been proceeding after an adjournment. A number of agreements announced on 7th June confirmed the Soviet suspicions. The economic policies in the three Western zones were to be co-ordinated. West Germany was to be encouraged to play a full part in the European Recovery Programme, the official name by which the Marshall Plan had now come to be known. A constitution for a Federal West German Republic was to be drawn up. The end of the Control Council also enabled the Western Powers at last to proceed with currency reform which they considered essential to German recovery. The British and Americans were the first to reach agreement in this and, after some hesitation, they were joined by the French.

Stalin, therefore, decided to act in order to show that he was in a strong position. The Soviet authorities halted all rail traffic between Berlin and West Germany for two days on 11th June, four days after the London communiqué. Next day they closed the main Helmstedt autobahn because of alleged repairs to the bridge over the Elbe, and later refused Western offers of help in repairing the bridge.

In the meanwhile, the American and British Governments were playing a daring and provocative hand from a delicate position of extreme military weakness. Britain's commitments in other parts of the world had stretched her forces to the limit. As for the United States, the only American reserves available without general mobilisation, if the Russians were to threaten to use force in Germany, was one division of 15,000 men. How did the Western Powers see the situation? After Clay's alarming telegram of 5th March, the Central Intelligence Agency had felt unable to go further on 16th March than to say that war was not likely within sixty days; an estimate that this body later extended to cover a further sixty days. If the Russians were to close off all routes to Berlin, neither the Americans nor the British wished to try to shoot their way through. They were in no position to do so. Also, there were various gloomy estimates as to the possible effect upon Berlin of a total blockade. Only one major trump card still remained in the hands of the Western Powers: it was the American monopoly of the atomic bomb.

The Western Powers, therefore, decided to go ahead with currency reform in their zones, specifically excluding Berlin. On Friday, 18th June, the first law affecting currency reform was announced, the main effect of which was to substitute one new Deutsche Mark for every ten of the old Reichsmark. The news was published shortly after the West German banks had closed for the week-end.

The Russian answer was not long in coming. On the next day Sokolovsky, the Russian Military Governor, made a disquieting statement addressed to the German population, claiming all Berlin as part of the Soviet Zone. He also imposed restrictions on travellers at the zonal frontier at the Helmstedt checkpoint in the British Zone. It was a strange and eerie scene in the morning—the silhouettes of British armoured cars drawn up to control the situation and a milling eastbound throng of travellers, including two Swiss and Dutch diplomats who were turned back with the rest. On 23rd June, the Soviet authorities announced currency reform for East Germany which they said would also apply to all Berlin. This faced the Western Powers with a dilemma which they decided to meet by introducing the new Western currency into their own sectors of Berlin, a course to which the French were most unwilling to agree.

Clearly the next forty-eight hours were to be critical and most confusing for the Berliners, who found themselves confronted with the choice of changing their money into two rival currencies. A special meeting of the City Assembly was called for four o'clock in the afternoon in the City Hall, which stood in the Soviet sector. Long before the meeting was due to take place a large crowd had begun to gather, nearly all of them Communists. The crowd then broke into the building, displaying almost military precision, and it forcibly took possession of the gallery in the Assembly and the upper floors of the building. The uproar and hooliganism became so bad that the Assembly's meeting was held up for two hours. When it was possible to begin the meeting, a resolution was put before the Assembly agreeing that the Soviet currency would operate in the Soviet sector and the Western currency in the other three sectors.

s.w.   257

This was opposed strongly by the Communists but—despite threats to confiscate the savings and social insurance funds of West Berliners that were held in the Soviet sector and the hostile mob in and around the building—the Assembly refused to be intimidated and voted strongly to accept this proposition. There followed one of the most ugly scenes in Berlin since the early days of Nazism. Communist thugs, some of them well known as former Nazis, assaulted the non-Communist members of the City Assembly as they emerged from the building. Their especial targets were the members of the Social Democratic Party. One Social Democrat Assembly woman, Jeannette Wolff, was singled out to be beaten up; and the fact that she had been in a Nazi concentration camp and had suffered a similar fate only pointed out the parallels. The Soviet Zone police stood blandly by, often aiding the Communist gangs of hooligans. "That's the car of that criminal Neumann," one was heard to say, indicating the chairman of the Berlin Social Democrats. Another gang of Communists struggled to overturn the cars of some Liberal Democrats. The mob surged back and forth for several hours before all the non-Communist Assembly members got away in the deplorable event.

Then came the blow which everyone had expected. At one o'clock in the morning of 24th June all rail and road communications between Berlin and the West were cut off. The city was now isolated, and to make matters worse the Soviet authorities cut off the electric power that came from the Soviet Zone to Western sectors also. "Technical difficulties" was the official explanation in each case. It was a very tense situation. Clay responded at once by making a public statement, saying: "Nothing short of war will cause the Allies to withdraw." Bevin, who was on a yacht cruise in the Solent, was fetched by a torpedo boat and rushed in a Navy car to London for a special meeting with the British Cabinet. In Washington, for the first time, the Truman Administration was forced to face the issue of what to do about Berlin if the city were blockaded.

That same afternoon some 80,000 Berliners attended a mass meeting. Franz Neumann, the Chairman of the Berlin S.P.D., who has been mentioned already, started the meeting with a fighting speech: "More than ever the eyes of the world are focused on Berlin. Yesterday the Communists, Grotewohl and Pieck, following the model of Hitler and the example of Prague, tried to seize power in Berlin by terror." This was a clear reference to the previous day's riots at the City Hall. "But they miscalculated. . . . Berlin will remain free; it will never become Communist."

But more important for the moment than even the city's morale—although that always had to be decisive—were the practical problems of stocks within the city and how they could be replaced. The Western Powers had to solve the problem of keeping alive 2,500,000 people who would have to live on reserve stocks and whatever could be supplied by air. An assessment of the situation showed that there was sufficient food for thirty-five days and enough coal for forty-five. It was also estimated that the Americans and British (for the French contribution was negligible) would need to carry out a daily airlift of 4,500 tons in order to maintain the civilian population and their occupation forces. It was a very formidable task.

The city was full of rumours—that the Western Powers were leaving, that there would be widespread epidemics because of the difficulty of disposing of sewerage and that it would be impossible to maintain civil government. The Soviet controlled news agencies exploited to the full any signs of weakness in the Western Press or defeatist remarks by Western politicians. A wave of fear was also caused when a barrage balloon was seen to be flying in the Soviet sector of the city, and there was a sense of relief when it was lowered following a vigorous protest by the British Air Force authorities.

It was a testing time for everybody—those in Washington and London no less than those in Berlin. The slightest sign of weakening resolution could have led to a collapse of the Western position in Berlin. Broadly, there were three schools of thought in Anglo-American circles. First, there were those who considered that the Western position was indefensible in the long run and that the facts of geography compelled the Americans, British and French to reach a compromise with the Russians. At the other extreme, there was the view that a resolute display by the Western Powers, with an armoured column driving up the Helmstedt autobahn, would compel the Russians to reconsider their attitude. This opinion was based on the belief that Stalin was not prepared to embark upon a major war involving the United States that still retained the monopoly of nuclear weapons. In between, there were groups who claimed to combine prudence and determination and who believed that the city should be supplied by air if such a course were practicable.

Clay, despite his earlier feeling shown in his telegram of 5th

March that the Soviet Union was ready to contemplate war, now appears to have believed that a display of force at the zonal frontier post might result in the lifting of the blockade. He wished to try it and sought instructions from Washington while he prepared at the same time for the maximum airlift of supplies. There has been subsequent dispute as to the origin of the airlift, and Attlee stated later that the idea began with a British R.A.F. officer. Clay states that he also had been considering the idea for some time, ever since the hold-up by the Soviet zonal guards of the military trains.

The Truman Administration in Washington was in considerable doubt and was deeply concerned by the dangers implicit in any attempt to call the Soviet "bluff" as it was termed. The British Cabinet at its meeting on 25th June came to the same view, although Aneurin Bevan, one of its supposedly most left-wing members, vigorously supported Clay's idea of an armoured column and clashed with the much more cautious Ernest Bevin.

While the various factors were being weighed, Clay and Robertson, his British opposite number, took the initial decision to start the airlift on 25th June. There is a story of Clay telephoning General Curtis Le May, Commander of the U.S. Air Forces in Europe, on that day (Clay himself puts the call a day earlier although other sources give 25th June as the day). "Curt," said Clay, "can you transport coal by air?"

There was a surprised pause at the other end of the line, and then General Le May replied, "Excuse me, General, would you mind repeating that question?"

The United States transport aircraft in the European theatre were limited, being all C-47s, with a load-carrying capacity of less than three tons, and the R.A.F. had even fewer aircraft. The French Government indicated that it would not be supplying any aircraft. Clay and Robertson both considered if an airlift by these aircraft could be demonstrated as a success, it would be possible to secure their reinforcement by available aircraft in other parts of the world at that moment.

On 26th June Bevin issued a statement in London firmly denying rumours that had been put about by Soviet sources implying that Britain was reconsidering her position. "This report is completely untrue," said the official Foreign Office announcement, "and is very far from representing the [British] Government's real attitude. The statement that we intend to stay in Berlin holds good. The opinion of the whole world will condemn the ruthless attempt by the Soviet Government to create a state of siege in Berlin and so, by starving the helpless civilian population, to secure political advantages at the expense of the other Allied Powers." That same day Churchill in a speech to a Conservative Party rally at Luton Hoo, Bedfordshire, was even more forthright. "This raises issues as grave as those we now know were at stake at Munich ten years ago," he declared. "There can be no doubt," he went on at a later stage in his speech, "that the Communist Government of Russia has made up its mind to drive us and all the other Allies out and turn the Russian Zone in Germany into one of its satellite states."

The Soviet answer, confirming Churchill's view, was given also on 26th June through the Communist mouthpiece in the Russian Zone, Wilhelm Pieck, who was Chairman of the Russian sponsored Socialist Unity Party. "The Berlin crisis," said Pieck, "can be settled only when the Western Allies leave Berlin."

Over the week-end Western policy began to clarify as the confidence in the airlift seemed to grow, although its potentialities remained unrealised. Truman authorised that the airlift should be put on a full-scale organised basis and that U.S. aircraft in other theatres should be used to reinforce it. He also approved a proposal to send two B-29 bomber squadrons to Germany, armed with nuclear weapons, to strengthen the Western position. This was a sombre threat to the Russians and an indication of what might happen if Stalin pressed matters too far. Immediately, aircraft from as far afield as Alaska and the Caribbean were reported to be heading for Germany. A vivid account of the situation was given by Major Edward Willerford of the U.S. Army Air Forces: "Along about 29th June we had a big staff meeting. I knew the C-54s [Skymasters] were coming in from all over the world. When we got to the point in the meeting where it was necessary to make a forecast on our potential performance, I was ready. General Smith called on me. I stood up and said: 'I estimate by 20th June we'll be flying in 1,500 tons every twenty-four hours.' I looked around proudly and everyone was studying me in consternation. You could read it on their faces: 'Poor old Willerford is gone in the head. Grab the strait-jacket, boys, before he gets violent.' For, you see, that day by straining ourselves black in the face we'd hauled in 384 tons, to quadruple that amount in a little over two weeks . . . looking back now seemed insane. . . . Anyway, if you run across anyone in the theatre who tells you he knew we could do it all the time, pass him up. We didn't know the answers all the time. We kind of astounded ourselves."

On 30th June Ernest Bevin made the strongest official statement so far by any Western leader in a speech in the House of Commons. Amidst cheers, this ponderous, staunch figure read a measured passage, approved by the British Labour Government, pledging that Britain would maintain her position in Berlin. "We recognise that as a result of these decisions," he went on, "a grave situation might arise. Should such a situation arise, we shall have to ask the House to face it. His Majesty's Government and our Western Allies can see no alternative between that and surrender, and none of us can accept surrender."

Three days later the Western Powers had final confirmation of the major development that had led the Soviet authorities to make the decision to blockade Berlin. A desultory correspondence between Robertson and Sokolovsky had given the British Military Governor the opportunity to seek an interview with the Russians. Somewhat reluctantly Clay and Koenig, the French Military Governor, agreed to accompany Robertson to Sokolovsky's headquarters near Potsdam. Sokolovsky greeted them politely but coldly. Robertson, who acted as spokesman, explained that the Western Powers regretted the deterioration in relations and expressed a hope that they could all reach a satisfactory settlement on the currency issue that had led to bitter relations. Clay, in his memoirs, described what happened next: "Sokolovsky interrupted to state blandly that the technical difficulties would continue until we had abandoned our plans for West German Government."

Robertson and Clay both confirmed that the currency issue, later given by the Soviet authorities as the official reason for imposing the Berlin blockade, never arose at this meeting on 3rd July. The Russians were clearly hoping to force the Western Powers out of Berlin by the winter.[1] They then hoped to seal off the Soviet Zone into a separate German state.

As the airlift mounted and aircraft followed each other in a quickening stream from American and British bases in West Germany into the West Berlin airports of Templehof and Gatow, the

---

[1] The Russian view was echoed by the London *New Statesman and Nation*, which stated on 10th July: "Every expert knows that aircraft, despite their immense psychological effect, cannot be relied upon to provision Berlin in the winter months."

diplomatic activity shifted to Moscow, Washington and London. On 6th July the ambassadors of the Western Powers delivered a protest to the Soviet Government. This was answered in a Russian note of 14th July. The formal excuse for the blockade was now given as the currency problem and not as it had been stated by Sokolovsky at Potsdam. The Russian note went on to state that it had no objections to negotiations but that they could not be limited to Berlin nor was the Soviet Union prepared to precede any such negotiations by lifting the blockade.

On 17th July the Western Powers took another very significant step. Sixty U.S. B-29 Superfortresses, similar to those that had been sent to West Germany and known to be carriers of the nuclear deterrent, arrived in Britain. The decision to send them followed an offer by Bevin on behalf of the British Labour Government to make available suitable airfields to the Americans. Whilst the flight was termed "a routine training mission," its significance was considerable and it led to the establishment of the first U.S. Strategic Air Command Base in Britain.

The Western Powers now sought to take the diplomatic initiative and their representatives in Moscow asked on 30th July for an interview with Stalin and Molotov. The American Ambassador, Walter Bedell Smith, who had been Eisenhower's Chief of Staff in the war, acted as the chief Western spokesman. At first, the Western delegates were rebuffed, being told that Molotov had started his vacation. However, this policy was reversed quickly, and they saw Molotov on 31st July and Stalin on 2nd August. Whereas Molotov was wooden, Stalin, as so often in the past, played the role of the avuncular and amenable leader. He explained that he wanted concessions in West Germany, including a Soviet voice in the control of the Ruhr. Pending these discussions he wanted the London decision on the formation of a separate West German state to be held up. He also offered to lift the Berlin blockade if the Soviet Zone *Ostmark* were accepted as the currency for all Berlin. At this point, Stalin appeared to be ready to accept the separate West German state. In the course of the talks Stalin and Molotov also maintained that the Western Powers had forfeited all rights in Berlin.

The Western Powers were still most anxious to reach an agreement and the talks continued with Molotov alone. But difficulties soon arose as Molotov, on his own, reverted to his intransigent role and, unlike Stalin, he continually sought the abandonment of the

West German state as the condition for lifting the blockade. It was a long drawn out negotiation. After several meetings with Molotov and a final meeting with Stalin on 23rd August, followed by more meetings with Molotov and Vishynsky, a very limited agreement was reached. This amounted to an instruction to the four military governors to agree by 7th September on practical measures for the simultaneous lifting of the blockade and the circulation of the *Ostmark* as the currency for all Berlin. The major problem of this directive was to be the terms under which the *Ostmark* was to be controlled—as the bank which issued it was to come under a four-power financial commission—and the talks by military governors soon broke down upon this issue.

Meanwhile the airlift was still growing and exceeding 4,000 tons daily. Of this tonnage, the Americans were contributing about two-thirds and the British the rest. The strain on pilots and ground crews was beginning to tell, but the possibility of being able to keep Berlin supplied throughout the winter was becoming a probability. The Berliners themselves were under constant pressures from Soviet propaganda and even by physical intimidation. The kidnapping during the late hours of the night of people with known anti-Communist views from the Western sectors also became a common practice. It added considerably to the macabre tensions of life in West Berlin. The City Assembly was also forced to leave the Soviet sector. The organised Communist hooliganism and intimidation which had begun with the scenes on 23rd June had continued. By the end of August it had become impossible for the Assembly to meet without bands of Communists rushing to demonstrate against the arriving Assembly men. A final effort to meet was made on 6th September, but Communist demonstrators using force occupied the official chamber, beat up reporters and drove out the non-Communist Assembly men. When the hall had been cleared of all but Communists, the demonstrators withdrew, leaving only the pro-Communist members in possession, who promptly voted Communist-sponsored measures.

The following day, a mass meeting was announced by the pro-democratic forces in Berlin to be held on 9th September in the square in front of the burned-out Reichstag. There had been many mass meetings in Berlin during this period, some in the same square, but Berliners still talk of this particular meeting as "The Reichstag meeting." It nearly did not take place as the British authorities, in particular, were nervous of the Soviet reaction to a gathering so close to the sector boundary. There is a story that Ernst Reuter, the Social Democrat Mayor of Berlin, whose election had been vetoed by the Russians, and Franz Neumann, the chairman of the S.P.D., discussed who should make the main speech. Neumann proposed Reuter. "Oh, no, Franz," Reuter replied, "I think it should be you. You will look much better in the part of the democratic martyr."

Neumann opened the huge meeting of at least 250,000 people with a minute's silence in memory of the victims of Nazi totalitarianism. "These people," he declared, "gave their lives in the cause of freedom. The concentration camps are still the same, but now the hammer and sickle flies over them instead of the swastika." Reuter appealed to the world to come to Berlin's aid. There were very few dry eyes in the vast gathering as speaker after speaker addressed it. By the end the crowd was in a frenzy. Whilst some thousands went off with Neumann to present a petition to American and British officers, many more thousands milled around the Brandenburg Gate which lay a few yards inside the Soviet sector. A youth climbed up to the top of this symbolic structure and seized the Soviet flag. A struggle followed between Berliners who were trying to burn the flag and the Russian soldiers who were trying to recover it. The Russians fired into the crowd, killing one person and wounding several others. Stones were thrown and cars were overturned. Fortunately British troops intervened to separate the two sides or matters could have become very much worse. The Communist commentary was given in *Neues Deutschland* under the heading "ONCE AGAIN REICHSTAG ARSONISTS." The article went on to accuse those who had taken part in the mass meeting as trying "to divide Berlin" and wanting a new war. "These criminal fools are now trying belatedly to win Adolf Hitler's war against the Soviet Union and want to enslave our people under the fascist yoke again . . . there are again Nazis and open warmongers in Berlin."

The Reichstag meeting and the breakdown of the talks between the Military Governors on the issue of the Four-Power Financial Commission to supervise the Soviet-controlled bank, that was to issue the *Ostmark*, meant the division of the city for all practical purposes although there still remained freedom of movement amongst the various sectors. The mood of the Reichstag meeting also made it clear that the people of Berlin were ready and determined to face the privations of winter in the blockaded city.

As the airlift thundered on and adapted itself to winter conditions, the Western Powers brought the Berlin issue before the
United Nations. This achieved little at first, but a counter-blockade
by the Western Powers, imposed at the end of July, 1948, stopping
the transit of all goods by rail into the Soviet Zone, began to be
increasingly effective. Various moves by neutrals in the U.N. broke
down, but the astonishing success of the airlift, which no one had
expected at the beginning, was placing the Soviet Union in a very
unfavourable posture before the world. By the turn of the year, the
Western Powers were actually on the political offensive.

The first sign that Stalin had realised that he could not force the
Western Powers out of Berlin short of war, which he was not prepared to countenance in the face of American nuclear weapons,
was an interview given by him to an American journalist on 27th
January, 1949. In this interview, the Soviet leader said he was
prepared to lift the Berlin blockade if the Western Powers were
ready to hold up the creation of the separate West German State,
pending a meeting of the Council of Foreign Ministers. Very significantly, he made no mention of the currency question.

Acheson, by now Secretary of State in succession to Marshall,
decided to follow this up. On his instructions, the American
Ambassador at the United Nations very casually asked Malik, the
Soviet delegate, on 15th February if the omission of the currency
issue had been accidental. Malik was nonplussed. He was in no
position to answer. Exactly a month later, on 15th March, he spoke
to the American Ambassador and said that the omission was "not
accidental."

The dropping of the currency issue represented a major victory
for the Allies and it showed again where the real point of difference
had arisen. Berlin had only been used as the lever by Stalin to stop
the establishment of the West German State. Truman and Acheson
authorised their U.N. Ambassador to undertake further inquiries
from Malik of the precise circumstances in which Stalin would be
prepared to lift the blockade. The negotiations were so secret that
even the British and French Governments were excluded at first,
and Clay in Berlin, somewhat to his chagrin, only learned about
them weeks later from the newspapers. Finally, Stalin let it be
known that if a definite date were set for the Council of Foreign
Ministers, the blockade could be lifted reciprocally and in advance
of the meeting. Therefore, a full meeting amongst the representatives
of the United States, Britain, France and the Soviet Union was held

on 5th May, after which it was announced that the blockade would be lifted on 12th May and that there would be a meeting of the Council of Foreign Ministers on 23rd May to consider the German question.

It was victory for the West. The lifting of the blockade was accompanied by many moving scenes. The first trains and trucks to reach Berlin were decked in flowers. A special meeting of the City Assembly honoured the Western Military Governors, in particular Clay, who had been so steady and staunch. The square outside Templehof airport was renamed Platz der Luftbrücke— Airlift Square. Nearly 200,000 sorties had been flown by American and British aircraft, carrying over a million and a half tons of freight. The biggest lift in one day had exceeded 12,000 tons— something which would have been inconceivable ten and a half months before. Many aircraft had crashed and forty-eight American and British airmen had died.

When they had embarked upon the venture of supplying Berlin by air, the American and British Governments—for France's contribution was negligible—had been in a quandary. The airlift was an idea that developed. It called for remarkable precision of planning and execution, yet it was worth the enormous effort and expense involved because it put off the necessity for challenging Stalin by a confrontation of ground forces in circumstances that would have exposed the lamentable weakness of the Western Powers, whose only real weapon of strength was the ultimate one— the atom bomb.[1] Stalin himself had assumed that Berlin would fall into his control in the course of a few weeks. When the Western representatives had seen him and Molotov the August before, they had been in a noticeably good humour and "with good reason" as one of the Western Ambassadors remarked later. They thought they were winning. But once the airlift had overcome the weather conditions of the winter of 1948-9, the Soviet leader was defeated. He had to make the choice of cutting his losses or of going much further and resorting to all-out war, and this latter he could not do. Clay has blamed himself in retrospect for not having secured in writing the basic access agreement to West Berlin back in 1945. Certainly his failure so to do was extraordinarily naïve, but it was understandable in the climate of American thinking immediately

[1] There is a striking parallel between the preponderance of American strength in "conventional forces" in the area in the case of the 1962 Cuba crisis and the Berlin situation of 1948.

before Potsdam; the true responsibility was carried by others higher up at the time.

The manifest resolution of the Berliners—Stalin's best hope was that Berlin's morale would fail—left the Russians with little bargaining power. Stalin decided, therefore, to make another attempt to achieve the domination of a united Germany by political manœuvre.

The period that began with the Prague coup and which included the Berlin blockade, ended with the signing of the North Atlantic Treaty in Washington, on 4th April, 1949. It is important to make clear briefly the sequence of events and why they took place.

Bevin's initiative in 1948 in establishing Western union, as stated already by implication, was intended only as the forerunner of the wider defence arrangement. Accordingly, with much secrecy, he dispatched Gladwyn Jebb to the United States to explain his intentions. Jebb found that the Americans were also thinking along similar lines. Bevin, with his shrewd sense of politics, invoked the aid of the Canadian Government. Thus the ink was scarcely dry upon the Brussels Treaty, signed on 17th March, 1948, before talks were proceeding at various levels throughout the prospective signatories of the wider Treaty which would include the United States. The United States Administration, seized of the urgency and gravity of the situation, decided to prepare the ground for Congressional support and, on 11th April, Marshall began exploratory talks with Senators Vandenberg and Connally on the security problems of the Western Powers. St. Laurent, the Prime Minister of Canada, then made the formal proposition speaking in the Canadian Parliament, on 28th April, that there should be a single mutual defence system, including and superseding the Western Union system. In the meanwhile, Vandenberg expressed to Marshall his readiness to promote a resolution in the American Senate recommending "the association of the United States . . . with such regional and other collective arrangements . . . contributing to the maintenance of peace by making clear its determination to exercise the right of individual or collective self-defence under Article 51 [of the United Nations Charter] should any armed attack occur affecting its national security." Bevin's and Marshall's ideas were advancing rapidly, but whilst the plans for the wider treaty went forward, Britain took the initiative in Europe by calling together the Western Union's Defence Ministers and Chiefs of Staff on 30th

April. Vandenberg's resolution passed the American Senate on
11th June, actually before the blockade of Berlin had begun, thus
clearing the way for the Truman Administration to open formal
talks with other countries.

The aircraft on the Berlin airlift were only beginning their great
build-up when the representatives of the five Western Union Powers,
Canada and the United States assembled in Washington on 6th
July, 1948. It was not surprising with the background of the critical
Berlin situation that progress was extremely rapid. On 9th September the Washington Conference ended, having examined the com-
plexity of implications of an integrated Western military alliance
with a common Commander-in-Chief. The Washington Conference
passed a recommendation to the Governments concerned that there
should be a treaty expressing their determination to resist aggression
in a defined area. The conference went further by suggesting that the
proposed treaty should be more than military and that it should promote "the stability and well-being of the North Atlantic peoples."
During the Washington talks it had also emerged that the concept of
a treaty including only the five signatories of the Western Union
(Britain, France, Belgium, Holland and Luxembourg) and the two
North American Powers, the U.S.A. and Canada, was not enough.
Approaches were, therefore, made to Iceland, Norway, Denmark,
Portugal and Italy, all of whom eventually joined, and to Eire and
Sweden, who refused to join.

Talks for the actual drafting of the North Atlantic Treaty commenced on 11th December and, after the essential consultations
amongst governments, the text of the treaty was finally published
on 18th March, 1949, two weeks before it was due for signature.

The crux of the North Atlantic Treaty was Article 5. This stated:

The Parties agree that an armed attack against one or more of
them in Europe or North America shall be considered an attack
against them all; and consequently they agree that, if such an
armed attack occurs, each of them, in exercise of the right of the
individual or collective self-defence recognised by Article 51 of
the Charter of the United Nations, will assist the Party or Parties
so attacked by taking forthwith, individually and in concert with
other Parties, such action as it deems necessary, including the
use of armed force, to restore and to maintain the security of the
North Atlantic area.

Any such armed attack and all measures taken as a result

thereof shall immediately be reported to the Security Council. Such measures shall be terminated when the Security Council has taken measures necessary to restore and to maintain international peace and security.

The Russian reaction was naturally sharp and bitter. Stalin had already decided to withdraw from his Berlin posture, which had only made easier the talks of the protagonists of the wider North Atlantic alliance; but his earlier inflexibility had made it too late for him to affect the outcome of the negotiations. He was facing a group of Western Powers that were by now thoroughly aroused and alarmed by his aggressive European policies.

As for Bevin, as he journeyed to Washington for the formal signing of the Treaty, he knew that he had succeeded in the most important aim which he had set himself during his years as British Secretary of State for Foreign Affairs. Others who have evaluated his career and his record in office have placed the emphasis on different achievements. Attlee, who was his personal friend over many years, ever since Bevin's resounding speech at the 1935 Brighton Labour Party Conference had brought about the downfall of Lansbury and the election of Attlee as Labour leader, has said that "Ernest Bevin's greatest achievement was Marshall Aid." Certainly the chain of events and proposals to the Marshall Plan, and Bevin's leadership in the European response to it, were decisive actions in the decisive year of the Cold War. But the North Atlantic Treaty Organisation was unquestionably his crowning achievement.[1]

Having been thwarted in Europe, Stalin now looked eastwards. And from Siberia there came the roll of atomic thunder. The Soviet Union exploded her first nuclear weapon four years ahead of Western expectations.

---

[1] The men who signed the North Atlantic Treaty in Washington on 4th April, 1949, should be recorded. They were the Foreign Ministers of Belgium (Paul-Henri Spaak), Canada (Lester B. Pearson), Denmark (Gustave Rasmussen), France (Robert Schuman), Iceland (Bjarni Benediktsson), Italy (Carlo Sforza), Luxembourg (Joseph Beech), Holland (D. U. Stikker), Norway (Halvard Lange), Portugal (José Caerrio de Matta), United Kingdom (Ernest Bevin), United States (Dean Acheson). The treaty was ratified by all the parliaments of the member countries within five months. Greece and Turkey joined in February, 1952.

CHAPTER 15

CHINA STANDS UP

Let China sleep. When it wakes, the world will be sorry.   *Napoleon*

The People's Republic of China was proclaimed by Mao Tse-tung in Peking on 1st October, 1949. He stood on the balcony of the Tien An Men—the Gate of Heavenly Peace—and looked down on the assembled thousands in his hour of victory, a commanding, dignified figure in a plain grey uniform unadorned by any distinctions of rank. There was spontaneous dancing for many nights in the streets outside the Tien An Men which—despite its name—used to be a place for public executions in earlier days. There have not been many scenes like it since the fall of the Bastille.

The background to the Chinese Communist revolution was very different from the Russian revolution. The struggle for power inside China had extended over nearly thirty years. Long before their victory was achieved, the Chinese Communists had become a state within a state and a much more formidable force in their own right than Lenin's inexperienced and motley band of Bolsheviks at their own moment of victory. Furthermore, by October 1949 the Chinese Communists were genuinely a popular movement. They would certainly have won a free election at that moment in time. Again it was a different situation from that of Russia in late 1917 when Lenin suffered a humiliating defeat at the polls after his own revolution.

The sequence of events in China leading up to October 1949 is significant in its implications for all that has followed. The Chinese Communist Party was founded in 1921, almost simultaneously in Paris and Shanghai. It owed its inspiration to the Russian revolution and it was, from the first, under the influence of the Soviet Communist Party. Amongst the founder members of the Shanghai group was Mao Tse-tung, the son of a rich peasant, who had become a young literary intellectual, whilst always retaining his sense of identification with the problems of rural China. In the French group was a cultivated young man of Mandarin background named Chou En-Lai.

China in those early 1920s was a land of fantasy, confusion and paradox. The Manchu dynasty had been swept away in the revolution of 1911. The prophet of the 1911 revolution and founder of the Kuomintang, Sun Yat-sen, was a man of strong nationalist views with a progressive liberal social policy, akin to the welfare state. The Western Powers, many of whom had extreme reactionary commercial and political interests in China, regarded Sun as an impractical visionary, and as he never really showed himself capable of administering the huge country, he was forced to retreat on Canton. After having his appeals for help turned down by the Western Powers, Sun eventually sought aid from the newly-emergent Soviet Union that had sent an envoy named Joffe to Peking, still the nominal capital of China. Joffe and Sun held talks that ended with a joint statement on 26th January, 1923, agreeing to Soviet help for Sun Yat-sen's Canton Government. A Soviet mission arrived in Canton shortly afterwards led by Mikhail Borodin as chief political adviser, together with two military advisers, Galen (who was also known as Blücher) and Kisenko.[1]

Borodin was a man of great personality. He had been trained as an engineer and had spent part of his life in the United States. He had also acted for a period as Soviet adviser to Kemal Ataturk. Borodin gave an illuminating interview to the *Manchester Guardian* correspondent in which he described his mission: " I came to Canton on a voyage of discovery and found Sun Yat-sen in very great difficulties. I took off my coat and settled down to help him in that horrible tropical climate, with insects of a size and ferocity I had never known in Russia, no snow, no winter and the sweat dripping on my papers. Horrible, it was loathsome and now Dr. Sun is being proved to have been not such a lunatic after all; you people turn round and curse me for doing what you might have done yourselves. It is not what you call sportsmanlike."

Borodin's main mission was to turn the Kuomintang into the cadre of the Chinese revolution that was to come. He persuaded Sun to set up a military academy at Whampoa, and its first Commandant was Chiang Kai-shek, who was sent to the Soviet Union

---

[1] Borodin and Galen were later to be amongst the victims of Stalin's purges. Borodin ended his life in a prison camp. Galen, who rose to be a Marshal of the Soviet Union and Commander-in-Chief in the Far East, was shot.

for training. The Kuomintang was also reorganised upon Communist party lines, with a Central Committee and political and military advisers guiding the civil administration and the army. Individual members of the Chinese Communist Party, aided by Borodin, quickly assumed positions of influence in Sun's Government.[1] Considering that the party then numbered only about 300, its achievement in infiltration was considerable and, by 1924, the Central Committee of the Kuomintang contained a number of Communists, including Mao Tse-tung. The strengthening grip of the Communists created a reaction amongst the non-Communists in the Kuomintang—many of them being rich landlords or businessmen who had been attracted to the party more by Sun Yat-sen's Chinese nationalism than by his social policies. They saw in the activities of the Chinese Communists, and in Borodin's influence over Sun Yat-sen, a threat to their own financial interests. As long as Sun was alive, it was possible to keep the right and left wings of the Kuomintang together, but he died in 1925 whilst on a visit to Peking. His successor became Chiang Kai-shek, the Commandant of Whampoa, who, despite his Soviet training, was no Communist. For a time, Chiang was also prepared to use Borodin and his mission, as long as they served his interests. However, it was soon clear that the coalition could not survive. Chiang proceeded to advance northwards to extend his area of suzerainty in 1926. Overtly, this struggle was between the Nationalist—or Kuomintang—Government based upon Canton and a weak Peking Government. In reality it was more a matter of Chiang asserting the authority of the Kuomintang régime over local warlords. The Kuomintang quickly established control over a wide area through local administrations answerable to it. But in the wake of Chiang's advancing troops, came Communist cadres inflaming the countryside against landlordism, feudal privilege and ancient customs. In Chiang's absence on his northern expedition, the Communists also forced the Kuomintang Central Committee to adopt the principle of collective leadership with Chiang Kai-shek in a subordinate position. Again in Chiang's absence they made the Kuomintang move the headquarters of the régime to Wuhan where the Communists were strong, whereas Chiang preferred Nanchang.

Sensing his danger, Chiang was forced to decide. In April 1927 he struck at the Communists, arresting and putting to death as

[1] This policy was known as the *yung-kung* period ("Let the Communists join as individuals").

many as he could seize. The survivors of the " April 12 Massacre "
fled to Russia or went underground and staged a series of ineffectual
uprisings in the cities where they believed themselves strong. Mao
Tse-tung attempted unsuccessfully to lead a peasants' uprising in
Wuhan later that year, against Russian advice, because it was a
rural area; and he was dismissed from the Chinese politbureau for
his activities, being accused of organising " a rifle movement."

The truth was that the Chinese Communists, under Borodin's
guidance, had overreached themselves disastrously. The conditions propitious to achieving power by " salami tactics," existing
in Eastern Europe from 1945 onwards, did not exist in the China
of 1927. There was no Soviet Red Army in the background to cast
its awesome shadows of overwhelming force. On Stalin's instructions
—for Borodin was only Stalin's agent—the Chinese Communists
had sought to achieve power through " co-existence " both with the
forces of nationalist capitalism and of social reform and had been
ignominiously routed in a trial of strength. It was an experience
that was to bite deeply into the memories of many survivors in
the Chinese Communist Party.

Eventually, Mao Tse-tung himself made his way with a few
followers to the mountain fortress of Chingkangshan where he
linked up, in time, with a Communist military force under Chu Teh
that had fought its way up from Nanchang. Cut off from the
outside world, Mao now proceeded to establish a small Communist-
controlled State, in the Chingkangshan area, implementing a policy
of land redistribution amongst the peasants as his principal political
programme. Several major attempts by Chiang Kai-shek failed to
dislodge Mao, until Chiang decided to end the stalemate by concentrating an overwhelming force against him in early 1934. An army
of 900,000 men in all was assembled by the Kuomintang; and in
the face of it Mao decided that his only course was to evacuate his
stronghold. It was a bold, desperate decision.

On 16th October, 1934, the Communists started their famous
" Long March " taking what equipment and supplies they could.
They began by marching south-west to the farthermost frontiers of
China. The local military governors and warlords that they met
on the way put up varying resistance. The Communists then
turned north and, skirting the borders of Tibet, they finally reached
the northern part of Shensi province, where they joined forces with
local Communist guerrillas. The " Long March " began with some
100,000 people. When it ended, on 25th October, 1935, the

numbers had fallen to 27,000. The surviving men and women had travelled nearly 6000 miles. Their average daily march had been 24 miles. They had fought numerous major battles and countless small engagements. They had crossed several mountain ranges and twenty-four rivers, including the wild gorges in the upper reaches of the Yangtze. It was during the " Long March " that Mao really stood out as a leader of men. The privations in adversity that he overcame, and his manner of doing so, evoked an extraordinary loyalty from his dwindling force—the sign of a great commander. It must be acknowledged that his achievement was without many parallels in recorded history and even the marches of Xenephon and Hannibal do not surpass his feat. In Yenan, Mao established a new Communist State, far from the reach of Chiang Kai-shek who was now facing threats from the Japanese in the north and east.

The smouldering Sino-Japanese war soon began in earnest—the War of Resistance against Japan, as it is known in China. During the long drawn out conflict between Japan and China, the Communists again proposed co-operation with Chiang. Because of the growing Japanese threat, Chiang was in no position to refuse. He even agreed, reluctantly, to recognising the Communist Administration in the Shensi-Kansu border region. The Communists were soon to show themselves as much more successful in their guerrilla attacks upon the Japanese than Chiang Kai-shek with his more orthodox and desultory military campaigns. Thus Mao now had a second issue, in addition to land reform, upon which to attract support to the Communists—his more effective challenge to the Japanese attempt to subjugate China.

Telescoping and simplifying the sequence of events, ten years were to be spent broadly like this. The Chinese Communists gradually strengthened their position in their autonomous state and behind the main Japanese lines of advance. During this period, Mao Tse-tung also established the Chinese Communist legend for incorruptibility, the third important factor in winning support away from Chiang Kai-shek.[1] Simultaneously, Chiang's area of

[1] Mao imposed three simple rules: prompt obedience to orders, no confiscation whatever from the poor peasantry, prompt delivery to the government, for disposal, of goods confiscated from the landlords. Other rules were laid down and put to music, so the Communists learned them as they sang, including, "Be courteous and polite; return all borrowed articles; pay for all articles purchased and be honest in all transactions with the peasants."

effective control was reduced steadily by the Japanese as he was driven out, first from the coastal cities and then from his own capital of Nanking, eventually falling back on Chungking.

By the time that Japan sued for peace in August 1945, after the use by the Americans of atomic bombs at Hiroshima and Nagasaki, the Chinese Communists had become established as a major political and military force and a rival government. They now had at least 750,000 regular troops at their disposal and then claimed the support of an armed militia of more than two million. What is more, they had done it almost entirely without Soviet aid, relying upon captured Japanese weapons to arm themselves. It soon became a race between Chiang's and Mao's forces to re-occupy the country in the wake of the retreating Japanese.

It was at this point that the United States Government became involved in the internal struggle for power in China. It was to have far-reaching consequences for Sino-American relations. The dilemma that faced President Truman at the time was clear, yet difficult. Obviously he could not permit the Japanese forces to remain in China merely to prevent the Chinese Communists from taking over parts of the country. Yet, after VJ-Day, it had become politically impossible for Truman to deploy American occupation troops on a sufficient scale and for an indefinite period in China. The only and quite proper alternative was to provide transport facilities for Chiang Kai-shek's forces to take over from the defeated Japanese. Yet there was also the reality of the internal Chinese situation and almost the American Administration's first action was to bring pressure on Chiang Kai-shek to invite Mao Tse-tung to Chungking for talks with a view to securing some form of arrangement. After insisting upon assurances about his own safety, Mao accepted Chiang's invitation and flew down in the American Ambassador's aircraft from Yenan on 28th August, 1945. The first confrontation between the two men since the far-off days of 1927, was a dramatic moment, both acting with cold formality and urbanity.

The Chiang-MaoTse-tung talks proceeded surprisingly satisfactorily. The reason was that Mao knew he was not yet in a strong enough position to take over the vast, ramshackle country; he had already proposed yet another coalition, and it was very much in his interest to secure an arrangement. After forty days of negotiations, a Kuomintang-Communist agreement was signed, resolving to avoid civil war and to build a free and independent China. Chiang and Mao also signed a pact pledging their desire for peace and unity. As might be expected, these amicable expressions carried little weight in the field where the real struggle for position was going on and fighting between Kuomintang and Communist forces was soon taking place in eleven provinces.

President Truman realised he had to do something much more dramatic to prevent total civil war. After a disagreement with the American Ambassador to Chungking, Hurley, he decided to send a special mission to China in an effort to rescue the situation. As an indication of the importance he attached to the solution of the China problem, Truman asked George Marshall, lately retired as United States Chief of Staff at the height of his great prestige, to lead the mission with the rank of Special Ambassador. Marshall's terms of reference were sent out in a document entitled *U.S. Policy Towards China*. In brief, the basic aim of American policy was a united China under what Truman conceived to be a democratic administration and not the single party state which Chiang's area of control had clearly become. Marshall was instructed to try to bring about a cease-fire between the Communists and Kuomintang and, in due course, to assist in the transportation of Chiang's troops to Manchuria to take over from Russian occupation troops that had invaded China in accordance with the Yalta agreement. Truman wanted Marshall to promote a national conference of the representatives of the major political forces in China, to bring about the country's unification. At this point, Marshall was also authorised to discuss frankly with the Chinese leaders the prospects of American financial, technical and military aid in establishing the new, united, democratic and independent China. The Americans had made a generous and magnanimous proposal. Its fault was that it was based upon the fallacy that permanent co-operation within a constitutional framework was possible between the Communists and non-Communists.

Marshall was appointed to his difficult mission on 27th November, 1945. He lost no time in preparing himself for his immense task. He left Washington by air on 15th December, having had virtually no time to enjoy his retirement from the U.S. Army. He found a very confused situation in China upon arrival but he made such good progress that he persuaded the Communists to accept him as a mediator on 3rd January, 1946. Again, on his initiative, a political consultative conference, including seven Communist delegates led by Chou En-Lai, met in Chungking from 10th to 31st January, and a cease-fire, brought about largely by Marshall's efforts, was announced on the first day. Furthermore, the political consultative conference ended in complete agreement on a reorganisation of the government on the basis of a coalition and on the appointment of a special committee to review the Draft Constitution.

Truman, sitting in Washington, could have been excused if he had thought that Marshall was transforming the situation. In the early stages, Marshall reported that the Communists were proving much less intractable than the Kuomintang. Marshall made a 3000-mile tour by air, interviewing local commanders to explain to them the truce, and in the course of this journey he saw Mao Tse-tung in his capital of Yenan. So much for the façade of goodwill: the truth again behind the painted lath of words was that both the Kuomintang and Communists were manœuvring as hard as ever for position as against the day when the Russians were going to withdraw from Manchuria and Marshall would go home. They both wanted power, not coalitions or agreements. At the end of March 1946 whilst Marshall was back in the United States for a few days, the Soviet authorities confirmed that all Red Army units would leave Manchuria by the end of April.

Thus the situation in Manchuria also was now ripe for dispute— it was the next major area of potential struggle between the Kuomintang forces and the Communists. Chiang Kai-shek began by detaining Communist members of the internal cease-fire teams in Mukden and arresting others in Peking. The Communists retorted by occupying towns and villages as the Soviet troops left, and they drove out Chiang's forces by force in some instances. Marshall's cease-fire and political agreement reached in January was now proven to be no more durable than the Chiang-Mao talks of the previous autumn and for the same reasons. On 15th April, 1946, Chou En-Lai announced " all-out " hostilities in Manchuria. The Communists took Changchun after fighting with Kuomintang forces and occupied Harbin, the industrial centre in northern Manchuria. Marshall's hurried return from America helped to bring about another truce in Central China but Chiang foolishly refused to consider a similar arrangement in Manchuria, although it was clear that he was not in a position to hold the Communists. Marshall, faithful to his task, even persuaded the Chinese Communists to accept an arrangement whereby the American member of the truce team held the casting vote in the event of a disagreement between the two sides, but again Chiang refused to accept his advice.

It was the Communists' turn to quarrel with Marshall as their strength grew. The situation was not helped by the extensive political lobbying for Chiang taking place in the United States, where demands were growing for " all-out aid " to Chiang Kai-shek. This exacerbated all the Communist suspicions of the American intervention and Mao made a public declaration on 22nd June calling for the Americans to cease military aid to Chiang and to withdraw all American forces in China.

All Russian forces had left Manchuria by midsummer 1946, and the Chinese Communists proceeded formally to set up an administration there. It proved to be the impregnable bastion from which they were shortly to advance to power, and Mao Tse-tung clearly realised the strength of his new situation. Even if Marshall had any hopes of success, in the first instance, these hopes were now disappearing fast as *both* sides had come to believe that they would win if it came to an internal military struggle—Mao from the solid basis of reality, and Chiang Kai-shek amidst his cloudy illusions of grandeur.

By the end of the same summer of 1946, Marshall realised that only a succession of Communist defeats could change the atmosphere as Mao Tse-tung had become implacable in his hostility to both Marshall and Chiang. Chiang Kai-shek, for his part, was maintaining that the Communists never meant to co-operate except as a tactical manœuvre in order to gain time and to gather strength. The desultory tripartite negotiations in Nanking were broken off and then briefly restarted only to break down again. As Truman wrote later in exasperation in his memoirs: " This is the way it goes. Someone makes a proposal which is accepted by the other side with three qualifications. They are then accepted by the other side with three qualifications to each of the first three qualifications. It was an old Chinese way to be sure nothing would happen." Considering the American temperament and their national desire to settle issues of foreign policy decisively and rapidly, it is easy to understand the feelings of depression that descended upon those responsible for American policy in China.

Truman now had no alternative but gradually to fall back upon a policy of giving military and economic aid to Chiang Kai-shek, without committing United States troops to the internal struggle. It was clear that Chiang Kai-shek lacked the administration, resolution and capacity to take advantage of this American help in money and kind—yet there was nothing else that Truman could do. As the policy of American aid developed, naturally so did the hostility of the Communists towards Marshall. The final breach between the parties came on 15th November, 1946, when the Communists boycotted a meeting of the National Assembly in Nanking. Marshall sadly admitted failure in his efforts to bring the Kuomintang and Communists together and returned to the United States on 7th January, 1947. He was already Truman's Secretary of State designate. He had undertaken his thankless China task with extraordinary resolution and integrity. The plain fact was that given the conditions existing in China in 1946, the long background to relations between the Kuomintang and the Communists and the basic beliefs in Marxist-Leninism of Mao Tse-tung and his colleagues, there was never any true prospect of success for Marshall.

Thus Chiang and Mao were left to fight out the civil war to its finish. The Kuomintang were handicapped fatally by corruption and lack of resolution. Chiang himself appeared incapable of providing leadership. Also the Communists had gained immeasurably in strength since the ending of the war. They were soon to gain yet further from American arms shipments to Chiang as many of the Kuomintang generals, with their armies and American equipment intact, went over to the Communists. For a period, in 1947, Chiang's hopes appeared to revive. In his drive northwards, his troops captured Yenan itself, but the Communists recaptured it the following year. A new Land Law was promulgated by the Communists at the end of 1947 for " liberated areas." Its intention was to confiscate the land of all landlords and redistribute it amongst the peasants. This political tactic led to the isolation of the cities held by the Kuomintang, in a countryside where the Communist support truly lay. From this point on, the Kuomintang's effort fell apart in incredible fashion after the loss of Manchuria. A decisive battle was fought at Suchow when, at the end of sixty-five days, Chiang lost nearly all his American equipment. Mao proceeded in two stages. First, he consolidated and built up his strength. Then, in early 1949, he began to advance south. Peking, China's historic capital, surrendered with its forces intact on 31st January, 1949. Nanking, Chiang's own capital, fell in April. Shanghai and Hankow were occupied in May. The rest of the country was soon to follow.

The leadership of the Chinese Communist Party won its struggle for power in a vast ramshackle country and achieved control over more than a fifth of mankind because it identified itself with the poverty-stricken lot of several hundred million Chinese peasants. The Communists had also stood out as good Chinese patriots in the long war against Japan. Chiang Kai-shek and the Kuomintang sought to defend a despot system of feudal landlordism in the countryside. They condoned corruption and exploitation in the cities. And they were defeated ignominiously. The parallel between Mao's policy, which had evoked such a deep response in rural China, and Lenin's slogan of 1917, " Peace, Land, Bread," is striking. Yet the parallel between Mao and Lenin cannot be taken too far. Although Mao Tse-tung was a convinced Communist from his earliest days in the Chinese Communist Party, he was never the cosmopolitan personality in the European world like Lenin. Rather his most striking quality was that he retained his indigenous Chinese mould of thought in his approach to all internal issues and this gave him an understanding of his own people's problems that is not common amongst political leaders whose out-look is fundamentally based upon doctrine.

The cool relationship between the Soviet Union and the Chinese Communists up to the moment of Mao Tse-tung's victory was striking. After the 1927 debacle, there had been little contact between Stalin and Mao's small Chinese Soviet at Chingkangshan. Formal relations between the two parties were restored in the 1930s although Stalin was most careful not to involve himself in China again. For his part, Mao Tse-tung was careful to stress the Chinese Communist Party's alignment with the Soviet Union. Stalin followed his policy of neutrality in the Far East during the war years because he considered himself too fully committed in his struggle against Hitler to risk conflict with Japan. In this period, he also underrated the growing strength of the Chinese Communists and laid all his plans for the future of Sino-Soviet relations with Chiang Kai-shek's administration. The 1945 Sino-Soviet Treaty, signed with Chiang's representative, following upon the Yalta concessions, was made with this end in view. Hurley, the American Ambassador in Chungking, is also on record as having said, after a conversation with Stalin in April 1945, that " he had established that the Chinese Communists were not really Communists and were not supported by the Soviet Government, and that the Russians wanted to establish good relations with the Chinese Government." It is true that Hurley, who was " rather an old-world American figure," to use Churchill's description, was not a perceptive political witness but many others took the same view, and it is possible that Stalin did likewise. At this period, Stalin also believed that the best course open to the Chinese Communists was to enter into a coalition with the Kuomintang. The official Soviet policy was stated thus: " It is no secret that China's progress has hitherto been hampered in no small degree by the disagreements between the Kuomintang and Chinese Communist Party. There are plenty of dubious well-wishers abroad who every now and again raise the cry that civil war in China is inevitable. There is no doubt that such a war would be disastrous to the country which now needs peace above all in order to repair the devastating consequences of the long years of Japanese occupation. All sincere friends of China look forward to closer co-operation between all the progressive and democratic forces of the Chinese people." It should be noted that in expressing this view Stalin was going much further than Mao Tse-tung in his calls for a coalition.

During the period of Soviet occupation in Manchuria and the eventual withdrawal, several charges were made in Kuomintang circles that the Red Army was aiding the Chinese Communists politically and even helping them with arms. There is little evidence to support this view and the Chinese Communists themselves denied it. In fact, the position was quite different: Chiang's administration in parts of Manchuria actually operated under Soviet protection in 1946. During the following year, 1947, Soviet policy in China appeared more to be motivated by general considerations and apprehension at American intentions rather than by specific Communist aims inside China. In January 1948 Vishynsky confirmed that Soviet policy in China was still based upon the principle of non-intervention. Indeed, the first sign of a change in Soviet policy and support for Mao Tse-tung did not come until as late as 10th April, 1949, when *Pravda* gave prominence to a Chinese Communists' statement that in the event of a third world war, they would support the Soviet Union. Even then, Stalin in his caution continued to maintain diplomatic relations with the Kuomintang Government whilst quietly opening Soviet consulates in Communist-held territory.

When Mao proclaimed the new Government in Peking on 1st October, Chou En-Lai handed a copy of the proclamation to the Soviet Consul-General. Next day Stalin broke off relations with Chiang Kai-shek's régime and recognised the new Communist administration. *Pravda* announced the decision on 3rd October.

Roshchin, the former Soviet Ambassador to the Kuomintang, presented his credentials to Mao Tse-tung on 10th October and the first Chinese Communist Ambassador to the Soviet Union did likewise in Moscow on 30th October. A major shift in world balances of power had taken place in the Orient.

The Communist revolution in China confronted the world with a challenge that was comparable in magnitude to the Russian revolution. This was no mere Soviet puppet régime whose leaders had been installed by the Soviet Red Army, as in so many Eastern European countries. The impact upon Asia was inevitable and very far-reaching. As far as the Western Powers were concerned, they were divided. The United States Administration in particular found itself in a difficult situation—her honourable record of good relations with China had ended in mutual bitterness and recrimination. The nation that America had sought to make a Great Power when her true position did not merit it was now aligned irrevocably against the United States. Ernest Bevin, at the British Foreign Office, was particularly determined not to repeat the same mistakes in British policy towards China that had been made towards Soviet Russia in 1917. But his difficulty was that his whole policy was committed to the maintenance of the Western Alliance, in which the special relationship between the United States and Britain still played the guiding role. Thus Bevin had to give great weight to American attitudes. As for the United States Government, it had just seen its China policy collapse ignominiously.

Bevin recalled his ambassador in China for " consultations " on 18th October, 1949, and announced that he was conferring with Britain's allies.

The United States, however, remained obdurate. Acheson announced in early December that the time had not yet come even to consider the matter. France took broadly the same view as the United States. But, inside Britain, the pressures for recognition of the new régime were soon mounting. They came in part from the left-wing elements but more weightily from businessmen who still had large commercial interests inside China and for whom diplomatic representation was essential.

Matters were brought to a head for Bevin with an announcement by India on 30th December that recognition was being accorded to the People's Republic of China. Pakistan followed suit on 4th January. These were two very important Asian Commonwealth countries whose decisions had been motivated by mutual interests and sentiments. Bevin decided he could wait no longer. Chou En-Lai received the British note on 6th January, 1950, announcing recognition. Several other countries followed suit. There had been no repetition of the long period of isolation that had marked the Soviet Union's early years, and many people assumed complacently that a new chapter in Sino-British relations had been opened and that Bevin had created a position from which the Western Powers might hope to come to terms with the Chinese revolution in a way in which they had not been able so to do in the case of Soviet Russia.

These aspirations were quickly to receive a rude shock. Instead of following the normal course of gratefully accepting recognition and proceeding to exchange ambassadors, Chou En-Lai replied to Bevin politely acknowledging the appointment of a British chargé d'affaires " for the purpose of carrying on negotiations concerning the establishment of diplomatic relations." This rejoinder showed that the Chinese Communists were not yet prepared to recognise Britain—an unusual experience for Bevin and his department.

The British Government cautiously attempted to discover what lay behind Chou En-Lai's chilly rejoinder. After some weeks, the Chinese Foreign Minister said that there were three unresolved questions: First, he complained earlier that the British had retained a consul on Formosa, Chiang Kai-shek's island of exile. This, in the Communist view, meant that Britain still accorded *de facto* recognition to the defeated Kuomintang régime, and the Peking Government was not prepared to allow the British to have it both ways. Secondly, Chou En-Lai accused Britain of abstaining in the United Nations debates on a proposal to replace the Formosa delegate sitting in China's seat by a delegate from Peking. In the Chinese view, this was another example of *Perfide Albion*. Thirdly, there were complex and outstanding issues of Chinese property abroad held by the Kuomintang, to which the Peking Government laid claim—and Chou En-Lai wanted a satisfactory settlement.

The bizarre situation was a forerunner to the almost arrogant trend that was later to mark many of Communist China's external policies. It was also a reflection of Chinese history. There was the famous case of Lord Palmerston appointing a Chief Superintendent of Trade whose duty, in Palmerston's own words, was " to place himself in direct communication with the local authorities at Canton in order to offer protection to British subjects, and to be the organ of communication between the British and Chinese Governments." On that occasion the Imperial Chinese Viceroy of Canton had been angry with Lord Napier, the British Superintendent of Trade, for daring to suggest that there would ever be mutually friendly relations between " the Occupant of the Dragon Throne and the ministering servants to whom he distributes his bounty." There was also the long-standing tradition that China did not wish for contacts with other countries nor the requirement that visiting ambassadors to the Imperial Court of China should prostrate themselves on the ground, knocking their heads on the floor. Indeed, Chou En-Lai's response to Bevin might have been drafted by Chien Lung who, in the first letter ever sent by a Chinese ambassador to a British monarch, George III, said: " There is nothing we lack, we set no value on strange and ingenious objects . . . and have no use for your country's manufactures."

Whilst the British Chargé d'Affaires, after six months, was still awaiting his opportunity to negotiate the exchange of ambassadors an event took place close to the northern borders of China that altered the prospect.

CHAPTER 16

MR. TRUMAN'S WAR[1]

What though the field be lost?
All is not lost; th' unconquerable will,
And study of revenge, immortal hate,
And courage never to submit or yield.
Milton

The Korean War broke out at dawn on Sunday, 25th June, 1950. The Russian-equipped armies of the Democratic People's Republic —North Korea—attacked the Republic of Korea—South Korea. It was still Saturday, however, when the telephone rang in Maryland where Dean Acheson, who was spending the week-end on his farm, was preparing to go to bed. It was Hickerson of the State Department calling the Secretary of State. " Something has happened in Korea," he said, " that may have world-wide repercussions." He told Acheson of the sketchy reports he had just received of an attack in force all along the 38th Parallel that was the frontier between the two rival Korean governments. The two men talked for a few minutes. Acheson then instructed Hickerson to telephone Trygve Lie, the Secretary-General of the United Nations, and ask for an emergency meeting of the Security Council on the following day. Already, he had a plan. He knew that the Soviet delegate, Malik, had returned home after the Russians started to boycott the proceedings of the U.N. in January 1950, as a vehement protest against the refusal to allow the Chinese Communist delegate to take China's seat. Acheson realised that if a Soviet delegate did not attend the emergency session on Korea, there would be no Soviet veto on any resolution condemning North Korea as the aggressor. He did not see how Malik could possibly get there in time.

He then telephoned the President who was also away for the

[1] As the Republicans called it.

CHINA

BORDER SETTLEMENT
Gained by S.KOREA
Gained by N.KOREA

Hyesanjin

Yalu R

NORTH

LINE OF NOV. 25·1950

Unsan

Hungnam

KOREA

Wonsan

Pyongyang

Kosong

Haeju

38TH PARALLEL

Panmunjom

Inchon

SEOUL

SOUTH

KOREA

Pohang

Kunsang

Taegu

PUSAN
PERIMETER
Sept.27·1950

Chinju

Pusan

Tsushima

Miles

0   100

week-end at his home at Independence, Missouri. Indeed, Acheson was the only senior member of the Administration within reach of Washington as Louis Johnson, the Secretary of Defence, was away on a visit to Japan. " Mr. President," said Acheson when he heard Truman's voice speaking from nearly 2000 miles away, " I have very serious news. The North Koreans have invaded South Korea." Truman offered to return to Washington at once, Acheson dissuaded him, explaining that the Security Council would be meeting next day anyway and that it would be far better for the President to fly back in daylight. He then added, " Mr. President, there is something you can do. As Louis Johnson is away I would like it if you could send word to the Defence Department that I am also acting Secretary of Defence until someone in authority shows up there, so that I can give instructions for the necessary military orders to be prepared." Truman gave the authority at once and, therefore, for a few hours the United States had the unusual constitutional position of having one man in charge of both the Departments of State and Defence.

Truman also ordered his aircraft for the morning and left Kansas City in such a hurry that two of his aides, who could not be found in time, were left behind. He realised that the moment of his greatest challenge had come. This was a far harder decision to take than the Berlin blockade. Korea, unlike Berlin, was a distant and little-known part of the world outside the declared defence perimeter of the United States. Secondly, before intervention in Korea could take place, the support of the United Nations had to be secured, which was also a very different matter from Berlin. There was the military problem: American armed forces had been run down since the war. If sudden new commitments were made, it would involve yet further major policy decisions for the President and Congress. Truman himself has summarised his thoughts on the flight back to Washington, and they indicate the stature of the man who had originally found himself in his great office without warning or adequate preparation: " I had time to think aboard the plane," Truman writes in his memoirs. " In my generation, this was not the first occasion when the strong had attacked the weak. I recalled some earlier instances: Manchuria, Ethiopia, Austria. I remembered how each time that the democracies had failed to act, it had encouraged the aggressors to keep going ahead. Communism was acting in Korea just as Hitler, Mussolini, and the Japanese had acted ten, fifteen and twenty years earlier. I felt certain that if

South Korea was allowed to fall, Communist leaders would be emboldened to override nations closer to our own shores. If the Communists were permitted to force their way into the Republic of Korea without opposition from the Free World, no small nation would have the courage to resist threats and aggression by stronger Communist neighbours. If this were allowed to go unchallenged it would mean a third world war, just as similar accidents had brought on the Second World War. It was also clear to me that the foundations and the principles of the United Nations were at stake. . . ." There have been few statements in recent years by a leading international political figure so clear in the basic integrity of their logic and deep appreciation of the grave issues that were at stake.

Far away from Truman as he flew to Washington was the Korean testing ground for the principles of collective security. This cold, hard, chastised land had already suffered the indignities of foreign domination in centuries that were past. For a long period during the Manchu dynasty Korea had fallen under China's influence whilst retaining the nominal title to independence. During the late nineteenth century, the country had been an area of struggle between the rival aspirations of Russian and Japanese imperialism.

Despite angry nationalist Korean movements, this situation remained until the end of the Second World War, when the Grand Alliance had the chance to implement the Cairo Declaration of 1943, laying it down that: " The aforesaid great powers [United States, Britain and China], mindful of the enslavement of the people of Korea, are determined that in due course Korea shall become free and independent."

Stalin accepted the Cairo declaration at the Yalta conference of 1945. Arrangements for occupation zones were carried a stage further at Potsdam when Rear-Admiral Matthias Gardner in discussions with the Russians pointed at the 38th Parallel as a suitable dividing line and remarked, " Why not put it there? " Shortly afterwards came the Japanese surrender, and the Russian and American troops arrived in Korea.

As in the case of Germany, the occupation of Korea gave rise to friction between the Soviet and United States military authorities. In the worsening climate of the Cold War, the two zones became two separate units of political development. In November 1947 a resolution was passed by the General Assembly laying it down that there should be elections in the spring of 1948 and calling for a nine-member United Nations Temporary Commission to supervise the elections. But the Soviet authorities refused to co-operate, and denied the Commission entry into North Korea. In these circumstances, two rival constitutions and governments were proclaimed in due course—the Republic of Korea with its capital of Seoul (the Korean word for capital), and the Democratic People's Republic of Korea, based on Pyongyang.

The Soviet occupation troops were withdrawn in 1948, leaving behind a Communist puppet administration. The United States forces were more slow to leave, partly because of American concern at the policies of the President of the Republic of Korea, Syngman Rhee, a man of fanatical nationalist views, attracting to himself extreme right-wing support. After much friction with Rhee, in June 1949, American occupation forces were withdrawn, and the position was made clear in a speech by Acheson to the National Press Club in Washington on 12th January, 1950. Acheson's statement excluded both Korea and Formosa from the American defence perimeter in the Far East. This perimeter, as he defined it, " runs along the Aleutians to Japan and then to the Ryukyus [and] from the Ryukyus to the Philippine Islands. . . . So far as the military security of other areas in the Pacific is concerned, it must be clear that no person can guarantee these areas against military attack. But it must also be clear that such a guarantee is hardly sensible or necessary within the realm of practical relationship." Acheson's so-called " Green Light " speech, as it came to be known by his bitterest critics, was followed by a statement from Senator Tom Connally, Chairman of the Senate Foreign Relations Committee, who said in May 1950 that Russia could seize South Korea without American intervention as Korea was " not greatly important."

The truth behind these statements was that Truman's Administration was under pressure from the military to reduce commitments and it was also suffering from the political and psychological consequences of the Chinese Communist revolution. There was a widespread feeling that Rhee's régime was even less worthy of support than Chiang Kai-shek's.

Stalin, on the other hand, obviously misinterpreted the American withdrawal. It is impossible to say what weight he attached to Acheson's speech of 12th January, but it is much more probable that he had been informed of the general hostile attitude of Congress towards Korea and had drawn his own conclusion that America had washed its hands of the country. He also ignored another statement by Acheson on 19th January asking Congress for economic aid for Korea. Checked in Berlin, he had been casting his eyes around for easy pickings and here, so he thought, was his opportunity. A successful Korean expedition would have the combined effects of regaining the initiative for the Soviet Union in the wider Cold War, inflicting a damaging blow at American prestige in the Far East where prestige is always an important political factor, and consolidating the Communist military position on the Asian continent. Stalin, therefore, proceeded with a steady build-up of the military forces of the Democratic People's Republic of Korea, directed by a Soviet military mission of approximately 3500 personnel.

MacArthur, in Tokyo, was not alarmed. On 25th March his Intelligence reported to Washington: " It is believed there will be no civil war in Korea this spring or summer. The most probable course of North Korean action this spring or summer is furtherance of its attempt to overthrow the South Korean government by the creation of chaotic conditions in the Republic through guerrilla activities and psychological warfare."

The surprise on 25th June, 1950, was complete.[1] The first indication that the North Koreans were attempting the invasion of South Korea came at 4 o'clock in the morning when the South Korean frontier guards found themselves the target of an artillery bombardment. The bombardment was followed by Russian T-34 tanks. The shells of the R.O.K. army's American 35 mm. anti-tank guns bounced off the Russian armour like tennis balls. As to the excuse for the invasion, a few hours after hostilities had started, Pyongyang radio station claimed that the action was taken in self-defence against an attempted invasion of North Korea from the South, by " the bandit-traitor Syngman Rhee." Pyongyang's announcement about Rhee was followed by a statement from Kim Il-sung, the Prime Minister of the Democratic People's Republic, calling upon the North Korean army and guerrillas " to liberate the southern part of Korea in a just war for its unification and independence." This was a clear statement of the military objectives involved.

The United Nations Security Council met at 2 o'clock in the

[1] An extremely balanced and thorough history of events is given by David Rees, *Korea; The Limited War.*

291

afternoon, New York time, also on 25th June, a moment at which the North Korean invasion was about to begin its second day's operations. As Acheson had foreseen, only ten of the eleven members of the Security Council were present. In the Soviet Union's absence, the Security Council promptly passed a resolution calling for an immediate cessation of hostilities and withdrawal of all forces to the 38th Parallel by nine votes to none, only Yugoslavia abstaining, as her delegate claimed that a North Korean representative should be heard first.

A great deal now depended upon Truman, who was met at the airport by Acheson as he flew in from Kansas City. His resolution and sense of dispatch were vital if any effective action were to be taken. The President immediately confirmed instructions that Acheson had drafted that MacArthur was to provide American naval and air support for the South Korean forces, but only south of the 38th Parallel. The President also confirmed orders that the U.S. Seventh Fleet, stationed in Far Eastern waters, was to move north from the Philippines to the sea between Formosa and the Chinese mainland to forestall any attack in either direction and to prevent the Chinese civil war from spreading, although he wisely suggested secrecy until the Fleet was in position.

In the meanwhile, the situation in Korea was continuing to deteriorate. The North Korean forces were meeting with little opposition from the R.O.K.s. Effective military reinforcements from the south were made impossible by the flood of oncoming refugees that jammed the roads. Seoul, the R.O.K. capital, fell on 28th June, just over seventy-two hours after the start of the attack.

Almost simultaneously, in New York, the Security Council took another step—a historic step. The Security Council declared:

Having noted the report of the United Nations Commission for Korea that the authorities in North Korea have neither ceased hostilities nor withdrawn their armed forces to the 38th Parallel and that urgent military measures are required to restore international peace and security, and

Having noted the appeal from the Republic of Korea to the United Nations for immediate and effective steps to secure peace and security, [The Security Council]

Recommends that the Members of the United Nations furnish such assistance to the Republic of Korea as may be necessary to repel the armed attack and to restore international peace and security in the area.

The alignment of the countries voting upon the resolution, which was carried by seven votes to one, with two abstentions, (and the Soviet Union as an absentee) should be recorded. The supporters of the resolution were: Britain, Nationalist China (still occupying China's seat), Cuba, Ecuador, France, Norway and the U.S.A. Yugoslavia voted against the resolution. India and Egypt abstained for want of instructions.

The Soviet retort to the resolution, trumpeted from far away Moscow, was to claim that in the absence of the delegates of the Soviet Union and Communist China, the Security Council had acted illegally. A fuller statement on behalf of the Soviet Govern ment was made by Gromyko in Moscow on 4th July, alleging provocation by Syngman Rhee, conspiracy by visiting American leaders to Japan and Korea and, finally, an act of aggression by the Republic of Korea on 25th June. From Peking, Chou En-Lai followed the Soviet statement by telegraphing the U.N. Secretary-General denouncing the Security Council's action as an illegal interference in the internal affairs of Korea and Truman's order to the Seventh Fleet as an act of open aggression.

There was a world-wide sense of alarm at the course of events. The American and British Governments regarded the situation as an act of naked aggression. The mood in Europe, with the memories of the Berlin crisis fresh in people's minds, was of grave fear lest Stalin was about to embark upon world war. In the United States, where public opinion was now fully awakened to the Soviet threat, the view was that the spread of Communism in Korea and China were all part of the machinations of international communism. In these circumstances, the attitude of the Indian Government as one of the leading neutrals was interesting. The Government of India announced belatedly on 29th June that it approved the two resolutions of the Security Council. On 3rd July the Indian delegate at the U.N. also stated that whilst India had no troops to spare for operations in Korea, India was not neutral.

The United Nations Security Council—the Soviet delegate still being absent—took yet another important step on 7th July. By seven votes to nil, with three abstentions (India, Egypt and Yugoslavia), it passed a British resolution setting up a unified U.N. command in Korea, the commander to be chosen by the United

States. Acting on this authority, Truman immediately nominated Douglas MacArthur.

The decisions had been made. The United Nations, through its chief agent, the United States, fighting under the U.N. flag, had embarked upon a war to resist aggression. The significant, puzzling and indeed extraordinary factor in the chain of these events between 25th June and 7th July was the absence of the Soviet delegate from the meetings of the Security Council. Stalin was guilty of a major oversight in not withdrawing the earlier instructions to boycott the proceedings that had been sent to the Soviet delegate to the U.N. But for this grave error, he would have been able to veto the actions of the Security Council and destroy much of the legal validity of the American action. The explanation is simpler than many realise—it lies in the basic incompetence that stemmed from the over-centralisation of major decisions in the Soviet Union, an inevitable consequence of the authoritarian régime. The episode must rank, along with Molotov's withdrawal from the 1947 Marshall Plan Conference, as one of the major Russian mistakes in the Soviet Union's drive for world domination.

The situation in South Korea was by now deteriorating even faster. It was obvious that the North Korean army was now driving full speed for the great prize of Pusan, the major supply port which lay in the extreme south. A quick end to the war was in sight unless Truman agreed to commit American ground troops. The President began by authorising the sending of a single U.S. regimental combat team, from which stemmed inevitably and very quickly the full American commitment after the U.N. meeting of 7th July.

The regimental combat team was flown into Pusan amidst scenes of great rejoicing on 1st July. Many of the young American troops were informed that they were performing " a police action " and that they would soon be back in Japan. Colonel " Brad " Smith who was in command of the unit, had been told by Major-General William Dean who saw him off at the Japanese airbase, " When you get to Pusan, head for Taejon. We want to stop the North Koreans as far from Pusan as we can. Block the main road as far north as possible. Contact General Church [the head of Mac-Arthur's advance mission in Korea]. If you can't locate him, go to Taejon, and beyond if you can. Sorry I can't give you more information. That's all I've got. Good luck to you, and God bless you and your men." Thus began the gravest American assignment since 1945.

Smith found Church in Taejon. "We have a little action up here," Church explained with a map. "All we need is some men up there who won't run when they see tanks. We're going to move you up to support the R.O.K.s and give them moral support." Through rain, mud and streaming refugees, Smith got his force, grown to 540 men, five 105 mm. howitzers and only six anti-tank shells, to Osan late 4th July a considerable feat as it had been the best part of 200 miles by road from Pusan. The first North Korean tanks were sighted in the early morning of 5th July. At exactly 8.16 a.m. the first American salvoes were fired, using the ordinary ammunition which bounced off the tanks just as the R.O.K. shells had done. The T 34, of which there appeared to be over thirty in the mist and rain went steadily on until two came within such close range that the six precious anti-tank shells were used, knocking them out. The crew of one T-34 surrendered. The crew of the other fired bursts at an American machine-gun nest, killing the first American in the Korean War. There was only one possible thing for Smith's force to do—to retreat as fast as it could from whence it had come. Osan fell without a fight. The action was a shattering blow to American morale for, as one American soldier put it, "Everyone thought the enemy would turn around and go back when they found who they were fighting."[1]

From now on the American attitude to the Korean War underwent a sharp change. Truman authorised more troops and asked Congress to remove limitations on the size of American armed forces altogether. MacArthur decided to commit the U.S. Eighth Army in Japan under General Walton Walker. Britain sent a Commonwealth Brigade. Many other countries sent small units. But the real burden had fallen upon the U.S.A. In the meanwhile,

---

[1] The American problem was illustrated by Philip Deane: *I Was a Captive in Korea*, p. 26.

"I don't get this. They told us it was a sort of police action. Some police action! Some cops! Some robbers! What is this police action?"

"Didn't your officers tell you?"

"Naw. We don't talk of such things with Bob."

"Who's Bob?"

"Bob. You know Bob. Our lieutenant."

"Well, didn't Bob tell you?"

"Naw. Not sure he knows himself. You tell me. What's Communism anyway? Why are we here?"

the North Korean drive for Pusan continued, as the 24th American Infantry Division now arriving fast in Korea performed a holding operation on the Osan-Taejon road. MacArthur was already evolving a strategy so bold and brilliant that it appeared to be incapable of success. Whilst the struggle for Pusan continued it seemed absurd to talk of victory, yet the record shows that a telegram sent on 20th July by MacArthur to Truman pointed out the North Korean weakness. "His supply line is insecure. He has had his great chance and failed to exploit it. We are now in Korea in force and with God's help we are there to stay until the constitutional authority of the Republic is fully restored."

Throughout the month of July, all the Soviet Union's propaganda agencies maintained a steady attack upon the United Nations' operation. *Pravda* described the Security Council's resolution on the appointment of a unified command in the most bitter terms: " By this resolution, the command of the American interventionist troops will operate under the cloak of the United Nations and will be supposed to be acting under the authorisation of the United Nations. For this purpose the troops of the American interventionists are to be supplemented by military formations from other countries. Thus under the flag of the United Nations an attempt is being made to form a coalition of plunderers for the bloody suppression of the Korean peoples." The Soviet Press also laid great stress on alleged American and South Korean atrocities. There were also frequent forecasts of an early end to the war. Yet, for four weeks, there was no indication of any kind that Stalin and Molotov had realised their catastrophic blunder in boycotting the proceedings of the U.N. It was not until 27th July that Malik suddenly announced that he would be taking the chair at the Security Council on 1st August.

When Malik actually returned to the U.N. he reiterated early Soviet statements to the effect that the Korean conflict was a civil war in which the United States was committing an act of aggression. He also made a number of attempts to secure a hearing for a North Korean representative.

Unfortunately, support to Soviet propaganda about alleged American intervention in China's internal affairs—something which Chiang Kai-shek naturally wanted—was given by a visit made by MacArthur to Formosa on 31st July. This visit to see Chiang Kai-shek arose out of an offer by the Chinese Nationalists to send 33,000 troops to Korea—which Truman had considered accepting, but which he had declined on practical as well as political grounds. MacArthur thereupon flew to Formosa to explain why Truman would not accept Chiang's offer, and his visit was immediately interpreted by critics of America throughout Asia as representing a shift in United States policy from neutralising Formosa to giving the Chinese Nationalist action backing. Sensitive to Asian opinion Truman was very concerned about what MacArthur may have told Chiang and he sent Harriman to Tokyo to warn the Supreme Commander against involvement with Chiang. As Harriman put it: " In my first talk with MacArthur, I told him the President wanted me to tell him he must not permit Chiang to be the cause of starting a war with the Chinese Communists on the mainland, the effect of which might drag us into a world war. He answered that he would, as a soldier, obey any orders that he had received from the President. . . . He had refused to discuss any political subjects whenever the Generalissimo attempted to do so. The Generalissimo had offered him command of the Chinese National troops. MacArthur had replied that it was not appropriate."

Harriman still had his doubts about MacArthur and reported to Truman: " For reasons which are rather difficult to explain, I did not feel that we came to a full agreement on the way we believed things should be handled in Formosa. . . . He accepted the President's position and will act accordingly, but without conviction. He has a strong idea that we should back anybody who will fight Communism . . . Chiang, on the other hand, had only the burning ambition to use Formosa as a stepping-stone for his re-entry to the mainland. MacArthur recognised that this ambition could not be fulfilled and yet thought it a good idea to let him land and get rid of him that way. He did not seem to consider the liability that our support of Chiang on such a move would be to us in the East. I explained in great detail why Chiang was a liability and the great danger of a split in the unity of the United Nations on the Chinese-Communist-Formosa policies."

MacArthur issued a statement on 10th August denying that his talks with Chiang had any political significance. Therefore, the President was feeling very relieved until a fortnight later, on 26th August, the White House Press Room brought him a message from MacArthur to the " Veterans of Foreign Wars " to be published on 28th August, copies of which had already been handed to the newspapers. MacArthur's statement was a direct challenge to Truman saying, " Nothing could be more fallacious than the threadbare argument by those who advocate appeasement and defeatism in the Pacific that if we defend Formosa we alienate continental Asia. Those who speak thus do not understand the Orient. They do not grasp that it is in the pattern of Oriental psychology to respect and follow aggressive, resolute and dynamic leadership—to quickly turn from leadership characterised by timidity or vacillation."

Truman was very angry indeed. Only the day before, in a letter to the Secretary-General of the United Nations, United States policy had been reaffirmed and it had been explained that the use of the Seventh Fleet in the Formosa Strait was intended only to prevent the Korean conflict spreading. What was even worse, MacArthur was the U.N.'s Commander. Truman acted quickly. He ordered MacArthur to withdraw his statement. The President also said later: " I gave serious thought to relieving General MacArthur as our military field commander in the Far East," (leaving him in charge of the Japanese occupation). But Truman hesitated and the moment had passed. He was to regret his sudden indecision and said sadly a year later, " I should have fired him then."

Nevertheless, for all his political folly, MacArthur was about to perform his remarkable Inchon operation. His strategy from the first week on had been to fight a delaying rearguard action down to the south, with the intention of using American command of the sea to make a landing far behind the North Korean lines at the appropriate moment. Therefore, he had concentrated his forces in Korea on holding the perimeter around Pusan.

MacArthur's plan, as it now developed, was for a landing by the U.S. Marines to be followed by the U.S. 7th Infantry Division. The Marines were to recapture Seoul which, apart from being the South Korean capital, was the vital centre of supply lines for the North Koreans driving for Pusan. The 7th Infantry Division was to wheel south in order to block the North Korean retreat whilst the forces within the Pusan perimeter were to break out to drive the North Koreans back into the 7th Infantry Division.

The Inchon invasion had to be prepared in Japan, which was a fertile operating ground for spies. It came to be known as " Operation Common Knowledge " but for all that the preparations went forward. MacArthur himself had complete confidence in the venture although there were many doubts. At a final conference on 23rd August, MacArthur claimed that the arguments against the plan were the reasons why it would succeed. He drew a parallel with Wolfe's victory over Montcalm at Quebec and said, " For the enemy commander will reason that no one could be so brash as to make such an attempt." MacArthur applied his dramatic sense to overrule, " I realise that Inchon is a five-thousand-to-one gamble, but I'll accept it. I am used to taking those odds." He dropped his voice, adding, " We shall land at Inchon, and I shall crush them! "

The landing itself, due for 15th September, was preceded by a very heavy naval bombardment on 13th September. Although the North Koreans realised what was happening, they lacked the forces and manœuvrability to resist effectively. Therefore, with surprising ease and comparatively few casualties, Inchon was captured on 16th September, the same day that the forces within the Pusan perimeter, which had been under all-out attack since 1st September, began to go over to the offensive. Steadily, the Pusan offensive gained momentum and by late September the North Korean army was in a state of demoralised rout, fleeing north.

Success now began to go to MacArthur's head and it increasingly affected those around him. The drive for Seoul by the Marines was commenced on 25th September. The first ominous sign of heady unreality was when Major-General Edward Almond, who had been MacArthur's Chief of Staff, announced its capture the same day. But very heavy fighting and casualties lay ahead in the three succeeding days—no mention of which was made in the communiqué. Much of the city was destroyed before resistance collapsed on 28th September.

MacArthur himself flew into Seoul to make a dramatic gesture in restoring the capital to Syngman Rhee. The U.N. commander's car, flying its five stars, swept through streets of rubble, littered with unburied dead, to the legislative chamber which by a miracle had been largely undamaged. Standing amidst falling glass splinters, MacArthur addressed Syngman Rhee: " By the grace of a merciful Providence our forces fighting under the standard of that greatest hope and inspiration of mankind, the United Nations, have liberated this ancient capital of Korea. . . ." MacArthur called for the assembled gathering to recite the Lord's Prayer with him and, turning to Rhee, he concluded, " Mr. President, my officers and I will now resume our military duties and leave you and your government to the discharge of civil responsibility." Syngman Rhee wept.

It was still MacArthur's hour. Congratulations poured in from all over the world. Truman cabled, " Few operations in military history can match either the delaying action where you traded space for time in which to build up your forces or the brilliant manœuvre which has now resulted in the liberation of Seoul." It took only a few more days to destroy the last of the invading forces south of the Parallel.

In less than a hundred days the U.N. action had succeeded—and succeeded brilliantly thanks almost entirely to the American Administration's vigour in Washington and the efforts of MacArthur and his forces in the field. If it had been left at that, the world's memory of the Korean War would have been very different.

CHAPTER 17

CATASTROPHE ON THE YALU

Where is the 38th Parallel? It is non-existent. I am going all the way to the
Yalu and the United Nations can't stop me! *Syngman Rhee*

The United Nations Organisation was faced by a major decision
following the defeat of the North Korean armies. Should it halt
MacArthur's forces on the 38th Parallel, the task magnificently
accomplished? Or should it authorise MacArthur to advance
northwards in order to unify Korea and to hold free elections in
both parts of the country, as originally envisaged in the United
Nations' resolution of 1948 which had been frustrated by the refusal
of the Soviet Union to allow the U.N. Commission north of the
38th Parallel? MacArthur himself had already been told on 27th
September, in advance of the U.N. meeting, by the U.S. Joint
Chiefs of Staff, that he could move his forces across the artificial
frontier to carry out " destruction of the North Korean Armed
Forces." This was a strictly limited objective, largely military.

The evolution of American political policy had begun to take
place much earlier than the military directive to MacArthur, and
as the United States Government was acting as agent for the U.N.
and supplying nearly all the forces and equipment, its views were
bound to be of crucial consequence. The American Ambassador at
the U.N., Warren Austin, issued a statement on 17th August,
saying: " The Security Council and the General Assembly have
built already a firm base for any future action which might be
decided upon. . . . The Security Council has set as its first objective
the end of the breach of the peace. That objective must be pursued
in such a manner that no opportunity is provided for another
attempt at invasion. . . . The United Nations must see that the
people of Korea attain complete individual and political freedom.
. . . Shall only a part of this country be assured of freedom? I think

not. . . . The General Assembly has decided that fair and free elections should be held throughout the whole of the Korean peninsula. . . . *The United Nations ought to have free and unhampered access to and full freedom to travel within all parts of Korea. . . .*" [1] This was an indication that the Americans, having seen the use to which Soviet military power had been put earlier in North Korea (and in Eastern Europe) were considering how best to redress the position in North Korea, whose Communist Government owed its very existence to Soviet force and not to logical boundaries.

This was the broad situation on the American side—the Administration being in favour of unifying Korea but strongly against extending the war to China—when the United Nations came to consider the position at the end of September. A resolution was put forward by Vishynsky on 2nd October, claiming the shelter of the 38th Parallel for the North Korean forces that had so recently violated it. The Soviet delegate also called for the withdrawal of all U.N. forces from Korea so that " all Korean elections [could] be held to establish unified, independent government "—something that the Russians had refused earlier. In the mood of the Inchon victory and under American influences, Vishynsky's proposals proved entirely unacceptable to the U.N. members and an Indian compromise resolution was also voted down. The debate then moved to the General Assembly's Political and Security Committee —where the Soviet veto did not apply. On 7th October, it passed by 47 votes to 5, with 7 abstentions, a resolution supported by the U.S.A. which was to have a vital bearing on the future:

. . . That all appropriate steps be taken to ensure conditions of stability throughout Korea:

That all constituent acts be taken, including the holding of elections under the auspices of the United Nations for the establishment of a unified, independent and democratic government in the sovereign state of Korea;

That all sections and representative bodies of the population of Korea, south and north, be invited to co-operate with the organs of the U.N. in the restoration of peace, in the holding of elections and the establishment of a unified government;

That United Nations' forces should not remain in any part of Korea otherwise than so far as was necessary for achieving the objectives specified;

[1] Author's italics.

That all necessary measure be taken to accomplish the economic rehabilitation of Korea; and

That a commission drawn from Australia, Chile, the Netherlands, Pakistan, the Philippines, Turkey, and one other nation be established to achieve the listed objectives.

The reference to unifying Korea clearly gave consent to the crossing of the 38th Parallel by MacArthur's forces. If the U.N.'s objective was now elections throughout the country, the corollary was that MacArthur would probably have to advance to the Yalu. Certainly this is how he saw it. The U.N. Interim Committee which consisted of seven small powers, four of them Asian, took a further step on 12th October, confirming the crossing of the 38th Parallel when it laid down that the responsibility for civil administration north of the Parallel came under the U.N. Thus it came about that MacArthur pressed on towards the Yalu and to the frontier between North Korea and China—and to disaster.

How did the situation as it had developed during these weeks look from the Chinese side? The evidence indicates that the North Korean venture, in the first place, had been a Soviet-inspired expedition, equipped by Russian arms and undertaken on Stalin's authority. The Chinese had only contributed to the extent of returning numbers of Korean expatriates who had served with the Chinese Red Army in the civil war and, naturally, these trained soldiers had proved valuable in the drive for Pusan. At the outbreak of the Korean War, the Chinese Communists had at first shown much greater alarm at the presence of the American Seventh Fleet off Formosa than at the remote possibility of U.N. operations beyond the 38th Parallel. But on 20th August, Chou En-Lai cabled the U.N. accusing the U.S.A. of having instigated the Korean War and saying, " Korea is China's neighbour. The Chinese people cannot but be concerned about the solution of the Korean question." Chou also demanded China's presence in the Security Council's discussions. This was an ominous warning. Four days later, Chou En-Lai sent another telegram accusing the Americans of direct armed aggression against the Chinese People's Republic, on the basis of the U.S. Seventh Fleet patrol off Formosa. These were angry words indeed. They were followed by the drum-beat of the internal Chinese Communist propaganda machine. The Chinese Press was soon filled with bitter anti-American stories. Mass rallies to whip up anti-American feelings became commonplace throughout the main

Chinese cities. The U.S.A. was depicted as " the paradise of gangsters, swindlers, rascals, special agents, fascist germs, speculators, debauchers, and all the dregs of mankind. This [the U.S.A.] is the world's manufactory and source of such crimes as reaction, darkness, cruelty, decadence, corruption, debauchery, oppression of man by man, and cannibalism."

On 30th September, Chou En-Lai issued yet another warning. He said that China would not stand idly by while the territory of a neighbour was wantonly violated. The day after MacArthur's troops crossed the 38th Parallel, Chou En-Lai dramatically sent for Panniker, the Indian Ambassador in Peking, at midnight. Chou told him that if U.S. troops invaded North Korea, China herself would enter the war.

All these Chinese statements were clear enough. They meant only one thing—intervention. MacArthur chose to discount the possibility. Truman, who was almost as optimistic as MacArthur, sent his Commander another message on 9th October:

> Hereafter in the event of open or covert employment anywhere in Korea of major Chinese Communist units, without prior announcement, you should continue the action as long as, in your judgment, action by forces now under your control offers a reasonable chance of success. In any case you will obtain authorisation from Washington prior to taking any military action against objectives in Chinese territory.

Whilst this permitted MacArthur to continue as long as success was in prospect, Truman also decided to see MacArthur personally. He considered MacArthur was by now out of touch with American opinion, after fourteen years in the Orient. As MacArthur had several times refused invitations to go to the United States, Truman took the decision to fly out to a rendezvous at Wake Island on 15th October. At this meeting, MacArthur was even more emphatic about the Korean situation and the possibility of Chinese intervention. " I believe that formal resistance will end throughout North Korea by Thanksgiving," he said and added: " It is my hope to be able to withdraw the Eighth Army to Japan by Christmas." When he was asked about the possibility of Chinese intervention he replied: " Very little. Had they interfered in the first or second months it would have been decisive. We are no longer fearful of their intervention. We no longer stand hat in hand. The Chinese have 300,000 men in Manchuria. Of these, probably no more than 100-125,000 are distributed along the Yalu River. They have no Air Force. Now that we have bases for our Air Force in Korea, if the Chinese tried to get down to Pyongyang there should be the greatest slaughter." The subsequent interrogation of prisoners showed that on the next day, 16th October, 180,000 Chinese troops started crossing the Yalu River.

Nevertheless, MacArthur ordered his forces on. There was very little resistance at first. Pyongyang, the North Korean capital, was entered on 19th October. Kim Il Sung, the North Korean Premier, fled. On 26th October, the R.O.K. 6th Division reached Chosan on the Yalu River and attacked some North Korean stragglers crossing by a footbridge into Manchuria.

Yet the omens of disaster were already to be seen. On 25th October R.O.K. troops in the west had run into Chinese road blocks near Unsan, south of the Yalu and the Chinese 124th Division struck at the R.O.K. 3rd Division at Sudong, above Hungham in the east. This sudden Chinese counter-attack had such weight that the R.O.K. forces were soon in panic-stricken retreat. More and more reports were reaching Eighth Army headquarters of the appearance of Chinese units. On 1st November the first Mig-15 jet aircraft appeared over Northern Korea—so much for Mac-Arthur's assessment of the situation in the air. The brutal fact had at last struck the U.N. Commander, and on 6th November Mac-Arthur announced: " A new and fresh army faces us, backed up by a possibility of large alien reserves and adequate supplies within easy reach of the enemy but beyond the limits of our present sphere of military action." That same day, 6th November, MacArthur gave orders to his Air Force commander to send 90 B-29 bombers to attack the bridges on the Yalu over which the Chinese were pouring.

Truman happened to be in Kansas City again for the American elections when Acheson telephoned him less than three hours before the B-29 bombers were to take off. Acheson anxiously explained the situation to the President and said that he had just had a hurried conference with the Under-Secretary of Defence, Robert Lovett, and the Assistant-Secretary of State, Dean Rusk. At this conference Rusk had pointed out that there was a firm commitment with Britain not to attack any targets on the Manchurian side of the Yalu without consultation. As Britain was the principal ally of the United States within the United Nations, MacArthur's action would be a breach of faith. Also it would raise serious political problems with other countries. Truman had to make a decision. He sent orders to MacArthur to postpone the bombers' mission unless there was " an immediate and serious threat to the security of our troops." MacArthur was also informed of the commitment to Britain. The President's message reached Tokyo only an hour and twenty minutes before the aircraft were due to take off. MacArthur's reply was immediate, bitter and angry:

> Men and material in large force are pouring across all bridges over the Yalu from Manchuria. This movement not only jeopardises but threatens the ultimate destruction of the forces under my command. The actual movement across the river can be accomplished under cover of darkness and the distance between the river and our lines is so short that the forces can be deployed against our troops without being seriously subjected to air interdiction. The only way to stop this reinforcement of the enemy is the destruction of these bridges and the subjection of all installations in the north area supporting the enemy advance to the maximum of our destruction. Every hour that this is postponed will be paid for dearly in American and other United Nations blood. . . . Under the gravest protest that I can make, I am suspending this strike and carrying out your instructions. What I had ordered is entirely within the scope of the rules of war and the resolutions and directions which I have received from the United Nations and constitutes no slightest act of belligerency against Chinese territory, in spite of the outrageous international lawlessness emanating there-from. . . . Time is so essential that I request immediate recon-sideration of your decision pending which complete compliance will of course be given to your order.

Truman, his cabinet and the Joint Chiefs of Staff were all taken aback by MacArthur's message. It was such a complete reversal of his earlier optimistic assessments of the Chinese threat that he had been giving only a fortnight before. Acknowledging the practical military danger, they were reluctant to refuse permission altogether to MacArthur, yet they had their political commitments, too. They compromised by instructing him to bomb the bridges only on the Korean side of the Yalu—something that could not be done effec-tively from the heights at which the American aircraft had to operate.

A strange thing now happened which enabled MacArthur to return to his previous state of heady optimism. For nearly three weeks, there was a lull in the Chinese activity. During this period there were also many frantic discussions at the United Nations in committees and in corridors. On 8th November, the Security Council invited the Chinese Communists to send a delegation to the U.N. The Chinese Communists arrived in New York on 24th November and the Security Council opened its full debate, on MacArthur's report stating that Chinese intervention had taken place, on 27th November. The Chinese reply charged the United States with intervening in the Chinese civil war, invading Formosa, encircling China and preparing for the Third World War. It was strong stuff. Two Russian resolutions in the Security Council containing, in substance, these Chinese charges were defeated by nine votes to one. A rival resolution reaffirming the U.N.'s intention of holding the Chinese frontier inviolate with a buffer zone in between but also accusing the Chinese of helping the North Koreans was vetoed by the Soviet Union on the same day. This significant move by the Communists showed that China was not interested in merely protecting Manchurian interests—it had decided upon a stake in the Korean War itself. There was a number of efforts attempting to reassure the Peking Government. Truman also stated publicly: " Speaking for the United States Government and people, I can give assurance that we are supporting and are acting within the limits of United Nations' policy in Korea and that we have never at any time entertained any intention to carry hostilities into China."

In the meanwhile MacArthur returned to his earlier objective of re-unifying Korea. His sudden alarm had disappeared as quickly as it had arisen He launched, on 24th November, his famous " Home by Christmas campaign " to end the war. His aim now was a two-pronged drive to the Chinese frontier in the east and west with the high mountains in between. Unfortunately for him, he had completely mistaken the purpose of the apparent lull in Chinese activity. This had not been the product of Chinese hesitation or apprehension. In fact, the period since 7th November had been used by the Chinese to strengthen enormously their forces across the Yalu, and there were by now some 300,000 Chinese troops in Korea. They were not " volunteers " but the organised divisions of the Third and Fourth Field Armies.

The first day of MacArthur's offensive saw U.N. advances up to ten miles. But, on the next day, the Chinese started probing counter-attacks. The main Chinese counter-attack came some hours later, breaking the R.O.K. forces, infiltrating the American units along the ridges and setting up road blocks behind them. A thousand blood curdling, eerie scenes were enacted under the full moon to an accompaniment of bugle calls as the Chinese armies were unleashed upon the surprised Americans. The situation was transformed.

By 28th November the U.N.'s victory was being turned into defeat itself. After an anxious meeting of the American National Security Council in Washington, Truman issued a prepared statement for a Presidential Press Conference on 30th November. It laid down the general lines of American policy for the rest of the Korean War:

> Recent developments in Korea confront the world with a serious crisis. The Chinese Communist leaders have sent their troops from Manchuria to launch a strong and well-organised attack against the United Nations forces in North Korea. This has been done despite prolonged and earnest efforts to bring home to the Communist leaders of China the plain fact that neither the United Nations nor the United States has any aggressive intentions towards China. Because of the historic friendship between the people of the United States and China, it is particularly shocking to us to think the Chinese are being forced into battle against our troops in the United Nations command.
>
> The Chinese attack was made in great force and still continues. . . . But the forces of the United Nations have no intention of abandoning their mission in Korea.
>
> The forces of the United Nations are in Korea to put down an aggression that threatens not only the whole fabric of the United Nations, but all human hopes of peace and justice. . . . If aggression is successful in Korea, we can expect it to spread throughout Asia and Europe to this hemisphere. . . .
>
> We have committed ourselves to the cause of a just and peaceful world order through the United Nations. We stand by that commitment.
>
> We shall meet the new situation in three ways. We shall continue to work in the United Nations for concerted action to halt this aggression in Korea. We shall intensify our efforts to help other free nations strengthen their defences. . . . We shall rapidly increase our own military strength. . . .

Truman's message was an implied abandonment of the aim of

unifying Korea by force. It was also an indication of a new American policy of finding a method of bringing about a cease-fire as quickly as possible, having established the principle of collective security against the North Korean invasion. At this Press conference there was an unfortunate incident which caused world-wide alarm. Truman had made a remark in response to a reporter's question, " We will take whatever steps are necessary to meet the military situation, just as we always have."

" Will that include the atomic bomb? " someone called out and Truman answered, " That includes every weapon we have," adding: " There has always been active consideration of its use. I don't want to see it used. It is a terrible weapon. . . ."

Realising what he had done, Truman put out a further statement immediately after the meeting attempting to correct any misunderstandings. It said, " Consideration of the use of any weapon is always implicit in the very possession of that weapon." But alarm had spread throughout the world. In Britain, particularly, the shock was profound. The news reached the House of Commons during a debate on the Korean situation. Over a hundred M.P.s signed a violent letter of protest to Attlee who immediately cabled Truman.[1]

The Conservatives also expressed grave concern at Truman's statement and R. A. Butler who spoke last in the debate from the Opposition front bench said, amidst ringing cheers from all parts of the packed House: " The British people as a whole wish to be assured before their fate is decided, that they are helping to decide their own fate." After Butler had spoken, Attlee announced to even louder cheers that he was flying immediately to Washington to see Truman. The President had accepted his suggestion within fifteen minutes of getting it.

---

[1] I was standing close to Attlee and Bevin when they received the news of Truman's statement which had first appeared in highly coloured form on the news agency tape. The paper, torn off from the tape machine, was passed along the government front bench by a Labour M.P., Ian Mikardo, to the Ministers. It was read first by Hugh Dalton and then John Strachey, the War Minister, both of whom looked very grave. The paper then reached Attlee, who appeared highly alarmed. In his turn, he showed it to Bevin, who only laughed outright and remarked, "Now I 'ave 'em!" It was as if the trade union official had seen that the employers had made a tactical slip which he could exploit. It was also an indication of the mood that afternoon—and also of Bevin's character, that almost alone of all those who read the news, he appeared entirely unworried and ready to treat the matter in its proper perspective.

The massive Chinese intervention that week and the retreat of MacArthur's forces created a sense of crisis almost akin to panic in certain quarters. In Europe there was widespread belief that the Third World War was about to begin. There were openly expressed fears that the Americans might rush headlong into it. Pleven, the French Prime Minister, and Schuman hurried to London to confer with Attlee before he left, to give him their views. From West Germany, there came stories that police officers were removing any identification symbols that might lead to victimisation in the Soviet occupation that might come any day. As for Britain—when the Korean War had broken out, the British Labour Government had embarked upon a major rearmament programme along with the much more massive American build-up. Under American pressure, this figure had then been raised to £3600 million in September and Parliament had been recalled to endorse it and to approve an extension of military conscription. By December 1950 the British mood of alarm had grown yet more. Attlee had been the recipient of the strongest representations about American impetuosity from Commonwealth countries, in the manner of Britain's constant consultation with her former Empire.

It was in this alarmist climate that Attlee flew into Washington with his mission on 4th December and went to the White House for his first meeting at 4 o'clock in the afternoon. In a sense he was also representing European and Commonwealth opinion to the Americans. Truman asked General Omar Bradley to explain the grave military situation. Attlee listened, doodling with pencil, as was his custom. He replied by saying that whilst his country strongly supported the United Nations and was doing what it could to help in Korea, its existing commitments were such that it would be many months before Britain could do more. Therefore, the continuing burden had to fall upon the United States and he was anxious that the Americans should pay due regard to the opinions of other countries. Here Attlee stressed his own contact with the Asian members of the Commonwealth and also the position of the Chinese Communists. Attlee felt that the Chinese, who were flushed with success, might demand a high price for a cease-fire.

In the discussion that followed, Acheson and Marshall both took the view that the Chinese Communists were operating within the grand design of Soviet-controlled strategy. If the Western Powers became too embroiled in the Far East, it would give Russia a free hand in Europe. Truman read Attlee a memorandum agreed by the American State Department and the Pentagon advocating a cease-fire in Korea if it were possible but warning that, " if the Chinese Communists reject a ccasc-fire and move major forces south of the 38th Parallel, the United Nations forces may face a forced evacuation of Korea." Truman emphasised strongly that this would not happen by agreement but only if they were driven out. Truman also spoke of a military pact or arrangements of some sort in South-East Asia—a forerunner to the subsequent South East Asia Treaty Organisation that came into being in 1954—and a form of Marshall Plan for South-East Asia. The atmosphere at the Anglo-American meetings was frank and grave.

A major difference between the two countries over the next three days was the recognition of Communist China. The Americans were strongly against any such proposal on the grounds that they " could not buy the friendship of the Chinese Communists." Attlee, on the other hand, maintained that nothing was gained by refusing to recognise them and it had the additional effect of driving the Chinese to dependence upon the Soviet Union. Attlee also saw the long-term prospect of Sino-Soviet differences which would work to the advantage of the West.

Acheson pointed out the extent of Soviet pressure all over the world and that they had to consider their Far Eastern policy in the light of the question: " How near is war? " If they considered that the Communist bloc was moving fast towards war they would be making a grievous mistake by trying to buy off the aggressor before he broke loose. " My own guess," said Acheson, " is that it won't work. All we might get is time but never enough time to do any good. Just enough to divide our people bitterly. Just enough to lose our moral strength." He was restating how deeply the main lessons of Chamberlain's appeasement of the German dictatorship and of their own post-war misjudgment of Soviet intentions had now gone in American thinking. Gradually it emerged that Attlee was succeeding in the two aims he had set himself at the conference: to convince the Americans of the need to take account of world opinion and also to convince them of Britain's reliability as an ally in the Korean venture. On the first point, the Prime Minister need not have had many fears, as Truman, Acheson and Marshall were all seized of its importance before ever he arrived. On the second issue, Attlee impressed Truman with his staunch sincerity. " You can take it from me," said Attlee to Truman, in his clipped manner and holding his pipe, " that we stand with you. Our whole purpose is to stand with you."

Attlee was shrewd enough not to raise the question of Truman's "atomic bomb statement" at a formal meeting. Of course, there had never been any American intention of using it and, very tactfully, he mentioned it privately to the President who explained exactly what had happened. With this in mind, a passage was inserted in the final communiqué: " The President stated that it was his hope that world conditions would never call for the use of the atomic bomb. The President told the Prime Minister that it was also his desire to keep the Prime Minister at all times informed of developments which might bring about a change in the situation."

Events moved fast. The weight of the Chinese attack was such that retreat only to the 38th Parallel was an optimistic appraisal of what might happen. A return to Pusan and evacuation became serious possibilities. MacArthur was told by Truman that the preservation of his forces was " now the primary consideration." The American casualty figures began to mount alarmingly. Pyongyang was recaptured by the Communists on 4th December, the day of Attlee's arrival in Washington. By the turn of the year, the Chinese Communist armies were massing on the 38th Parallel for the second invasion of South Korea.

The two major decisions that had been taken since the Inchon landings must be examined in the aftermath of MacArthur's disaster. First, there was the U.N. decision to cross the 38th Parallel followed by the drift in policy from the more limited objective of resisting aggression to the wider aim of unifying Korea by force and using force of arms to implement the U.N.'s 1948 resolution. Secondly, there was the Chinese decision to intervene.

There is no doubt that the victory at Inchon affected some political leaders far from battlefields, as well as intoxicating those around MacArthur himself. Nor was this mistake confined to American leaders. The British Labour Government, amongst others, was a willing party to the fateful U.N. decision authorising MacArthur to cross the 38th Parallel and re-unify the country.[1] In fairness, however, to many of those outside MacArthur's circle who acquiesced or supported the decision, they were broadly under the impression at this point that the purpose of advancing across

[1] Ernest Bevin said in New York a few days before the day of the U.N. resolution of 7th October: "No South Koreans. No North Koreans. Just Koreans."

the Parallel was to destroy the forces of aggression and to render impossible another attack. And this was a defensible position especially bearing in mind the artificial nature of the frontier. But the evidence shows American policy, followed by Britain, had looked beyond this limited aim to re-unification of the country. As military success brought re-unification within their grasp, the temptation to go ahead became yet greater and the policy-makers under the guidance of MacArthur's misconceived reports could not bring themselves to believe that the Chinese Communists would fight, any more than the Russian and North Korean Communists had believed earlier that the United States would intervene in Korea. The fact that MacArthur himself was the U.N. Commander also played its part. He had occupied his lonely and autocratic position as Supreme Commander in Tokyo for so long that he was indifferent to many of the political considerations that formulated opinion in the United Nations. As he said, he believed in success itself and its psychological effect in the Orient. He had won a brilliant victory and he was determined to exploit it to the full. There was always a strong measure of logic on his side insofar as the U.N. resolution of 1948 was valid and he could also claim its implementation was most desirable. But the real political fault did not lie with MacArthur at this stage but with the nature of the U.N. directives (which specifically gave him authority to advance) and in the constant conflict between practical military requirements and the lack of clear political decisions on limited objectives. The situation was further complicated by the varying opinions within the United Nations, all of which imposed responsibilities upon the U.N. Commander in the field. Answering in the famous subsequent Senate inquiry in 1951, he said:

I was operating in what I call a vacuum. I could hardly have been said to be in opposition to policies which I was not aware of even. I don't know what the policy is now. You have various potentials:

First is that you can go on and complete this war in the normal way and bring about just and honourable peace at the soonest time possible with the least loss of life by utilising all of your potential.

The second is that you can bring this thing to an end in Korea by yielding to the enemy's terms and on his terms.

The third is that you go on indecisively, fighting with no

mission for the troops except to resist and fight in the accordion fashion—up and down—which means that your cumulative losses are going to be staggering. This isn't just dust that is settling in Korea, Senator, it is American blood.

When one considers further the political limitations imposed upon military operations by conceding that Manchuria was "a privileged sanctuary"—to use MacArthur's own words—it is impossible not to have some sympathy for him. MacArthur's mistakes were different ones. First, in his duties as the Supreme Allied Commander in the Far East and during the Japanese occupation, the great American proconsul had inevitably assumed a leading political role. In time of peace, while this role was limited to the Japanese occupation, MacArthur had been extremely successful on occasion, although he had come into conflict with Washington. With the onset of the Korean War and his appointment as U.N. Commander, MacArthur's thinking changed to the point that he was soon ready to exceed his U.N. authority, as shown by his real attitude to Chiang Kai-shek in his irresponsible message to the American Veterans. Thus, in his political naïvety, MacArthur became unable to differentiate between his responsibilities to the U.N. and his concept of what American policy should be towards China in order to redress the Communist revolution that had changed the balance of power in the Orient. To that extent MacArthur, by his ill-judged public utterances and his undoubted lobbying behind the scenes, of which evidence emerged later, reduced the great moral authority of the U.N.'s historic decision to intervene in Korea, although the action itself was of such moment that its basic importance will always withstand the passage of years.

MacArthur's second major blunder was military. He wantonly disregarded the possibility of Chinese intervention and he failed to undertake proper military arrangements to safeguard against the dangers of a Chinese counter-attack. He left himself with an 80-mile gap between his forces in North Korea, and there was no way to bridge it.

On the Chinese Communist side, the explanation is more simple. The Chinese civil war had just ended in circumstances in which American policy had been identified with support for Chiang Kai-shek. It is also inconceivable that the Peking Government was not informed in advance of the North Korean expedition. Indeed some observers claim that Stalin informed Mao Tse-tung of his intentions during Mao's presence in Moscow in the early part of 1950. Nevertheless, it is probable that the Chinese Communists attached even less importance to the possibility of American intervention in Korea than the Russians, as their thoughts were concerned with the aftermath of civil war. This explanation would also show why initial Chinese reaction to American moves concentrated upon the neutralisation of Formosa. However, Chinese policy changed quickly, as Chou En-Lai's warning mentioning Korea on 20th August showed.

The Chinese Communists suddenly sensed danger in Korea as the route of a possible counter-revolution by force of American arms. They saw in MacArthur's visit to Chiang Kai-shek—and in Chiang's offer of troops for Korea—evidence to support this assessment. After the Inchon landings, this danger became very acute in Chinese thinking. With their background of Marxist analysis of capitalist intentions and with the distorted history in Communist books of the precedent of the Russian " Intervention," the U.N. Korean operation to them became merely a cloak for a new " Intervention." In these circumstances, the American challenge was real and a fight for the survival of the Chinese Communist revolution. And in the closed climate of a Communist state, the Chinese leaders soon became as much victims of their own propaganda as MacArthur had become already in his proconsul's splendour in Tokyo. It explains why the Chinese rejected all U.N. assurances about the safeguarding of the Chinese frontier and also why the Chinese themselves were not prepared to stop at the 38th Parallel any more than MacArthur had been. They, too, were determined to destroy the enemy's military potential in Korea and saw their opportunity of so doing.

In short, it was another extraordinary two-way failure in communications and judgment in which both MacArthur and the Chinese Communists made exactly the same mistakes.

The Korean War now entered its third and final phase. The Chinese Communists scornfully rejected all thoughts of a cease-fire as their forces stood poised upon the 38th Parallel. They launched their great attack aimed at driving the United Nations troops into the sea, on the night of 31st December, 1950. By mid-morning on New Year's Day they had made substantial advances along snow-covered ridges and frozen paddy-fields. Again it was the R.O.K. forces that broke. General Matthew B. Ridgway, a tough, hawk-like ex-paratroop officer with considerable tact, who had just succeeded

General Walker [1] as Commander of the U.S. Eighth Army, described the scene he met:

> Only a few miles north of Seoul, I ran head-on into that fleeing army. I never had such an experience before and I pray to God I never witness such a spectacle again. They were coming down the road in trucks . . . only a few had kept their rifles. Their only thought was to get away, to put miles between them and the fearful army that was at their heels. . . .

Seoul fell for the third time on 4th January, fires from huge quantities of fuel and napalm lighting up the countryside in a great funeral pyre as the U.N. forces retreated south.

Then, suddenly, for the second time in the Korean War, the Chinese forces halted. There was considerable apprehension in United Nations circles and wonder, too. But on this occasion, the Chinese had halted for a very different reason from their earlier withdrawal near the Yalu on 7th November—they had now discovered that supply lines had become too long and they lacked sufficient air and tank support even to stay where they were, let alone press home their attack. The United Nations' retreat had been conducted too skilfully. By 15th January the Chinese had been halted some distance south of Seoul.

Very cautiously, Ridgway made a personal reconnaissance on 24th January in a light aircraft: " For two hours we flew over that lonely, empty land, skimming the ridge tops, ducking into the valleys, circling over dead villages. Over all this snowy land, which covered our entire battle front, we saw no sign of life or movement." On his return, the Eighth Army Commander ordered his counterattack for the next day, 25th January.

The U.N. counter-offensive only gathered momentum slowly. February 1951 was a period of heavy slogging as the Chinese forces retreated under pressure. On 14th March R.O.K. units reached Seoul and found the South Korean capital—or what was left of it—abandoned by the Chinese. On 31st March the United Nations' forces reached the 38th Parallel and the Korean War was back where it had started for the second time.

During this period of military struggle in Korea, the debate in the

---

[1] Lieut.-General Walton Walker was killed in a motor accident on 23rd December. The jeep he was travelling in collided with an R.O.K. truck that suddenly decided to overtake blindly. Walker was killed instantly.

U.N. had proceeded in parallel to the operations in the field. The Chinese advance gave great impetus to the activities of the delegates of those countries, such as India, that were in " a peace-at-any-price mood." But the American representative was instructed by Acheson to say that his country flatly rejected any cease-fire agreement which included dishonourable conditions. A compromise resolution put forward by Lester Pearson, of Canada, and carried by 50 votes to 7 on 13th January, was not supported by the U.S.A. in the first instance, although the American delegate agreed reluctantly to vote for it on the grounds that it appeared to be the general wish of the U.N. This resolution went a long way to meeting the views of all countries except the Communist bloc and embodied three very important proposals: (1) An immediate cease-fire in Korea. (2) Withdrawal of all "Non-Korean" troops and an interim administration for all Korea to be approved by the United Nations. (3) The General Assembly would also set up a special body, including Britain, Communist China, the Soviet Union and the United States to discuss a general settlement of Far Eastern issues, notably the future status of Formosa and China's representation at the U.N.

Unfortunately the resolution proved quite unacceptable to American public opinion. A storm of protest swept the angry country and there were many demands for Acheson's resignation although he personally had opposed the policy strongly. The criticism reached such proportions that Truman even felt it necessary to make a public defence of his Secretary of State.

Paradoxically, the United Nations' proposals were also quite unacceptable to the Peking leaders who were clearly not in touch with the operations and still thought at this point that all the military advantage lay with them—just as MacArthur had done in October. Instead, Chou En-Lai put forward impudent counter-proposals that political negotiations should actually be conducted as the fighting went on. He said also that the conference itself on Far Eastern problems—at which he suggested Britain, China, Egypt, France, India, the Soviet Union and the United States should be represented—must be brought to Peking, almost as though the rest of the world were suppliants to China. The Chinese rejoinder so angered opinion generally at the U.N. that it soon emerged that Chou En-Lai had overplayed his hand most foolishly and his political blunder was made all the more humiliating when it was followed by the unexpected collapse of the Chinese military offensive.

317

The Truman Administration was by now under considerable pressure. Both Houses of Congress passed strident resolutions demanding that the United Nations should brand China as an aggressor. Truman bowed to the storm. To carry these resolutions further, the American delegate promptly introduced in the U.N. itself a resolution to this effect on 20th January. However, the new American attitude was against the views of the British Government and of a number of other countries, despite Chou En-Lai's preposterous demands. These more cautious governments were particularly concerned that sanctions against China might have the effect of invoking the 1950 Sino-Soviet Treaty of mutual assistance, thus leading on to the Third World War. The difference became so acute that for a short period there was a serious danger of a rift amongst the supporters of American policy, to say nothing of a serious split in the Anglo-American alliance. Eventually a compromise was reached in which, whilst the U.N. branded China as an aggressor, a Lebanese motion of amendment deferred any application of sanctions until further efforts at conciliation had been made. The British delegate, Sir Gladwyn Jebb,[1] made clear his country's coldly conditional support of these proposals and several other N.A.T.O. country delegates did likewise. The formal steps to brand China as an aggressor were, therefore, taken by the Political Committee on January 30th and ratified by the General Assembly on 1st February. A new and still unresolved chapter in China's conflict with the United Nations was opened.

The Indian delegate, Sir Benegal Rau, acting on Nehru's instructions, bitterly attacked the decision, saying that it would end all further hopes of negotiated peace. Like the leaders of other "non-aligned" countries, Nehru did not appreciate that the balance of force in the field played the major part in any Chinese attitude to a cease-fire and not the wording of resolutions.[2]

February 1951 came and went, during which the U.N. forces continued to advance. The British Government played an important part throughout in restraining American policy by maintaining its objections to any form of sanctions. And during this same period yet more efforts were made by MacArthur and the more extreme American elements to change yet further those American policies

[1] Now Rt. Hon. Lord Gladwyn.

[2] This was borne out later when Malik, the Soviet delegate, proposed a truce on 23rd June, 1951, when the military situation had turned decisively against the Chinese and their forces were in danger of catastrophe.

to which they had been opposed all along. Truman had already patiently and magnanimously set out yet again in a letter to Mac-Arthur on 13th January, the political background to the Korean situation. MacArthur, however, reopened the whole debate in a dramatic statement read from a pencilled manuscript to war correspondents hastily collected in a tent on Suwon airfield on 7th March. He warned: " Vital decisions have yet to be made—decisions far beyond the scope of the authority vested in me as the military commander." Despite the fact that he knew that a draft statement of conciliatory peace aims in Korea had just been prepared for Truman, which gave up the idea of unifying the country by force, MacArthur threw out a challenge to the Chinese Commander in the field to negotiate or face the possibility of Chinese military collapse. He was determined to sabotage the attempts at a cease fire.

Again the Americans found themselves embarrassed at the United Nations, where distrust of MacArthur's intentions was out of hand. As for MacArthur, as yet unknown to Truman, he had already taken another step on 20th March. He had replied to a letter from an American Republican Congressman, Joseph Martin, in extraordinary terms. MacArthur's letter, which was for publication, gave the U.N. Commander's support by implication to a suggestion by Martin that Chiang Kai-shek's forces should be used to open " a second front in Asia " by landing on the mainland. MacArthur concluded with a paragraph that summarised the basic differences between himself and Truman's administration: " It seems strangely difficult for some to realise that here in Asia is where the Communist conspirators have elected to make their play for global conquest, and that we have joined the issues thus raised on the battlefield; that here we fight Europe's war with arms, while the diplomats there fight it still with words; that if we lost the war to Communism in Asia the fall of Europe is inevitable; win it, and Europe would probably avoid war and yet preserve freedom. . . . There is no substitute for victory."

As Truman said later, this last paragraph was " the real 'clincher' and the time had come to draw the line." Martin read Mac-Arthur's letter to the House of Representatives on 5th April with a dramatic flourish. Truman sent for Acheson, Bradley, Marshall and Harriman next morning to decide what to do. Harriman thought that MacArthur should have been dismissed even before the Korean War had started because of his earlier disputes with the

Administration over policy in Japan. Marshall saw the political dangers of relieving MacArthur of his command and urged caution. Bradley was more deeply shocked by MacArthur's insubordination to the President than anything else: he thought MacArthur should go but he wished to consult the Chiefs of Staff. Acheson explained that he, too, was in favour of dismissing MacArthur but considered that it was most important to get a unanimous recommendation to this effect from the Joint Chiefs of Staff. He said, " Mr. President, if you relieve MacArthur, you will have the biggest fight of your administration."

When the same five men met again next morning—it was Saturday—Marshall began by saying that he had read in the Pentagon file all the messages that had passed to and from Mac-Arthur and he now agreed with Harriman—he should have gone two years before. Bradley was still a little hesitant, so he was asked to make a final recommendation by Monday. At 9 o'clock on Monday, 9th April, Bradley reported unanimous agreement amongst the Joint Chiefs of Staff. Marshall, Harriman and Acheson all stood by their earlier views. Truman now told the others something that they did not all know—he had already decided MacArthur must go after his statement of 24th March prejudicing the conciliatory cease-fire proposals.

The major decision having been taken, the problem then was how the deed should be done. The original intention was that the Secretary of the Army, Frank Pace, who was on a visit to Korea, should be instructed to inform MacArthur. However, on the evening of 10th April, Bradley hurriedly arrived to tell Truman that the news had reached the Press and Truman thereupon telegraphed the orders to MacArthur direct and convened a Press conference at one o'clock in the morning of 11th April. Unfortunately there was a delay in transmission and news of Truman's Press announcement reached Tokyo some twenty minutes before the telegram. Mac-Arthur was entertaining some guests to lunch and laughing and talking when an anguished aide, who had heard the news on the radio, called Mrs. MacArthur from the dining-room. She returned and whispered to her husband. MacArthur's face froze. His guests sat uncomfortably wondering what had happened. Then MacArthur turned to his wife who was still holding his shoulder and said quietly yet so that everyone could hear, " Jeannie, we're going home at last."

Acheson was right. The news that so relieved large parts of th world, stunned America. The reaction that followed was violent. Truman's opponents were in uproar. To add a focal point to the campaign against the President, MacArthur returned home amidst extraordinary scenes. In each city that he stopped, he was accorded a form of Roman triumph—Honolulu, San Francisco, New York and, finally, Washington. Television carried his words to the whole American continent. Nor did MacArthur miss his political opportunity. To the charges that he had been interfering in politics, he retorted, " The only politics I have is contained in the simple phrase known well by all of you: God bless America."

Finally, on 19th April, MacArthur was accorded an unusual honour and stood up on Capitol Hill before the joint Houses of Congress. It was his moment. He said, " I stand upon this rostrum with a sense of deep humility and great pride; humility in the wake of those great American architects of our history who have stood here before me; pride in the reflection that this forum of legislative debate represents human liberty in the purest form yet devised." A gale of applause swept the auditorium. " That which I have to say," continued MacArthur, " is solely expressing the considered viewpoint of a fellow American. I address you with neither rancour nor bitterness in the fading twilight of life with one purpose in mind, to serve my country." (Applause.)

MacArthur's speech, delivered with all his histrionic ability, was a very powerful plea to reinforce the last paragraph of his fateful letter to Congressman Martin, claiming that the Communist challenge in the Far East must receive overriding priority above all other theatres of hot or cold war. After criticising Truman's lack of decision, he went on, " While no man in his right mind would advocate sending our ground forces into continental China—and such was never given a thought—the new situation did urgently demand a drastic revision of strategic planning. Apart from the military need as I saw it to neutralise sanctuary protection given to the enemy north of the Yalu, I felt that military necessity in the conduct of the war made necessary:

First, the intensification of our economic blockade against China.

Second, the imposition of a naval blockade against the Chinese coast.

Third, removal of restriction on air reconnaissance of China's coastal areas and of Manchuria. (Applause.)

Fourth, the removal of restrictions on the forces of the Republic of China on Formosa with logistical support to contribute to their effective operation against the Chinese mainland. (Applause.)

At points in his speech, MacArthur received ovations. There was cheering when he claimed, " War's object is victory—not prolonged indecision," and again when he said, " Why, my soldiers asked of me, surrender military advantages to an enemy in the field? I could not answer." MacArthur concluded with the same sentimental appeal with which he had begun, " I am closing my fifty-two years of military service. . . . The world has turned over many times since I took the oath on the plain at West Point, and the hopes and dreams have long since vanished. . . . But I still remember the refrain of one of the most popular barrack ballads of that day which proclaimed loudly that ' Old soldiers never die, they just fade away.' And like the old soldier of that ballad, I now close my military career and just fade away—an old soldier who tried to do his duty as God gave him the light to see that duty. Good-bye."

MacArthur's return was followed with an inquiry by the combined Senate Committees on Armed Forces and Foreign Relations. Around the inquiry developed the internal American debate. Hearings began on 3rd May and continued intermittently into June. Whilst many Americans appeared to imagine that the central issue was Truman's right to relieve MacArthur, there could be only one finding upon this, which the inquiry acknowledged. Much more serious for the Western Powers was the way in which the whole of American strategy in the Cold War was exposed publicly. Although steps were taken to delete passages from the record on security grounds, the large number of people involved made it impossible to prevent damaging information appearing in the Press. MacArthur himself was the first to give evidence, which he did for a number of days. He was followed by Marshall as Secretary of Defence and it soon became clear that there was a fundamental difference between the two, in that Marshall was much more anxious than MacArthur about Soviet military strength in the Far East, coupled with the possibility of Russian intervention if the war were to spread to the Chinese mainland.

Marshall said, " There can be, I think, no quick and decisive solution to the global struggle short of resorting to another world war. The cost of such a conflict is beyond calculation. It is, therefore, our policy to contain Communist aggression in different fashions in different areas without resorting to total war, if that be possible to avoid. This policy may seem costly, if maintained over a period of years, but those costs would not be comparable at all to what happens if we get involved in what you might call an atomic war. . . ."

General Bradley was perhaps Truman's most effective defender. The crux of his testimony was given in a prepared statement at the beginning of his evidence on 15th May in which he said: " In Berlin, Greece and Korea, the free nations have opposed Communist aggression with a different type of action. . . . Each incident has cost us money, resources, some lives . . . Korea, because of the importance of the engagement, must be looked upon with proper perspective. . . . The course of action often described as ' a limited war ' with Red China would increase the risk we are taking by engaging too much of our power in an area that is not the critical, strategical prize. Red China is not the powerful nation seeking to dominate the world. Frankly, in the opinion of the Joint Chiefs of Staff, this strategy would involve us in the wrong war, at the wrong place, at the wrong time, and with the wrong enemy." Bradley's words did much to reassure America's allies. But too much was said in the public debate for Truman and Acheson in particular not to suffer in the collective American mind as the principal Republican scapegoats for " the mess in Korea " and for " Mr. Truman's War," despite the fact that history would always honour them for what they had done.

After Ridgway's promotion to Tokyo to take MacArthur's place there, the new commander of the U.S. Eighth Army became Lt.-General Van Fleet, a tough and capable operational commander. Van Fleet arrived in Korea to meet a new Chinese offensive that was opened on 22nd April. Again, the Chinese made some gains at considerable cost in casualties but they lacked sufficient air support to break through. They were also held up by a particularly gallant rearguard action by a British unit, the First Battalion of the Gloucestershire Regiment, that made a remarkable stand south of the Imjin River and held up the advance on Seoul. A second Chinese spring offensive was halted by 21st May, and on 24th May Van Fleet was able to launch his counter-offensive which drove the Chinese north of the 38th Parallel once more.

The military balances in Korea had changed substantially in the weeks preceding Van Fleet's advance. The United States had poured in arms and aircraft since the Chinese intervention on a vast scale. By the middle of May 1951 the firepower at the command of the United Nations forces was so great that it came to be known as " the Van Fleet load." However, it took Van Fleet's capture of Chorwon and Kumwha in the so-called North Korean "iron triangle" on 13th June to make the Peking Administration accept finally the peril of their forces. To make matters easier for the Chinese Communists, conciliatory statements were made on behalf of countries supporting the United Nations action, notably a speech by Lester Pearson saying that complete capitulation might not be necessary and that it was sufficient for the United Nations to achieve their objective—which was the defeat of aggression against South Korea. Acheson followed Pearson's path on 2nd June when he was appearing before the Congressional Inquiry into MacArthur's dismissal. He drew a distinction between the cease-fire and " the long-term political objective of the United Nations in Korea which has been to establish a free, independent and democratic Korea. . . . The United States has been in favour of that [latter] result since 1945." Acheson went on, " Obviously if the defiance of the U.N. is removed, and if the attack on the U.N. forces ceases and if the Korean business is settled, then these other questions go back where they were before the whole trouble started."

Along with these conciliatory remarks in public, Acheson secretly arranged for Stalin to be given a grim warning that unless peace talks were commenced the Americans would intensify the war. A casual word to this effect was passed with Malik at the U.N. by George Kennan, the American Ambassador-designate to the Soviet Union. Malik expressed indifference but promptly reported back his conversation. And within a few days he appeared on a weekly U.N. nations' broadcast on 23rd June. He spent fifteen minutes abusing American policy and then gabbled, as he overran his time, " The Soviet peoples further believe that the most acute problem of the present day—the problem of the armed conflict in Korea— could be settled also. This would require the readiness of the parties to enter on the path of peaceful settlement of the Korean question. The Soviet peoples believe that, as a first step, discussions should be started between the belligerents for a cease-fire and an armistice providing for the mutual withdrawal of forces from the 38th Parallel." This was a most significant remark and great importance was attached to it in view of the Berlin precedent. Confirmation as to its importance was soon in coming. The Peking *People's Daily* endorsed Malik's words on 25th June. Ridgway was authorised to make a broadcast that he understood that the enemy wished for discussions and he proposed that negotiations for a truce should take place on board the Danish hospital ship *Jutlandia* in the port of Wonsan, some eighty miles north of the 38th Parallel. Ridgway was answered by a joint North Korean and Chinese Message suggesting Kaesong as a more suitable site than the *Jutlandia*.

Ridgway agreed to the proposal of Kaeson and soon regretted it. When a preliminary meeting took place[g] the United Nations party was forced to fly white flags as it entered Kaesong and it was immediately surrounded by armed Communist troops. Thus Communist journalists and photographers were able to record a staged scene in which Ridgway's men looked like defeated emissaries suing for peace. The Chinese also attempted to detain the U.N. party overnight.[1]

The first full meeting took place on 10th July. It soon emerged that a considerable gulf separated the two sides. The Communists were not just asking for an armistice. They had determined to have it on the 38th Parallel and to couple it with a withdrawal of *all* foreign troops from Korea, which could have created a new and dangerous situation in advance of any peace terms. Several days were spent in discussing whether an agenda came before issues. On the second day the Communists prevented the entry into Kaesong of twenty Western newspapermen when their own appeared to have freedom even to enter the conference room. After protests by the United Nations, they were then forced to give way. The relatively minor issue indicated the prevailing atmosphere.

After a number of stops and starts—the official transcript of the talks, based on Communist translations, records remarkable obstruction tactics by the Communists and bewildered anger on the part of the Americans—the Communists staged two incidents. First, they claimed that a patrol at Kaesong had been ambushed on 19th August. The Communists dropped this complaint because of lack of confirmatory evidence and, on 22nd August, instead charged

[1] Alan Winnington, a British newspaper Communist correspondent who sided with the North Koreans, later told Western journalists: "This is the first time Oriental Communists have sat down at a conference table on terms of equality with Americans and they intend to make the most of it."

the U.N. with bombing Kaesong with the intent "to murder" their delegation. The U.N. investigating officer was presented by a North Korean colonel with bits of twisted metal and a small unexploded rocket of a kind that the U.N. forces had not used for over a year. When the U.N. officer declined to sign a complete acknowledgment of guilt on the spot, the North Korean colonel suddenly announced the suspension of the Armistice talks. That a comparatively junior officer should have taken this step, indicates that the "incident" was a high-level decision as a prelude to a resumption of hostilities. The Chinese had evidently decided that they had by now redressed the dangerous situation in which they had stood in June.

Therefore, a fierce Chinese attack was launched on 27th-28th August, breaking through the R.O.K. Fifth Division in the central sector. Van Fleet counter-attacked on 31st August and his troops advanced slowly and steadily throughout September until the Chinese realised their danger once more and suddenly decided to resume the talks. Ridgway determined this time to avoid the invidious Kaesong situation and so he insisted upon a genuine demilitarised meeting place at Panmunjom, a miserable and desolate village of three or four ruined mud huts near the line. Again there was haggling amongst liaison officers. Finally, the Armistice conference was resumed at Panmunjom on 25th October. A month later, the Communists agreed to the proposition that the truce line should be the line of contact between the forces *at the time the truce was signed.*

The next stage, after it was agreed where hostilities were to cease, was to discuss the exchange of prisoners. A deadlock was now to arise upon a new principle in the history of warfare—that a prisoner should not be compelled to be repatriated against his wishes. The specific circumstances of the conflict between Communism and the free world dictated the importance of this principle. Yet nobody had foreseen that it would arise. The issue became the subject of a conflict within the American Administration, Acheson insisting upon the principle of a free choice for each prisoner, against the military who saw no point in it. Significantly, however, Marshall supported Acheson and the Secretary of State's view prevailed. Between 11th December, 1951, when this subject first came under discussion, and the date upon which the Korean War ended on 27th July, 1953, the U.N. forces were to suffer 140,000 further casualties. Of these, 32,000 were Americans including 9000 dead.

Truman put it in most graphic language, " *We will not* buy *an armistice by turning over human beings for slaughter or slavery.*"[1]

The United Nations at this time held 132,000 prisoners of war and it had a further 44,000 captives on its hands—men who came originally from South Korea but who had been conscripted into service by the Communists after the invasion. The Communists listed only 11,559 U.N. and R.O.K. prisoners although Pyongyang radio had, at one time, claimed 65,000 prisoners. Ten thousand Americans were known to be missing but only three thousand were acknowledged as being still alive. There were many other grizzly discrepancies in numbers. Fifty thousand South Koreans had disappeared altogether. "Released at the front!" was the Communist explanation. The most remarkable fact, however, was that only 70,000 out of 132,000 Communist prisoners wished to return despite extraordinary circumstances of gang warfare and intimidation by the Communists in the prison camps on Koje Island. Syngman Rhee also organised his intimidation gangs and after his hold was broken the figure willing to return rose to 75,000. Even so, the number of nearly 60,000 refusing to return was remarkable considering the circumstances in which the Communists had organised themselves inside the camps where they defied all discipline for a period, even capturing the commanding American brigadier on one occasion and threatening him with his life. When the Communist-controlled camps were finally restored to a semblance of order, there was discovered in one compound alone an arsenal of 3000 tent pole spears, 1000 Molotov cocktails, 4500 knives and large numbers of hatchets, hammers and flails. In another compound were the bodies of sixteen men "sentenced to death by the People's courts."

The debate at Panmunjom on the prisoners continued for a whole year throughout 1952. It became a vital matter of prestige for the Communists that such a large number did not wish to return to North Korea or China despite Lee's efficient tactics.

A new factor as yet was injected into the situation in 1952 when the Chinese Communists accused the Americans of using methods of bacteriological warfare in Korea. The bacteriological warfare campaign was preceded by a severe outbreak of typhus in North Korea in December 1951. This epidemic was certainly aggravated by the circumstances of war and the breakdown of such primitive safeguards to the water supplies and sanitation as had existed in the

[1] Author's italics.

larger communities. Chinese prisoners captured in January and February 1952, continually reported the widespread extent of the typhus epidemic. On 22nd February the North Korean Foreign Minister formally accused the United States of dropping the germs of smallpox, typhus and other diseases. These charges were promptly repeated by Chou En-Lai. They were denied by Acheson on 4th March, who asked that the International Red Cross should undertake an investigation, which the International Red Cross agreed to do. Malik, however, sought a formal condemnation of the U.S.A. in the United Nations in advance of any investigation and rejected the proposal to use the International Red Cross on the grounds that the body was really Swiss in composition. Instead, the Chinese Communists established their own " International Commission " inviting to China Dr. Joseph Needham, a well-known British bio-chemist and Sinophile, supported by a team of scientists who were either Communists or fellow-travellers. The Needham inquiry was not allowed to visit the scenes of many of the alleged incidents, nor did it arrive in China until many months after they were said to have taken place. Nevertheless, it had no hesitation in declaring the charge against the United States proven.

The charges against the Americans became a major propaganda weapon in the Cold War throughout 1952 and mass demonstrations were staged in every Communist country. The most probable reason for this attack on the Americans is that it may have begun as an easy excuse by the Communists for the breakdown in health arrangements in North Korea and Manchuria, and it was then seized upon and magnified by the Peking authorities as excellent propaganda. The campaign was used to the full in China. Hygiene was carried to extraordinary lengths and led to the virtual elimination of the flies in Peking for a period. The propaganda, however, collapsed at the United Nations and rebounded against the Communists when the barbaric methods, by which "confessions" by U.S. airmen had been obtained, were made known.

Then, on 5th March, 1953, Stalin died. His death enabled the Communist bloc at last to abandon its defeated venture. The Communist commanders in Korea took the first step on 28th March by agreeing to an exchange of sick and wounded prisoners adding most significantly that they considered that this would lead to " the smoother settlement of the entire question of prisoners of war, thereby achieving an armistice in Korea." Chou En-Lai, who had just returned to Peking from attending Stalin's funeral in

Moscow, issued a statement on 30th March that the prisoners who wished repatriation should be exchanged and that those who refused should be handed over to a neutral state to ensure " a just solution." Truce talks were resumed speedily but a solution was still elusive as the Communist representatives refused U.N. proposals on the neutral arrangements for dealing with the prisoners. Eventually an agreement was reached on 8th June for a Neutral Nations Repatriation Commission to consist of a representative each from five countries—Sweden, Switzerland, Poland, Czechoslovakia and India.

Unfortunately both the United Nations and Communists had reckoned without Syngman Rhee. The South Korean leader turned out to be strongly opposed to the Armistice terms, as he still wished to re-unify Korea by force. This obstinate and fiery old man had already made the most embarrassing pronouncements from time to time throughout the protracted negotiations and, like General MacArthur, he was indifferent to the risks of a Third World War. An angry exchange took place between Syngman Rhee and the Americans, acting as the agents for the U.N. Rhee thereupon took it upon himself, on 18th June, to order the South Korean guards to permit a mass escape of prisoners. Although a few were killed or recaptured by the small number of Americans at hand, some 27,000 got away. Rhee hoped that his action would force the Communists to break off the negotiations. But he miscalculated the Communist anxiety to end the Korean War.

When the negotiating delegations met at Panmunjom on 20th June the Communists handed over a letter from Kim Il Sung accusing the U.N. command of complicity in Rhee's outrageous breach of faith but adding that it could not affect the ultimate fulfilment of the proposed armistice.

The signing of the Armistice took place on 27th July at 10 o'clock in the morning. The two delegations filed in silently. They signed eighteen copies of the agreement, nine in United Nations blue, nine in Communist red. They then rose and walked out without exchanging a word. Twelve hours later, at ten o'clock at night, all firing ceased.

There still remained the extraordinary affair of the prisoners. Some of the confrontations were later described by an American officer who was present: " Each prisoner would be brought in by guards, in half the cases dragged in kicking, biting, and flailing his arms. This first compound manufactured masks to avoid identification by the Communists. The Pole, of course, objected to this but was overruled by the Indian chairman—they could come nude or in suits of armour if they pleased. . . . Every quarter of an hour or so a prisoner would throw a chair, upset the explainer's table or start chanting or reciting poetry at the top of his lungs. . . . While the Indians ruled out spitting and throwing benches at the explainers they allowed the prisoners to call them any names they could think up."

The extraordinary affair continued until 21,805 Communists still refused repatriation. These were set free in January and February 1954. Most of the Chinese decided to make a new life in Formosa. The political conference to decide their fate was never held. The Great Powers were anxious to forget the Korean War—a fact that was underlined at the Geneva Conference of 1954 when no agreement was reached on the unification of Korea and there were few meetings upon the subject although the two Korean delegations had come across the world to discuss matters.

Thus Korea returned to the international obscurity from which it had emerged with traumatic suddenness. "Mr. Truman's War" had established new principles in international affairs. Whereas Stalin's tactics had been always to exercise remote control and to let others do the actual fighting, the American President and his countrymen had borne by far the major burden—despite the mistakes and their impetuosity—with high courage and honour. The Chinese had been guilty of military blunders as great as those of MacArthur, and yet their stature amongst Asian nations had also been raised immeasurably by their armies. As for the Korean people—they had suffered grievously and returned now to reconstruct their ruined land.

CHAPTER 18

ENDING THE EUROPEAN CIVIL WAR

We must learn to trust each other again.   *Robert Schuman.*

The Soviet Union's miscalculation of the American reactions to the invasion of South Korea had a parallel in Europe that was no less serious for Stalin's drive for world domination. The Korean War led specifically and directly to West German rearmament; and eventually to the burying of the ancient European enmities. To that extent, the importance of the chain of events that began on 25th June, 1950, had repercussions beyond even the establishment of the principle of collective security through the United Nations. It was the catalyst that began the process that eventually led to the transformation of the vague and heady ideals of post-war European unity into the reality of the Treaty of Rome in 1951.

The Western Powers had decided to set up the German Federal Republic in 1949. This decision was consequent upon the division of Germany. The Soviet Union followed the action of the Western Powers by announcing, later in 1949, that the administrative functions of the Russian military occupation would be transferred to the provisional government of the German Democratic Republic. Two German states had come into being.

In the contractual arrangements setting up the West German government, the West German leader, Dr. Adenauer, undertook not to create new German armed forces. His undertaking was intended to make provision for the situation until the end of 1950, by which time, it was generally understood, matters would be clearer. But no such conditions were laid down by the Soviet occupation authorities upon the East German régime and the Russians gave ready sanction to the setting up of the East German *Volkspolizei*, a military force of some 40-50 thousand men, armed with small-arms and armoured cars.

The Americans generally, and Acheson in particular, had already had doubts about the Petersberg Agreements. They considered the policy of coupling the establishment of a West German State with the denial of arms to it as illogical and impractical in the long term. They had also come round to the view expressed by the British Chiefs of Staff several years beforehand, even before the war had ended, that a West German contribution to European defence would become important in the face of expansionist Soviet policy. These strands of American thinking now began to form the basis of the arguments in favour of West German rearmament put forward by some Europeans—that the successful defence of Western Europe could not be undertaken without West German help; and that it would be better to concede with good grace something to German national pride that might be extorted later, in less propitious circumstances. There was an additional and even more powerful argument associated with the new North Atlantic Treaty Alliance—N.A.T.O. itself was being called upon to defend Western Europe in circumstances that made the defence of West Germany the critical factor in all Western military planning. Without West German participation, the military situation became impractical and illogical.

On the other side of the argument—against West German rearmament—there was a very large number of political obstacles. The most powerful opposition was based upon emotion. European memories were still fresh with the circumstances of the German occupation. At the time that the German rearmament debate began, less than five years had elapsed since the Nazi concentration camps had been discovered. There were thousands of victims, or the relatives of victims, of the Nazi concentration camp system spread throughout Europe. There was also recognition by Western European opinion of how the East European countries, particularly Poland, had suffered at German hands. The one inevitable consequence of any plans to rearm Western Germany, so the argument ran, would be the strengthening of the Soviet hold upon Eastern Europe. Finally, there was the imponderable factor of the possible reaction of the Soviet Union itself—the country that had paid the greatest price of all to German militarism. Communists and fellow-travellers put out warnings that Stalin now possessed the atomic bomb, and felt so strongly about Germany that he may even regard West German rearmament as a *casus belli*. The fact that the Russian people had suffered so grievously at German hands after 1941 largely because of Stalin's own miscalculated treachery was ignored.

The Defence Ministers of the N.A.T.O. countries met at the Hague on 1st April, 1950. At this meeting, it became clear that a decision would have to be reached about Western Germany because geography had cast it for the vital role in the military situation.

Acheson, therefore, decided to visit Paris and London to see how far the U.S.A. could satisfy its Allies by giving them guarantees against German militarism. In Paris, on 7th May, Acheson saw Robert Schuman, the French Foreign Minister, a man who was known for his support for the concept of European unity.

When Acheson arrived, Schuman told him in great secrecy of plans that he and his associates, including Jean Monnet, had formulated for a single authority to control the French and German coal and steel industries. At this point Schuman had not even told the French cabinet. Acheson saw at once that the plan, if successful, would be a historic development towards Franco-German rapprochement. Acheson travelled on to London on 9th May with a sense of elation, in advance of Schuman who was also to meet Bevin on 11th May for a conference of the Foreign Ministers of the three Western Occupation Powers. Acheson found his old friend Bevin ill and in great pain, and when he had told Bevin of Schuman's plan, he realised that the British Foreign Secretary no longer possessed the physical resilience to see its imaginative sweep, as Bevin had done three years before in the instance of the Marshall Plan. Instead Bevin, who had already expressed publicly his misgivings about West German rearmament, now also regarded the Schuman Plan (as it came to be known) as a threat to his own policy instead of being the logical extension of it which it really was. Bevin obstinately remained hostile to and suspicious of Schuman's proposals. The story is all the more poignant because of the fact that Bevin should have had his judgment clouded in part by his own state of health, but it must be emphasised that the later decision not to join the Schuman Plan was the collective decision of the British Labour Cabinet that stemmed in part from its mistaken belief that British industry, less damaged by the war, was better off in the long term operating independently of Europe.

Throughout the London discussions of 1st to 13th May, 1950, the issue of German rearmament cropped up. The two European foreign ministers—Bevin and Schuman—explained to Acheson the problems of public opinion in their own countries, and it was agreed that whilst no mention of the subject should be made in the communiqué, the discussions would continue. The Korean War, six weeks later, transformed the situation. A wave of fear swept Europe.

Konrad Adenauer, the new Federal German Chancellor, formally requested the High Commissioners of the occupying Powers to strength their forces in Germany. Adenauer's appearance on the European stage should be noted. He was soon to play an important part. He had become the first Federal Chancellor by only one vote less than a year before on 15th September, 1949. At that time he was seventy-three, having been Burgomaster of Cologne from 1917 until he was forced into retirement by Hitler in 1933. Later he had been brought out of retirement by the British military occupation authorities only to be dismissed by them for alleged " incompetence." The first objectives of this shrewd, determined man had been to end the occupation, to stop the dismantling of plant, and to secure the release of minor Nazi war criminals. Now he was concerned with the military security of his country—and yet later with the great issue of Franco-German rapprochement. In response to Adenauer's request, McCloy, the United States High Commissioner, had to explain that his government remained opposed to the creation of a German army, as in the contractual Agreements, but in view of the new circumstances, McCloy added that it was " very difficult to deny the Germans the right and the means to defend their soil." American policy had begun to shift.

When the Consultative Assembly of the Council of Europe [1] met in Strasbourg on 7th August, in the grave mood sweeping Europe, delegates immediately proceeded to raise the crucial issue of defence. In the presence of eighteen German members, taking their seats for the first time, Paul Reynaud, the former French

[1] The Council of Europe owed its existence to the great desire for European unity manifest after the war, given impetus by the signing of the Brussels Treaty in 1947. For a period there had been a divergence between European aspirations and Bevin's foreign policy—the British Foreign Secretary wishing to limit the organisation to a Council of Ministers—but the British Government gave way to the proposal for a wider consultative assembly which was duly established on 5th May, 1949. The original members of the Council of Europe consisted of Britain, Belgium, Denmark, Eire, France, Italy, Luxembourg, the Netherlands, Norway and Sweden. These were joined later by Greece and Turkey. West Germany accepted associate membership in June, 1950, after bitter opposition from Kurt Schumacher, the German S.P.D. leader, who contended that "the road to Strasbourg was only a stage on the road to German rearmament," to which the S.P.D. at that time was opposed, although it was to modify its views subsequently.

Prime Minister, proposed the appointment of a European Minister of Defence. That this far-reaching step should have been urged gave an indication of the prevailing anxiety. It was supported by Churchill, leading the Conservative M.P.s in the British delegation. A resolution proposed by Churchill himself and amended by the French was then carried by 89 votes to 5 (with 27 abstentions) [1] calling for " the immediate creation of a unified European Army, under the authority of a European Minister of Defence, subject to proper European democratic control and acting in full co operation with the United States and Canada." Churchill later explained that his proposed European Army should include German units— something to which the French had been opposed in the course of the Strasbourg debate.

Across the Atlantic, the United States Government was under the severe pressures of the Korean War—the full implication of which, in terms of manpower and arms, was only beginning to dawn. It was most anxious to take steps to strengthen the position in Europe. Accordingly, Acheson warned Bevin and Schuman, who were both journeying in early September by boat to the United States for a further meeting of the Western Powers, that he wished to raise the whole issue of German units for the defence of Europe. When Bevin and Schuman arrived, Acheson discovered that a very wide gulf separated the resolution passed at Strasbourg and its implementation, let alone its acceptability to European opinion. Opposition in France had hardened so much that the French Government was in danger of falling because of the threatened resignation of many of its members. In particular, the French had become particularly opposed to the raising of German forces until their own French Army had been re-equipped. Acheson learned also that Bevin, supported by his own British Labour colleagues, was against hasty West German rearmament, partly because he foresaw serious political difficulties within the Labour Government that held office by a very narrow majority since the general election of February 1950.

The deadlock was broken by René Pleven, the French Prime Minister, on 24th October. The so-called Pleven Plan was supported two days later by the French National Assembly by 349 to 235. The Plan made five proposals: (1) A European Defence

---

[1] The abstentions in the main were made up by British, German and Swedish Socialists. One British Labour M.P., R. W. G. Mackay, however, voted in favour of the resolution.

Minister, responsible to a European Assembly, should be appointed. The status and constitution of the Assembly were yet to be worked out, but the body could be either the Consultative Assembly of the Council of Europe or a new body to be elected in accordance with new electoral laws. (2) A European Defence Council, made up by Ministerial representatives and with a single European defence budget, should be decided upon. (3) Each European country should contribute military forces from their own national forces. Pleven's intention was that these units should be merged at the lowest possible level—probably battalion strength—in order to avoid any danger of independent action by the troops of a single country. (4) Although West Germany was to contribute forces, there should be no German national army and no German Defence Minister. (5) Pleven wanted to make his proposals conditional upon the acceptance of the Schuman Plan for coal and steel.

The Pleven Plan was an impractical compromise proposal, based upon the need to conciliate French public opinion that was even more deeply apprehensive of Germany than of Soviet expansionism. There were many grounds for objection. The West Germans also had an important objection: Adenauer was really only prepared to rearm behind a Western defence screen, as his fear of action by the Red Army was very strong. Yet the Western Powers—particularly the U.S.A.—had a conflicting objective. They saw West German rearmament primarily as a means of strengthening the existing weak state of European defences and helping to create the military screen that Adenauer sought as a prerequisite.

Adenauer, nevertheless, made a strong appeal to support Pleven's concept in a speech in Stuttgart on 4th November. In terms of the Western Alliance it was a brave and magnanimous statement. He asked the French people to trust Germany because there was no time to lose in facing the common danger and he called upon his own countrymen to share in European defence provided that they were not being used as mere cannon fodder. In the Bundestag, Adenauer went further by commending the Pleven Plan itself, especially if British forces were to join the European Army—something which Britain had shown no inclination to do, partly because of her world-wide commitments but also because Bevin and the Labour Government still saw Britain as a country maintaining her special relationship with the United States, and her world influences, by preserving her independence of Europe. Acheson made a further effort. By his skilful diplomacy at the end of 1950, a compromise between the urgent American demand for German units to strengthen European defence and the more nebulous Pleven Plan was reached. At the N.A.T.O. Council in December, German rearmament was accepted in principle. Pleven agreed to modify his Plan and he succeeded in getting the French cabinet to accept German units of five or six thousand men in the ratio of one German unit to five raised by the other countries. To meet another French objection, West Germany was also to come at the end of the queue for military equipment. Under American pressure, Bevin agreed to support the proposal. The six months since the Korean War began had thus brought about its major change in the European situation, including the opening up of new prospects for the West German people. The initial stimulus had come from fear of Russian intentions. The plans had been carried further by American initiative and out of the fear that the Americans might not participate in supplying the N.A.T.O. Supreme Commander—an essential commitment from the European viewpoint—unless and until agreement had been reached on the German issue.

The Soviet reaction to the changing military position of West Germany was to issue a series of vehement protests. On 20th October, 1950, Molotov arrived in Prague and he was joined by the Foreign Ministers of Bulgaria, Czechoslovakia, East Germany, Hungary, Poland and Rumania. The conference of eight Communist countries speedily issued a lengthy document suggesting that the four Occupation Powers should agree upon a statement of opposition to German rearmament. They also proposed the unification of Germany on the basis of a conference of an equal number of representatives from East and West Germany, who would meet to prepare a constitution and help in the drafting of a Peace Treaty. Molotov carried the Prague declaration a stage further on 3rd November, by calling for a meeting of the four Foreign Ministers to consider it. After an exchange of a number of notes, in which Molotov appeared to accept a Western condition that any conference on Germany should consider "other principal causes of international tension" including Austria, a preliminary conference to discuss the agenda for the Foreign Ministers met in Paris on 5th March, 1951.

The Palais Rose Conference, as the preliminary conference came to be known, lasted from March until 21st June. It was an astonishing affair. It occupied seventy-four sessions. The four men who attended this gathering were Gilbert Jessup (Ambassador-at-large,

U.S.A.), Gromyko (Senior Soviet Deputy Minister for Foreign Affairs), Ernest Davies (British Foreign Under-Secretary), and Alexandri Parodi (Secretary-General at the Quai d'Orsay). The exchanges deteriorated to a low level of abuse and recrimination at meeting after meeting. The French and British Governments were more anxious than the Americans to prolong the conference after it was clear that Gromyko was determined on a wholesale attack upon N.A.T.O. Gromyko's claim was that the Western attitude "put the Soviet Union in a position of unequal rights" and that his government had no objection to a discussion of its own treaties of friendship and mutual assistance. But, whatever their differences, the Western Powers preserved their united front. On 21st June Davies, speaking on behalf of his colleagues, said that further meetings had been rendered futile by the Russian attitude. He also announced that a Western invitation to a conference of Foreign Ministers was still open. Thus the Palais Rose Conference ended with more recriminations as to who was responsible for the breakdown.

Even before the abortive Palais Rose Conference had met, the French Government had initiated a conference on the Pleven Plan to which all the member states of N.A.T.O. and West Germany were invited. The first meeting took place on 15th February. After receiving a French memorandum it adjourned for a week. Under the terms of the French memorandum, the German contribution was not to exceed one-fifth of the whole, which was to be 100,000-140,000 men in the first stage, rising to 250,000-300,000 eventually. There were to be ten to twelve divisions, each consisting of two or three national combat teams. There was to be a European Commissioner of Defence responsible to an Assembly which would have the right to dismiss him. There was also to be a Committee of Ministers. A long series of Paris meetings, lasting many weeks, followed in which the details were argued out between the representatives of the new West German Government and the representatives of France, Italy, the Netherlands, Belgium and Luxembourg.

The British and Americans stood on one side. They considered that the Pleven proposals, as unfolded in detail, were still somewhat impractical—a view they had held earlier. Bevin left the Foreign Office in March 1951 with only a month to live. Amongst his last telegrams were some sent to Acheson, expressing his dark gloom about the Pleven proposals, which he did not think could be accepted by Britain and which he also feared would delay the setting up of any effective system of defence in Western Europe. He died on 14th April, 1951, leaving behind him such a legacy of affection and respect in the great department of state over which he had presided that his name is always recalled with great warmth by those who served under him. By any standards, he was a great man and he had left his stamp upon Europe and upon his own country.

The Paris discussions proceeded throughout the early summer of 1951. By late June, at the time that the Palais Rose Conference was ending, it became clear that the French would only accept West German rearmament within the framework of a European Defence Community. The British and American Governments, giving way, made a declaration in support of the French proposals. However, neither the Americans nor the British were prepared to join the European Army itself—although the British Government desired "the closest possible co-operation with the European Continental Community at all stages of its development"—a refusal that was a particular blow to the European supporters of E.D.C., as it gave support to opponents who claimed that it would become dominated by West Germany.

A new situation arose in the autumn of 1951. There were great hopes in Western Europe that the new Churchill Administration which followed Labour's narrow defeat in the General Election of October 1951 would reverse Britain's negative attitude to the European Defence Community. Thus there was a sense of dismay when a senior Conservative Minister, Sir David Maxwell-Fyfe, informed the European Consultative Assembly on 28th November that it would be quite unrealistic for Western Europe to expect Britain to join anything akin to a European federation. Furthermore, he held out no hope of anything more than a minor association with the European Defence Community.

The cold douche administered by the incoming British Conservative Government placed the European Army proposals in even greater jeopardy. The European reaction may have been illogical; but as Eden, the new Foreign Secretary, put it in a private minute to Churchill, " We are being made the whipping boy," adding: " This appears to be Strasbourg's only activity at this time." The truth was that there had been a partial misunderstanding in Western Europe as to Churchill's real attitude. He himself argued subsequently that his main aim was an ending of the traditional conflict between France and Germany and, in the furtherance of this aim, he had used expressions about European unity that had been taken wrongly to imply that he would be prepared to support full British participation.

Acheson, Eden and Schuman met in London in February 1952 to see what they could do to save E.D.C. Acheson explained to Eden, in a private conversation after he flew in, that he was contemplating a new "Monroe Doctrine" for Europe, in which the Americans would promise that if any European country threatened the peace, the others could count on American support. He hoped that this would help meet the French position. Schuman wanted more. He said, when he arrived, that if France could be certain of "the political presence" of Britain in such a way as not to leave France face to face with Germany, he thought that "French opinion would be satisfied." Adenauer, who also came to London, then joined the three men. He was assured that no steps would be taken which would discriminate against Germany, and this relieved him enormously. From the German point of view, Adenauer was making great progress. It appeared to Eden that at last something had been achieved and the European atmosphere "had been lightened" as he put it, although Britain obviously remained unaware of the commitment required of her—a consideration that was not lost upon Schuman.

The British Government received a formal request to join from all the E.D.C. countries in due course—France, West Germany, Italy, Belgium, the Netherlands and Luxembourg. In an impressive joint note delivered on 14th March, 1952, Britain was asked to enter into treaty relations and reciprocal promises with the European Defence Community on the lines of Ernest Bevin's Brussels Treaty of 1948. Under this latter Treaty, the signatories were already bound to go to the assistance of any of the other signatories if attacked; but Churchill and Eden were still not prepared to go as far as to include West Germany and Italy in the Brussels Treaty, which had forty-five years to run. A conversation over dinner on 19th March (in Paris where Eden had gone in quest of a solution) between Eden and Dirke Stikker, the Netherlands Foreign Minister, did a great deal to awaken the British Government at last to the danger of E.D.C. collapsing altogether. Stikker, a forthright man, told Eden in very frank terms that unless some treaty was agreed upon, the Netherlands Parliament was almost as unwilling as the French to enter the European Defence Community. Eden returned home to warn Churchill and his colleagues, and the British Government was now forced to make a counter-proposal that it was prepared to give the separate European member states a guarantee under Article 51 of the United Nations Charter—the Article specifically referring to the rights of individual states to take action when a member of the U.N. was attacked—as an alternative to extending the Brussels Treaty. It was a half-step forward as it gave a guarantee against German aggression, but the question was: was it sufficient? For the moment the situation appeared improved by the move and the Paris discussions on the European Defence Community Treaty went forward towards completion.

In the meanwhile, more discussions had been taking place between the Allied High Commissioners and Adenauer, aimed at revising the earlier Contractual Arrangements and the occupation status of the three Western Powers, parallel to the incorporation of West Germany into the E.D.C. The new discussions were long and involved. Adenauer's task in satisfying both the High Commissioners and the Bundestag was an extremely difficult one and he was branded by his opponents as " the Chancellor of the Allies." The principal issues involved occupation costs—a matter of particular concern to Britain because of her parlous balance of payments position—and the occupying powers' right to declare a state of emergency and to reassume control.

Compromises were made, however, and gradually the two sides came closer together. It was decided that the Contractual Agreements and Defence Treaty were to come into force on 1st October, 1952. The occupation costs were to be met by the Federal Republic until then, and there was to be a sliding scale thereafter. Nothing was said about occupation costs after June 1953 although it was assumed that the Federal Republic would pay a share. Everything seemed ready for the signatures to the Contractual Agreements, but just as Schuman was actually on his way to Bonn on the night of 22nd-23rd May to meet Acheson and Eden, the French cabinet suddenly demanded new conditions. The French Government said that it would not sign the Contractual Agreements without a stronger Anglo-American guarantee on aggression by one country against another with the E.D.C. and it would not place the Agreements before the National Assembly for ratification unless France received larger orders for offshore purchases and more support for her policies in Indo-China and North Africa. It was an indication of the mood in France. From the French point of view there had been growing alarm at the revival of German industry. France's economy was in a parlous state and the effects of her colonial wars were telling heavily. Acheson and Eden found themselves in a grave dilemma. Schuman telephoned the French cabinet in Paris repeatedly whilst the deadlock continued. The Anglo-American guarantee was strengthened reluctantly by Acheson and Eden to read: " Accordingly, if any action from whatever quarter threatens the integrity or unity of the [European] Community, the two Governments will regard this as a threat to their own security. They will act in accordance with Article 4 of the North Atlantic Treaty." Equally reluctantly, the French cabinet accepted this offer and temporarily dropped their insistence upon the other issues which Acheson had coldly stressed were outside the scope of the discussions. There were now to be problems on the German side. The Western Powers agreed to modify their position on war criminals. Thus it came about that at last the Contractual Agreements were signed on 26th May, 1952 —an auspicious day in European history and the first major step by Germany towards sovereignty and the Franco-German rapprochement.

The way was now open for the signing of the European Defence Community Treaty. The gathering of Foreign Ministers in Bonn moved on to Paris where, in the elegant Salon de L'Horloge of the Quai d'Orsay, the E.D.C. Treaty was duly signed by the representatives of the six European countries—France, West Germany, Italy, Belgium, the Netherlands and Luxembourg. The Treaty was to last for fifty years and the Defence Community was declared to be supra-national in character. Acheson and Eden looked on at the proceedings hopeful that a new European dawn had appeared.

They were soon to discover that the drafting and signing of the E.D.C. Treaty, and its corollary, the Contractual Agreements, had been difficult enough. The European Defence Community Treaty's long quest in search of ratification by the various European Parliaments was to prove even more difficult.

CHAPTER 19

DEATH OF A TYRANT

When tyrants' crests and tombs of brass are spent. *Shakespeare*

Stalin died at ten minutes to ten on the night of 5th March, 1953, at the age of seventy-three. There had been strange stirrings within the Soviet Union since the turn of the year. *Pravda* had announced on 13th January, 1953, that a conspiracy by nine doctors of the Kremlin medical administration had been unmasked. The doctors were accused "as secret enemies of the people" who had " deliberately subjected their patients to harmful treatment." They were stated to have murdered a number of prominent men, including Andrei Zhdanov, one of the most important figures in the Politbureau and a potential successor to Stalin. Five of the Kremlin doctors were accused of having connections with the American secret service and with the Jewish international organisation, " Joint." The doctors were pilloried in the Soviet Press as " poisoners " and as " hired murderers."

The sensational announcement was clearly a means of increasing fear and uncertainty and it led immediately to a witch-hunt throughout the Soviet Union in the succeeding fortnight. The obvious conclusion was that Stalin was preparing for a return to the purges of 1937. This belief turned to near-certainty when the Soviet Press gave prominence, on 6th February, to Stalin's earlier call for "vigilance" that had heralded the purges of sixteen years before. The Indian Ambassador in Moscow, who was the last foreign envoy to see Stalin alive, on 17th February, noticed during their conversation that Stalin repeatedly made drawings, in red pencil on a piece of paper, of wolves. The Soviet dictator then began to talk of wolves. He told his surprised visitor that Russian peasants knew how to deal with wolves. " They have to be exterminated," said Stalin, " but the wolves also know this, and they will act accordingly." Five days later, on February 22nd, the Soviet Press

343

campaign for "vigilance" was suddenly brought to an end. References to Stalin stopped abruptly. Instead, the Press referred at length to industrial production figures, the supply of vegetables and even to the latest fish landings at Soviet ports. Just over a week later, on 3rd March, a special announcement was made by the Council of Ministers declaring that Stalin had suffered a cerebral hæmorrhage the day before. Two further bulletins on 4th and 5th March showed that Stalin's condition was deteriorating fast. He had a relapse. Finally, the formal announcement of his death some hours before was made at 3 o'clock in the morning of 6th March.[1]

During the night of Stalin's death, Moscow was surrounded by M.V.D. troops. Appeals were broadcast asking urgently for solidarity. The streets leading to the Red Square and to the important buildings in the city were discreetly closed.

The changes in the Soviet Administration were announced within twenty-four hours. Stalin's successor as Chairman of the Council of Ministers was declared to be Georgi Maximilianovich Malenkov —who had made the main speech at the Nineteenth Party Congress the previous autumn and who was clearly Stalin's own choice.

The new Praesidium of the Soviet Government was to be reduced in size and, apart from Malenkov, four other names were announced

---

[1] Whether Stalin died from natural causes or was murdered may never be known. The available evidence, at the time of writing, points to an "Open Verdict." Three facts, apart from the strange sequence of preceding events, stand out: (1) After years of fulsome and laudatory comment on Stalin, *Pravda* restricted itself to some short tributes by minor officials and foreign Communist leaders. (2) Stalin's private secretariat, under General Alexander Poskrebyshev, who was privy to his secrets, was immediately disbanded. Poskrebyshev himself, awarded the Order of Lenin in 1939, disappeared altogether from the scene. He has never been mentioned again except once, derogatorily, by Krushchev in his "secret speech" to the Twentieth Congress. (3) On 4th April, 1953, less than four weeks after Stalin's death, *Pravda* announced that the Kremlin doctors had been released from detention and rehabilitated. I have a vivid memory also of a talk with Churchill one evening in the Cabinet Room at 10 Downing Street some months later. The Prime Minister, who was bidding me a safe journey on a long trip I was undertaking across the Soviet Union and through China suddenly dropped his cheerful banter. "Who knows the savageries they can perpetrate?" he asked dramatically; and then, with a sweep of his cigar, "Who knows how Stalin died? There is every reason to suppose he was foully murdered. Who knows . . . ? Who knows . . . ?" he said, as he stared on into his glass of whisky, before turning again to me. "I wish I was coming with you," he added. The story does not contribute to the evidence but it gives an indication of the widespread suspicions that existed in other countries.

in the first list, Beria, Molotov, Bulganin and Kaganovich. Molotov was to return to his old post as Foreign Minister.

Stalin's funeral took place on 9th March. The funeral orations were delivered by Malenkov, Beria and Molotov and from this it was apparent that Beria—Stalin's head of the secret police and now Minister of the Interior as well—stood second to Malenkov in authority. The men who bore Stalin's coffin to the Lenin mausoleum, to be renamed " The Mausoleum of Lenin and Stalin," were obviously the new rulers of Russia. Apart from the five men already mentioned, there was Voroshilov as titular Head of State, Anastas Ivanovich Mikoyan and Nikita Sergeyevich Krushchev— this last a new name for the general public in the Western countries.

The Supreme Soviet, called for 14th March to confirm the Soviet Government changes, was mysteriously postponed for a day. Instead, the Central Committee of the Soviet Communist Party met on 14th March and relieved Malenkov "at his own request" of his post as Secretary of the Central Committee that he had held under Stalin. Instead, Krushchev was appointed to the leading position in the reorganised Central Committee Secretariat. With these changes in the leadership, the Supreme Soviet's meeting on 15th March duly endorsed Malenkov's appointment. The true significance of the changes was only now apparent. There had been a struggle for power in which the others had been unwilling to concede the supreme authority to Malenkov. A form of compromise had been reached. Finally, Krushchev had emerged as a potential rival to Malenkov.

The characters and backgrounds of the two men—whose struggle was to dominate Soviet internal politics for the next four years— were so dissimilar that it is easy to see in retrospect that a clash was inevitable. Malenkov was the sophisticated bureaucrat personified. He had been a member of Stalin's secretariat at a very early age in 1925. In the late 1930s he had wielded great power as head of the Personnel Department. He became Secretary of the Central Committee in 1939, and, after the war, he was made Deputy Chairman of the Council of Ministers of the Soviet Union. This suave, polished man was the antithesis of his much more crude and older rival Krushchev, the son of a miner, who was said to have reached manhood before he taught himself to read and write.

Krushchev's initial rise had been slower than Malenkov's but, after a spell in Moscow in 1935, he came suddenly into prominence in 1938 when he was appointed First Secretary of the Ukrainian Party and a candidate member of the Politbureau—this latter a position that Malenkov did not reach until 1941. During the war Krushchev played a prominent part first in the Kiev area and then on the Stalingrad front. In 1943, he was given the rank of lieutenant-general, and, after the war, Krushchev was in turn Chairman of the Council of Ministers of the Ukraine, First Secretary of the Ukrainian Party again and, in December 1949, First Secretary of the Moscow Party and a full member of the Politbureau (which Malenkov had become in 1946). In the Politbureau, Krushchev was responsible for agricultural policy until he was publicly repudiated in *Pravda* on 5th March, 1951, and transferred to a post in charge of internal party affairs—a fact that was greatly to strengthen his personal position two years later.

Whereas Malenkov's overt good humour, tact and charm—qualities that were shown to the full in the West during a brief visit to Britain in 1955—led to his being described as " the man who would make a good parliamentary candidate in a free society," [1] Krushchev's public postures were less attractive and much more belligerent. Nevertheless, Krushchev had already proved himself in the Stalin era as "The Great Survivor" and his political agility had been demonstrated fifteen years before by a speech that he had made in the Red Square, Moscow, on the day of announcement of the verdict in the trial of Trotsky's followers. Krushchev, as quoted in *Pravda*, then had spoken of " these infamous nonentities who wanted to break up the unity of the Party and of Soviet Power. . . . They raised their murderous hands against Comrade Stalin . . . Stalin—our hope, Stalin—our expectation, Stalin—the banner of progressive mankind, Stalin—our banner, Stalin—our will, Stalin—our victory." His words make strange reading in the light of his famous speech to the Twentieth Congress three years after Stalin's death.

The changes in the Soviet Union were received cautiously in the West. The great Russian tyrant who had forged his country's position of world power out of the raw material of an uneducated and pitifully poor people and a backward continent had suddenly gone. He had so completely filled the Soviet scene that his successors were largely unknown outside Russia. Yet, the doctrines of Communism remained and there was every reason to suppose that

[1] A description of Malenkov by Morgan Phillips, General Secretary of the Labour Party.

Russia's new rulers subscribed to them as ardently as Stalin and Lenin had done in their own ways before. Nevertheless, there were early indications of a new and slight easement in East-West tensions. A British aircraft was shot down, on 12th March, by Soviet fighters over Germany, and it came as something of a surprise when the Soviet Government proposed talks on air safety. A fortnight later, the Soviet spokesman in the United Nations was at pains to explain the Soviet Union's peaceful intentions. More significantly, agreement was suddenly reached in Korea on the exchange of sick and wounded prisoners on 30th March. Then, Chou En-Lai, who had just returned from Moscow after attending Stalin's funeral, called for the repatriation of *all* prisoners. And, equally suddenly, the East-West deadlock at the U.N. over the appointment of a successor to Trygve Lie as Secretary General, was broken by the appointment of Dag Hammarskjöld.

The first Western leader to make a major move of conciliation in response was Churchill. After some weeks of cogitation, in which he had spoken most cautiously in public, he delivered a speech in the House of Commons on 11th May that had a world impact. Churchill said, " It would be, I think, a mistake to assume that nothing can be settled with Soviet Russia unless or until everything is settled. A settlement of two or three of our difficulties would be a very important gain. . . ." He went on to mention the hopes of peace in Korea and the abortive Austrian Peace Treaty for possible settlement as two examples; and he made it clear that he wished to assure the new Soviet leaders that he acknowledged the necessity of reconciling Russia's own desires for security with the freedom and safety of Western Europe. Churchill put forward the first of his two main proposals, saying, " The Locarno Treaty of 1925 has been in my mind. It was the highest point we reached between the wars. . . . It was based upon the simple provision that if Germany attacked France we should stand with the French, and if France attacked Germany we should stand with the Germans.

" The scene to-day," continued Churchill, " its scale and its factors, is widely different, and yet I have a feeling that the master thought which animated Locarno might well play its part between Germany and Russia. . . . Russia has a right to feel assured that as far as human arrangements can run the terrible events of the Hitler invasion will never be repeated, and that Poland will remain a friendly Power and a buffer, though not I trust a puppet State."

Churchill now came to his second proposal: " I believe that a conference on the highest level should take place between the leading Powers without long delay. The conference should not be overhung by a ponderous or rigid agenda, or led into mazes or jungles of technical details, zealously contested by experts and officials drawn up in cumbrous array. The conference should be attended by the smallest number of Powers and persons possible. . . ."

The reception to Churchill's initiative was mixed—in part favourable and part hostile. He was supported in France but his speech was received with suspicion in the United States where there were accusations of appeasement and mentions of " Munich." President Eisenhower, who had assumed office five months before, was coldly non-committal—an indication of reservations in the new American Administration, if not hostility. Churchill's speech was also represented in sections of the American Press as the last desperate throw by an ageing statesman who had always had a predilection for personal diplomacy during which it was clearly feared he would outwit, and even deceive, Britain's allies. The term "Locarno" was unfortunate, too. It had different connotations from those in Churchill's mind for the Soviet Union, where the Locarno Treaty had been regarded as a move to guarantee Germany's position in the West in order to give her a free hand in the East. Nevertheless, the American hostility was the principal obstacle as it was soon apparent that there was a major divergence between Churchill's views and the attitudes of Eisenhower and Dulles, his new Secretary of State. Churchill persisted. He felt very strongly that the opportunity should not pass and he compelled Eisenhower to agree to a preliminary conference of Western Powers to be held in Bermuda at the end of May, amongst the United States, Britain and France to prepare themselves on Far Eastern as well as European issues before a meeting with the Soviet Union. On the same day as the public announcement of the Bermuda meeting, the French Government of René Mayer fell and France was to remain without a government for the next month—an unfortunate situation that compelled the postponement of the Bermuda Conference.

The Soviet reaction to Churchill was more slow in coming. *Pravda* gave it on 24th May. While objecting strongly to the prospect of three Powers concerting their policy before meeting the fourth, it quoted sections of his speech with approval. Particular praise was given to Churchill's view that the problem of reconciling the Soviet Union's own claim for security with the security of Western Europe was not insoluble.

The machinations of the hobgoblins that sometimes seem to bedevil events now took a further hand. After a month of political crisis in France, Joseph Laniel was confirmed as Prime Minister on 26th June. But a bald announcement from Downing Street next day, on 27th June, stated that Churchill's doctors had advised him to take a rest. In fact, the British Prime Minister had suffered a stroke at the same moment that the new French Government was taking shape. To make matters worse, the British Foreign Secretary, Eden, was in a Boston hospital recovering from an operation that left him with a prolonged convalescence. Without Churchill, its moving spirit, or the only man who could deputise for him effectively, the original Bermuda Conference was clearly an impossibility. Instead, a meeting of the three Western Foreign Ministers was called in Washington for 10th July. Bidault was again to represent France and in Eden's absence Lord Salisbury was appointed acting Foreign Secretary.

In the meanwhile, the Soviet leadership had also been suffering its own troubles. The Russian Control Commission in East Germany was abolished on 28th May and it was replaced by a Soviet High Commission. The arrival of the new High Commissioner, Semeonov, was marked by a sudden shift in the East German Government's policy away from heavy industry " to the needs of the workers, farmers, the intelligentsia and all members of the middle class." This surprising official announcement went on, " The coercive measures for the collection of taxes and social security contributions in private industry shall be rescinded. Requests for permission to resume business from persons who have closed or handed over their concerns shall be granted immediately." Permission was given for refugees, who had fled to the West, to return with impunity. Other measures, including a major law reform and amnesty were forecast. The effect of these remarkable events in East Germany was offset by a decision to increase the norms of workers and thus to reduce the basic wages they received.

Very soon there were strikes against the norms, ending up with an incident in East Berlin that was to have startling repercussions. Some three hundred building workers marched down Stalinallee at ten o'clock on 16th June. By the time the march reached Alexanderplatz it was nearly two thousand strong. It stopped in the square outside the "House of the Ministries" in the Leipzigerstrasse. There were shouts for Grotewohl, the East German Prime Minister, and Ulbricht, the East German Communist leader. After some delay, two lesser East German Ministers appeared. They were shouted down. When neither Grotewohl nor Ulbricht appeared, someone suggested calling a general strike for the next day, 17th June. The cry was taken up and the whole crowd endorsed it. This call was sent forth, by telephone and messengers on bicycles and trams. Three demonstrators also made their way to an American radio station in West Berlin, with a demand for a return to the old "norms"—free and secret elections—immediate measures to reduce the cost of living—and no victimisation against the strikers. News of these demands and the happenings of the day were broadcast from West Berlin that evening.

Seventeenth June, 1953, became a day of uproar leading to uprising in East Germany. Throughout the Soviet zone men were on strike and demonstrating. By midday the Marx-Engels Platz in East Berlin—known as the Lustgarten in earlier days and now the scene of traditional Communist demonstrations—was full. Russian tanks suddenly appeared and charged the stampeding crowd. The tanks pursued the crowd down the Unter den Linden, leaving behind the first casualty of the day, the mangled body of a man caught by the tank tracks, in a large pool of blood. Three youths climbed the Brandenburg Gate and tore down the red flag despite warning cries about the machine-guns that were being trained on them. Several public buildings were set alight. Many East German police and soldiers showed sympathy with the demonstrators. The insurrection spread quickly to Halle, Jena, Leipzig, Görlitz and Magdeburg. On 18th June, a West Berlin inhabitant, Willi Gottling, was executed as a Western agent who had helped to instigate the uprising.

The news of the "Seventeenth of June" was a severe shock to Stalin's heirs in the Kremlin. It posed grave problems for the Communist régime within East Germany which had implications for every Communist state in Eastern Europe. As for the rest of the world, it was now able to see that eight years of Communist rule and indoctrination had failed completely to win the support of the people upon whom it had been imposed, despite all the overwhelming weight of Soviet propaganda.

The next shock within the Soviet Union was the fall of the Lavrenti Pavlovich Beria, who stood second only to Malenkov in the hierarchy. *Pravda* announced sensationally on 10th July that

Malenkov, addressing a full session of the Central Committee at the end of June, had indicted Beria for " criminal and treasonable acts." The *Pravda* account went on to say that Beria had tried " to put the Soviet Ministry of the Interior above Party and Government " and that he had sought to undermine the state " in the interests of foreign capital." Beria, it was stated, was relieved of all his Party positions " as an enemy of the Communist Party and the Soviet people." Before his fall, the last time Beria had been mentioned in the Soviet Press was on 10th June. *Pravda*, on 27th June, reported that the Party and State leaders, Malenkov, Molotov, Voroshilov, Krushchev and Bulganin had attended a Bolshoi Theatre performance on 25th June. As Beria was not present, it must be assumed that he was arrested sometime between these two dates. A subsequent news item in *Pravda* dated Beria's formal dismissal as having taken place on 26th June. There are some signs, too, that Beria's downfall was associated, in part, with the events in East Germany. He was certainly connected, during the months of May and early June 1953, with the policy of easement. It is known also that when the East German situation threatened danger on 16th June, the East German Communists immediately asked for the intervention of Soviet troops, and that their demand was not met at first. More than twenty-four hours was to go by before the first Soviet tanks were allowed to move and this happened only when mob violence appeared imminent. There is also a report from East German sources that, some weeks later, the S.E.D. Politbureau received a letter from the Soviet leaders stating that Beria had been in favour of policies that might have led to the abandonment of East Germany. The effect of these two events— the uprising and Beria's arrest—and their relationship was, temporarily, to shake the confidence of the Soviet leadership and restrict its capacity for manœuvre.

In the meanwhile, the three Western Foreign Ministers had been meeting in Washington. Their talks concluded on 14th July with the proposal that there should be a Four-Power meeting of Foreign Ministers to discuss free all-German elections for a single free all-German government and the elusive Austrian Peace Treaty. This was a quite different suggestion from Churchill's earlier idea of a small, personalised meeting of the leaders of East and West and it represented a major victory for Dulles over Salisbury and Bidault. In terms of practical European politics it also meant that there could be no question of the E.D.C. Treaties being ratified in France and Germany before the Foreign Ministers had made one more attempt to solve the German problem.

The preliminaries to the Foreign Ministers' Conference took up the late summer and autumn of 1953. Notes passed to and fro as each side manœuvred for position. The differences were easy to see. As far as the Western Powers were concerned, their view was that an all-German government should participate in the drafting of the peace treaty but, for this to be the case, there had to be free elections first. The Soviet Union started from quite different premises: the provisional all-German government was to be established first, by an amalgamation of the two German régimes. This provisional government was then to prepare for the peace treaty, and, finally, it was to be responsible for holding free elections. The Russians also maintained that any ratification of the E.D.C. Treaty would conflict with the purpose of any conference whose aim was German unity, as it could only mean that West Germany was tied irrevocably to the Western defence system. Thereby they exposed a major political weakness in the Western position. A series of diplomatic notes passed during which Molotov pressed for the inclusion of China at any East-West meeting—a demand that was carefully calculated to place the United States Administration in difficulty.

A sense of direction was given again to British foreign policy in October by the return to their duties of Churchill and Eden. Addressing the annual Conservative conference rally on 10th October Churchill made his first speech on international affairs since 11th May, and he explained his country's priorities—the American Alliance that he considered vital, and the long-term association of Germany with the West. He dropped his original demand for a meeting of heads of government and he also confronted the Malenkov Government with its own major dilemma. If the Soviet Union continued with policies that made permanent the division of Germany, it might not be able to prevent West Germany being integrated into the West. On the other hand, the Soviet Government also realised, especially following the events of 17th June, that an all-German government arising out of any sort of free elections was certain to lean to the West—and, according to Churchill on 10th October, it would be encouraged so to do. Clearly neither of the alternatives was in the Soviet interest and Molotov was, therefore, forced to agree to the Four-Power Foreign Ministers' Conference to meet in Berlin in January 1954. However, the Soviet Foreign Minister reserved his right to put forward his own solutions to the German problem and to raise again the proposal for a Five-Power meeting, to include China, to consider the situation in the Far East, including Korea. Molotov knew only too well that the twin Soviet objectives that his government wished to pursue— the withdrawal of American troops from Europe and the prevention of a resurgent, united Germany allied to the West—could only be furthered if he were able to gain time and create conditions for a specific and quite possible eventuality, the rejection of E.D.C. by the French National Assembly.

At this same time, Dulles and Eden realised that French opinion was the vulnerable factor in their own strategy. To meet it, Dulles attempted to take the initiative himself before the Four-Power meeting. At the N.A.T.O. Council meeting in Paris on 14th December he gave a grave warning. He said that if E.D.C. did not " come into effect and France and Germany remained apart as potential enemies, it was doubtful whether the continent of Europe could be made a place of safety." In these circumstances, the United States would be compelled to make " an agonising re-appraisal of their basic policy." Dulles believed that he was serving notice on France in a manner that would eventually force her to the point of ratifying E.D.C. but, in fact, he achieved an effect almost contrary to his objective. There was an immediate storm of French protest against Dulles's remarks. At the same time, Dulles, by his tactless move, had limited yet further any hopes amongst the Western Powers that the Berlin Conference could achieve success because it was apparent even to the most partisan Western supporter that the Soviet Union would never agree to the unification of Germany in circumstances that could lead to the new all-German government joining E.D.C. and yet this was just what Dulles was demanding in effect, if not in fact.

Thus the first major attempt to reach agreement between East and West at the conference table since 1949 was held in circum-stances in which the two sides were entrenched in irreconcilable positions from the start. The Berlin prospects seemed as bleak as the European winter. The long awaited conference's meeting-place was also a mistake as it gave rise to preliminary arguments as to the actual building in Berlin in which the meetings should be held —a tiresome issue that was only resolved by the Western Powers agreeing to hold meetings alternately in East and West Berlin, instead of insisting upon a rotation of meetings in the sectors of each of the occupying Powers.

s.w.   353

The Berlin Conference opened on 25th January. Bidault spoke for the three Western Powers when he outlined proposals for an agenda. He suggested four points: (1) The problem of German unity, (2) The Austrian Peace Treaty, (3) Security in Europe, (4) Other matters. Molotov replied in a long speech which, although conciliatory in tone, reiterated all the familiar Soviet positions. At the conclusion of it he put forward his own alternative agenda: (1) Measures for reducing international tension and the convening of a Five-Power conference to include China, (2) The German question and the problem of European security, (3) The Austrian Peace Treaty.

The Western Powers, after consultation overnight, decided to accept Molotov's agenda. It was a good move which conceded nothing in principle but which showed a spirit of conciliation. As Dulles put it, " It is an agenda which we will take for the sake of getting on with our work. We do not want to turn this conference into another Palais Rose." The first item, although Dulles sought to limit the scope of negotiations which involved China, also led to a comparatively easy agreement. The Foreign Ministers accepted a proposal to hold a conference at Geneva in April on Korea and the increasingly dangerous situation in Indo-China, where Communist forces were threatening the French position.

The four delegations were now faced by the hub of the issues dividing them—Germany. Eden presented the Western plan for reunification. It fell under four main headings. The first essential prerequisite, according to him, was to hold " free and secret elections " throughout Germany. The Four Powers would supervise the elections and any disputes amongst them would have to be settled by a majority vote. The new all-German Assembly thus elected would then proceed to the drafting and approval of a constitution, and to the setting up of an all-German government which would be free eventually to enter into international commitments. During the interim period, whilst the establishment of this administration was taking place, the Four Occupation Powers would supervise the country. Finally, the German peace treaty would be signed by all the former belligerents and it would come into force when it was ratified by the Four Occupation Powers and by Germany. Molotov's rejoinder to Eden's plan was to claim that if the German elections were under foreign supervision, they could not possibly be free. It was a spurious argument at first sight to the Western delegates, but less so in the Soviet mind because of the way in which Molotov regarded "supervision" as it had been practised in his country, in Poland and other East European countries. He also demanded that the E.D.C. agreements should be abandoned —a more understandable claim. His position was made more clear when he tabled a draft peace treaty on 1st February, under which a unified Germany would " undertake not to enter into any coalition or military alliance directed against any Power whose armed forces took part in the war against Germany." In short, whereas the Western Powers wanted a free choice for Germany, Molotov wanted neutralisation. It was back to the old positions again, and it augured ill for the outcome. To underline this disagreement Molotov made a revealing remark to Eden over dinner one evening. He told the British Foreign Secretary in private that whilst he subscribed to the concept of free elections, he considered that the occupying Powers should agree upon the nature of the government that they wished to come out of the free elections. The repeated arguments now showed that he had no intention of relaxing his determination to resist free elections as the West understood the meaning of the term—even to the point of insisting on no elections.

This attitude of Molotov's and his demand for German neutrality were to be central issues for discussion throughout the rest of the Berlin Conference. The discussions on the Austrian Peace Treaty were equally fruitless. One of Molotov's demands was that the Occupation Forces should remain in Austria until the German Treaty had been signed because this would prevent any recurrence of the 1938 *Anschluss*. The conference ended on 18th February with a pathetically forlorn communiqué recording the Foreign Ministers' inability to agree.

The Berlin Conference of 1954 set the seal on the division of Germany—perhaps for several generations. If Molotov had been more flexible and less maladroit, the Western Powers could have been faced with the military consequences of agreeing to a settlement that might, in theory, have excluded Western Germany from the N.A.T.O. defence pattern. Alternatively, Molotov could have driven them to a point at which the continued division of Germany became the sole responsibility of the West. Fortunately for Dulles, Eden and Bidault, the Soviet Union had also been faced by the consequences of the failure of the Communist doctrine to establish any hold on the German people, and Stalin's successors had decided in advance of Berlin to reject disengagement and to stand on the Western frontier of Stalin's own conquests—the wide, winding

River Elbe. In the light of this it is difficult to see why Molotov went to Berlin at all. The answer is that he had no alternative if he were to keep alive the struggle against E.D.C. which, from his point of view, was not lost by any means. As for the Western Powers, they knew they now had to secure the ratification of the E.D.C. Treaty and thereby integrate West Germany into the North Atlantic Treaty Alliance, or face a European situation that would become more fluid and dangerous as time went on.

The Benelux countries and West Germany soon ratified the treaty but the real struggle was in France. There, the Laniel Government was forced, again and again, to postpone bringing the issue to a head because of the balance of forces existing in the National Assembly. To most Frenchmen, old hatreds and experiences had left their mark. Germany still remained the traditional enemy. Any proposal involving the rearmament of Germany evoked their strongest emotions. The fact that E.D.C. had been a French creation was a source of embarrassment to some, and certainly not an effective argument for mass French support. The Gaullists in the Assembly remained bitterly opposed to it. So were the Communists. These together represented a large bloc of votes. The Socialists were divided, despite the support for E.D.C. by Guy Mollet, the French Socialist leader, and this division within the Socialists was enough to prevent Laniel taking action. The French political situation became even more confused when the Laniel Government fell on the Indo-China issue on 12th June—where the French military situation had become critical. Nor was it clarified in any way when Laniel was succeeded on 17th June by Mendès-France, a dynamic and somewhat brittle and intransigent figure, leading a Gaullist-Radical administration.

In these uncertain days the French decision could have gone either way. Eden had long come to the private conclusion that a majority did not exist in the French Assembly for E.D.C. but Dulles could not bring himself to accept this view. Instead he demanded action and, to put pressure on Mendès-France, the American and British Governments announced at the beginning of July that they were proposing an examination of how West Germany could be granted her sovereignty despite France's failure to ratify the E.D.C. Treaty, upon which Germany's status was conditional under the Bonn Agreements. The pistol was now really being held at France's head in a most brutal manner. Under the threat, Mendès-France felt he had no alternative than to offer to meet the other five E.D.C. Powers in a last vain attempt to secure some formula that he could get past the National Assembly. This Five-Power meeting took place in Brussels on 19th August. Mendès-France's suggested amendments to the Treaty which discriminated openly against Germany and also incorporated the right of secession from the Defence Community—both unacceptable points to the others and to Dulles who was determined to get his way. The French delegation was now in a minority of one. In his isolation and desperation, Mendès-France now turned to Churchill and Eden. The French Prime Minister could see that if the controls on West German rearmament, as laid down in the E.D.C. Treaty, were not accepted by his countrymen, Europe would end up by having West German rearmament inside N.A.T.O. without any controls. At the same time, he knew that the task of getting E.D.C. ratified by his own National Assembly looked impossible. Mendès-France flew to see Churchill, at Churchill's own home of Chartwell, on 23rd August. Eden, who was on holiday when he heard of the proposed meeting, had also flown back to England to be present. The British spokesmen were anxious to help but they were full of grave warnings as to the consequences to France if the Treaty were not ratified. Mendès-France felt cornered. The issue now had to go to the vote and the following week it came before the Assembly. The bitter debate lasted for two days. Mendès-France took the extraordinary course of declining to commit himself or his government in support of the Treaty's terms. As Eden described it subsequently, he was " more referee than advocate." The vote was taken on 30th August. It now turned out that Eden had been right. The Treaty was defeated by 314 to 264, with 43 abstentions. It is possible that a more positive lead by Mendès-France could have secured a narrow majority, but it was by no means certain. In that case Dulles would have been right, but it is an academic point. The European Defence Community was dead. The supra-national organisation upon which Western policy had been based lay in ruins. The political consequences to Europe were most alarming, as the Western Powers were now committed to West German rearmament and could not draw back without creating a critical situation in West Germany. To make matters worse, Dulles's earlier forecasts of a possible American return to isolationism had suddenly become a serious possibility. Only in the Soviet bloc, from which a concentrated propaganda campaign had been directed on French opinion, was there jubilation. The Soviet Foreign

Ministry issued a Press statement calling for a new conference on Germany and European security which Molotov knew would be held in very different circumstances from the Berlin confrontation.

The Western disarray was complete until Eden took the initiative. First, the British Foreign Secretary convened a Nine-Power conference in London, consisting of the six E.D.C. countries, the United States, Canada and Britain. His aim was to consider a solution by which Western Germany was granted sovereignty and was rearmed within a N.A.T.O. framework. As a preliminary, Eden also decided upon a hurried tour of European capitals. In his bath on a Sunday morning—a place in which Eden claims he often gets inspiration— he suddenly came to the conclusion that the Brussels Treaty of 1948 might be used as the substitute for E.D.C. if it were extended to include West Germany and Italy. It also occurred to the Foreign Secretary that the Brussels Treaty had certain positive advantages, including freedom from the supra-national features of the European Defence Community that had precluded British participation. And if Britain now came in to buttress this wider framework, might it not remove some of France's inhibitions? He communicated his enthusiasm to his colleagues and secured their support.

Taking only one adviser, Sir Frank Roberts, Eden set out for Brussels on 11th September. He met with a very cordial reception from Paul-Henri Spaak, the Belgian Foreign Minister, who liked the idea at once of a modified Brussels Treaty as the method of rearming Germany inside a controlling framework. At a meeting of all three Benelux representatives, Eden's rescue plan was endorsed. The British Foreign Secretary had an equally cordial reception from Adenauer in Bonn, where the West German Chancellor's policy and entire personal future had been pledged to E.D.C. and was on the brink of disaster. By the time he had visited Rome, Eden felt he had some chance of success for his plans. But his last and most difficult city of call remained ahead. On arrival in Paris, Eden found Mendès-France unyielding. He retired to bed dispirited. There was a dramatic change next day. The French Premier appeared unexpectedly to take the chair at a meeting of the permanent N.A.T.O. Council at the Palais de Chaillot, which Eden was to address. Afterwards, Mendès-France asked to see Eden alone and told him that after a sleepless night he had come to see Eden's arguments about the impossibility of not having West Germany in N.A.T.O. However, Mendès-France required the strongest safeguards that were practicable, and to that extent he wanted Eden's help desperately. It was the great chance of a breakthrough that Eden was not slow to take.

Thus the Foreign Secretary returned to London with the belief that the nine-power conference now had a real chance of success His main aim was to secure West Germany's entry into N.A.T.O. with safeguards over German rearmament of a non-discriminatory character acting through the N.A.T.O. Command. His task was to create these safeguards in such a manner as to make the plan acceptable to French opinion. Eden also had a secondary aim of great importance—the extension of the Brussels Treaty as a means of strengthening West European political unity. This, in itself, commended his ideas to the former E.D.C. Powers.

The London Conference assembled on 28th September. Eden worked frantically behind the scenes to bring the success that was really assured by two major concessions—from Britain and West Germany. On the second day, Eden gave the great assurance that France had sought in vain previously. " The United Kingdom," he said, " will continue to maintain on the mainland of Europe, including Germany, the effective strength of the United Kingdom forces now assigned to SACEUR [1]—four divisions and the tactical air force—or whatever SACEUR regards as an equivalent fighting capacity." The Foreign Secretary announced that his government also agreed that these forces should not be withdrawn against a majority decision of the Brussels Treaty Powers except in an extreme overseas emergency for Britain. The second concession was made by Adenauer, who had as much as anyone to lose by failure. He gave a unilateral undertaking that West Germany would not manufacture atomic, biological or chemical weapons, thereby allaying the feelings of those who feared a German military resurgence.

Eden had, in truth, snatched success out of disaster for the West. Dulles called it the " near-miracle of London." The central problem created by the collapse of E.D.C. had been overcome and the task now was to embody the London Conference decisions into a formal treaty—work that was done very quickly in the Paris Agreement of October. The German Federal Republic had become a member of N.A.T.O. whilst Western European Union had been accepted by the N.A.T.O. Council as part of its defence system. It might be thought that no more disasters could now take place, but the architects of the great remoulding of Western Europe were

[1] Supreme Allied Commander, Europe.

still to undergo a most anxious moment. On Christmas Eve, 1954, the French National Assembly rejected, by 280 votes to 258, Article 1 of the Bill ratifying the Paris Agreements. In a mounting flurry of excitement and apprehension Mendès-France made it a confidence issue to reverse the vote. He succeeded. The year 1955 opened in Europe in circumstances that were very different from those that had gone before.

Events of profound importance had taken place since the first tentative proposals for a European Army, including a West German contribution, had been made as far back as 1950. The Soviet strategy, conceived by Stalin, to secure Communist domination over the whole of Germany had been defeated after a desperate political struggle. For the way things turned out at the end, most of the credit must go to Eden. His effort was a remarkable diplomatic achievement that has made its lasting contribution to the security of the West. Yet in the intervening years since the Strasbourg meeting of 1950, there were many others who played their parts also—from Acheson to Dulles, from Schuman to Mendès-France, to say nothing of Bidault and Spaak. The roll call of names is not complete, however, without the steadfast story of Konrad Adenauer. He will undoubtedly rank as one of the most significant figures of the period, and, after passions have stilled, the stature of this elderly Rhinelander will certainly grow until he comes to be regarded as one of the great leaders of German history.

The long struggle to integrate West Germany into N.A.T.O. had, of course, been stimulated in the first place by the Korean War. In its immediate sense, it was also a most important success for the West in the quest for security against the perpetual Soviet threat in Europe. But the wide sweep of history will record the year 1954 as the beginning of a much greater achievement—the ending of the European Civil War that had lasted ever since 1914.

CHAPTER 20

THE TRAGEDY OF DIEN BIEN PHU

Diplomacy has rarely been able to gain at the conference table what cannot be gained or held on the battlefield.   *Walter Bedell Smith*

The year 1954, in addition to the struggle by the Western Powers for the physical body of Western Germany, included the Indo-China crisis that threatened, briefly, to light the nuclear blaze of a third world war. In the six months between the Berlin Conference that ended in February, and before the final death agonies of E.D.C. in August, the climate of official opinion in the United States changed so sharply that it reached the point at which the Eisenhower Administration was prepared to take actions that could have led on to a direct military conflict with Communist China on the Chinese mainland, and to the possible involvement of the Soviet Union. For France, with her national ethos shaken bitterly by war-time experiences, it was a time of anguish, disillusionment and an agonising choice. Amongst the Asian neutrals, the anti-American moods created by the Korean War and by American policy towards China reached new levels of hostility so that it appeared that it might be years before Asian suspicions of the United States would die. During this same period, British foreign policy, under the direction of a revitalised Eden recovered from his severe illness and supported by Churchill, asserted itself in a restraining role upon the United States. The Soviet Union also emerged for the first time in a new and apprehensive attitude at the 1954 Geneva Conference, acting as a restraining influence within the Communist bloc upon Chinese policy. It was the first authentic sign of the Sino-Soviet conflict that was yet to come. In all, the spring and summer was a period of crises, misunderstandings, strained alliances and intense diplomatic activity in the Cold War.

The Indo-China struggle had its roots in the great Asian movements for independence that marched in the wake of the retreating

Japanese. On 2nd September, 1945, a Democratic Republic of Vietnam was proclaimed. It was led by the Viet-Minh National Liberation Committee [1] with Ho Chi Minh, a dedicated Communist, at its head. This government soon came into conflict with the returning French, who regarded the three States of Indo-China —Vietnam, Laos and Cambodia—as their traditional sphere of colonial influence. A long and bitter struggle developed that increased greatly in intensity after the Chinese Communist revolution. There was never much evidence that Chinese forces were directly engaged, but from 1949 onwards the Viet-Minh armies had a ready base for supplies and training on their country's frontiers. This new factor transformed a desultory and sporadic campaign into a determined military operation that soon threatened French suzerainty. It is true that for a brief period in 1950 the personality and military skill of General de Lattre Tassigny, holding both posts of French High Commissioner and Commander-in-Chief, regained the initiative for France but de Lattre's tenure was cut short by a fatal illness.

The overall Indo-China situation was in itself an example of one more rearguard action by European colonialism but it also threatened to change the balance of power throughout South-East Asia. The French political leaders of the day had much to answer for—in particular they were nearly always slow to consider greater freedoms for the Vietnamese, despite incessant American pressure. They decided to champion a puppet Emperor, Bao Dai, who was effete, corrupt and unpopular. Reluctantly they agreed to granting Vietnam the status of an Associate State of the French Union, which was not enough to assuage nationalist sentiment. For a long time, the United States also bore a large proportion of the costs of France's struggle in Indo-China, increasing their aid as time went on. Yet it was to little avail. By the end of 1953, the outlook was extremely bleak for the French, and the prospect of the Communists over-running Indo-China led on to the dangers of new threats to Burma, Thailand and Malaya.

It was against this background that Bidault, in Berlin, advocated that Indo-China should be included in the agenda for the forth-coming Geneva Conference on Korea—which it was agreed, finally, would assemble on 27th April, 1954. After the Berlin Foreign Ministers' Conference broke up on 18th February, the French

[1] The word Viet-Minh is in itself a Vietnamese abbreviation for "League for the Revolution and Independence of Vietnam."

military situation—already grave—deteriorated further. Whilst the French had been holding the towns, the Viet-Minh forces had infiltrated the countryside with skilful guerrilla tactics. The French had found themselves fighting a phantom enemy by day, and suffering severe and incessant losses, mainly by night. They developed an understandable longing for some spot where they could fight a major battle on conventional European lines, in which they could outgun and destroy their elusive enemy.

In November 1953 the French decided upon this place for the pitched battle. It was in a small mountain valley, in the area west of the Red River Delta, a few miles in from the frontier of Laos and so far north that it was comparatively close to the Chinese border. The village in the valley, translated into English was called "The Seat of the Border Country Administration" but its Vietnamese name—soon to echo round the world—was Dien Bien Phu. The French immediately set about fortifying and garrisoning the village which had changed hands at earlier stages of the Indo-China war and whose main strategic significance was that it stood on the invasion route to Laos. Ten thousand of France's best troops were sent to Dien Bien Phu and they were reinforced yet further as the weeks went by. It is difficult now to see why General Navarre, the French Commander, ever chose this remote spot. Later, after the Viet-Minh had laid siege to it, it was described by a French journalist as " an immense stadium, at least 20 kilometres in length and 7 or 8 wide. We [the French] hold the floor of the stadium. The tiers of the mountains all around belong to the Viet-Minh."

Early in 1954 it became apparent that the Viet-Minh intended to accept the French challenge at Dien Bien Phu. They invested the " stadium " with their forces and to Navarre's surprise they equipped them with artillery and anti-aircraft guns supplied from across the Chinese frontier, brought in part by a new fleet of Molotova trucks that moved along hurriedly constructed roads. The French landing strips on the floor of the "stadium" quickly came under fire and an air-lift of supplies, upon which Navarre was relying, developed into a most hazardous operation. With French arms and prestige already committed in this remote valley, the Viet-Minh began on 12th March the first of their many attempts to take Dien Bien Phu by storm in an offensive that lasted nearly four days. The bitter sense of having made a fatal mistake sapped the roots of confidence in the French command in Indo-China and demoralised the politicians in Paris.

This was the situation on 20th March when General Paul Ely, the French Chief of Staff, flew into Washington on his way back from an inspection tour of the military position in Indo-China. Ely's American visit extended over a number of days. He saw the Chairman of the American Joint Chiefs of Staff, Admiral Arthur Radford, John Foster Dulles and, finally, President Eisenhower. In the course of his talks a dramatic new American policy swiftly developed. Ely, on his way to Washington, had already come to the conclusion that Indo-China would be lost without American intervention. He posed the question on arrival: What would be the American reaction if MIGs piloted by Chinese were used to attack Dien Bien Phu? From this it was only a short stage for Ely, Radford and Dulles to be discussing seriously the possibility of an American air strike at the Viet-Minh positions around the Dien Bien Phu " stadium." Dulles was immediately seized of the critical nature of the French situation and he sounded a warning note in public in a speech to the Overseas Press Club of America on 29th March. Referring to the extension of Communism, the Secretary of State said that this " should not be passively accepted but should be met by united action. This might involve serious risks, but the risks are far less than those that will face us in a few years from now if we dare not be resolute to-day." As the Press had been alerted before Dulles spoke and the key paragraph in the speech had been passed to the British and French Ambassadors, there could be no doubt as to the implications of Dulles's words. Four days later, on 3rd April, Dulles and Radford met Congressional leaders at Eisenhower's request to discuss the possibility of American intervention. A possible Congressional resolution authorising the use of American air and naval power in Indo-China—but not ground forces—was discussed by Dulles in this Saturday meeting with the group of astonished men from Capitol Hill. Accounts of what happened at the meeting vary but they are agreed on the fact that there was a consensus of opinion of those present, including Dulles himself, that the United States should not act alone. Next day—Sunday, 4th April—Dulles and Radford went to see Eisenhower at the White House, privately, after dinner. By now, particularly Radford and, to a slightly lesser extent, Dulles had convinced themselves that Ely—who had returned to France with the American advice that the French Government would have to request military

action officially—was right and that the United States must intervene. They persuaded the President to cable Churchill that same
night, " I fear that the French cannot alone see this thing through.
. . . And if they do not see it through and Indo-China passes into
the hands of the Communists, the ultimate effect on our and your
global strategic position with the consequent shift in the power
ratios throughout Asia and the Pacific could be disastrous. . . .
This has led us to the hard conclusion that the situation in South
East Asia requires us to take urgent and far-reaching decisions."
Eisenhower went on to suggest " a new *ad hoc* grouping " to check
Communism. In addition to the United States and Britain he
proposed France and the Associated States—Australia, New Zealand,
Thailand and the Philippines. He concluded, " *The important
thing is that the coalition . . . must be willing to join the fight if necessary.*[1]
I do not envisage the need of any appreciable ground forces on
your or our part. If I may refer again to history, we failed to
halt Hirohito, Mussolini and Hitler by not acting in unity and in
time. That marked the beginning of many years of stark tragedy
and desperate peril. . . ." Eisenhower urgently asked Churchill to
see Dulles who was prepared to fly over at once.

The British Government was taken aback. They found themselves
faced by a difficult decision. Both Churchill and Eden had long
considered the possibility of some wider alliance that could contribute to the security of the British position in Hong Kong and in
Malaya where, in more favourable circumstances than in Indo-
China, the British had fought a successful campaign against Communist guerrilla forces. Indeed, this alliance had been put forward
by Schuman, amongst others, in earlier years. The British had
also resented Britain's exclusion from the so-called A.N.Z.U.S. Pact
in which America had formed a defensive alliance with Australia
and New Zealand. On the other hand, the Geneva Conference
was less than four weeks away at the time of Eisenhower's telegram
and any such action in advance of it, in Eden's view, would destroy
all hopes of any possible agreement that could save South-East
Asia from further Communist territorial gains. Churchill himself
doubted very strongly that any action would be effective without
considerable ground forces,[2] and both the British Conservative
Administration and British public opinion were as strongly opposed
as ever to fighting a campaign against the Chinese on the mainland.
Whilst Eisenhower, Dulles and Radford waited impatiently for his

[1] Author's italics.   [2] Incidentally, Dulles held similar views.

reply, Churchill decided to take his time. After three days, the Prime Minister cabled Eisenhower that he and his government would see Dulles in London on 12th April—a full week after the President's urgent appeal.

In the meanwhile, Dulles had taken the bit between his teeth. On 5th April he told the House of Representatives' Foreign Affairs Committee that China was only avoiding the charge of aggression by technicalities. He went on to say specifically that Chinese personnel and arms were involved in the battle around Dien Bien Phu, which was now completely surrounded. Dulles named a Chinese general at Viet-Minh headquarters and stated that Chinese guns were "shooting through the clouds to bring down French aircraft." He called for "a unity of action" although he still "would deprecate" action by America alone. The Americans were baffled and surprised when Dulles's speech had a mixed reception in France, where weariness with the conflict had extended to a wide section of the public. Also, despite Ely's views, the Laniel Government was most undecided.

International tension mounted as the Dien Bien Phu perimeter grew smaller and the garrison's struggle became more desperate. The Viet-Minh forces were driving hundreds of communication trenches to within a few feet of the French positions and at some points they were within a thousand yards of the heart of the French fortifications. The French garrison was by now completely cut off. The last aircraft to land on the Dien Bien Phu strip had been a casualty evacuation transport which had been destroyed by Viet-Minh gunfire as it was preparing to take off on 29th March, marooning the crew that included a French nurse.[1] Air drops of supplies were now most difficult operations and the defenders often had the chagrin of seeing them fall into enemy hands, so small was the defended area. In Paris there were rumours, defeatism and a multitude of conflicting emotions.

Dulles, the most intrepid air traveller in the history of modern diplomacy, reached London on 11th April. His arrival was awaited with apprehension by the British. The cabinet had decided already that it did not consider Dulles's threats of intervention, even if they were to be carried out, would cause the Chinese to draw back. The position was, in fact, to the contrary in the opinion of the British, and they believed that in the event of

[1] Her name was Mlle Geneviève de Gallard-Tarraubes, who became known in the Press as "The Angel of Dien Bien Phu."

an American-Chinese conflict the Soviet Union might be drawn in with the gravest consequences to all. The British favoured instead a solution by the partitioning of Vietnam and they considered that the right time to warn the Chinese was after this partition had been agreed. The cabinet paper concluded, " On the other hand, the proposal to organise collective security in South-East Asia is in itself attractive, and there is an advantage in expressing our views to the Americans whilst their own ideas are still not fully formed." A clear decision had been made also to resist the American proposals in advance of the outcome of the Geneva Conference. Dulles drove immediately to the American Embassy and after dinner he and Eden had a preliminary discussion that covered the main issues. The American Secretary of State first expanded his ideas which, he said, depended upon two conditions—the French must grant the Associated States real independence at last, and the Americans must be able to carry the British, Australian and New Zealand governments with them in any intervention. Eden, who was very concerned about reactions throughout the rest of Asia, particularly in India and Burma, and the implications for the still delicate situation in Malaya, tried to separate the American proposals into two groups—those involving immediate action, and the longer term suggestion for a pact. He stated his opinion that the warnings to the Communists at this point should not go beyond saying that the Western Powers would not allow the Geneva Conference to be prejudiced by Viet-Minh military action. When it came to the proposed new pact, Eden was strongly against anything that excluded India and the other Asian countries in the Commonwealth and, therefore, he urged a careful study of the idea before action was taken. The more formal talks on 12th and 13th April covered the same ground and served only to show the difference between the two governments. Dulles used a number of analogies of the situation as he saw it, including the Japanese invasion of Manchuria and Hitler's reoccupation of the Rhineland. He also attempted to equate the idea of Indian membership of the pact which he regarded as controversial, with Formosa, which was anathema to the British. He made no headway.

The joint statement after the talks, agreed by Dulles, indicated in the light of cool study that Eden had prevailed. On the afternoon of 13th April as Dulles was flying on to Paris, Eden informed a tense and suspicious House of Commons that " The Governments of the United States and United Kingdom are ready to take part with other countries principally concerned in an examination of the possibility of establishing a collective defence within the framework of the Charter of the United Nations to assure the peace, security and freedom of South-East Asia and the Western Pacific." In response to an angry intervention by Aneurin Bevan accusing him of surrender to Dulles, Eden said: " He [Bevan] is completely inaccurate if he suggests that there is *a definite commitment* [1] to take certain action in certain sectors," and went on to repeat the exact terms of the agreement to examine " the possibility of establishing a collective defence."

Dulles himself had left London with a completely different view of what had been agreed—paradoxically more close to Bevan's—and he was certain that he would now proceed with his plans for a formal pact along the lines of an Asian N.A.T.O. Later, he claimed that he had reached this understanding with both Churchill and Eden. In Paris, he met a somewhat confused situation, but the Laniel Government did not have the same caution as the British to an immediate South East Asian Pact. Rather, the French Government was more concerned with the efficacy of any American airstrike at Dien Bien Phu. The breach between the American and British Governments became public almost at once when Dulles, by now back in the United States, announced to the Press on 16th April that a meeting was being called in Washington for the Ambassadors of Britain, Australia, New Zealand, France, Thailand, the Philippines, and the three Associated States—Vietnam, Laos and Cambodia. The object of the meeting was to set up a working party to draft the Asian pact. To the British Ambassador, Dulles also repeated the threat that any attempt to include India would be countered by bringing in Formosa. The British reaction to this was extremely sharp. Eden instructed Sir Roger Makins, the Ambassador, not to attend the meeting " which was entirely contrary to the spirit of our agreement in London." On hearing the news, Dulles was angry. He felt let down. A long-standing antipathy between the two men came out into the open.[2] Dulles realised that there was no time to change the advertised "mass meeting", as Eden had called it scathingly. At the same time, he recognised that he dared not proceed without the British. There-

---

[1] Author's italics.

[2] In the autumn of 1952, before Eisenhower had been installed as President, Eden had made an attempt to prevent him from appointing Dulles as his Secretary of State.

fore, Dulles turned his meeting into " a briefing conference " before the Geneva negotiations and flew to Paris on 22nd April for the N.A.T.O. Council where he could meet Eden and Bidault again.

The Paris discussions at the time of the N.A.T.O. Council were crucial in what was to come. Dulles took Eden on one side at an official dinner on 23rd April and told him of a cable from Navarre which said that only a powerful airstrike by the Americans in the next seventy-two hours could save Dien Bien Phu. He clearly believed that the loss of Dien Bien Phu might mean the fall of the Laniel Government. He foresaw its replacement by a neutralist one which would jettison E.D.C.—a view that was supported strongly by General Gruenther, Eisenhower's successor at N.A.T.O. headquarters. Two American aircraft-carriers were already on their way to the area and the Americans were considering the use of sixty B-29 aircraft that would operate from Manila and drop their bombs from a height of 20,000 feet. Eden was extremely alarmed by Dulles and cabled a warning to Churchill that night. Next day, he had more talks with Dulles and Radford, who had also come to Paris as he was the most enthusiastic of all " the interventionists." In the afternoon Eden saw Dulles again and Bidault. At the last meeting he felt that Dulles was speaking as though Britain was committed already to armed action and pointed out sharply that this was not the case. That same evening, 24th April, Eden flew back to London and drove at once to see Churchill at Chartwell. A cabinet had been called for next morning, which was a Sunday. After approving Eden's recommendation that the Americans and French should be told again that no British undertaking would be given in advance of the Geneva Conference, the cabinet broke up. In the early afternoon, news arrived that Dulles was proposing an immediate declaration on behalf of the governments of the United States, Britain, France, the Philippines, and Associated States showing their determination to check Communism and to use " eventual military means." Churchill was also told that Eisenhower was ready to seek Congressional approval for intervention as soon as he heard that Britain was ready to participate. American aircraft were to go into action over Dien Bien Phu in four days' time on 28th April. The cabinet was therefore recalled for a tense and angry emergency session at 4 o'clock in the afternoon. It promptly decided to reject Dulles's plan. It authorised Eden to convey this decision. To make matters perfectly clear, it was also decided that Churchill should make a formal public statement in Parliament. In the Prime Minister's statement there were four significant sentences that indicated the British view: " The siege of the French fortress of Dien Bien Phu, the fate of which now hangs in the balance, creates a violent tension in many minds at a time when calm judgment is most needed. . . . It must not be allowed to prejudice the sense of world proportion. . . . Her Majesty's Government are not prepared to give any undertakings about United Kingdom military action in Indo-China in advance of the results of Geneva. We have not entered into any new political or military commitments." These firm words were intended for Dulles and they hit him as if they were a stinging rebuke.

However, Churchill had not yet spoken when Bidault was waiting anxiously for the British decision at Orly airport, as Eden arrived on the night of 25th April *en route* for Geneva immediately after the emergency cabinet meeting of that Sunday afternoon. Bidault did not seem surprised. As for Dulles, he flew on to Geneva, full of foreboding and chagrin but recognising that the United States could not act alone. Far away, amidst the jungle heat and flies, the Dien Bien Phu garrison was at the end of its strength.

The events of the preceding few days had obviously made Eden the key figure at the Geneva Conference when it assembled on 26th April. It was appropriate that this should be so in the white Palais des Nations building that used to house the ill-fated League of Nations and where Eden had been such a prominent figure nearly twenty years before. Many of Geneva's cafés still carried pictures and cartoons of the ghosts of those inter-war years of hopes and disillusionments—Briand, Streseman, Litvinov—and of the young Eden himself. For Eden, too, it was also something of a homecoming. To start with, he even stayed in the Hotel Beau Rivage, the traditional home of all British delegations to Geneva in the 1930s. But he was somewhat startled to find the Chinese delegation of all people in the same hotel and, as a security precaution, he moved to a large villa standing alone on some rising ground overlooking the lake, some distance out of the city.

The Geneva conference was divided into two separate sections that had little in common. The Korean Conference, which was to settle the political future of Korea, was a Sixteen-Power conference consisting of the sixteen United Nations countries that had sent forces to Korea, except for South Africa which had declined. However, the conference included South Korea. On the Communist side, the Soviet Union, China and North Korea were all represented. The Indo-China Conference, when it finally started, formally contained nine Powers—France, Britain, the United States, the Soviet Union, China, the Viet-Minh and three Associated States—Vietnam, Laos and Cambodia. Nevertheless, because of its fluidity other countries took a hand. For example, at one point Krishna Menon of India arrived and appeared to be the most active "delegate" of all.

Korea took up the first week of the formal conference. The South Koreans began by demanding free elections in a united Korea on the Western pattern. The North Korean delegate, Nam Il, retorted by putting forward a plan in which the North and South Korean authorities should appoint an all-Korean commission to arrange for the holding of elections. Nam Il also asked for the withdrawal of all foreign troops. As Dulles soon pointed out, this plan was very similar to Molotov's proposals for bringing about German reunification put forward in Berlin—and the same criticism in reverse could well have been made of the South Korean proposals. The delegates met in the mornings in plenary sessions on Korea whilst the afternoons and evenings were taken up by incessant private discussions on the Indo-China situation, the background to which was the impending fall of Dien Bien Phu and its repercussions in Asia and on the French political situation in Paris.

Chou En-Lai made a formal speech on 28th April in the plenary session on Korea. This was Communist China's first appearance at a major international conference. The Peking Government had sent one of the largest delegations to the conference and the Western Powers awaited with interest—and some apprehension—their first encounter with the man who was both China's Prime Minister and Foreign Minister at the time. Chou's well-cut, completely plain, revolutionary tunic, without badges or insignias, and his controlled and dignified expression made him an impressive figure as he rose. It was not surprising in the circumstances that the opening part of Chou's prepared speech was a defiant justification of the Peking Government's position. He asserted, " No force in the world can prevent the Chinese people from marching along the road of making China strong and prosperous." He denied that China had committed aggression or would do so. He accused the United States of trying to impose "the Kuomintang remnant clique" by force upon the Chinese people. His defence of China's intervention in the Korean War was that " quite obviously the United States was playing the old game of the Japanese militarists of invading Korea, to establish a base for invasion on the mainland of China." Chou's manner was calm. His voice was a dull, high-pitched monotone. But his words conveyed an unmistakably arrogant truculence. At the end of his speech, however, Chou introduced a new and positive note. He struck at the weakest point in the American position over Dulles's proposed South-East Asian Pact when he deplored the absence of India, Burma and Indonesia. As a counter-move, he demanded that the Asian countries " should consult among themselves with a view to seeking common measures to safeguard peace and security in Asia."

This last remark was clearly intended for the Asian Conference in Colombo that was taking place simultaneously and attended by the Prime Ministers of India, Pakistan, Burma, Indonesia and Ceylon. It had begun originally as a way of mediating in the recurrent India-Pakistan dispute but inevitably it had become pre-occupied by the Indo-China crisis. The Colombo Conference now showed clearly how the Asians saw Dulles's manœuvres, for they regarded them as a simple attempt to perpetuate French colonial rule and to extend the domination of the Western Powers over Asia. Throughout the period of the two conferences—Geneva and Colombo—the British delegation at Geneva and the Indians in Colombo maintained close contact. Nearly all the participants in Geneva attached great weight to Nehru's influence in Asia and this unique link added to Eden's authority in his conduct of negotiations.

The first week of the Korean Conference showed that there was little chance of progress. It appeared as if the thoughts of the principal delegates were elsewhere, and the Korean situation presented little room for manœuvre. Dulles and Eden had a long and unpleasant meeting on 30th April. To be fair to him, Dulles's main reason for pressing his South-East Asian Pact was to strengthen the French position at the conference and to save the Laniel Government in Paris out of fear of what might replace it. Bidault, who was leading the French delegation in Geneva, was in a very depressed state. He had already remarked to Dulles and Eden that he had no cards in his hand, " Perhaps just a two of clubs and a three of diamonds! " Eden, on the other hand, was quite determined not to allow the long-term South-East Asian defence plan to start its life by being roundly condemned by the Asians at the Colombo meeting. He explained to Dulles that he had already got some support for the pact from Ceylon and Pakistan and that he had also diverted Nehru for the moment from declaring open opposition. The British were anxious to go ahead, he assured the American Secretary of State, with an immediate secret examination of the proposal, but this was not what Dulles wanted. His aim was something much more overt.

At root, there was a basic difference of assessment of the situation between the United States and Britain. Dulles believed that all French resistance in Indo-China was about to collapse after Dien Bien Phu. He foresaw that this would lead to the fall of Laniel and Bidault, with the gravest consequences to Western hopes in Europe. Eden, on the other hand, did not take such a pessimistic view of French morale. Whilst recognising the psychological symbol of Dien Bien Phu, he could not accept that the loss of some thousands of troops could end resistance by the very large army in Indo-China under French command of nearly 550,000 men—most of whom, it is true, were Vietnamese troops. As to Europe, he had already come to the conclusion privately that E.D.C. would never come into being and that the Western Powers would have to consider rearming West Germany within a N.A.T.O. framework. Therefore, Eden was still determined to try to achieve an Indo-China agreement based on partitioning the country.

After this talk with Eden, Dulles realised finally that his policy was unacceptable to Britain. He announced that he personally was withdrawing from the Geneva Conference. Instead, the American Under-Secretary of State, Walter Bedell Smith, would be flying out to take over the leadership of the American delegation. This was a dramatic turn of events. When Eden went to see Dulles off at Geneva airport three days later, the atmosphere between the two men was chilly and bitter on the American's side, and not all Eden's attempts to overcompensate by affability could hide the true situation from the large array of Pressmen from both sides of the Iron Curtain. Dulles's departure transformed the conference. Eden now had even greater freedom. His position became all the more important because there was no conference secretariat in the normal sense and it had been agreed that he and Molotov should act as joint-chairmen and as the conveners of the meetings.

In subsequent years, various biographers of Dulles have defended his bizarre and erratic behaviour at Geneva by claiming that his militant approach strengthened Eden's hand immeasurably and that it actually made possible the Indo-China agreement that emerged subsequently. There is enough truth in this assertion to warrant a brief examination of its premises. First, it is true that Dulles had gravely alarmed Molotov and the Soviet Government —as well as the British—to say nothing of the Asian neutrals. Indeed, the Russians had come to regard the situation in Indo-China as one that was partly outside their control, largely because of Chinese belligerence towards America and all the more dangerous because of this. At the same time, the Russians were conscious that their commitments in the Communist bloc might lead to the involvement of the Soviet Union in a wider conflict. For these reasons, the Malenkov Government had decided that it was in the Soviet interest for Molotov to co-operate with Eden in the plans he was promoting and seek to avert American armed intervention.

Dien Bien Phu fell on 7th May. The last radio message from its commander was sent with the Viet Minh forces only a few yards away. The French had lost 15,000 men, of whom 10,000 were taken prisoner. As these were nearly all troops from Metropolitan France, the loss was severe but not decisive, as Eden had correctly forecast. The impact in France was bitter and widespread, never-theless—and understandably so.

The central problem from now on was the political negotiations at Geneva which had had to be pressed before the military position took charge again. Next day the negotiations began, having been held up for the arrival of the Viet-Minh delegation. Bidault's opening speech—made in these tragic circumstances for his country —proposed the regrouping of all the regular forces on both sides into separate zones in Vietnam and the disarming of all the guerrillas. He also called for the release of prisoners of war and an international commission to supervise the truce. This was very much along the lines that Eden had been working. The Viet-Minh counter-proposal was for a cease-fire and the withdrawal of all French troops, which would have left the Associated States at the Communists' mercy. It also included elections in the three states of Vietnam, Laos and Cambodia and interim administrations by the *de facto* governments—either legal or rebel as the situation specified. The Viet-Minh delegate, somewhat surprisingly, also expressed his readiness to examine the question of entry into the French Union and to recognise French economic and cultural interests. It was a big gulf, which Eden realised he must try to bridge from a position of French military weakness.

Eden and Molotov had by now established a working under-standing perhaps better than at any time since Eden's first visit to

Moscow in the spring of 1935. At one private meeting in Geneva, Molotov unbent so far as to acknowledge that there had been a time when the Soviet leaders had thought a great deal of Chiang Kai-shek and that the speed of the Chinese Communist success had surprised them. The Soviet Foreign Minister had also tended to agree with Eden about the danger of various other elements on both sides who might take control if the conference failed—an indication of the alarm created by Dulles and the Chinese.

But Eden found that he had no such working arrangement with Chou En-Lai who, so Molotov acknowledged privately, was very much his own master at the conference. A meeting between Eden and Chou on 20th May made no progress. The Chinese Prime Minister was exceedingly stiff and unyielding and showed that he was the force behind the Viet-Minh negotiators. During the next few days, in a round of individual private meetings that slowed down the pace of the conference, Eden suggested that representatives of the two military commands should meet immediately in Geneva to work out any regrouping of forces that might be possible if hostilities were ended.

He felt that this might be a start and sought Molotov's aid. He was delighted to get a telephone call at breakfast time on 29th May from the Russian delegation to say the Chinese would accept the idea—here was another indication that the Viet-Minh were under Peking's strong influence, if not orders. Now Eden faced a new difficulty, for the American delegation appeared most dissatisfied at this, and Bedell Smith said he wanted to make his reservations public. As Eden put it in a dispatch to London: " The Americans seem deeply apprehensive of reaching any agreement, however innocuous, with the Communists." Nor was this all: the spectre of American intervention had suddenly revived. In telegrams from Paris, Eden learned that the Laniel Government had almost reached the point of asking for American intervention and Eisenhower appeared again on the point of ordering military action. The slow progress at Geneva had caused American patience to evaporate. Dulles in Washington now felt that he was about to be proved right and that the conference would collapse. It looked like this, too, when the conference reached deadlock on the composition of an international commission to supervise any armistice arrangements. Whereas Eden had suggested the five Colombo Powers who were both " Asian and neutral," Molotov and Chou were demanding Poland and Czechoslovakia in addition to India and another Asian country.

And this was clearly unacceptable to anybody on the Western side as it meant that the commission would have two Communist representatives and none from the West.

The situation was again balanced on a knife edge when the prospects for American intervention received another major setback and the Geneva Conference was infused with new life. The Laniel Government tottered and then fell, thereby creating a new situation, as the Americans could not order military intervention without a French Government to request it. Laniel had been under severe pressure ever since early May and he had escaped defeat by only two votes after the fall of Dien Bien Phu. His chief critic, Mendès-France, who had not been in office since 1945, made a devastating attack on the French Prime Minister on 10th June. He accused him of planning intervention by the Americans. Instead, Mendès-France proposed a peace offer to the Viet-Minh on honourable terms before it was too late. The vote in the French National Assembly was taken on 12th June and when the figures were announce Laniel had been defeated by 306 votes to 293. The French President immediately asked Mendès-France himself to form an administration. When the new Prime Minister designate came before the National Assembly on 17th June, he made one of the shortest investiture speeches on record. He said his aim was peace. He would seek it openly; and he set himself and the Viet-Minh a time limit of four weeks. Thus, if no solution had been reached by 20th July, Mendès-France promised he would resign. It was a bold idea that astonished everyone. When the Communists in the Assembly offered their support, Mendès-France declined it, saying he would only take office if he had a clear majority without the French Communist votes. Suddenly, people seemed to feel the war had gone on long enough. In the mood of the moment Mendès-France was swept into office by 419 votes against only 47.

In the meanwhile, Eden had been applying pressure at Geneva as a last desperate effort. On 11th June he had solemnly warned the conference that it must admit failure if it could not reach agreement on two issues that were deadlocked—the composition of the international commission and the future of the other two Associated States, Laos and Cambodia, which the Viet-Minh delegate had called into question in his opening statement. The British Government had by now realised that it could not countenance a major breach in the Anglo-American Alliance and that steps must be taken to repair the damage. A visit to Washington by Churchill

377

and Eden had been under consideration for some days, and Churchill decided that the time had been reached when it could not be postponed any longer. Therefore, on 12th June, it was announced that the Prime Minister and Eden would be going to Washington on 25th June. Whilst the object of this visit was to bridge the widening gulf, it was also to persuade the Americans to give the French more time to reach agreement at Geneva. As it so happened, this is not how the Communist Powers interpreted it. They now feared that Britain also was reaching the end of her patience. Molotov particularly was only too well aware of Dulles's off-stage noises. Therefore, he hurried to make amends and brought pressure on the Chinese. Next day Chou En-Lai accepted a formula that allowed for a Viet-Minh withdrawal from Laos and Cambodia and their virtual exclusion from the conference, and he went on to confirm this in a private talk with Bidault who had remained behind in Geneva after Laniel's fall to continue the conference. Molotov also indicated that the Communist Powers were prepared to be more flexible about the membership of the international commission.

The Communist change of policy had come only just in time. Bedell Smith had received a telegram from Eisenhower instructing him to wind up the conference as soon as possible. And the Americans were already packing their bags after their weeks of frustration in one of the strangest and most impotent situations in which they had found themselves at any international gathering for years.

With these concessions, the first part of the conference was over. The detailed work in the preparation of an agreement continued. Eden had to go to Washington, having been at Geneva for seven weeks. The new French Premier had to define his terms and perhaps meet the Chinese. Molotov, the veteran of a hundred stubborn encounters, also felt the need for a rest as he had been at Geneva as long as Eden. Therefore, the two co-chairman seized the opportunity and flew back to their capitals on 10th June. The veil that covers personal reactions in the Soviet Union prevents us from knowing how Molotov was received after his work, but Eden found a united House of Commons awaiting him with congratulations; before he and Churchill left for Washington on 24th June. In a speech in Parliament on 23rd June he also paid a gracious tribute to Molotov, something that few people could have envisaged before the conference began on 26th April. Mendès-France, meanwhile, travelled to Switzerland to meet Chou En-Lai at the French

Embassy in Berne. It was, of course, the most decisive meeting of the conference, although it did not actually take place within the Geneva framework. To the French Prime Minister's relief, Chou was conciliatory. He recognised at once that Vietnam could be partitioned successfully for a number of years. This meant that provided a suitable line could be agreed, a major agreement was in sight. Secondly, Chou did not press Mendès-France for early elections in the French area, although he could have done so at considerable advantage to the Communist cause because the Viet-Minh would almost certainly have triumphed. The news of Mendès-France's meeting was received with relief in Western quarters. Chou himself now left for India and Burma on his way back to Peking. In Delhi he was garlanded with flowers and he made a deep impression by the peaceful sentiments he expressed. Communist China was overtly seeking popularity amongst the Asians.

Thus Churchill and Eden arrived in Washington in a better atmosphere than might have been expected, partly because of events but largely because they had been preceded by a long letter from the Prime Minister to Eisenhower welcoming the South-East Asian Defence Pact. Dulles was more amenable, too, during the talks than the British had feared. Eden was at pains to explain the delicate situation reached by the Geneva Conference. For Mendès-France's benefit, Dulles and Eden agreed the minimum terms that they would be prepared to accept at the conference. These included "the independence and integrity of Laos and Cambodia" and "at least the southern half of Vietnam and, if possible, an enclave in the [Red River] delta." They also demanded "effective machinery for international supervision of the agreement." And armed with these agreed terms, Eden returned by sea for a rest and reached Geneva on 12th July. At the same time, Dulles flew direct to Paris to meet Mendès-France who appealed to Eden to join them in order to persuade Dulles to return to the conference itself. This, however, Dulles was not prepared to do. And he now refused to associate himself with any settlement, as he would have preferred that things had gone otherwise.

The next few days in Geneva were a flurry of activity. The two major outstanding issues were now the line of partition in Vietnam and the membership of the international commission. Furthermore, Mendès-France's deadline was approaching, although he was holding out for the 18th Parallel whereas the Viet-Minh had moved north in their claim from the 13th to the 16th. As zero hour approached, Chou En-Lai, back also from Peking, suddenly suggested to Eden on 18th July that the supervisory commission should consist of Poland, Canada and India. This augured for success. On 20th July, the last day of his time limit, Mendès-France and the Viet-Minh delegate agreed on the 17th Parallel. The final agreement was reached at 2 o'clock in the morning of 21st July. Eden took the chair for the last time at 3 o'clock on the afternoon of that same day to announce the terms of the settlement—a division of Vietnam on the 17th Parallel, with Hanoi going to the Viet-Minh, a bitter blow to the French.

There remained the South-East Asian Pact. Progress upon this was so rapid that although India, Burma and Ceylon refused to join, an agreement was ready in a few weeks. But the draft treaty, when it came, was not the formidable and organised military alliance that Dulles had envisaged on the lines of N.A.T.O. It was a pact to resist aggression in the area, with a standing council whose headquarters were to be in Bangkok. The ceremonial signing of it took place at Manila on 9th September, the eight signatories being the United States, Britain, France, the Philippines, Pakistan, Thailand, Australia and New Zealand.

Reactions to the Geneva settlement were varied. Eden was cheered again in the House of Commons, mainly from the Labour benches. The French reaction was relief tempered by a feeling of having suffered a major and inevitable setback. Chou En-Lai naturally hailed it as " a tremendous success." The Vietnamese Foreign Minister resigned on the spot. The American view broadly was that it had been a Communist victory.

Yet, the fact was that, given the French military situation, there had been no alternative, apart from Dulles's policy of intervention. In the background, there had been the constant threat of nuclear weapons which, undoubtedly, was a factor in Molotov's calculations and the cause of the conciliatory posture that he had adopted throughout. Within narrow limits, Eden had negotiated with considerable skill. Without him, it is possible that there would have been no agreement. Mendès-France's unusual methods had played their part. As Eden put it later, " He was a good man for the short lap." And, as he claimed rightly, Chou En-Lai had achieved a considerable success, even if it could be argued that he had compelled the Viet-Minh to accept terms that were less good than those to which their military position entitled them. The argument, therefore, comes back in its full circle to Dulles. His attitude had undoubtedly earned his country a great deal of needless hostility. His interventionist policy had really failed because it was militarily untenable, despite Radford's advocacy, unless it were implemented on a scale that very few people were prepared to support. Nevertheless, the modified South-East Asia Treaty Organisation stood to Dulles's credit, and, even amongst the Asian neutrals, there was muffled praise for this achievement.

The Great Powers had stepped back from a crisis that had threatened a major war. For a short while, the guns were silent all over the world. It was the first time that this had happened for over twenty years—since Japan had invaded Manchuria in 1931.

PART FOUR

THE DEADLY STALEMATE

CHAPTER 21

THE REVENGE OF HISTORY

Nero was a product of his time. Nevertheless, when he was dead, his statues were destroyed and his name everywhere erased. The revenge of history is greater than that of the most powerful secretary-general.   *Trotsky*

Soviet foreign policy, from Stalin's death in March 1953 until Krushchev's decisive victory over his rivals in June 1957, vacillated, hesitated and was often defensive in character. There were good reasons for this. An internal struggle for power was taking place. A generation of Communist doctrinal teaching, in which Stalin's name had been a central thread, was being jettisoned. Inevitably, there were bitter arguments and these turned into open conflicts. A complicating factor in the situation was that no clear dividing line existed between Stalinists and anti-Stalinists. Sometimes the personalities changed sides or formed new alliances. The crescendo of debate was reached in Krushchev's so-called " Secret Speech " to the Twentieth Congress of the Soviet Communist Party on 24th February, 1956. The speech itself caused varying emotions, from dismay and anger to great relief as the news of it spread slowly from the centre of the Soviet Union to the periphery of the Soviet Communist Party. Outside the Soviet Union, Krushchev's denunciation had an even greater and more traumatic impact upon the various Communist parties. The Twentieth Congress led directly to the ferment of 1956 in Eastern Europe that culminated in the Hungarian revolution.

Parallel to the Communist doctrinal argument and the personal struggle for power within the Soviet Union, there was the internal Soviet defence debate. It stemmed from the belated recognition of fast changing military technologies. At first, the Soviet leadership was slow to appreciate the foreign policy implications of nuclear weapons—the inevitable handicap of having no free discussion in a Communist society. Malenkov was the first to speak of the dangers of nuclear war. Krushchev, himself, began to face the new situation only later, by the end of the 1950s; but the more conservative Communists, including Mao Tse-tung still clung to their earlier interpretations of the world struggle. These years, from 1953 onwards, also included periods during which many superficial Western observers, supported by the apologists for Communism, claimed that the Cold War was about to end. In the event, no such thing happened.

Whilst the post-Stalin Soviet leadership set about the tasks of ending the Korean War in 1953, and grappling with the issues of Indo-China and with the European Defence Community, a major struggle was taking place inside the Kremlin over the Soviet Union's internal policy. The Malenkov Administration's proposals for more consumer goods—the "New Course" as it was termed officially—which had come to the fore at the time of the East German uprising, met with increasing resistance. Opposition to it came from those who still advocated the traditional emphasis on heavy industry. At this period the protagonists of the "New Course" included Malenkov and Mikoyan. Their opponents were led by Krushchev, Bulganin and Zhukov, the last two being Minister and Vice-Minister of Defence respectively. As it turned out, the practical considerations proved decisive. The consumer goods programme showed itself to be incapable of being fulfilled because heavy industry was still allocated the main priorities for investment. Despite the adoption of the New Course, no proper provision was made for the essential change in the Five Year Plan to give consumer goods their place, or to resolve the conflicting priorities. And the Soviet economy soon showed that it could not achieve both targets simultaneously. To illustrate the complications that now set in; the "New Course" demanded increased food supplies. This led to the renewal of the Virgin Lands project to supply the food. In its own turn the Virgin Lands programme required more investment in heavy industry, in order to build the plants to manufacture the farm machinery, that would make possible the greatly increased production from the Virgin Lands. The Soviet economic muddle was both created and intensified by its own spiral.

From mid-1954 the supporters of heavy industry appeared to get the upper hand. Their claims were assisted by a delegation led by Krushchev, Bulganin and Mikoyan to the fifth anniversary celebrations of the Chinese People's Republic on 1st October, 1954. The Soviet delegation to China was the first of many that were to be undertaken jointly by Krushchev and Bulganin and it entered into agreements with the Chinese Communists to equip a large number of heavy industrial projects in China. About this time, too, there were a number of indications, manifested by Soviet official resolutions and directives, that showed power was slipping from Malenkov. Wolfgang Leonhard in *The Kremlin Since Stalin* has shown clearly that the Soviet Prime Minister's fate was almost certainly determined from 14th to 17th December, 1954, when Viktor Abakumov, the former Minister of State Security was tried and sentenced to death for his alleged responsibility in the "Leningrad Affair"—an event which had taken place in the early part of 1949 involving a ruthless purge of the supporters of Zhdanov, the former Politbureau member who had died on 30th August, 1948. As Abakumov had worked closely with Malenkov, the implication was obvious. There were also reports that certain documents were circulated within the Soviet leadership at this time, accusing Malenkov himself of the " Leningrad Affair." The Abakumov verdict was announced in the Soviet Press on 24th December, alongside a statement made by Krushchev as far back as 25th September, emphasising the importance of heavy industry. The associations were not accidental. A month later, on 24th January, 1955, *Pravda* contained an article by Dimitri Shepilov justifying the priority for heavy industry. Mikoyan was simultaneously dismissed from his post as Minister of Internal Trade.

Malenkov resigned on 8th February, 1955, at a meeting of the Supreme Soviet. A self-critical statement by Malenkov was read for him in his presence. Included in Malenkov's statement were the words, " I recognise clearly that my insufficient experience in local work has had an unfavourable effect on the fulfilment of the complicated and responsible duties of the Chairman of the Council of Ministers, as well as the fact that I have not had the opportunity of being directly responsible for individual branches of the economy in another ministry or any other economic body. I also regard it as my duty to state in this declaration that to-day, when the Communist Party of the Soviet Union and the workers of our country are concentrating their efforts on the rapid development of agriculture, I recognise particularly clearly my responsibility for the unsatisfactory situation that has developed in agriculture, because earlier, for a number of years, I had been entrusted with the task of controlling and directing the activity of the central agricultural organs and the activities of the local Party and Soviet organisations in the field of agriculture." Reports said that most members of the Supreme Soviet were taken completely by surprise. Nevertheless, when the vote was taken as to whether to accept Malenkov's statement, they all held up their hands in agreement except one woman. Malenkov's successor was proposed by Krushchev on behalf of the Central Committee. He was Nikolai Alexandrovich Bulganin, whose career had included such diverse experiences as being Chairman of the Moscow Soviet, a director of the State Bank, membership of the War Council on various fronts, Deputy Chairman of the Council of Ministers (from 1947 to 1949) and Minister of Defence.

The change in the Soviet leadership had immediate repercussions in other European Communist countries. In Hungary, Imry Nagy who had been appointed Prime Minister because of Malenkov's influence in June 1953 was forced to resign on an indictment of administrative incompetence that was very similar to the one on which Malenkov had pleaded guilty. The new Soviet leadership that had emerged was a coalition of party and army leaders and economic technocrats. Two leading economists, Saburov and Pervukhin were promoted to being First Deputy Prime Ministers and four other economists were made Deputy Prime Ministers. The enhanced power of the Red Army was reflected on 11th March, when eleven new Soviet Marshals were appointed. As for Krushchev, he also had been strengthened in his party position by virtue of Malenkov's down-grading, although he was not yet able to assert complete authority over the administration.

The impact upon Soviet foreign policy of Malenkov's fall did not take long to appear. At the same session of the Supreme Soviet that had received Malenkov's resignation, Molotov delivered a long report on foreign affairs in the course of which he insisted, " The Austrian problem could not be considered apart from the German problem." This was the view to which Soviet policy had adhered throughout the long German struggle. But, less than three weeks later, Molotov informed the Austrian Ambassador in Moscow that he was ready to propose the withdrawal of the occupation troops of the Four Powers, provided that a satisfactory way could be found to insure Austria's future neutrality. Molotov invited the Austrian Chancellor, Julius Raab, to Moscow.

The Austrians were very apprehensive in case the Western Powers should object to direct Soviet-Austrian negotiations but when they received encouragement, from Washington and London, the invitation to Raab was accepted. At the Moscow talks, Molotov insisted that neutrality guarantees should rule out the joining of any alliances by Austria and the withdrawal from Austrian territory of foreign bases. The Austrians also found that they were being called upon to pay a heavy price in settlement of certain Soviet economic claims. But they considered that these demands were outweighed by the fact that the country would regain her independence at last. The proposed new Austrian arrangements proved acceptable—indeed welcome—to the Western Powers. Thus, on 15th May, there was the surprising spectacle of the four Foreign Ministers meeting the Austrian Foreign Minister to complete the formalities of the Austrian Peace Treaty.

What motivated the Soviet Union in its volte-face over Austria? The probability is that there were two factors. First, there was always the hope that a solution of the Austrian problem, with its safeguards of neutrality, might act as a tempting example to parade before a German public opinion that was still preoccupied with re-unification. Secondly, and more important, the Soviet leaders had faced, at last, the inevitability of West German rearmament. In order to meet it, and concurrently with the Austrian Treaty preparations, they decided to reorganise the Communist defence pattern.

As the date of the final ratifications of the Paris Agreements approached in 1955, the Soviet Union denounced the Anglo-Soviet and Franco-Soviet Treaties of Friendship and convened a conference on East European security in Warsaw. The participating states were the Soviet Union, Poland, Czechoslovakia, Hungary, Rumania, Bulgaria, Albania and East Germany. The Chinese sent a delegation of observers led by the Defence Minister. The text of the Warsaw Treaty, establishing a joint Communist command and staff under Marshal Koniev, was announced on 14th May, the day actually preceding the formal signing of the Austrian Treaty. A point of interest in the Warsaw text was the exclusion of East Germany—although East German armed units had been in existence since 1948.[1] Thus, in these circumstances, the continuing occupation of Austria was a military liability rather than an asset to the Soviet Union, as it played no part in the new defence arrangements.

The next shift in Soviet policy was even more surprising, though there had been indications for some time that it was coming. The bitter dispute with Yugoslavia, that had caused such upheaval in

[1] East Germany was admitted to the Warsaw Pact in 1958.

the Communist bloc since Tito's break with Stalin in June 1948, became the subject of a gauche attempt at rapprochement by Bulganin and Krushchev. The original Soviet-Yugoslav argument had arisen because of Stalin's attempt to impose Soviet domination upon Yugoslavia. The circumstances leading up to the expulsion of Yugoslavia from the Cominform on 28th June, 1948, were complex. They revolved around the Soviet Union's demands for key rights —including access to secret information—demands that had been accepted in other European states. To be truthful, Tito and his colleagues had once envisaged the eventual absorption of Yugoslavia into the Soviet Union but they were not now prepared to act the part of satellites. As Stalin saw it, the Yugoslav Communists were suddenly parading as "*National* Communists" and "Revisionists." Tito denied this hotly—from his standpoint, there were no such things and he claimed that the Yugoslavs were the true Marxist-Leninists. In short, the Yugoslav dispute and its wider significance was the logical development of the spread of Communism to more than one state—an event that was to have yet greater implications in different circumstances in Sino-Soviet arguments.

The Yugoslav régime's fate hung in the balance after the break. A Soviet economic blockade compelled Tito to turn to the West for trade and credits. Thus he became "a reluctant Revisionist" [1] under Soviet pressures. Extreme tensions racked the country whilst pro-Soviet elements in the Yugoslav Communist Party were eliminated. Border incidents were common. The threat of armed invasion preoccupied the Yugoslav Communists with good reason as it appeared in 1949 that Stalin was seriously considering military action. In the East European states, many leading Communists were tried or imprisoned or executed—on Stalin's orders—as being Titoists. Although many confessed to the charges under duress, the indictments really foreshadowed what might have been, rather than what had actually taken place. And the Communist judicial charades were intended to be a warning to all independently-minded Communists. Indeed, in Stalin's lifetime, Tito's name became the focal point for more doctrinal abuse than any man since Trotsky. [2]

After Stalin's death, Soviet policy toward Yugoslavia changed only slowly. There were several indications of a possible rapproche-

---

[1] Alfred Sherman, *Tito—A Reluctant Revisionist*, an essay in *Revisionism*, edited by Leopold Labedz.

[2] An excellent and documented account of the Soviet-Yugoslav break is given by Adam Vlam, *Titoism and the Cominform*, Harvard University Press, 1952.

ment. Nevertheless, the news in 1955 that a Soviet delegation containing Krushchev, Bulganin, Mikoyan, Shepilov and Gromyko was to visit Yugoslavia caused a sensation. The surprise announcement was nothing to the dramatic manner of the delegation's arrival. At Belgrade airport, on 26th May, after the Soviet airliner had landed, Krushchev stepped forward to read a prepared statement before Tito and assembled reporters. He made the most complete apology for Stalin to have been delivered up to that time. The Yugoslav authorities, who had approached their Soviet guests with chilly formality and suspicion were as astonished as the Western newspapermen who were present. " We sincerely regret what happened," said Krushchev, " and are removing with determination everything that has accumulated during this period. In this, we, for our part, without any doubt include the provocative role which the enemies of the people, Beria, Abakumov and others who have now been unmasked, played in the relations between Yugoslavia and the U.S.S.R. We have carefully examined the material on which the serious accusations and insults, which were made against the Yugoslav leaders, were based. The facts show that this material was invented by the enemies of the people, despicable agents of imperialism who had joined the ranks of our party through deception."

After allowing for the jargon of Marxist leadership and its customary contempt for human intelligence, nevertheless Krushchev's speech at Belgrade has few parallels. Tito cut short the attempt to translate his remarks into Serbo-Croat and bustled the Russians into the waiting cars.

Throughout the subsequent talks, the Yugoslavs insisted that they were being conducted between representatives of two states and not between two fraternal Communist parties. For this reason, the final communiqué was not signed by Krushchev, although he was the leader of the Soviet Delegation, but by Bulganin as Prime Minister.

The leaders of the Western Powers observing the changes, decided that the time might be appropriate for the first meeting of heads of Government since the Potsdam Conference ten years before. (Churchill's initiative of May 1953 had reached fruition but Churchill himself had given way to Eden as Prime Minister on 6th April, 1955. Mendès-France, who had given purpose and direction to French policy for a short period, had fallen from power in January over Algeria and had been succeeded by Edgar Faure.) Through diplomatic channels a date and place were fixed—18th July at Geneva. The problem facing the West was: What were they going to say to the Russians? Eden attempted to arrange a meeting between Eisenhower, Faure and himself to co-ordinate their policies in advance of Geneva. Eisenhower, however, would only go as far as to agreeing to a meeting of Western Foreign Ministers in Paris on 15th July, which turned out to be extremely valuable. The various delegations began to arrive in Geneva on that week-end. Once again the city had become the centre of international nego- tiation and large crowds thronged the airport to catch glimpses of the visiting celebrities.

The Geneva Conference opened most harmoniously. After the opening speeches, the agenda was quickly agreed by the four Foreign Ministers on behalf of their delegations: 1. Re-unification of Germany. 2. European security. 3. Disarmament. 4. The development of the East-West contacts.

Bulganin presented the Soviet viewpoint with precision and courtesy in a manner that was very different from previous East- West meetings. Yet there was steel behind his soft-spoken words. Neither he, nor Krushchev, were prepared to consider the German question except in the context of European security. To try to meet his point, the Western Powers agreed to take the two issues together. Bulganin then produced a draft agreement in which he envisaged that the N.A.T.O. and Warsaw Treaty alliances would remain in being for a period. He foresaw that progress would be made by the gradual reduction of troops on both sides, the solemn renunciation of force and—eventually—a single European Treaty. On the crucial German question, Bulganin made it clear that the Soviet Union would never agree to an armed united Germany joining the Western camp. He accused the Western Powers of creating the major obstacle to Germany re-unification by the re-militarisation of Western Germany under the Paris Agreements. The implications of Bulganin's speech were only too clear—the Soviet position on the most contentious issues had not changed since Stalin and German re-unification was being postponed indefinitely until the Communist bloc considered that the moment was ripe for an all-German government in which the Communists would have the leading part.

The Western counter-proposal on Germany returned to the claim for free elections as a first stage. Eden added his own conception of a demilitarised zone on both sides of the line of East-West confrontation, with control and inspection of armed forces in Germany and her neighbours as part of an agreement on the limitation of armaments. This was the so-called Eden Plan upon which there has been a great deal of discussion in subsequent years.[1] Bulganin was frankly disbelieving about Eden's proposals and after some confused exchanges the two proposals were referred for detailed consideration by the Foreign Ministers at a new conference to be held later. The Heads of Governments' directive to the Foreign Ministers stated: " The re-unification of Germany by free elections should be carried out in conformity with the national interests of the German people and the interests of European security." These were loose terms of reference. The Soviet Government was to exploit them later.

The conference passed to disarmament. It was Eisenhower's turn to seize the initiative. On the morning of 21st July he said, " I propose that we take a practical step, that we begin an arrangement, very quickly, as between ourselves—immediately." It was a dramatic introduction followed by his offer to exchange military blueprints and charts, giving descriptions and the locations of all military and naval installations of any kind, both in their own countries and abroad. He proposed that each nation should have a fixed number of airfields and aircraft equipped for photographic reconnaissance to inspect each other's territory; and, to avoid the plans being rejected by the Soviet Union on technical grounds, he suggested an early agreement in principle with the details to be worked out later. This was Eisenhower's " Open Skies Plan." As the President concluded his offer, there was a clap of thunder. The lights suddenly went out and the members of the conference stared at each other with amazement in the gloom of the storm outside the meeting hall. It was some minutes before the lights and equanimity were restored.

Bulganin, always suave, promised sympathetic study of the proposals and the hopes of the Western Powers rose briefly. These were quickly dashed during the adjournment when Eisenhower and Krushchev were walking out to the cocktail lounge. " I don't agree with the Chairman," said Krushchev coldly, meaning Bulganin. When the conference resumed Bulganin did not make a formal reply to Eisenhower's plan. Instead, he returned to earlier Soviet proposals and agreed that both schemes should be

[1] The precise terms of Eden's proposals are contained in the R.I.I.A. *Documents*, 1955, p. 43.

referred to the United Nations Disarmament Commission. Russian xenophobia was as firmly entrenched as ever.

The Heads of Government turned finally at the end to East-West contacts. They instructed the Foreign Ministers to examine " such free contacts and exchanges as are to the mutual advantage of the countries and peoples concerned." A Four-Power Foreign Ministers' conference was fixed for October at Geneva.

The achievements of the 1955 Summit Conference appeared meagre on paper. In fact, it turned out to be a premature confrontation. However, the apparent good humour and courtesy that had marked the meetings were in such contrast to earlier bitter East-West confrontations that a new atmosphere was created called the " Geneva spirit." There were many examples to show that the new atmosphere of goodwill was deceptive. After Geneva, it was only when the Soviet attitude to Germany was studied more closely that the permanent nature of the differences re-emerged. Krushchev on his way back from the conference paused in East Berlin to say, " We are convinced that the workers of the German Democratic Republic will not agree to a solution which puts the interests of the Western groupings ahead of the interests of the German Democratic Republic." He meant that the Soviet leaders were just as determined as ever not to agree to any solution of the German problem that would jeopardise the Communist régime in East Germany. And the Foreign Ministers' Conference, when it met again at Geneva in the autumn, made the position even more clear. In response to a Western proposal for free all-German elections in September 1956 Molotov answered: "It has been suggested here that a plan should be adopted for all-German elections. . . . Such a plan ignores the real conditions in Germany, in as much as the question of holding such elections has not yet matured. Such mechanical merging of the two parts of Germany through so-called free elections, held moreover in the presence of foreign troops as envisaged in the Eden plan, might result in the violation of the vital interests of the working people of the German Democratic Republic, and we cannot agree to that."

Those people in the West who—after Geneva—had assumed that a new era in East-West relations had dawned were again proved premature. Nevertheless, the internal changes that were taking place—largely within the Soviet Union—were continuing apace. The preparations for the Soviet Communist Party's Twentieth Congress were pressed forward, after Geneva, in the last weeks of 1955. The Congress was due to meet on 14th February. The Party journal *Bolshevik* indicated, in advance, a major shift in doctrine by stating that in the new situation it had become possible to "utilise parliamentary forms of struggle for power and for the peaceful development of the Revolution." In his opening speech to the Congress, Krushchev appeared to be taking a similar position when he said that it was no longer necessary to hold the view that a war between the socialist and capitalist states was inevitable. At the same time he warned again that the capitalist nations might start a war.

The first major sensation at the Congress was a speech by Mikoyan on the third day in which he openly criticised Stalin. He admitted, "For some twenty years we actually had no collective leadership." Instead "the cult of the individual" had prevailed. He went on to criticise Stalin's *Economic Problems of Socialism in the U.S.S.R.* Mikoyan's speech had an electrifying effect upon the assembly as a whole although there is no doubt that the more sophisticated party leaders had been criticising Stalin for some time in private. The Congress then proceeded to take very important decisions in which it recognised the non-inevitability of war and the possibilities of revolution without violence. But the major act was still to come. On the morning of 25th February the Congress went into secret session for an address by Krushchev. Krushchev now fully exposed Stalin's reign of terror and admitted that thousands of loyal party members had been tortured into confessing crimes that they had never committed and many more thousands had been condemned to death or dispatched to labour camps. Of course Krushchev's revelations were nothing new to informed observers of Communism but their significance lay in their admission by the First Secretary of the Soviet Communist Party. Krushchev stood before the Twentieth Congress to say in effect that for years it had been the Communist practice to lie, cheat, twist, torture, murder and grovel. The savage and primitive nature of Soviet society, with its appetites for power, its desperate struggles for survival and its craven cowardice in high places, was exposed to all.

Yet there were important omissions from Krushchev's speech, including any major criticisms of Stalin's foreign policy. For example, there was no attack upon the Molotov-Ribbentrop Pact, which had precipitated the war and had brought disaster to the country. Stalin's post-war expansionist policies—with the exception of his attitude to Yugoslavia—also went unchallenged. There was no mention of the major events, from the Prague coup and Berlin blockade in 1948 to the outbreak of the Korean War which had brought into being the Western Alliance. Krushchev was also careful to omit those events in Stalin's career in which he, himself, shared a measure of complicity in the crimes of the dictator. Finally he took great care not to extend his attack to the dictatorship of the party itself and he limited himself to harsh criticisms of Stalin personally, the cult of personality and the perversion of party aims.

The significance of these changes was profound. Whilst they never meant that the Soviet Union would not be prepared to go to the brink of war when it suspected Western weakness, as in Berlin and Cuba in 1961-2, they still form the basis of Soviet policy in the developing countries at the time of writing.

Krushchev's speech was intended for internal consumption. The leading Communists who heard it, whilst many of them were dazed with shock, knew its truth. An expurgated version was circulated later, on numbered copies, and read at local Communist meetings in the Soviet Union, the numbered copies then being returned to Moscow. The speech's impact could have been controlled and its effect limited if it had stopped there. Unfortunately for Krushchev, the American State Department secured a copy through clandestine sources and, after leaking selections, published the document in full on 2nd June, 1956. Indeed, 2nd June turned out to be a historic day. Marshal Tito arrived in Moscow to be hailed by *Pravda* in glowing terms. Molotov, who had signed the Cominform resolution against Yugoslavia, was dismissed from his post as Foreign Minister and replaced by Dimitri Shepilov, the former editor of *Pravda* and a Krushchev protégé. These were happenings of great significance, and four days later Kaganovich, another Stalinist, was dismissed from his post in the administration.

Matters now got out of hand. A wave of hysteria swept through the Communist parties of the world. To them, it was as if the Pope himself had appeared suddenly on the steps of St. Peter's and denounced Jesus Christ. The secret speech struck at the central conviction of every Communist in the world. It showed to each the true nature of the creed to which he had committed himself body and soul. There was an immediate reaction in other Communist countries where the local leaders found themselves in very difficult situations. De-Stalinisation was set in motion throughout Eastern Europe. In Poland Wladyslaw Gomulka, the former First Secretary of the Polish Communist Party, who had been under arrest on treason charges since 1950 was "rehabilitated" on 6th April. An Amnesty Bill was published in Warsaw announcing the release of 30,000 political prisoners and reducing the sentences on 40,000 more—a staggering indication of the nature of the struggle that had been going on in Poland since the Communist régime was established. The Czechoslovak Government released two prominent Communists who had been accused of "Titoism" but it was careful not to refer to the Slansky trial of 1952. The Bulgarian Prime Minister, Vulko Chervenkov, was forced to resign in the presence of a visiting Yugoslav delegation—an act of great significance. Matyas Rakosi, the veteran Stalinist of Hungary, "confessed" to his faults in May.

It must be emphasised that all this had been taking place *before* the American publication of Krushchev's secret speech. The effect of its publication was to raise the political temperature to the point that there was a riot in Poland before the eyes of hundreds of Western businessmen attending the Poznan Trade Fair. The riot arose out of the dissatisfaction on wages and conditions in a large engineering factory in the city. The workers had sent a deputation to Warsaw. On 27th June, when this deputation returned, it was learned that it had come back empty-handed. There were even rumours that some of its members had been arrested. The next day, a huge crowd assembled in Poznan's main square and sought to attract the attention of the visiting foreigners in the main hotels adjoining. The authorities appeared to be taken by surprise. Some shots were fired by members of the Security Police and a running battle developed. Sympathisers amongst the Polish Army handed their weapons to the demonstrators. A prison was attacked and opened and an abortive attempt was made to seize the headquarters of the Security Police who fired upon the crowd. More troops were called out and by next day order had been restored. The official figures stated that fifty-three people had been killed (including nine members of the Government forces) and over 300 wounded.

Conflicting explanations were proffered. The Polish Government's first reaction was to attribute the riots to " Enemy agents and imperialist centres," as in the case of the 1953 East German uprising. But Eduard Ochab, Beirut's successor as the First Secretary of the Polish Party [1] reversed the party's attitude on

---

[1] Beirut was taken seriously ill after the Twentieth Congress and died on 12th March. A popular jest in Poland was that "the truth had killed him!"

18th July. Ochab told the Seventh Plenum of the Polish Central Committee, " It would be wrong to concentrate attention above all on the machinations of provocateurs and imperialist agents. It is necessary to look first of all at the social roots of these incidents which have become for our party a warning signal. . . ." Three days later, on 21st July, Bulganin arrived in Warsaw, for the overt purpose of attending the Polish Communist National Day and he informed the Poles that Ochab's explanation was unacceptable. In his speech he said, " The recent events in Poznan, provoked by hostile agents, provide fresh evidence that international reaction has not yet discarded its mad plan for the restoration of capitalism in the socialist countries." Bulganin's warning made little difference to the Poles. Gomulka was formally readmitted to the Polish Communist Party in August. Shortly afterwards, Ochab paid a visit to Peking, in September, in which he appeared to have secured Mao Tse-tung's sympathy and support for a more independent attitude towards the Soviet Union. At the beginning of October, certain leading Stalinists in the Polish hierarchy resigned and on 16th October it was announced that Gomulka would be taking part in the Central Committee's Eighth Plenum to begin on 19th October. Ochab then asked Gomulka to present the report—an obvious prelude to his reinstatement as First Secretary.

All this was too much for the men in the Kremlin whose denunciation of Stalin by Krushchev had never been intended to destroy the Soviet Union's grip on Eastern Europe. At the very moment that Gomulka was preparing to address the Central Committee, a Soviet aircraft appeared over Warsaw. There was consternation when it was learned it contained Krushchev, Molotov, Kaganovich, Mikoyan and a number of military leaders. The Polish leaders hurried to the airport to meet their guests. At the confrontation, Krushchev is reported to have said, " We gave Russian lives to liberate your country and now you are determined to give it to the Americans! " Pointing at Gomulka he demanded, " Who's he? " Gomulka is said to have answered, " I am the former First Secretary of the Party whom you and Stalin flung in prison. My name is Gomulka." The Russians went straight to their huge embassy on the city's outskirts whilst the Poles returned to their meeting in the Party offices in the centre.

Ochab was quite undeterred. He announced to the Central Committee that the Politbureau was nominating Gomulka for the post of First Secretary. A further Soviet-Polish meeting took place that evening at the Belevedere, Warsaw's historic palace, in circumstances of great tension. Reports had been coming in all that afternoon of Soviet troop movements towards the capital. At the outset of the meeting, Krushchev attempted to bully Gomulka but the First Secretary-Designate threatened not to answer at the meeting but on Radio Warsaw. Gomulka is also believed to have told Krushchev that the Polish Communists would fight rather than be trampled upon by the Russians. The Soviet delegation realised that it was in a very vulnerable situation and decided to leave as quickly as possible. The Red Army units in Poland and Polish home forces both remained on the alert as the Central Committee proceeded to elect Gomulka whose speech to the Central Committee, outlining his programme, was broadcast over the national radio network—a most unusual course. In it, Gomulka showed that he remained a loyal Communist despite his experiences but that he insisted on certain measures of Polish independence. The speech did much to reassure the Russians, who now realised that Gomulka had no intention of taking Poland out of the Communist bloc. On the other hand, the Polish Stalinists had been decisively defeated and Krushchev decided to accept gracefully by telephoning his congratulations to Gomulka.

The next day was a day of great rejoicing in Warsaw. A quarter of a million people thronged the square outside the Soviet Palace of Culture to greet Gomulka, the hero of Poland's October Revolution.

In the meanwhile even more dramatic events were in prospect in another Communist country—Hungary—where, parallel with the upsurge of feeling in Poland, events had been moving quickly. A meeting of the Petofi Circle—a literary and cultural organisation —on 27th June had turned itself into a huge public demonstration against Stalinism. Beginning at 6.30 in the evening it lasted until the early hours of the morning, as speaker after speaker attacked the crimes that had been committed in the name of the brotherhood of man. The audience numbered several thousands and every mention of the name of Imre Nagy—the dismissed ex-Premier of the Malenkov period—brought thunderous cheers. Nagy's name had become synonymous with the pent-up hopes of the Hungarian peoples but the significance of what was happening was lost on the Russians, preoccupied as they were with Poland.

Throughout the late summer the Russians paid little attention to the growing Hungarian discontent but the Petofi Circle took great encouragement from the changes in the Hungarian leadership, in which Rakosi, the arch-Stalinist, was replaced by a slightly less rigid Stalinist, Erno Gerö. As the feeling continued to grow, at the end of September Krushchev summoned Hungarian party leaders to a conference in the Soviet Union at which Tito was present. The reason for this conference was that Krushchev himself was now in difficulties over the storm he had caused and anxious to invoke Tito's aid. He had begun by going to see Tito in Belgrade on 19th September and had then persuaded Tito to return with him to try to persuade the Soviet leadership of the rightness of Krushchev's course since the Twentieth Congress. At the Russian Conference Gerö grovelled to Tito and he was ordered to lead a goodwill mission to Belgrade. Whilst Gerö was away in Belgrade the situation in Budapest suddenly got out of hand, partly under the impact of the news from Poland.

A huge student demonstration took place in Budapest on 22nd October. A deputation from the demonstration appeared at the Budapest radio station at 8.30 that evening demanding that its claims for a sixteen-point programme—including free elections and the withdrawal of Russian troops—should be broadcast. The demands were refused. The students retaliated by printing a manifesto overnight and the next day, 23rd October, saw the point of no return. From now on the Hungarian Communist Government lost all authority. It first attempted to ban another demonstration. Then it rescinded its ban. Huge crowds marched up and down in the city singing patriotic songs. Actors recited poetry. The city was drunk with excitement. Slogans demanded the recall of Nagy. Finally, the cry went up for Nagy to appear.

Imre Nagy was at his home in Orso Street when a deputation arrived to persuade him to come to the Parliament building, outside which thousands were waiting for him. When he got there he found that someone had attempted to disperse the crowd in advance by turning off the electricity but it had responded by lighting newspapers and bundles, transforming the darkened scene into one of torchlight defiance. Nagy appeared on the balcony around 8 p.m. He spoke briefly and appealed to the people to go home. In words that were obviously addressed to the Central Committee, he talked of settling the country's problems " by negotiation in the bosom of the party." It was an attempt to control the situation but Nagy's efforts were undermined by a hectoring broadcast by Gerö, just arrived back from Yugoslavia.

A crowd of demonstrators went again to the radio station to repeat their demands and were fired upon by the Secret Police. Several people were killed and many more wounded. An Army detachment appeared and refused to fire upon the crowd. The Secret Police thereupon fired at the Army detachment. Simultaneously, another crowd attacked Budapest's huge monument to Stalin with hammers and blowlamps. The dramatic scene as Stalin's figure tottered and fell, symbolised the logical end to the chain of events that had been set in motion by Krushchev's speech at the Twentieth Congress.

Gerö was desperate by now. An emergency meeting of the Hungarian Central Committee began just before midnight and ended with the nominal election of Nagy as Prime Minister, although he was to remain without effective authority for some hours. Three hours later, the first Red Army tanks appeared in the streets of Budapest having been asked for by Gerö before the Central Committee met.

At first the Soviet tanks seemed content to patrol the streets as demonstrations of strength. Firing broke out when this failed to impress the Hungarians. A Soviet attack on the large Corvin block failed. The Hungarians staged a brilliant military operation using improvised weapons and barricades. Much of their inspiration came from Colonel Pal Maleter and by next day it was apparent that there was little the Red Army could do. Indeed its tanks were in a very dangerous situation militarily, caught up as they were in the street fighting. The struggle now spread to the whole country, being waged largely between the populace and the Security Police.

Gerö was dismissed on 25th October and he was replaced by Janos Kadar who professed himself a staunch supporter of Nagy's policy. Mikoyan suddenly appeared in Budapest that same day and apparently began negotiations with Nagy.

Nagy announced his new Government on 26th October. He also stated that the Red Army forces would be returning to their bases after order had been restored, presumably on Mikoyan's authority. In Nagy's administration, Pal Maleter, by now a general, was named as Minister of Defence. At dawn, on 29th October, the Red Army began its withdrawal and by 1st November Budapest was free of troops.

Nagy announced that the one party system was abolished; and a new sense of freedom was in the air by the time Mikoyan flew back to Moscow on 30th October. The next day—31st October—

Tass issued a statement that the Soviet Government was " ready to enter into negotiations with the Government of the Hungarian People's Republic and other Governments which are party to the Warsaw Pact on the withdrawal of Soviet troops from Hungary." Nagy appointed a delegation led by the Minister of Defence, Maleter, and Chief of Staff, General Kovacs, to negotiate the Soviet withdrawal. He announced also that Hungary had withdrawn from the Warsaw Pact.

For a few hours it appeared as though an unprecedented event was about to happen—the Soviet Union seemed to be on the verge of granting complete freedom to a Communist State. But some other disquieting events were also being reported. The local radio transmitters at Nyiregyhaza and Miskok in north-east Hungary broadcast warnings on 31st October—the day of the *Tass* statement and before Nagy's announced withdrawal from the Warsaw Pact— that Red Army forces were coming through in very large numbers from the Soviet Union. On the evening of 1st November, the new First Secretary of the Hungarian Communist Party, Janos Kadar, disappeared. All seemed well, however, on 2nd and 3rd November. The talks between Maleter's delegation and the Russians began amicably at Tokol at 10 p.m. on 3rd November. The Hungarians reported progress to the Government in the Parliament building by telephone until the connection was suddenly broken at midnight. Reports have it that General Ivan Serov, the head of the Soviet Security Forces marched into the meeting and ordered the arrest of the Hungarians despite the protests of the Russian generals.

Nagy was in bed that night of 3rd-4th November when he was awakened by the news that the Red Army was attacking Budapest. He asked about Maleter and his colleagues but there was no news as to their fate. There could be only one conclusion now, and at 5.20 a.m. on Sunday, 4th November, Nagy broadcast to the world. His words were picked up in many Western countries and rebroadcast upon their national networks. " This is Imre Nagy, President of the Council of Ministers of the Hungarian People's Republic speaking," he cried. " To-day, at dawn, Soviet forces launched an attack against the capital with the obvious purpose of overthrowing the legal Hungarian democratic Government. Our troops are fighting. The Government is at its post. I notify the people of our country and of the entire world of these facts."

The fighting was bitter but sharp and sporadic. This time the attack had been well planned and the defenders had been taken by

surprise. At 6 a.m. a pro-Soviet administration led by the missing
Kadar was proclaimed and it turned out that Kadar had been at
Soviet headquarters at Szolnok all the time, having returned on
Russian instructions from his position of being a spy in Nagy's
circle. There could be no question of any prolonged resistance to
the Russians. Thousands fled across the border into Austria.
Nagy, himself, sought asylum in the Yugoslav Embassy along with
a small group. He remained there for nearly three weeks and left
only after he had been granted a safe conduct by Kadar. At 6.30
p.m. on 23rd November Nagy wrote a letter to the Yugoslav
Government expressing gratitude and got into a bus sent by the
Kadar Government along with others who had taken refuge at the
time. For an inexplicable reason there were two Soviet M.V.D.
officers in the bus and Nagy insisted that they should leave. However, as the bus was moving off, the M.V.D. officers leaped on
board and the bus drove straight to a building occupied by the
Soviet Military Command. Nagy and his associates were dragged
out forcibly and into the building.

Only the bare outlines of the rest of the story are known but they
are sufficient. Nagy and those who had been arrested with him
were held in captivity in Rumania. An official announcement
said he had been granted " asylum." It was then stated that he
was brought to trial with eight co-defendants. Four of these,
including Nagy and Maleter, were condemned to death and shot.
One of the defendants died " under interrogation," and the announcements of the trial and of their deaths were made simultaneously on 16th June, 1958.

The Polish and Hungarian revolutions had threatened the whole
fabric of Stalin's empire in Eastern Europe. Krushchev's secret
speech to the Twentieth Congress, which in terms of Soviet internal
politics had been skilful enough a move to indict those most closely
associated with Stalin and to manœuvre Krushchev himself into a
position in which he could dispose of them, had caused very different
effects outside the Soviet Union. In Poland, the existence of a man
like Gomulka and the shrewd and sensitive management of the
situation by the Polish Politbureau narrowly averted uncontrollable
movements developing in Warsaw. The Soviet leadership had
been very alarmed by what happened, as witness the sudden
arrival of the Kremlin delegation at the beginning of the Eighth
Plenum, but once it had been realised that Gomulka had no intention of taking Poland out of the Warsaw Alliance if left to his own

devices the Russians were not in a position to use armed force merely to prevent the Polish Communist Party from appointing its own Politbureau.

But Hungary was a very different story. Nagy himself was a less experienced and dominating personality than Gomulka and the Hungarian Communist leadership under Rakosi and later Gerö were always far more rigid than their Polish counterparts. Indeed, their record of oppression and murder in Stalin's later days was far worse than the Polish Communists. For example, there had been no event in Poland comparable to the Rajk affair. Nor did the Hungarian Politbureau ever show the same sense of cohesion as the Poles. Finally, Nagy chose to associate himself with a far more radical movement than Gomulka was prepared to do.

It has been claimed that the Russian decision to intervene militarily in Hungary, but not in Poland, was in some way motivated by the Anglo-French expedition to Suez which took place around the same time. The dates are important therefore. The first use of Soviet force took place on the night of 23rd/24th October. Soviet armour and infantry for the second attack was reported crossing the Russian frontier on the evening of 31st October, before Nagy made his announcement of Hungary's withdrawal from the Warsaw Pact. And for this latter to have happened, a major decision must have been taken in Moscow on at least the previous day and probably on 28th or 29th October, immediately after the first Soviet defeat and as the withdrawal was proceeding. The sequence of events in the Suez operation, on the other hand, began with the Israeli invasion during the night of 29th October. The Anglo-French ultimatum to Egypt only became public at 4.30 p.m. of 30th October. Even allowing for Soviet anticipation of the course of action that Britain and France were likely to pursue, the logical deduction is that the Soviet Union's decision to remain in Hungary regardless of the consequences was taken in advance of their full knowledge of what was likely to happen at Suez. This is not to condone in any way the crime of the Suez venture but to separate accurately the reality of events from the emotional associations that linked the two crises in certain people's thinking.

The impact of events in Hungary was felt throughout the world. Outside the Communist bloc, the Soviet action in Hungary dealt a further shattering blow to the morale of the various Communist parties, again particularly in Europe. Within the bloc there was the gravest perturbation, which was shown by the steps that were taken hurriedly to redress the situation.

On 29th December the Chinese Communist Party made its first major contribution to the evolution of Communist theory with an article in the *People's Daily*, entitled *More on the Historical Experience of the Dictatorship of the Proletariat*, following discussions in the Chinese Politbureau. It referred specifically to the Polish "deviation" and to the Hungarian uprising. The writer drew a distinction between the "fundamental contradictions" to be found in capitalism and the "non-fundamental" differences that might appear within Communist parties. The Chinese view was that there were correct and incorrect courses in Communist policy; and that Stalin had followed the incorrect policy. The Soviet Union so the article said, had also made mistakes including "Great Power chauvinism." But the Hungarian situation had gone far beyond the non-fundamental contradictions in Poland and it had become a clash between those who wanted Hungary to remain a Communist country and those who wished to revert to capitalism. Thus, according to Chinese reasoning, the Soviet action was justified. *Pravda* printed the Chinese article next day, including even the criticisms of the Soviet Union.

Krushchev was quick to act himself. He convened a conference of Communist leaders in Budapest on 1st January, which reaffirmed the solidarity of the bloc. Chou En-Lai assisted him by undertaking a tour of European capitals. In Budapest, Chou delivered a bitter attack on " the Nagy clique." In Moscow, he spoke of "the glaringly ill-intentioned and shameful attack" that had been made on the Soviet forces in Hungary.

Finally, Mao Tse-tung carried the doctrinal reappraisal yet a stage further in a major speech on 27th February, 1957, which was not published until 18th June. This was the speech that came to be associated with his earlier slogan, " Let a hundred flowers bloom, let a hundred schools contend." Mao's theme was again the two kinds of contradiction—antagonistic and non-antagonistic. According to him the antagonistic contradictions had to be eliminated by action but the non-antagonistic contradictions could only be eliminated by persuasion.

The question arises: What motivated Krushchev's February speech in view of all that followed? The Twentieth Congress was intended as an exercise in de-Stalinisation and the earlier speeches, particularly those by Krushchev, Mikoyan and Anna Pankratova, demonstrate this clearly. The secret session, however, at which Krushchev spoke on 25th February, was an afterthought. Originally there was to be a mass demonstration in the Red Square on that day and up to 23rd February Moscow radio was still calling upon the population to attend. But the earlier speeches had caused so much ferment that pro-Stalinist as well as anti-Stalinist movements developed in the course of the Congress. Action had to be taken. Krushchev decided to put himself at the head of the anti-Stalinist forces. He used his opportunity with skill because by implication he indicted all his main rivals for the leadership. His opening sentences also have great significance, " Because of the fact that not everyone as yet fully realised the practical consequences of the personality cult and the great harm caused by the violation of the principle of the collective leadership of the Party, which results in the concentration of unlimited power in the hands of a single individual, the Central Committee considers it absolutely necessary to make the material pertaining to this matter available to the Twentieth Congress."

June 1956 had been the climax of de-Stalinisation. Immediately after the Poznan riots, the process was placed in reverse as the columns of *Pravda* showed in early July. On 23rd August the Soviet leaders had issued a clandestine warning against "Titoism" to the East European Parties—and there was Krushchev's visit to Yugo-slavia in September, showing an internal Soviet struggle. To add to the evidence Kaganovich, who had been dismissed in June, returned in mid-September, and Molotov was appointed Minister of State Control with wide powers on 22nd November. The Stalinists were now in the ascendant and this was confirmed at a Plenary Session of the Central Committee held in Moscow from 20th to 24th December at which Krushchev and his supporters were kept in the background.

The internal struggle then took another turn in the new year of 1957. The Central Committee met again on 13th February and Krushchev emerged again in a dominating role in his advocacy of economic reforms. His plans were not accepted immediately but in the succeeding weeks he appeared to have won the day with the announcement of the decentralisation of the Soviet economy and the establishment of local *sovnarhozy*—or economic planning committees—throughout the Soviet Union.

His enemies were preparing to strike back. A Party Praesidium was called for 18th June, 1957, on the invitation of Molotov and

Malenkov. Krushchev had been away in Finland with Bulganin and returned to Moscow on 14th June to receive a rapturous reception. *Pravda* published next day a large picture of Krushchev being greeted by Malenkov, Molotov, Kaganovich, Mikoyan and others, their faces beaming with pleasure. But when the Praesidium met, Molotov and Malenkov launched their attack. " Talk less and give the people more to eat," Molotov is supposed to have said.

Reports have it that Krushchev's removal from the post of First Secretary was demanded. He was to be replaced by Molotov, and Malenkov was to become Prime Minister. Krushchev was outnumbered in the Praesidium and he appealed to the Central Committee. Time was essential. His few supporters in the Praesidium resorted to filibustering. The only woman present, Yekatrina Furtseva, is reported to have spoken for six hours, while Krushchev's supporters in the Central Committee were flown in from all over the Soviet Union in army aircraft made available by Marshal Zhukov, who had no reason to like the Stalinists following his post-war humiliations at Stalin's hands.

When the full Central Committee met on 22nd June, Krushchev was now in a majority. In the bitter struggle that followed certain people changed sides, including Shepilov, who guessed wrongly that Krushchev would lose. Over 300 people were present and 215 asked to speak. In fact, some sixty did so.

Krushchev's victory was published on 4th July. Malenkov, Molotov, Kaganovich and Shepilov were branded as " The Anti-Party Group " in the manner of Communist practice. They were all dismissed from their great offices—Molotov, the veteran of the Bolshevik Revolution, to go to exile as Ambassador in Ulan Bator after all his years of great influence at the centre; and Malenkov to manage a power station at Ust-Kamenogorsk. Shepilov was sent to Frunze and Kaganovich to the Sverdlovsk area. Five of the eleven members of the Praesidium were dismissed. Nine new ones were appointed. It was the greatest single upheaval in the history of Communist leadership.

Nor was this all; Zhukov who was promoted for his services in June, was dismissed on 27th October, because his strength and outspokenness suddenly represented a new threat to Krushchev. Finally, Bulganin was dismissed some nine months after the struggle in the Central Committee on 28th March, 1958. Later he was to confess to siding with " The Anti-Party Group " in these events.

407

Thus the wheels had turned full circle. History had taken its revenge on Stalin. His associates in the main, had been driven from power. At last, Krushchev was in control of power in the Soviet Union and in position to give a new confidence and purpose to Soviet policy.

CHAPTER 22

COLLISION COURSE

But our rest is as far as the fire-drake swings
And our peace is put in impossible things
Where clashed and thundered unthinkable wings
Round an incredible star
Chesterton

The Soviet Union launched the first man-made earth satellite in history on 4th October, 1957. The satellite was twenty-two inches in diameter and it circled the earth every ninety-five minutes at 18,000 miles an hour. The great achievement excited the imagination of the world. In particular, it staggered—and alarmed—the American people, who had not grasped fully the extent of Soviet technological advance. Behind the event, and the successful firing of a Soviet intercontinental missile some weeks before, lay military implications that challenged the entire basis of modern defence theory. It marked a new stage in international politics as important, in its own way, as the first atomic explosion twelve years before.

Very little of this was realised by the public at the time. Throughout 1957, the Soviet Union and the East European countries had been largely preoccupied with their own internal problems since the Twentieth Congress. United States policy, also, had appeared to be becalmed. This was due in part to the fact that John Foster Dulles, who had dominated American foreign policy ever since Eisenhower's inauguration, had been stricken by cancer in late 1956. Although he was soon back at his desk, his energy was diminished. But the substantive reason for American policy stagnation was that the United States leaders of the day had no clear ideas to pursue. Dulles's earlier doctrine of the "liberation of Eastern Europe" had gone—as the United States' refusal to intervene in Hungary showed. Furthermore, because in 1957 Soviet policy was temporarily defensive, the pressure was removed from the American leaders to consider new possibilities. As for Britain—she was still nursing her wounds after the Suez disaster.

Only in Western Europe were there significant movements. The war-time dreams of a United Europe had been carried several stages towards practical realisation, beginning with the so-called Schuman Plan for the European Iron and Steel in 1950 and leading on to the conference at Messina in June 1955 to consider wider economic integration. It is true that the European idea had received a major rebuff from Britain's reluctance to participate in the detailed working out of a closely-knit economic community; but in early 1957 France, Germany, Italy and the Benelux countries had come much closer together. The British leaders, in the face of this, preferred a looser European free trade area and they now bent their energies towards establishing it, believing the Messina concept to be an impractical dream. History already shows how wrong they were. And, under the stimulus of Jean Monnet's Action Committee for a United States of Europe, the Treaty of Rome, setting up the European Economic Community, was signed on 25th March, 1957.

Krushchev, in the autumn of 1957, finding himself suddenly in a much stronger political situation than most people could have foreseen a few months before, was determined to gain the maximum advantage. He did so, at the biggest international Communist meeting for many years, held immediately after the fortieth anniversary of the Bolshevik Revolution which was attended by sixty-four Communist parties. The first speech at the conference was made by Mao Tse-tung who said that the world Communist movement had to have a head like any individual Communist party. This role must belong to the Soviet Union, he argued. And, although the Soviet State (as a state) was later substituted for the Soviet Communist Party, Mao was supported by the conference.

In his newly acquired position of strength Krushchev was able to make political capital out of pressing for a summit conference and renewing certain disarmament proposals. Parallel to Krushchev's overtures, a separate and apparently independent plan for the limitation of weapons and forces in an area of central Europe was put forward by the Polish Foreign Minister, Adam Rapacki.

The Communist bloc's recovery on the political stage was assisted by the American reaction to the *Sputnik*. In Washington, the cry was to redouble the United States defence effort and to speed up the American missile programme. Initial United States failures at launching an American satellite accentuated Krushchev's political advantage. When the United States finally succeeded with the satellite *Explorer*, at the end of January 1958, it was a much smaller satellite weighing only 30 lb. as compared with the 184 lb. *Sputnik* of the previous October. The inference again was obvious. The new American demand was now to close the " missile gap." In these circumstances, the United States was reluctant in early 1958 to undertake another summit conference from what the West believed to be a position of weakness. But the pressures for such a meeting mounted and Krushchev appeared as the most ardent believer in it.

The international scene was made confused in the summer of 1958 by events in the Middle East and by a French settlers' rebellion in Algeria. A sudden revolution in Iraq, in which King Feisal and the Prime Minister, Nuri-es-Said, were assassinated, destroyed the core of the Baghdad Pact and placed the region in jeopardy. However, the United States and British governments, having at last co-ordinated their Middle East policies, responded quickly by landing forces in the Lebanon and Jordan. It was an action which, despite Soviet warnings and threats, stabilised a situation that looked as though it could get out of hand.

The significance of the rebellion in Algeria was that it brought back to power Charles de Gaulle, who had led the French resistance in war-time. Prime Minister at the end of the war, De Gaulle had lived in retirement for a number of years whilst the French political system and the status of her leaders had declined. He accepted office again in June 1958 at the invitation of a dismayed National Assembly. Nobody had any clear idea what he intended to do, but he was strongly supported by the French right wing who believed he would retain French control of Algeria; ironically, he proceeded to do the exact opposite. Yet his immense prestige and romantic patriotism was soon to invest France with a new sense of purpose in affairs.

The Middle East crisis led to further Soviet pressure for a summit meeting. Krushchev himself proposed on 19th July, that " a meeting should be held without delay between the heads of the governments of the U.S.S.R., the United States, the United Kingdom, France and India with the participation of the Secretary-General of the United Nations." He suggested a meeting " any day and hour! " The American and British responses were frigid at first. But as the days went by first Macmillan and then Eisenhower both came to the point at which they would have accepted a meeting within the framework of the Security Council. By the end of July, it appeared as though Krushchev only wanted the date to be settled. Preparations went forward hurriedly for a special meeting of the Security Council to meet his demand.

On 31st July Krushchev suddenly flew to Peking accompanied by Malinovsky, the Minister of Defence, after references on the Chinese radio to " a deceptive plan . . . full of pitfalls," meaning the proposed U.N. meeting. The Soviet visit remained secret until a communiqué was issued after four days of talks. Krushchev and Mao both declared themselves in favour of an early meeting of heads of government, but they were strangely silent about it being held within the Security Council framework. Another significant point was that great stress was laid on unity in the Communist *bloc*. *Pravda* returned to the theme on successive days as a clear indication that there had been some disagreements. It was not very long before reports also reached the West that there had been disagreements between Krushchev and Mao on defence policy. The Chinese were said to have asked for aid for an attack on Formosa —a request which the Soviet delegation firmly refused—although Krushchev is believed to have agreed to the Soviet Union going to Chinese aid in the event of any American attack on the mainland arising out of the Formosa situation.

Krushchev's visit to Peking ended the prospects for a summit conference for the time being. Demonstrations were held throughout China supporting the decisions of the Krushchev-Mao conference. Particular stress was laid by the Chinese upon a sentence in the communiqué to which Krushchev had been compelled to agree, in which the two leaders pledged themselves " to wage an uncompromising struggle against revisionism, the chief danger in the Communist movement, which is clearly manifested in the League of Communists in Yugoslavia." Considering the key position of Yugoslavia in Krushchev's strategy and his attempts to court Tito in the preceding two years, the full significance of Krushchev's capitulation was clear.

Immediately after Krushchev left Peking, the Chinese Communists began to concentrate aircraft and troops on the mainland opposite the island of Formosa. A mounting battle of words developed between the Chinese and the Americans over Chinese accusations of American aggression. A Chinese attack on the off-shore islands appeared imminent in mid-September. Heavy and prolonged bombardment of Quemoy added to the tension until suddenly, on 6th October, the Chinese Communists announced a unilateral cease-fire which led to the gradual ending of the crisis. A feature of the Formosa crisis was that Krushchev insisted on several occasions that in any conflict with the United States " aggressors," the Chinese would be supported by the Soviet Union—another indication of the nature of the meeting in Peking.

If Krushchev had been compelled to make some concessions in Peking, he was now even more anxious to secure concessions from the Western Powers at their weakest point militarily—Berlin. The Middle East crisis about which he had asked for a summit conference had evaporated, and a new crisis in East-West relations had to be created. It was not long in coming. Addressing a rally in the Moscow Sports Palace on 10th November, in honour of Gomulka, who was visiting the Soviet Union, Krushchev spoke of handing over to the German Democratic Republic the Soviet occupation rights in and around Berlin.

The Western Powers realised that, whether they liked it or not, they might now be placed in the position of having to deal with the East German régime which they had consistently refused to recognise. They knew, also, that if this were to happen, it would mean *de facto* recognition, an act which would go a long way towards accepting the division of Germany and the Communist bloc's western frontier as being on the River Elbe. Krushchev's threat was underlined in a formal Soviet note to the other Occupation Powers and the two German Governments on 27th November. He suggested that all occupation forces should be withdrawn from Berlin and that West Berlin should become a demilitarised free city. The Soviet proposal stated that an agreement to this effect should be negotiated within the next six months. It was, in effect, an ultimatum.

Krushchev denied the ultimatum element subsequently, but he took the unusual course on 27th November of holding a news conference to support his demand in the panelled room of the Council of Ministers in the Kremlin. The import of Krushchev's words was most ominous. He referred repeatedly to his determination " to liquidate that cancerous tumour that is West Berlin." *Pravda*, on 29th November, added that, if the Berlin occupation statutes were not changed, " fairly unpleasant consequences may arise."

Any indications of hesitation or weakness on the part of the Western Powers could have led to disaster. In the tense situation the American General commanding the U.S. troops in Europe responded on 30th November. He warned, " any infringement of West Berlin would be the equivalent of an attack on the United States and plans existed to deal with it." Willy Brandt, the Social Democrat Governing Mayor of West Berlin since 1957—a man in the tradition of the courageous Ernst Reuter—added acidly that Krushchev's six months ultimatum was " Concentration camp by appointment."

The considered Western answer to the Soviet Union was decided at a meeting of the N.A.T.O. Foreign Ministers held in Paris in December. It rejected the Soviet demands, and stated that the Western Powers refused to negotiate " under menace of an ultimatum."

But the year ended on a worse note. Gromyko, addressing the Supreme Soviet on Christmas Day, warned that Berlin could become " a new Sarajevo." Krushchev's retort to the Western answer was to propose a peace conference and summit talks on Berlin and Germany with both German Governments taking part. Somewhat surprisingly, he made no mention of the six months' deadline; and in order to come some way to meet him, the Western Powers promptly suggested a Four Power Foreign Ministers' Conference to which East and West German "advisers" should be invited.

The world had been brought face to face with the consequences of the shift in the balance of military power that had stemmed from the Soviet break-through in rocket technology. It was at this point in early 1959 that Macmillan decided to undertake a "probing" mission to Moscow. Macmillan's visit to the Soviet Union came as a shock to his partners in the Western Alliance. There was talk again of "a new Munich" in both Bonn and Washington. Krushchev provided a menacing overture for the Prime Minister in a speech at Tula, four days before Macmillan arrived. The Soviet leader announced that another Berlin airlift " could not be tolerated." Krushchev went on to renew his threat to sign a separate treaty with East Germany if the Western Powers refused to agree to withdraw from West Berlin.

Macmillan reached Moscow on 21st February wearing a fur hat. He was subjected to the usual rigorous schedule that both Russian hospitality and Communist policy impose upon visiting Heads of

State, from formal dinners and receptions to visits to factories. In between, time was set aside for exploratory talks between the two delegations.

When Krushchev discovered that Macmillan had not come to make concessions but merely to learn what lay behind Soviet statements and to advocate the Western proposal for a Foreign Ministers' conference, he changed his tactics abruptly. On 24th February, whilst Macmillan's party was visiting a factory, Krushchev delivered himself of "an election speech" to "a delegation of Soviet citizens" who were said to have waited upon him in order to support his candidature for the Supreme Soviet. The Soviet leader spoke in very sharp terms of Western attitudes—meaning the views Macmillan was putting forward in the private talks—and denounced the idea of the Foreign Ministers' Conference as "a bog without an exit" and " a waste of time." Macmillan was shocked when he learned the news of Krushchev's *ex cathedra* manœuvre. He immediately cancelled the following day's programme and asked Krushchev for the loan of a *dacha* outside Moscow at which he could meet the Soviet leader for lunch. The strange confrontation, which took place on the Minsk road, began with Krushchev in his most belligerent mood. He refused to concede anything to Macmillan's position and maintained that the Western troops were only in Berlin because of the Potsdam Agreement, which was nullified. He would not listen to any suggestion that the Allied Powers had entered Berlin in the first place as part of the German Instrument of Surrender and had the right to remain there until the full peace treaty was signed. He brushed aside the Western suggestions for the Foreign Ministers' Meeting and demanded an Allied withdrawal and a summit conference. At the end of this tirade, which greatly depressed Macmillan, who was also suffering from a chill, the Prime Minister replied quietly that Krushchev must face the consequences of his policy. " If you go on like this," he said, " there will only be a war and where shall we all be? " Krushchev leaped to his feet and stormed over to the window shouting, " You have insulted me! "

It was the end of the effective discussion. To parade the deadlock publicly, Krushchev refused to travel with Macmillan to Kiev. Krushchev announced he had "toothache" and proceeded to receive a visiting mission from Iraq. Macmillan, for his own part, had to decide whether to cut short his visit to the Soviet Union or to proceed as planned in the hope that the Russians would change their attitude. It was a forlorn gamble. But so reluctant was he to admit failure in the face of the criticism that he had received that the Prime Minister carried on despite a temperature from his chill. A very gloomy British party arrived at Kiev on 27th February and the gloom was accentuated when they heard that Mikoyan also had been attacking the West in another " election speech." Their astonishment was all the more great next day when they reached Leningrad to be met by Mikoyan, wreathed in smiles. Shortly afterwards, Macmillan received a telephone call from Krushchev saying that his toothache was better and that " a British drill had cured it! "

The British party returned to Moscow in a new atmosphere. A Soviet note of 2nd March, accepted the despised Foreign Ministers' conference. Macmillan was permitted to deliver an uncensored television broadcast. One item in the communiqué at the end of the visit, however, caused alarm in Western capitals because it implied a form of disengagement. The British and Soviet Governments undertook to make " a study of method of limitation of forces and weapons in an agreed area of Europe, coupled with a system of inspection." The result was that Macmillan, who had undoubtedly achieved a limited success, returned home to face Western criticism. He visited De Gaulle in Paris and Adenauer in Bonn, immediately, before flying to see Eisenhower.

Macmillan's visit to Washington in March 1959 coincided broadly with a new phase of American foreign policy. Dulles's illness had taken an increasing grip on him and his life was drawing to its close. In the previous December, he had made a great effort, in pain, to attend the N.A.T.O.'s Foreign Ministers' Meeting in Paris to discuss Krushchev's Berlin ultimatum. Dulles exercised less and less influence on American policy as the weeks went by. He lingered on in office until 16th April.

The strong personality of Dulles had overshadowed all American actions in world affairs since early 1953. When this articulate, indiscreet, evangelical, craggy man was buried with full military honours in the Arlington Cemetery on 28th May, 1959, there were some to praise and many to condemn his record. At times, because he often attuned his own ear more to American opinion, he had miscalculated the mood of world opinion. Europe had always viewed him with mixed feelings. He had been regarded as an ogre in Afro-Asia for a period and he had been feared by the Communist bloc and hated by the Chinese. But his policy in the later stages of the Suez crisis, which angered so many in Britain, won a new respect for his crusading sense of international morality amongst the neutrals. There were some occasions when the actions he proposed were extremely dangerous—as with Indo-China in 1954. Yet Dulles's instincts had usually been right. When he was wrong, it was more often than not for the right reason. It was a measure of his stature that his illness and death left a great gap in the Eisenhower Administration—a gap that was filled by Eisenhower taking greater initiatives himself.

The Foreign Ministers' Conference that Macmillan's visit had contributed to, met at Geneva on 11th May, 1959. By now, Krushchev's six months' ultimatum had been dropped quietly, showing yet again that Communist threats can be met successfully by resolution. Gromyko began by attempting to get the two German delegations admitted as full members of the conference—an act which would have meant a form of recognition for the East Germans. When this manœuvre failed, he sought to make the Western Powers negotiate on the basis of a Soviet draft of the German Peace Treaty. This draft showed again how little the Soviet aim of dominating all Germany had changed. For example, Articles 16 and 17 of the Soviet draft laid down that the Communists should have "unhampered activity" in West Germany; whereas "all revanchist and revisionist" groups would be banned in East Germany. Since it had long been the Communist practice to describe any liberal Western political views as "revanchist" or "revisionist," the draft treaty was merely an open return to the basic objective. Gromyko introduced new proposals on 9th June, which differed little except that the Western Powers were to be guaranteed a year's security in West Berlin—a most unsatisfactory concept—while the details of German re-unification were to be argued out between rival delegations of equal status from East and West Germany. The conference lost importance after an adjournment, first because Vice-President Nixon visited Moscow to open an American exhibition and later when it was announced on 3rd August that Krushchev and Eisenhower would be exchanging visits. It was Eisenhower's first major initiative. In preparation, Eisenhower visited Europe to consult with his Allies.

Krushchev arrived in Washington on 15th September accompanied by a party of 100, including nearly all his family and holding a replica of a pennant that had been carried by a Soviet rocket to the moon the day before—a symbol of Soviet technological achievement and a shrewd reminder of the military power that went with it.

The story of Krushchev's rumbustious journey has been told fully—his anger at the National Press Club at being asked questions about his record under Stalin and the Hungarian Revolution, his controlled outburst in San Francisco and his adroit skill on a number of occasions. There is no doubt that Krushchev was deeply impressed by much that he saw, from the high level of American industrial activity to the standard of living of the American worker. To any man coming from the grey life of the Soviet Union, with its spartan daily existence, the richness of the American society was an inevitable shock. The visit gave Krushchev cause for much thought about the practicalities of industrialisation and—despite the great achievements of rocketry—Soviet backwardness.

As the tour proceeded, American generosity and warmth gradually overcame political inhibitions. By the time Krushchev was on his way back across the continent, his ebullience had gained American respect. He, too, appeared to draw inspiration from the American reaction.

In the course of his visit Krushchev addressed the United Nations General Assembly. He advocated a sweeping proposal that all nations should disarm down to police units within four years but he made no attempt to deal in depth with the fundamental difficulties of arms control and inspection that would be essential for its implementation. Krushchev's U.N. speech naturally caused a flurry among left-wing circles in the West but it was received with appropriate scepticism by the more serious observers.

Nevertheless, it would be a mistake to dismiss Krushchev's American visit as a mere exercise in propaganda. Apart from the impact that the tour made upon Krushchev and his party, the Soviet Government attached great importance to it. Therefore it was an attempt of a kind at a *détente* on Soviet terms. The Soviet Press at first presented it as the ending of the Cold War. A remark by Krushchev in Washington—" The ice of the Cold War has not only cracked, but begun to melt "—was given great prominence. Krushchev was impressed, too, by his two days of talks with Eisenhower at Camp David, and he said on his return to Moscow that the "responsible" leaders of America were opposed to war. He admitted that the greatest danger of war might come from a miscalculation or mistake. He spoke of Eisenhower's "farsightedness" and withdrew his suspended Berlin ultimatum. Clearly he thought he could make progress towards his unchanged goal in other ways.

Krushchev flew to Peking on 30th September, immediately after his return from America. The official report of his talks with Mao referred on 30th September to " a cordial and friendly talk "; on 1st October to "cordial"; and on 3rd October, the report stated only that Mao and he had met. At a banquet in his honour on 30th September Krushchev referred to his American visit. After stressing the military strength of the Communist Powers he said, " But we must think realistically and understand the contemporary situation correctly. This, of course, does not by any means signify that if we are so strong, then we must test by force the stability of the capitalist system." Krushchev's words received no answering warmth from the Chinese.

Krushchev in Washington had won his objective at last of a summit conference. He was determined that Chinese intransigence was not going to prejudice the meeting. During the course of Eisenhower's visit to Europe that preceded Krushchev's arrival in Washington, the American President had also been won over to the idea, largely by Macmillan. The talks with Krushchev at Camp David confirmed Eisenhower in this intention and with no Dulles at his elbow to warn otherwise he allowed the preparations to go forward through diplomatic channels. From now on, Krushchev took every precaution against something untoward happening before the summit meeting.

The Soviet objectives at the forthcoming meeting were easily definable. First, Krushchev and colleagues had long been concerned about the problem that was posed by West Berlin. The glitter of West Berlin's shops, the vitality of its life and the free speech of its people represented an unanswerable challenge a hundred miles inside the hinterland of Communism. West Berlin was also the only open point in the frontier that circled the entire Communist bloc, stretching from the Elbe to the Pacific. The constant hæmorrhage of refugees through West Berlin constituted a major threat to the East German régime. Even more important, the Soviet leaders hoped to use their relatively new position of strength, applied at the West's weakest point of Berlin, to compel recognition of the German Democratic Republic. In this way, they hoped simultaneously to achieve three further objects: the consolidation of the uncertain Pankow régime; the creation of a new and fluid political situation in West Germany, which had had remained firmly pro-Western since integration into N.A.T.O.; and official recognition by the West of the frontier of the Communist bloc as being on the River Elbe, thereby extinguishing all remaining hopes in the East European countries that eventually they might be free to resume their traditional contact with Western Europe.

The Western aims were less clear. Macmillan personally believed that an accommodation could be reached with Krushchev's administration provided the negotiations were conducted at the highest level. He based his hopes on two factors. First, he assumed that Krushchev and his immediate circle had come to appreciate at last the consequences of nuclear war and that it presented an unacceptable alternative to genuine co-existence. Secondly, Macmillan's reading of history and outlook led him to the conclusion that the Soviet Union was on the point of becoming a "satisfied power" in the sense that its leaders now recognised that they had more to lose than to gain by aggressive actions that threatened the peace. Eisenhower was not so precise. He had become attracted to the idea of "summitry" since Dulles's death. He believed, like Macmillan, that the Soviet leaders may have reached the point at which they wished to make some limited agreements. De Gaulle was, by far, the least optimistic of the three Western leaders. He hoped for nothing. He expected little. He could see no logic in the propositions that the West should—or could—make concessions on Berlin and he saw no prospect of the Soviet leaders making any concessions at all. As for Adenauer, the remaining Western leader who would be absent inevitably because of the German situation—he also was opposed to the conference and broadly shared De Gaulle's view that nothing should be expected from it.

The date and place of the meeting upon which so much was supposed to depend was announced: Paris, 16th May, 1960. Shortly afterwards it was also made public that Eisenhower would visit the Soviet Union from 10th to 19th June. As the time went by the two sides began to prepare themselves. The more they considered the issues involved, the less they saw of room for negotiation and manœuvre. The moment of truth in Russian thinking probably came during a visit that Krushchev made to France in late March. De Gaulle, with his lofty formality, left the Soviet leader in no doubt as to the Western determination to maintain its position in Berlin. Krushchev began to see that the prospects of *détente*—which he tended to equate with a Soviet victory in the negotiations on Berlin, upon which he had placed so much store—

were dissolving fast. He found that his threats made no impression on De Gaulle; and before he left Paris, he said again on 2nd April that when the Soviet Union signed a separate peace treaty with East Germany, it would nullify "all rights" of the West in Berlin. Two American speeches—by Herter at Chicago on 4th April and by Dillon at New York on 20th April—warned Krushchev against his threatening attitude. Krushchev retorted by saying at Baku that the West would " obviously lose the right of access to Berlin by land, water or air " after the Peace Treaty.

All this might have been interpreted as the manœuvring before a major negotiation if that is as far as it had gone. However there are good reasons for supposing that there were powerful elements in the Soviet leadership who had remained opposed to Krushchev's policies. They were given their opportunity when a U-2, an American photographic reconnaissance aircraft, on a flight across the Soviet Union from Peshawar to Bodo in Norway, crashed in the Sverdlovsk area. The truth was that the United States had been in the habit for some years of undertaking aerial reconnaissance missions under the guise of "weather flights" as a routine procedure to collect military intelligence. The particular aircraft that crashed near Sverdlovsk was unique for two reasons. First, the mission was undertaken with the summit meeting only fifteen days away. Secondly, unknown to everyone except the Russians, the pilot landed unhurt by parachute.

The first news of what had happened was given by Krushchev at the end of a long report to the Supreme Soviet on 5th May. His speech followed an important meeting of the Central Committee on the day before. He suddenly announced that early on the morning of 1st May, " at 5.36 a.m. Moscow time an American plane crossed our border and continued its flight into Soviet territory. The Minister of Defence immediately notified the government of this aggressive act. The government told him: ' The aggressor knows what to expect when he invades foreign territory. If he goes unpunished he will commit new provocations. The thing to do, therefore, is to act—shoot down the plane . . .' The plane was shot down." There was stormy applause and shouts of " Quite right! " and " Shame on the aggressors! " at this point. " The first investigation," Krushchev went on, " has shown that the plane belonged to the United States. . . ." When he said this there could be clearly heard on the broadcast relay an interjection from a member of the audience, " How does this agree with Eisenhower'

421

pious speeches?" At another stage in his speech Krushchev asked "Who sent this aircraft?" and sought to draw a distinction between "Pentagon militarists" and Eisenhower, inferring that it might have been done without the President's knowledge.

Assuming that Krushchev had told virtually the whole story, the American State Department after hurried consultations in Washington issued a statement to the effect that "an unarmed plane, a U-2 weather research plane based at Adana, Turkey, piloted by a civilian has been missing since 1st May. During the flight of this plane the pilot reported difficulty with his oxygen equipment which could result in the pilot losing consciousness . . . It is entirely possible . . . the plane continued on an automatic pilot . . . and accidentally violated Soviet air space." That same evening an indiscreet remark made by a Soviet official that the Russians had "got the pilot" reached the ears of the American ambassador in Moscow who immediately sent a warning cable which arrived too late to stop the State Department statement.

Krushchev made another statement to the Supreme Soviet on 7th May: "Comrades, I must let you into a secret. When I made my report I deliberately refrained from mentioning that the pilot was alive and healthy." He added that the pilot's testimony was that he was a member of the Central Intelligence Agency. Krushchev continued, "This is a regular reconnaissance plane . . . for collecting espionage information." He then produced enlarged photographs made from developed film of Soviet airfields taken by the aircraft's cameras and various other impediments found on the pilot including money, jewellery and means for committing suicide. Krushchev made the maximum capital out of his opportunity but he was still careful not to indict Eisenhower personally.

The Americans were in a difficult situation. Whilst Eisenhower was calmly playing golf after having been informed of Krushchev's revelations, frantic meetings were being held in Washington. One view at the meetings was that the Americans should adhere to their original story and, if necessary, find a lowly scapegoat. This proposal was rejected largely on the initiative of Christian Herter —Dulles's successor as Secretary of State—and Foy D. Kohler, Assistant Secretary for European Affairs. Their reasoning was that with the possibility that Gary Powers, the pilot, might confess, flat denial of espionage was not a tenable position. Therefore a statement was drawn up admitting the spy flight. There was discussion as to whether Eisenhower should or should not be asked to take personal responsibility. Herter then telephoned Eisenhower, who had just finished his round of golf. Eisenhower at first wanted to accept the responsibility, but was dissuaded by Herter. Yet another statement was issued saying, " it appears that in endeavouring to obtain information now concealed behind the Iron Curtain, a flight over Soviet territory was *probably* undertaken by an unarmed civilian U-2 plane." The American statement of 7th May went on to defend such a practice on the grounds of the state of the world, but it also said clearly: " As a result of an inquiry ordered by the President it has been established that insofar as the authorities in Washington are concerned, there was no authorisation for any such flight. . . ."

Next day Eisenhower changed his mind. When he got back from Gettysburg, he told Herter to announce that the flight had been undertaken by Presidential authority. His basic reason for so doing was that he felt very strongly that he had a defensible position on the constant need to gather military intelligence as being essential to the security of the West. He also realised that for him to disown responsibility laid him open to the humiliating charge of not being in control of affairs. Yet another American statement was drafted pointing out how the Soviet Union had rejected Eisenhower's "Open Skies" plan in 1955 and that it would be dereliction of American duty to all free peoples if steps were not taken to overcome the " danger of surprise attack." Saying that programmes for over-flights had been developed and were no secret to the Soviet leaders, the new statement added: " In accordance with the National Security Act of 1947, the President has put into effect since the beginning of his administration directives to gather by every possible means the information required to protect the United States and the Free World. . . ." The new statement did not say that flights had been suspended pending the Paris Conference, although this was in fact the case. The reason was that Eisenhower wished to keep the Russians in suspense.

Krushchev's attempt to differentiate between Eisenhower and those responsible for the U-2 was at an end. The Soviet Press from then on attacked the Americans violently but as late as 14th May—the day that Krushchev left for Paris—*Pravda* declared that Krushchev's party would be going " with a pure heart and good intentions " and " would spare no efforts to reach a mutually acceptable agreement."

Paris lay under a cloudless May sky as the delegations began to

arrive that week-end. Krushchev was the first to come, bringing
with him Gromyko and Malinovsky, the Minister of Defence. He
pledged himself at Orly airport to "exert all effort" to make the
conference a success. Eisenhower flew in next day and remarked
that it would be a " pleasure to meet my old friends," De Gaulle
and Macmillan. Macmillan's arrival in a small red aircraft,
wearing an old suit and suède shoes, amused the large crowd of
Pressmen but his words were sombre, as he warned of the possible
" extinction of civilisation." The conference, to him, represented
the fulfilment of great effort and he set much store by it.

The atmosphere in pre-conference rounds of courtesy calls was
ominous. Krushchev attempted to browbeat both De Gaulle and
Macmillan in turn. But there was no attempt at arranging a
Soviet-American meeting. Macmillan tried unsuccessfully to
persuade Eisenhower to announce publicly that the U-2 flights had
been suspended. Thomas Gates—the American Secretary for
Defence—by one of those bizarre actions that stem from lack of
political insight, suddenly cabled the Pentagon to order a military
alert for all American forces. His reason was that he was convinced,
on hearing of Krushchev's angry interview with De Gaulle, that
a dangerous situation threatened.

The Summit Conference began at 11 a.m. on 16th May in the
Elysée. De Gaulle, acting with frigid and dignified courtesy,
escorted first Krushchev and then Macmillan into the exquisite
salon that had once been Madame de Pompadour's dining-room.
Krushchev remained seated and showed no sign of recognition when
Eisenhower arrived. De Gaulle opened the proceedings by asking
if anyone had a statement to make. Krushchev immediately said
" Yes," before Eisenhower, whose prerogative it was to open the
proceedings by virtue of being head of state as well as head of
government. De Gaulle attempted to call upon Eisenhower, but
Krushchev insisted. Taking no notice of anyone, he put on his
metal-rimmed spectacles and began to read: " A provocative act is
known to have been committed with regard to the Soviet Union
by the American Air Force. . . ." His hands were shaking as he
went on to use such phrases as "treacherous nature" and "incompatible with the elementary requirements of normal relations between
states." He accused the Americans of putting out several different
versions and said that the flights had been authorised by " the
President personally." Krushchev ended by demanding that "the
United States government . . . must first condemn the inadmissible

provocative actions of the United States Air Force . . . secondly refrain from continuing such actions . . ." and thirdly " call strictly to account those who are directly guilty." Krushchev continued that he saw, " no possibility of productive negotiations . . . at the Summit . . . where one of them had made treachery the basis of his policy with regard to the Soviet Union." His crushing insult to Eisenhower was capped when he concluded by informing him that the American President's forthcoming visit to the Soviet Union was cancelled and the Summit Conference should be postponed for six months, by which time there would be another American President.

The men in the salon were taken aback. Macmillan wilted sadly. Eisenhower was extremely angry. De Gaulle alone preserved his poise. Eisenhower pulled himself together. Speaking from scribbled notes, he asserted that the U-2 flights had no aggressive intent. He said specifically, for the first time, that the Americans would not be sending any more. As he went on his tone became moderate and dignified although he said later that he had controlled himself with difficulty. He explained that the flights could not be the issue, as they had been suspended. A sharp exchange took place between De Gaulle and Krushchev when the French leader pointed out that France had been over-flown repeatedly by a Soviet space-ship that had been launched a few hours before and that for all De Gaulle knew it might have cameras on board. Krushchev denied this. De Gaulle referred to excellent Soviet pictures of the far side of the Moon. Krushchev flung his arms up crying, " as God is my witness, our hands are clean and pure."

Macmillan made a sad and eloquent plea for negotiations to begin. He and De Gaulle both attempted repeatedly to put into perspective what De Gaulle described as " a minor incident of espionage." They had agreed to adjourn the meeting until next day when Krushchev suddenly announced that he intended to publish his personal attack upon Eisenhower. He refused to be dissuaded when it was pointed out to him that he was taking a very grave step. De Gaulle, however, was determined to have the last word. " You have inconvenienced us," he told Krushchev acidly.

Krushchev walked out leaving behind him a mixture of emotions. That evening Macmillan, calling upon the delegations in turn, strove desperately to rebuild the shattered conference. His last meeting with Krushchev ended near midnight. The Soviet leader remained unyielding. The surprises were not over. Early next morning Krushchev appeared on the pavement outside the Soviet

Embassy. Seizing the first loitering reporter, he proceeded to announce that he would be leaving Paris next day if Eisenhower did not apologise. He said gaily that he was off into the country that morning with his friends, Malinovsky and Gromyko. Shortly afterwards, Krushchev's motorcade swept out of Paris on its way to the Marne battlefield where Malinovsky had fought in a unit of the Tsarist army.

The Western leaders met gloomily at the Elysée at 10 a.m. Macmillan recounted his failures of the previous evening. De Gaulle suggested that he, as the host, should issue a formal invitation to the participants to another meeting at 3 p.m. " to ascertain whether it is possible for the Summit Conference to begin and calling for a written reply." Eisenhower and Macmillan then left for a drive in the country in the direction of Eisenhower's former home when he had been N.A.T.O. commander at Marnes-la-Coquette.

De Gaulle's two dispatch-riders found Krushchev clowning in a farmyard at Sézanne, with chickens fluttering and reporters agog. Krushchev hurried back to Paris immediately, reaching the Soviet Embassy only seven minutes before the meeting was due to begin. He ordered one of the Embassy officials to telephone the Élysée to find out whether the meeting that was about to begin was a preliminary meeting to clarify the previous day's discussion. In that case Krushchev would attend. But if it was the Summit Conference proper, he explained, he would not come as Eisenhower had not agreed to his requests. Eisenhower and Macmillan arrived, watched by a small crowd and the immaculate guard. The traffic was held up to allow Krushchev's car easy access to the Elysée courtyard. More telephone inquiries from the Soviet Embassy were made. De Gaulle replied coldly that he wanted an answer to his invitation in writing. The minutes ticked by. At 4.45 a communiqué was issued from the Elysée stating that De Gaulle had invited the other three leaders to a meeting. It added, " President Eisenhower and Mr. Macmillan were present. The absence of Premier Krushchev was noted. President de Gaulle noted that in these circumstances the planned discussions could not take place."

The Summit was over but Krushchev felt that he had not yet achieved his fullest impact. He called a Press conference next day in the Palais de Chaillot which was attended by some 2000 newspapermen and anyone else who could secure admission. The extraordinary gathering took the form of a public meeting. Krushchev appeared rotund and beaming before the crowd. He was flanked by Gromyko, suave and dark-suited and the massive Malinovsky in uniform. The Soviet leader was cheered fervently by a small group of faithful French Communists for whom seats had been reserved in front but booed by émigré East Europeans and some Americans. He proceeded to answer written questions that had been handed up from the floor, which were sifted carefully by Gromyko in order to eliminate difficult ones. The Soviet Premier lashed the Americans mercilessly for an hour and a half. At times he appeared to work himself up into a passion of rage and his manner and language shocked the conference deeply. Yet it was a con-trolled performance throughout as his relaxed hands showed and he was careful to make no commitments on Berlin. Next day, as the leaders departed, behind the smokescreen of the world's headlines for his Press conference, Krushchev stopped in East Berlin to say that there would be no separate peace treaty before another summit meeting in six or eight months' time.

The Summit Conference of 1960 presents an enigma. Did the U-2 incident really destroy the conference? Or were the Soviet leaders determined to destroy it anyway for reasons of their own and was the U-2 made the excuse? Events in the Soviet Union immediately preceding the conference point to the latter conclusion. First, a strange rumour circulated in the second half of April that Mikoyan had been dismissed. At the celebrations for the fortieth anniversary of Soviet rule in Armenia, on 25th April, Mikoyan, who was the only Armenian in the Soviet leadership, was inexplicably absent. A few days later, on 4th May, a meeting of the Central Committee was convened suddenly and proceeded to make sweeping changes. Two leading members of the Party Praesidium were dismissed and three former candidate members promoted to full membership. The Central Committee Secretariat consisting of ten members was reduced to six. Amongst those dismissed were certainly Krushchev's supporters such as Furtseva. Shortly afterwards Voroshilov resigned from the office of Soviet President. There were a number of other important changes at this time, all pointing to a struggle within the leadership. During the period of transition, Krushchev appeared still to be safeguarding Eisenhower's personal position in all his comments on the U-2. But when Eisenhower accepted responsibility Krushchev's position was undermined. Nevertheless, he still seems to have hoped for a successful conference as was shown in the *Pravda* editorial on the day of his departure for Paris. Robert Conquest in *Power and Policy in the U.S.S.R.* suggested that the final decision to sabotage the conference was actually taken at Moscow Airport at an emergency meeting of the Praesidium and he has pointed to the individuals present and the surprising length of their deliberations. Wolfgang Leonhard in *The Kremlin Since Stalin* asserts: " It is probable that Soviet policy was changed between 11th and 15th May, that is to say after the failure of the attempt to make a distinction between Eisenhower and the military ' clique '."

Krushchev's conduct in the latter half of 1959, when he returned from the United States, placed alongside his behaviour in Paris, fully supported these conclusions. Every action in Paris, from the reading and publication of his prepared speech at the Élysée on 16th May to his Press conference at the Palais de Chaillot indicated that his performance was being conducted for the benefit of an audience in Moscow. He may have assumed that the positions of military strength that had been won by Soviet developments would recapture the diplomatic initiative and force the West at last into making concessions over Berlin. Certainly he had used the new situation to generate tension on issues that had been dormant for some years. Nor had he been averse to using the threat of war to raise the tension yet again, because he knew that he could always withdraw his threats without difficulty. At the same time, Krushchev still showed himself ready to retreat from untenable positions at the first hint of danger.

The period of Soviet activity that began with the sputnik in 1957 and ended in Paris in 1960 had many lessons. The most important of these was that the West would not allow itself to be pushed too far when its vital interests were at stake. Ironically, the Soviet leadership had not yet learned this particular lesson.

CHAPTER 23

DUEL AT THE BRINK

Once to every man and nation comes the moment to decide. *Lowell*

President Kennedy's inauguration in January 1961 ended the hold-up in East-West negotiations on major issues. The Western Powers had expected and feared a major crisis after the fiasco of the Paris Summit Conference. They were relieved when Krushchev did not press his Berlin claims or carry out his threat to sign the separate peace treaty with East Germany until a new American President had been installed. Kennedy, for his part, did not take long to put out feelers for a meeting with Krushchev. He was spurred on by a deteriorating situation in Laos, where Communist guerrillas were threatening to seize the country, as they had done in North Vietnam in 1954. All the same Kennedy, as the new leader of the West, was compelled to move cautiously in order not to alarm opinion in Europe, particularly in West Germany. Kennedy's exploratory moves started in March 1961 and by early May he had secured sufficient agreement in the Western Alliance to make arrangements to meet Krushchev in Vienna on 3rd and 4th June.

Kennedy's object in seeking the meeting was primarily to make an accurate assessment of Soviet policy. He also wished to make clear to Krushchev the limits on such issues as Berlin, beyond which the Western Powers were not prepared to go. Kennedy's own description of the encounter was "sombre." The extent of this understatement became apparent as the days went by. After an amicable beginning to the Vienna talks on the first day, at which Krushchev had appeared bland and affable, the two leaders turned to the Berlin and wider German issues. At this point Krushchev adopted his previous belligerent manner. He said baldly, "West Berlin is a bone that must come out of the Soviet throat." Kennedy who had never encountered anything quite like the Soviet leader before sought to narrow the argument. He soon found this to be impossible. Krushchev then launched into a tirade against the position of the Secretary-General at the United Nations and demanded that he should be replaced by a "troika"—or three men, two to be drawn from the Soviet and Western blocs and one from the neutral countries. He handed Kennedy two long memoranda setting out the Soviet views on Germany and disarmament. In exasperation, Kennedy asked Krushchev if there was one single question upon which the Soviet position was open to negotiation or modification. Krushchev answered, " No." Kennedy persisted, asking if there was not one area in which the Soviet Union might be prepared to make a concession to demonstrate its desire for peace. Krushchev retorted, " Only if it suits our purpose."

The new American President came away from the meeting obsessed by the bleak prospect that Krushchev had held out. It was only too clear that the Soviet bloc meant to prosecute its aim of world domination with renewed vigour. Kennedy said later that he had no idea whether he had made any impression on Krushchev. All the indications were that he had not. The Soviet leader mistook Kennedy's restrained manner for weakness.

The West had not long to wait for the next Soviet move after Vienna. Krushchev's repeated threats to sign a separate peace treaty and drive the Western Powers out of Berlin had caused an unprecedented flood of refugees to the west. Thinking that they would soon be cut off from all means of escape, the East Germans were fleeing at the rate of over 1000 a day in July 1961, and this could not continue. The Western Foreign Ministers met in Paris at the beginning of August in a state of mounting international tension. The Soviet Government, on 4th August, proposed talks to terminate the Western Powers' occupation rights. Dean Rusk, Kennedy's new Secretary of State, speaking to the N.A.T.O. Council on 8th August, offered six additional American divisions to be stationed in Europe if the Berlin crisis grew worse. Ulbricht, the East German Communist leader remarked significantly on 10th August that new measures might be enforced to halt the flow of refugees. His words showed how seriously the Communists now regarded the drain of people.

Then it happened. The East German Communists suddenly sealed off the Eastern half of the city in the early hours of 13th August. At first, very few people seemed to grasp what was taking place as trucks and troops rushed down the Unter den Linden and improvised barriers were flung across streets near the Brandenburg

Gate. The Russians expected grave trouble and units of the Red Army had been brought in from the hinterland to surround the city. But the Western Powers, having got over their initial surprise, did nothing beyond delivering a very strong protest on 17th August. By this time a wall across Berlin was in the course of construction and Soviet and American tanks were confronting each other at the few remaining crossing points.

A wave of resentment at Western inactivity swept the people of West Berlin. A huge crowd of over 200,000 stretching as far as the eye could see gathered outside the Schoneberg on 16th August to hear Willy Brandt, the Governing Mayor, attempt to reassure his city. It was a great speech, containing the blends of courage, hope and caution that the crisis demanded. At the end, when the German national anthem was played, Brandt was not the only man who was weeping in the face of this tragedy for all Berliners. Kennedy, sensing the feeling of West Berlin's disillusionment, sent Lyndon Johnson to Berlin, and the American Vice-President flew into the city on 19th August making warm speeches and distributing ball-point pens.

A coup had taken place. Krushchev and Ulbricht, between them, had actually annexed East Berlin to the Communist state. This had been done in defiance of the German Instrument of Surrender that had decreed that Berlin should be jointly occupied by the Four Powers of the Grand Alliance. The West had not been able to take any steps to counteract what had happened, any more than they had been able to act at the time of Hungary. Once more, the military situation in the area had dictated prudence by the West. To some extent the Berlin position had been analogous to Hitler's remilitarisation of the Rhineland in as much that it had taken place in the sphere of Soviet power. But, whilst it had never been the original Communist plan to take the step of putting up the Berlin Wall—Krushchev had hoped to avoid the painful admission of Communism's failure to stand the test of competitive co-existence —the Communists had achieved an important part of their objective by eliminating the danger to East Germany constituted by West Berlin. As for the people of West Berlin, who had lived up to this point in the hope and faith that one day there would be a change in East Germany, they felt dispirited as never before.

Could the Western Powers have acted differently? The answer is an imponderable. The facts are that Berlin was surrounded by the Red Army and that only a small Western garrison was stationed in the city itself. The Russians could have crushed Western resistance easily. The West Berlin populace were in a highly inflammatory mood and any action by Western troops might have been supported by rioting across the Brandenburg Gate. No one could have said, in these circumstances, that Soviet and Western forces throughout Central Europe might not have been engaged quickly and that escalation to the Third World War would then have begun.

Krushchev, however, was still not yet satisfied. He continued to maintain tension on the issue of Berlin for nearly another year until midsummer 1962 when he suddenly gave an undertaking not to raise the Berlin issue until after the mid-term American elections on 6th November. His attention had by then become centred on affairs in the Caribbean and he had devised a much more daring and decisive attempt to cripple the Western position.

Almost unnoticed by Western public opinion a dangerous situation had been developing gradually in Cuba from the early 1950s onwards. On 11th March, 1952, one of the candidates in the Cuban Presidential election, Fulgencio Batista, had seized control of the country in a military coup before ever the election could be held. He proceeded to establish a dictatorship that increased in ruthlessness and corruption as time went on. One of Batista's earliest opponents was a quixotic and romantic young lawyer called Fidel Castro. After a brave but ineffectual attempt to challenge Batista's authority in the courts, Castro took part in an attempt at armed insurrection on 26th July, 1953. The plan completely miscarried. Some 200 insurgents, mainly students, attempted to storm Fort Monteada, the country's second largest military depot. Many were killed and some, including Castro and his brother Raúl, were taken prisoner and given long prison sentences. Castro's trial was notable for the régime's attempts to intimidate the judges and for an extraordinary speech by Castro lasting five hours after he had spent seventy-six days in solitary confinement. From this speech it was clear that Castro was a romantic socialist revolutionary motivated by the strongest spirit of protest at the corruption, poverty and exploitation of the Cuban people.

Fidel Castro was sentenced to fifteen years in prison after " The July 26 Movement," as it came to be known. He and those of his associates who survived were released under an amnesty in May 1955 and they promptly set to work to organise another revolutionary force on Mexican soil. Castro himself played a large part in collecting money to equip the expedition from rich Cubans who had no love for Batista. Castro's second revolutionary army consisting of eighty-two men set sail for Cuba on 25th November, 1956, in a fifty-eight-foot yacht, the *Granma*, laden with small arms. On their arrival, scheduled for 30th November, the party was to be met by a rebel force of 100 men, and diversionary shootings and bomb explosions were to take place in a number of places. The plan was to equip guerrillas with the arms carried on the *Granma*. By staging a general strike in support of the guerrillas, Castro hoped to bring down the unpopular Batista régime.

The yacht's voyage turned out to be a nightmare. It failed to reach Cuba on the appointed day. It ran aground off the Cuban coast. Castro and his party were forced to abandon most of their supplies and get ashore as best they could. The majority of the party were killed or taken prisoner shortly after landing. Only Castro, his brother Raúl and ten others escaped to the mountains inland.

The truth was that Castro's venture was not as absurd as it seemed. The deep social unrest in Cuba gave him ready support, especially amongst the peasants—the *campesinos*. Showing remarkable determination, Castro built up guerrilla forces who behaved very circumspectly towards the peasants and won their support yet further. By preaching land reform, Castro also ensured a solid political base for his movement. The Batista régime, although it often captured and killed or tortured supporters of " The July 26 Movement," failed to extinguish it. As time went on, Castro's position grew stronger. The months went by and the extraordinary struggle continued in sporadic yet desperate fashion. In May 1958 Batista launched a major attack backed by 12,000 men. It failed miserably, partly through corruption but largely because Batista had lost all vestige of support and received little co-operation from the countryside. At the end of 1958 a small rebel force won a decisive victory at Santa Clara. On 1st January, 1959, as the city was on the point of surrender, Batista fled. Fidel Castro had become the leader of the Cuban nation.

Castro's movement had begun by being ridiculed by the *Partido Socialista Popular*, the Cuban Communists. As his extraordinary survival turned into success, the Communists gave him their support and infiltrated the ranks of Castro's movement. The programme proposed by Castro was still far from orthodox Marxist-Leninism.

Yet it was quite sufficient in its socialism to alarm United States opinion, where there had been no great support for Batista. The Agrarian Reform Law in May 1959 was the first major step in a succession of events. Large sugar estates—many of them American owned—were broken up or confiscated. More and more foreign property was seized. Each action led to a fresh outburst of anti-Castro feeling in the United States and it was usually followed by a reaction of yet greater anti-American feeling in Cuba. The Castro movement owed its first impetus to a revolt against poverty, illiteracy and exploitation but it soon acquired a strong nationalist flavour.

In 1958 the United States Government had proclaimed its neutrality in the Cuban Civil War and had suspended arms shipments to Batista. It was also among the first to recognise the Castro régime on 7th January, 1959. By midsummer, the American people began to have second thoughts about the event that had taken place so close to their shores. After a visit by Castro to the United States in April 1959, at which Christian Herter gave a lunch for him, Cuban-American relations deteriorated fast. Executions and mob law, with mass trials for former Batista supporters, revolted American opinion. Castro refused to permit free elections and soon there were allegations of Communist infiltration in the government. In July, both the Commander of the Cuban Air Force and the anti-Communist President Utrutia resigned on these grounds. Nevertheless, in January 1960, Eisenhower reiterated his country's policy of non-intervention and Castro's right to make reforms, whilst demanding proper compensation for the American property that had been seized.

Up to this point it could have been argued that Castro was not under the influence of the Communist bloc and that he was following his own romantic and revolutionary socialist policy. However, his country was already in severe economic difficulties, partly because of the inevitable lack of foreign capital for development and partly from the restriction on Cuba's traditional trade with the United States.

In February 1960, however, Mikoyan arrived in Havana offering Soviet credits and trade. The Soviet leadership had appraised the situation in Cuba and they had decided to take advantage of the obvious opportunity to establish a foothold in the most traditional of all American spheres of influence. Mikoyan, on this visit, concluded a five-year treaty with Cuba undertaking to buy 5 million tons of sugar at world market prices, and he guaranteed a $100 million credit to Castro to buy machinery and materials. In June and July 1960 Castro seized two American oil refineries and then started to seize all American property. In the face of the angry American reaction to this situation, Krushchev made a most belligerent announcement offering Soviet atomic retaliation against any possible American threats of invasion. The Soviet-Cuban alliance had moved into a new phase which was emphasised by a public demonstration of friendship by Krushchev and Castro at the United Nations in September 1961.

After first reducing and then suspending all American purchases of Cuban sugar, Eisenhower took the grave step of breaking off diplomatic relations at the beginning of 1961. It was one of the very last acts of his administration. By now American policy had reached the point at which it had been decided that Castro must be removed at all costs. The question was: How could it be achieved? A group of Cuban exiles were trained in Florida and Guatemala by officers of the Central Intelligence Agency, in circumstances that are now well known. Kennedy allowed himself to be persuaded that Castro possessed such little support that their invasion would succeed. Thus the so-called " Bay of Pigs " invasion was launched on 17th April. Its humiliating failure damaged Kennedy's reputation before his own country and the world. Castro emerged in a stronger political position than ever before and the threat to American influence throughout Latin America became extremely grave. Castro therefore felt himself able to announce at last what many suspected—that he was a Marxist-Leninist. In the meanwhile, other plans were being prepared in the Soviet Union. In the summer of 1962, Raúl Castro, the Cuban Foreign Minister and Ché Guevara, the Finance Minister, travelled to Moscow to undertake the negotiations for a new treaty under which Cuba received arms and technicians " to resist the imperialists' threats." It was also to emerge soon that the Soviet Union was going to help Castro build "a fishing port at Havana" and that the Russian Atlantic fishing fleet would harbour there. The clouds were gathering.

From the American point of view the situation had become critical. Kennedy was in no position to risk another "Bay of Pigs" fiasco. Nor did he have any evidence to confirm that there were any offensive Soviet weapons or forces in Cuba although intelligence reports in August stated that there were Russian SA-2 rockets in Cuban hands. This was the ground-to-air missile that had been credited with helping to bring down Francis Powers's U-2 in 1960. On 11th September the Soviet Union announced through *Tass* that only defensive arms were being sent to Cuba. On 13th September Kennedy was forced to accept this statement at its face value although he warned that his administration could not tolerate any Soviet action that directly threatened American security. As a precaution and as an overt indication of his determination, he obtained powers from Congress to call up 150,000 reservists in an emergency. He proceeded also to mobilise public opinion in the Americas at a conference of twenty Foreign Ministers from the American states that condemned " the attempt to make Cuba into an armed base for Communist penetration of the Americas. . . ."

Because the situation was so tense, Kennedy and his colleagues decided to proceed very cautiously. There was still nothing they could do, unless Castro committed aggression in some form or until there was conclusive evidence of Soviet forces or long-range missiles in Cuba. A number of intelligence reports kept coming in of feverish building activity on certain sites that were closed to native Cubans. This news seemed very ominous indeed. Aerial reconnaissance was limited throughout September, partly because two incidents involving U-2 flights—one over China and one over Sakhalin—had embarrassed Kennedy.

Finally, because of further intelligence reports of building activity, the Central Intelligence Agency decided to resume the U-2 flights over Cuba. These were held up in early October by the seasonal typhoons that made conditions impossible. The first good flying day over Cuba was Sunday, 14th October. Thanks partly to very heavy rain a few hours before, which put out of action the electric controls of the Cuban defences, a U-2 piloted by Major Rudolf Anderson made a perfect run at low level over the area of the reported building activity. Its photographs were developed overnight and reached Washington next morning. When they came to be examined by photographic interpretation experts they showed beyond doubt that launching pads were being built in more than ten places for medium-range and intermediate-range ballistic missiles. The M.R.B.M.'s had a range of 500-1000 miles and the I.R.B.M.'s could reach targets up to 2000 miles away. It was possible to make out the outlines of the rockets under their tarpaulin covers. The pictures also showed over twenty Ilyushin-28 aircraft capable of carrying the nuclear bomb to nearby American targets. The extent of the work done, when compared with earlier pictures, confirmed the earlier reports of how rapidly the military build-up was being pressed forward.

That night, 15th October, General Maxwell Taylor, the Chairman of the Joint Chiefs of Staff, considered the news over dinner with his intelligence officer, Lieutenant-General Joseph Carroll. He informed McGeorge Bundy, the Secretary of the National Security Council at his home and ordered a special report for Kennedy. When Bundy called at the White House next morning, 16th October, he found the President in the act of reading it.

Kennedy received the news calmly. It was not unexpected. He ordered Bundy to call together a group of twelve men at 11.30 a.m. In the meanwhile, he decided to act as if nothing had happened and continued to fulfil his scheduled engagements. The twelve men summoned were Bundy himself; Vice-President Lyndon Johnson; General Maxwell Taylor; General Marshall S. Carter of the C.I.A.; the Secretaries of State and for Defence, Douglas Dillon; the Secretary of the Treasury; Under Secretaries George Ball and Roswell Gilpatric; Robert Kennedy, the Attorney-General; Edward Martin, Assistant Secretary of State for Inter-American Affairs; and Theodore Sorensen, the President's Special Counsel. The twelve were joined by Dean Acheson; Robert Lovett, the former Secretary for Defence; Llewellyn Thompson, the former Ambassador to Moscow and Alexis Johnson, Deputy Under-Secretary of State who acted as the group's secretary. It was to be Kennedy's War Council.

Kennedy and his advisers all realised that they faced one of the greatest decisions in history, perhaps the supreme decision. They had to determine the fullest implications from the evidence in their hands. They asked themselves: were their main problems centred around Krushchev, in which case Soviet withdrawal must be their aim? Or did the central threat to American security stem specifically from Castro's régime, as that would mean that Castro himself would have to be driven out? Kennedy personally was undecided. General Maxwell Taylor, supported very strongly by Acheson and Bundy—and later by John McCone, Allan Dulles's successor as head of the C.I.A.—were for immediate action even to the extent of an American air strike to wipe out the bases before they could be brought into operation. They argued that if Krushchev and Castro succeeded in getting the Soviet rockets operational the inevitable consequences—political as well as military—would be a major and possibly decisive shift in the world balance of power.

Others took a different view. Some even argued that it would be better to wait. These two points of view have been described subsequently as dividing the War Council into " hawks " and " doves." The so-called " doves " at various points included Sorensen, Robert Kennedy, Lovett and McNamara. Adlai Stevenson was soon brought into the discussions because of the key position he would have to play as the American spokesman at the United Nations, and he too could be classified broadly as a " dove." The President, himself, was by inclination a " dove " too.

Writing so soon after the event and in a period before the minutes of the discussions have become available in the normal practice of publication after a suitable term of years, it is impossible to ascribe with accuracy specific views to individuals. Only the men who were present at each meeting know exactly what happened. Nevertheless the broad outlines of the story are clear enough. The American War Council—or "Excom" as it came to be called [1]—decided that the strictest secrecy must be preserved until they were sure of what action they were going to take. This was extremely difficult in Washington where most things soon become common gossip. Yet this was the only way in which they might be able to regain the initiative at the appropriate moment. They all agreed to carry on with the greatest show of normality, keeping even their social engagements to avoid suspicions being aroused. The President, above all others, had to adhere to his arrangements.

Therefore, on the next day, 17th October, Kennedy addressed rallies for the mid-term elections due on 6th November in New Haven, Stratford and Waterbury, Connecticut. In the meanwhile, the War Council proceeded with its deliberations, this time at the State Department. They were still uncertain what to do when Kennedy got back near midnight. The possibilities ranged from a naval blockade to stop the Russians sending any more equipment to Cuba, to an ultimatum that might end in invasion and even in nuclear war. Mobilisation was being considered. One member believed strongly that destruction of the actual sites by an air strike might be the best course provided it could be done suddenly and cleanly. Others said that the Cuban air force would have to be destroyed first, to avoid unnecessary loss of American lives, a course which would have defeated all hope of surprise and killed thousands of Cubans instead.

[1] "Excom" is the abbreviation for Executive Committee of the National Security Council.

Gromyko, who was heading the Soviet delegation at the current session of the U.N. had sought an interview some days previously with Kennedy for a general talk. It was due to take place in Kennedy's office in the early evening of 18th October and it was eagerly awaited. Kennedy knew that he must be extremely careful not to disclose any of the knowledge he possessed and yet he had to probe Gromyko as far as possible without creating suspicions that the United States Administration had been alerted to the danger. It was not an easy task. Gromyko, a capable, experienced functionary but not a policy maker at high level, arrived bringing with him the Soviet Ambassador. Kennedy had asked Llewellyn Thompson to be present. Gromyko began by raising the issue of Berlin which had been dormant for nearly a year and which Krushchev had obligingly promised in midsummer that he would not raise until after the 6th November American elections. Gromyko reiterated Krushchev's promise about 6th November and added that after that date the Berlin question would have to be reopened. He spoke of " normalising " the situation, by which he meant a German peace treaty that would include a Western withdrawal from Berlin. If no agreement was reached, Gromyko continued, the Soviet Government would be "compelled" to sign a separate peace treaty and to take the consequential actions. Gromyko is said to have used "compelled" twice, emphasising it the second time by raising his finger in warning.

Kennedy said later that he realised in that instant of time the pattern of the various Soviet actions. Krushchev's promise to postpone the Berlin issue yet again until after 6th November had always puzzled him. Why the American elections? Gromyko was now sitting there in his office warning him to expect a Berlin ultimatum shortly. And by 6th November, or thereabouts, Krushchev knew he would have established nuclear bases actually within the traditional American sphere of influence. Whilst it may have been argued that this did not alter the military balance decisively, the political and psychological consequences could be shattering to American morale.

The two men continued to discuss Berlin, going over the familiar arguments. The talk eventually turned to Cuba. "Cuba belonged to the Cubans" according to Gromyko. "What could Cuba do to the United States? It was a baby facing a giant. Cuba could not use a threat to anyone," he said. Gromyko also told Kennedy that the Soviet training of Cubans in certain weapons was purely defensive. The Soviet Government would never have risked anything else. At a later stage in the conversation, Gromyko repeated the defensive nature of the weapons supplied to Cuba. Gromyko's words were strictly correct. The weapons actually in Cuban hands were the defensive ground-to-air missiles. The M.R.B.M.'s and I.R.B.M.'s were to remain firmly in Soviet control. Kennedy subsequently accused the Soviet Foreign Minister of lying but this was not really true. But there was no doubt that Gromyko attempted very hard to deceive the President by carefully concealing the true Soviet policy. In many ways the wheel had now turned its full circle and Kennedy was in the position to humiliate Krushchev, just as Krushchev had humiliated Eisenhower in Paris.[1]

The Gromyko interview on 18th October was an important factor in determining the American course of action. As Krushchev's intentions and not those of Castro were identified as the principal danger, the arguments in favour of invasion weakened. At the same time, the attractions of a naval blockade increased. A naval blockade would leave the United States with the greatest freedom of manœuvre. It limited the risk of war. It was the course most likely to be supported by the Organisation of American States, a key body in the situation. Finally, if successful, the naval blockade would humiliate Krushchev effectively before the world. That same evening, the War Council decided provisionally upon the naval blockade although the final decision was deferred.

Next day—Friday, 19th October—was to be the day of decision. Sorensen wrote the first draft of Kennedy's speech to announce the naval blockade. The preparations to implement it and to justify it legally and morally before the world went forward feverishly. As every hour passed on the Friday, more and more people learned of the secret. Therefore it was important that Kennedy himself should make the announcement as soon as possible. However, Kennedy had been compelled to keep an engagement on that Friday for another election speech at Cleveland. Thus, while the War Council was coming to its final decision, he was in Chicago, passing a campaign poster demanding that he showed " Less Profile and More Courage! " With the decision taken, the President had to return to Washington. Pierre Salinger, his spokesman,

[1] Gromyko dined with Dean Rusk in the State Department immediately after his talk with Kennedy. Although the Soviet Foreign Minister did not know it, the War Council was meeting in a room underneath where he was having dinner.

calmly announced in the Sheraton Hotel, Chicago, on Saturday morning, 20th October, that Kennedy had a cold and was having to fly back.

The world knew immediately that a crisis was afoot but speculation on the subject of it ranged from Berlin to Laos and included Cuba. Kennedy reached the White House in the early afternoon and accepted the War Council's recommendation. General Norstadt, the American Commander at N.A.T.O. was alerted. Plans were set in motion for informing America's allies. Acheson flew off to Europe with copies of Kennedy's draft speech and the revealing photographs taken by Major Rudolf Anderson the previous Sunday for distribution to America's main partners in the Alliance. Acheson's aircraft landed briefly in Britain where he handed over one copy of the documents to the American Ambassador who had driven out to meet him. The former Secretary of State then flew on to Paris where he had a secret meeting with De Gaulle personally. The British Government, although seriously alarmed, decided unhesitatingly to support the American action. De Gaulle, when he saw Acheson, swept the photographs aside and concentrated on the President's draft speech which he approved. Adenauer, who was also informed, accepted the news calmly and with determination.

The time of Kennedy's announcement was fixed for 7 o'clock on the evening of Monday, 22nd October. Rusk arranged to see the Soviet ambassador an hour before. By Sunday, some American newspapermen had discovered the truth in part and one newspaperman had unearthed the whole story. A naval blockade was confidently predicted in newspapers around the world on Monday. Nevertheless, the aim of tactical surprise had been achieved.

Speaking calmly and very seriously Kennedy appeared before the television cameras with the words, " Good evening, my fellow citizens. This Government, as promised, has maintained the closest surveillance of the Soviet military build-up on the island of Cuba. Within the past week unmistakable evidence has established the fact that a series of offensive missiles is now in preparation. . . . The purpose of these bases can be none other than to provide a nuclear strike capability against the Western Hemisphere." Kennedy went on to describe what had happened. He itemised the American response. A naval blockade against shipments of "offensive weapons" was to be imposed. "We are not at this time," he continued, " denying the necessities of life as the Soviets attempted to do in their Berlin blockade of 1948." The armed forces had been

441

told to prepare for " all eventualities." Then came his gravest warning, " Any nuclear missile launched from Cuba against any nation in the Western Hemisphere " was to be regarded by the U.S. Government " as an attack by the Soviet Union on the United States, requiring full retaliatory response upon the Soviet Union."

The effect of Kennedy's speech upon the minds of ordinary people in various countries was a striking illustration of the way in which they had come to regard the Cold War. The staunchest support for the President in Europe came in West Germany and to a lesser extent in France and Italy. In Britain, where Communist infiltration of the Campaign for Nuclear Disarmament movement had created a deep mood of appeasement, part of the public and nearly all the Press were openly hostile. The Afro-Asian countries, as might have been expected, expressed horror and shock. Demonstrations sprang up around American embassies all over the world. The Communist Press reacted with fury against "the gang of militaristic criminals" in Washington. The Latin American countries suddenly appreciated a threat to their security from outside the Hemisphere and their thoughts immediately turned to the Monroe Doctrine.

The Soviet Government appeared to have been taken aback completely. It submitted a long statement to the Security Council which was largely repetition of earlier statements. The Cuban Government showed more spirit. It attacked Kennedy for " an act of war."

When the Security Council met on the afternoon of 23rd October, the Soviet delegate appeared to have no instructions. Stevenson presented the American case at the United Nations with great clarity. His display of photographs were most telling. But the truth was that the United Nations suddenly found itself powerless and the Afro-Asian delegations discovered that they were of little importance in the great clash between Soviet and American power. The crunch would come when the first Soviet ship was intercepted by the American forces. As the world waited for this to happen, American Polaris submarines put to sea and aircraft of the nuclear strike force took to the air.

Indications of how the Soviet ships bound for Cuba would react came on Wednesday, 24th October. Some Russian freighters appeared to be slowing down. The first encounter between an American and Russian vessel was on Thursday, 25th October. The captain of the Soviet tanker *Bucharest* acknowledged an American naval inquiry and stated that he was carrying oil to Havana. This information was immediately accepted and the *Bucharest* proceeded unhindered. Later that same day, twelve Soviet ships out of twenty-five that were bound for Cuba suddenly turned back. It could only mean that the Soviet Government had decided not to challenge the blockade.

In the meanwhile, the United Nations Security Council had been meeting. With Zorin, the Soviet delegate in the chair, the first Soviet-American confrontation on Tuesday, 23rd October, had achieved nothing. Zorin, without instructions, obtained an adjournment. Krushchev also manœuvred. He addressed an open letter to Bertrand Russell, the British philosopher, on 24th October—in response to a personal appeal by Russell in which Russell had spoken one-sidedly of Krushchev's "continued forbearance"—in which the Soviet leader said, " we shall do everything possible to prevent this catastrophe. But . . . if the United States carries out the programme of piratic actions . . . we shall have to resort to means of defence. . . ." U Thant, the Burmese Acting-Secretary-General of the United Nations, also attempted with the aid of the neutral countries to compel the United States to compromise. Adlai Stevenson was instructed to inform Thant that the Americans were only ready to negotiate on the dismantling of the missile sites and their verification. Thant, addressing the Security Council that evening said he had appealed for " the voluntary suppression of the naval blockade." Clearly this was of no value to the Americans as it left the Soviet rockets still in Cuba, and in the meanwhile aircraft reconnaissance confirmed that the work on the launching pads was proceeding as fast as possible.

Stevenson therefore flung down the American challenge to Zorin in the Security Council. " Do you, Ambassador Zorin," he demanded addressing the Russian in the chair, " deny that the U.S.S.R. has placed and is placing medium and intermediate range missiles in sites in Cuba? Yes or no? " Stevenson's words rapped out at Zorin who speaks fluent English, " Yes or no? Don't wait for the translation—yes or no? "

Zorin retorted, " I am not in an American court-room, sir. Therefore I do not wish to answer a question that is put to me in the fashion in which a prosecutor puts questions. In due course, sir, you will have your reply." Stevenson was not to be daunted, " You are in the court-room of world opinion right now," he snapped.

443

" You can answer yes or no. You have denied that they exist. I want to know whether I have understood you correctly." Zorin continued to seek an escape, " Will you please continue your statement, sir? " he appealed to Stevenson. " You will have your answer in due course."

" I am prepared to wait for my answer until hell freezes over, if that is your decision," said Stevenson. " I am also prepared to present the evidence in this room."

Zorin knew he was cornered. " I call on the distinguished representative of Chile," he announced desperately. But there was to be no evasion. The Chilean delegate promptly offered to yield the floor to Zorin: Stevenson intervened, " I had not finished my statement. I asked a question, Mr. President, and I have had no reply to that question. I will now proceed, if I may, to finish my statement." Zorin was immensely relieved, until Stevenson dramatically produced new photographs of the work on the rocket launching pads. Zorin promptly queried their authenticity. In response, Stevenson asked calmly, " I wonder if the Soviet Union would ask their Cuban colleagues to permit a United Nations team to go to the sites? " He concluded, " Our job is not to score debating points. Our job, Mr. Zorin, is to save the peace. If you are ready to try, we are."

The Soviet Union had been indicted before the world most effectively, but to what avail? The Russian ships that had turned back indicated that Krushchev was not prepared to flout the American blockade. Yet the issue reverberated: What action could the United States take now to prevent Krushchev completing successfully the rocket bases in Cuba and winning the greatest political and psychological battle so far in the Cold War?

Kennedy's War Council decided to step up its threats of action. It let it be known on Friday, 26th October, through diplomatic channels and newspapermen that "further action" was being considered. In fact, it was considering an air strike, but the world—and Krushchev—immediately assumed that an invasion was being prepared.

It was at this point that Krushchev seems to have decided to capitulate. At 9 o'clock in the evening of 26th October—4 a.m. 27th October, Moscow time—the celebrated and mysterious telegram arrived from Krushchev which indicated that he had lost his nerve. Those who have seen the telegram, which remains unpublished at the time of writing, say that it was confused and somewhat hysterical. Krushchev appeared willing to dismantle the launching pads and withdraw the rockets from Cuba in return for a guarantee to Cuba against invasion. It is reasonable to assume that members of the Soviet Praesidium must have argued far into the Friday night and Krushchev himself dictated his agitated message in the early hours. This view is confirmed by the fact that the Soviet Foreign Ministry on the Saturday morning, 27th October, published a formal and truculent message offering to dismantle the Cuban bases in return for America giving up her bases in Turkey. (This was a view that had been expressed first in London, when the crisis began, by *The Times* and *Guardian*.) A second Soviet note that arrived next day contained little indication of Krushchev's readiness to withdraw given the night before. It had all the appearance of having been drafted carefully in contrast to the first note. It was most puzzling.

Certain members—notably Robert Kennedy and McNamara—of the War Council advocated that the President should ignore the second note. He should reply only to the previous night's strange message, accepting it in principle. Kennedy telegraphed Krushchev on the evening of 27th October to this effect, referring to Krushchev's apparent agreement to withdraw the Soviet rockets.

It was a shrewd and calculated gamble. If Krushchev capitulated formally and publicly, agreeing that Kennedy had understood his secret note correctly, the United States had won. If he did not, the War Council had reached the point at which it either had to recommend much stronger action or lose the initiative. Kennedy could only await the outcome. As seen in Washington by the men responsible, the world stood at the brink of nuclear war that Saturday night of 27th October, 1962.

Krushchev too, felt that the crisis was really upon him. Both Krushchev in Moscow and Castro in Havana mistakenly believed that an invasion of Cuba was imminent. As Krushchev put it, " Not days but hours were left before the invasion of Cuba."

Krushchev's anxiously awaited answer reached Kennedy early on Sunday morning, 28th October. The Moscow radio first announced that the Soviet Government had an important statement to make. It was a Soviet note from Krushchev which began by thanking Kennedy for his " sense of proportion." It continued, " I regard with great understanding your concern . . . in connection with the fact that the weapons you describe as offensive are formidable weapons indeed. Both you and we understand what kind of weapons these are. In order to eliminate as rapidly as possible the conflict . . . the Soviet Government . . . has given a new order to dismantle the arms which you describe as offensive and to crate them and return them to the Soviet Union. . . . As I had informed you in the letter of 27th October [the unpublished letter], we are prepared to reach agreement to enable representatives to verify the dismantling of these means. . . ."

It was capitulation! Kennedy promptly welcomed " Chairman Krushchev's statesmanlike decision." The Cuba crisis had ended, less than six days after Kennedy had made his momentous speech and a fortnight to the day after the lone U-2 aircraft flown by Rudolf Anderson had brought back its terrifying evidence. Anderson himself—whose role had been so vital—had not lived to see the end, being killed on 27th October flying yet another sortie over the rocket bases.

The dismantling of the bases and the packing up of the missiles began immediately. Krushchev also accepted Kennedy's demand that the U.N. should send a team to verify that this was being done, and Thant flew off to Havana with a crowd of forty advisers to see Castro to make the arrangements. During the two days that he was there, Kennedy suspended the blockade.

Castro, however, was adamant when Thant met him. He could do nothing about Krushchev's capitulation but he refused flatly to permit the U.N. team on to Cuban soil on the grounds that it infringed Cuban national sovereignty. The dialogue was fascinating, " What right does the United States have to ask this? " demanded Castro. " Is it based on genuine legal right or is it based on force? Is it a demand based on a position of strength? " Thant, whose conduct throughout the crisis had stamped him more as the representative of a neutral Afro-Asian country, had already conceded Castro's point in advance by saying that the inspection could only be carried out with Cuban agreement. Thant now replied significantly: " This is my point of view, that it is not a legal right, that dismantling could only be carried out with the approval and acceptance of the Cuban Government."

Thant had failed. Mikoyan was now pressed into the breach and flew from Moscow with Kennedy's agreement. He met an even more difficult situation than Thant, as Castro was clearly determined to extract the maximum compensation from his Soviet ally to offset the disaster. Mikoyan had to remain in Havana arguing feverishly with an angry and voluble Castro for nearly four weeks. He could not even return to Russia for his wife's funeral. In the end, he left Cuba with Castro quite unmoved and determined to resist the inspection team.

Kennedy and his War Council now faced the last of their major decisions. Should they accept Krushchev's word and the evidence of their intelligence services that the bases were being dismantled and the arms brought back to Russia? Or should they insist that Castro should be humiliated further and forced to accept the inspection team? Indeed, could they do this? Certain members of the Council considered that the blockade and tension should be maintained until Castro was forced to yield—with the resulting effects upon his political position in Latin America. Kennedy and others thought otherwise. They had decided that they had gone far enough. One member of the American War Council remarked bitterly afterwards, " The President was too like his father. He believed in taking a quick turn round on the New York Stock Exchange before twelve o'clock, rather than running the risk for the larger prize." The truth was that Kennedy—like Krushchev— had emerged from the Cuba crisis as a man who had walked too close to the brink of nuclear holocaust and who was now as deeply anxious as the Soviet leader to retreat before he tempted the fates too far.

Kennedy's confrontation with Krushchev over Cuba must rank as one of the classics of a skilfully played diplomatic hand. The Americans, by the manner of their handling of the crisis, had succeeded throughout in retaining the initiative whilst preserving the maximum freedom to retreat or manœuvre should they have considered it necessary. To that extent, it was in marked contrast to the Anglo-French reaction to Nasser's seizure of the Suez Canal. Kennedy and his advisers were helped considerably—and decisively —by the geographical and military situation. Cuba was too far from the Soviet Union to enable Krushchev to render any effective assistance that was certain not to lead on to general war. The overwhelming American superiority of conventional weapons in the Caribbean area enabled Kennedy's invasion threat to appear credible to the Soviet Praesidium sitting in the Kremlin. The American President's posture of calm control and implacable determination had a profound effect upon world opinion by the end of the crisis. It emphatically regained the initiative for America in the Cold War and it restored the West's confidence in the American capacity and will to lead.

Krushchev subsequently admitted that in effect he had been caught in the act of attempting a political coup of major importance and had been forced to beat an ignominious retreat. The Soviet Union's actions of the previous few months—from Krushchev's surprising postponement of a Berlin crisis in the summer until the November, to some cutting down in the second half of 1962 of Soviet aid to neutral countries—had all fallen into a pattern. His aim had been Western humiliation over Berlin, in the situation of alarm and disarray that would have followed the successful establishment of nuclear rockets in Cuba. But this aim had perished, with severe consequences to the morale of the Soviet leadership. Krushchev, like a man whose gamble has cost him dearly, was forced for a while to adopt cautious policies of retrenchment abroad and consolidation at home.

The United Nations, although it served a useful purpose as a centre of communication during the crisis, had proved impotent on the central issues. The reason for this was that power and talk are separate factors—and power counted at the time of the Cuba crisis. The Afro-Asian neutrals, who had come to dominate the U.N. in terms of votes, suddenly found themselves ignored. They also learned that their moral authority, based on their claims to genuine neutrality, had been eroded by their constant applications of a double standard of judgment as between what they themselves claimed the right to do and that which they criticised the Western Powers for doing. Thus, they were shown to be what they always were—the avaricious and parochial proponents of self-interest and not the upholders of the principle of law. And until the Afro-Asian neutrals come to accept the principles of the rule of one law in the abstract, to be applied universally, they will remain morally as well as militarily ineffective.

Finally, there was Castro—a crazed and proud political romantic who probably believed that he was exploiting the Communist bloc. He had suffered a major set-back in a way different from Krushchev. But, in the longer term, the appeal of his revolutionary ideas remains a most important factor in Latin-America. Furthermore, he had attached the Soviet Union to the coat tails of *Fidelismo* in a stronger manner than ever before.

Seven weeks after the Cuba crisis, on 19th December, Krushchev sent a message to Kennedy, for whom he now had the most healthy respect. He said, " It seems to me, Mr. President, that the time has come to put an end to nuclear tests once and for all, and to draw the line under them." This did not mean that Krushchev had suddenly forsaken his basic aims of Communist world revolution —far from it—but that he had decided that an end to nuclear testing, at least temporarily, was in the interests of Soviet policy. The proposal gave the Soviet economy a minor respite. It continued to remain what it had always been—a war economy governed by dictatorship and impelled by the evangelical desire to extend its power.

The move on nuclear testing also gave Krushchev an opportunity of meeting head-on his newest threat: the Chinese challenge to the Soviet claim to leadership of the Communist bloc.

CHAPTER 24

THE BROKEN MONOLITH

Thy truth is as dark to me as my truth is dark to thee until the Lord enlighten all our seeing.
Saltmarsh

Krushchev's "Secret Speech" to the Twentieth Congress has marked a turning point in the history of World Communism. Not only did it create the convulsions in Eastern Europe later that year, and the "rightist" deviations of European Communists but it must be considered as the true starting point of the dispute with "leftist" China that now racks the Marxist-Leninist movement in every land and challenges all previous concepts of the Cold War.

The reactions of the Chinese leaders to Krushchev's amazing attack upon Stalin in 1956 were a sense of anger, mingled with astonishment. Although Krushchev spoke in February and thereafter de-Stalinisation moved forward rapidly in Europe, the Chinese Press ignored the debate which was taking place throughout the rest of the bloc. Instead, Mao convened an enlarged meeting of the Chinese Politbureau to consider how the event should be treated. The outcome of the discussion within this very small circle of Chinese leadership was that they should take all possible steps to limit the attack to Stalin himself and not allow it to spread to the Communist system as a whole. At the same time, they decided to protect Mao from any accusations that he was adopting Stalin's course.

The Peking Administration followed the three policies carefully throughout 1956 and, as we have seen, it emerged for the first time during the Polish and Hungarian revolutions as a mediator in the crisis that affected the Communist bloc. During this period, Mao was unquestionably considering what steps he could take to establish the Chinese Communist Party as the alternative source of leadership for the Communist movement. At first, Mao thought in terms of a more liberal Communist philosophy. The lamentable failure of the "Hundred Flowers" policy and increasing economic pressures within China led, however, to a sudden and traumatic change in the outlook of the Chinese leadership between the National People's Congress of June 1957 and the Chinese Central Committee's plenum in September. Up to June 1957 the Chinese Press warned repeatedly that "dogmatism" was the main danger to Communism. From September on, the Chinese leaders took a different view for the very practical reason that they had discovered suddenly—with the "Hundred Flowers" uproar—that the Communist philosophy had won very few adherents amongst the Chinese people despite eight years of power. They were faced also with a grave economic crisis that same year because of the failure of production to keep up with population. The Chinese leaders, taking the view that a revolution in retreat is no basis for its survival, decided during this period upon radical new measures including the communes policy that was to emerge the following year—1958.

When Mao Tse-tung went to Moscow for the Communist Conference of November 1957, he had shifted his position from one of earlier sympathy for the Polish Communists to a much more rigid approach. He had come to the view that the bloc must be a tightly-knit unit and that there was little room for liberal policies. In a speech at Moscow University on 17th November he said bluntly, " The socialist camp must have a head and this head is the Soviet Union." At the conference itself Mao emerged as the most severe critic of "revisionism"—a reversal of his earlier fears about "dogmatism." Gomulka, amongst others, is said to have come away from Moscow bitterly disappointed with the new Chinese view.

China's "Great Leap Forward" programme including the communes was launched in the summer of 1958. "The Great Leap," with its spectacular backyard steel furnaces, aimed at over-taking the production of such highly industrialised countries as Britain by 1970. The programme was a radical attempt to break the ring of economic difficulties that threatened to drag down the revolution and it was based upon the effective mobilisation and direction of China's surplus raw material—manpower. Implicit in the whole concept of "The Great Leap" was the introduction of the theory of permanent revolution. Speaking at the 8th Party Congress in May 1958 Liu Shao-chi claimed, " Marx, Engels and Lenin often pointed out that the watchword of the working class should be uninterrupted revolution." The commune policy also represented a major challenge to the Soviet policy because the

451

Chinese were stating publicly that they proposed to follow a new course determined by China's poverty and backwardness. They were claiming, by implication, that the Chinese experiment had greater relevance to the needs of all other under-developed countries than the Soviet Union's different methods of advance.

Nevertheless, the Soviet reaction was slow in coming, almost certainly because of bad reporting of the events in China within the Soviet Union. It is also possible that Krushchev knew little of the communes policy development when he flew to Peking at the end of July 1958; only then did he realise the implications of what was taking place. Whilst the Chinese began to find out the practical difficulties of the ideas and to slow down their plans, Krushchev appears to have kept his feelings largely to himself. The Russian Press contained no criticism of the Chinese policy. Indeed, Krushchev's first recorded opposition to the Chinese schemes was during a conversation with Senator Hubert Humphrey on 1st December, 1958, when he described the communes as old-fashioned and reactionary. He added, " You can't get production without incentive." Krushchev denied ever having said this shortly afterwards at the Twenty-first Congress of the Soviet Communist Party that opened on 27th January, 1959. " The very idea," he remarked, " that I could have been in any way confidential to a man who boasts of his twenty-one year struggle against Commnuism can only serve to raise a laugh." He went on to ask, " How unthinkable a confidential talk with Humphrey would be on questions of the policy of the Communist parties, on our relations with our best friends, the leading people in the Communist Party of China? " At the same Twenty-first Congress, Krushchev speaking overtly to the Chinese said it was impossible to *"leap"* into Communism. The Twenty-first Congress itself, Donald Zagoria has pointed out in *The Sino-Soviet Dispute 1956-1961*, must be seen as Krushchev's attempt to forestall the Chinese challenge that he could see to be growing.

Later, in that same year of 1959, Krushchev astonished and angered the Chinese, as we now know, when he visited Peking immediately after his trip to the United States by the way in which he spoke of the American scene. His rosy view of American achievement and good faith was not how the Chinese Communist saw the United States that had played the decisive part in isolating their country. It was also around this time that the Soviet Union rejected Chinese requests for nuclear weapons.

Mao Tse-tung must have realised that the gulf between the two Communist parties was very great indeed and a bitter struggle lay ahead. The Summit Conference of May 1960 served briefly to hide the differences in a union of condemnation for Eisenhower but during the next month the dispute came out into the open.

What people had long suspected was confirmed dramatically during the summer of 1960. The discovery stemmed, in the first place, from Chinese accusations of Soviet "insincerity" in their disarmament proposals at a meeting of the World Federation of Trade Unions in Peking. Shortly afterwards, Communist delegates from all over the world were travelling to Bucharest for the opening of the Congress of the Rumanian Communist Party on 20th June, 1960. Krushchev himself suddenly decided to head the Soviet delegation, perhaps because of the Chinese charges at the W.F.T.U. meeting. The Chinese delegation was led by Peng Chen, the Mayor of Peking and an important member of the Chinese Politbureau. The Russian leader decided to use the occasion to mobilise overwhelming support for the Soviet position against the growing signs of Chinese hostility. A Soviet letter was circulated to the delegates accusing the Chinese of departing from the decisions of the 1957 Moscow Conference. The Chinese, the letter said, had failed to understand "the character of the present era." Whereas the Chinese were describing the period as one of "imperialism, wars and revolutions," the Soviet view was it also included "the disintegration of imperialism, transition to socialism and the formation and consolidation of the world system of socialism." The terms of the dispute may have appeared to the outsider as being presented exclusively in theological terms but it nevertheless contained the hard reality of a struggle for power for the leadership of the bloc. To the assembled foreign delegates, the Soviet circular must have been an astonishing revelation because it went on to attack Chinese behaviour and point out the folly of certain of China's internal policies.

In the open conference, Peng Chen was moderate and restrained. He claimed that the Chinese were in favour of co-existence. He noted the criticisms of the Chinese and would report upon them. But Peng went much further in private. He published, for the first time, a bullying letter from the Soviet Party to the Chinese Party which showed Krushchev in a very different light. The publication of this second letter provoked Krushchev into a violent tirade against the Chinese, in the manner of his outburst in Paris a month earlier. Peng replied to it coldly and sharply, accusing Krushchev of " revisionism." The conference broke up with the foreign Communist delegates stunned and bewildered by the extent of the cleavage. The only agreement was a decision to pursue the matter further at a major conference in Moscow in November 1960.

It is important to understand that parallel with the Russian-Chinese argument there had been also the continuing dialogue between Krushchev and Tito. Krushchev's clumsy attempt at rapprochement in 1955 had been followed by the gradual rebuilding of Soviet-Yugoslav relations which reached their highest point during the late summer of 1956. It was then that Krushchev journeyed to Yugoslavia and returned to the Soviet Union bringing Tito with him in an effort to answer the criticisms of his de-Stalin-isation policies. The Hungarian revolution and the Nagy affair led to yet another brief period of estrangement in early 1957. But, by the autumn of 1957, after a secret meeting with Krushchev in Rumania, Tito was able to send a delegation to the celebrations of the Fortieth Anniversary of the Bolshevik Revolution although he claimed that he could not go himself because he had " lumbago." The Moscow Conference's declaration had referred to " the necessity of resolutely overcoming revisionism and dogmatism " and continued " the main danger at present is revisionism or, in other words, right-wing opportunism." This last was too much for the Yugoslav delegation to the conference and they had refused to sign the declaration.

Soviet-Yugoslav relations turned for the worse again in 1958. The Seventh Congress of the Yugoslav Party met at Ljubljana in April 1958 to find that the Soviet Party had reversed its decision to be represented and that the other Communist bloc parties had done likewise. The Chinese now took a hand and the *Peking People's Daily* announced on 5th May that Stalin's decision to expel Yugoslavia from "the socialist camp" had been "basically correct." By implication this was a public rebuff to Krushchev for his 1955 attempts to apologise for Stalin.

The Soviet Party was forced to adjust itself to the Chinese demand and Tito learned yet again of the difficulties of Communist independence when Voroshilov, the Soviet President, cancelled his visit to Yugoslavia due to begin on 11th May, 1958. The Soviet Government also suspended credits and all other economic assistance that had been promised to Yugoslavia. The announcement of Nagy's execution followed shortly afterwards and it was related

to the new situation. Throughout the period after the Chinese turn
to the left in 1957 it is apparent that Krushchev's public hostility
to Tito was associated with pressure from the Chinese Communists.

However, Krushchev then decided that he must take steps to
redress the position. After Bucharest in 1960, he carried forward
the attack he had launched upon the Chinese to the point of attempting to silence them. He began to apply pressure by withdrawing
Soviet technicians in China. In August the *Agence France Presse*
reported that the departure of the technicians had turned into a
" veritable exodus." A preliminary conference of twenty-six
Communist parties was held in Moscow in late September 1960 to
prepare a draft declaration for the great November conference.
Once more the Sino Soviet differences flared up and the rival
delegations led by Kozlov and Suslov on the one hand and by
Teng Hsiao-ping and Peng Chen on the other argued every
paragraph.

The Moscow Conference has often been described as one of the
most important gatherings in the story of Communism. This is
not merely because it was attended by eighty-one Communist
parties and remained in almost permanent session until it disbanded
on 2nd December. Much the most significant point was that the
delegates meeting within the walls of the Kremlin included men
who were to challenge frontally determined the Soviet Union's
ideological supremacy that had extended over forty years. It is
said to have begun quietly enough. Furthermore, because of the
normally inarticulate character of the Communist mind—the power
of persuasion always comes hard to the convinced Communist and
very few Communist leaders are capable of making an attractive
public speech—the proceedings were often dull. Only on a few
occasions did the true drama of the gathering transmit itself to the
delegates in session and much of the argument was conducted in
corridors.

The conference started on 11th November. A large number of
attacks was made upon the Chinese by the smaller Communist
parties from outside the bloc. The first Chinese intervention was
by Teng Hsiao-ping on 14th November. The tough, brisk, Chinese
Secretary-General claimed Chinese adherence to the 1957 declaration. He also protested yet again that the Chinese believed in
co-existence. He said that the Chinese position was misrepresented
and he accused the Russians of producing arguments that were,
in fact, lies. His words shocked the assembly deeply. Teng

proceeded to lecture the conference on the true Chinese position. He claimed that the Chinese belief in an aggressive foreign policy was the only way to further the revolution and help the peace. He did not believe that the peace could be preserved by the apparent Soviet belief in the goodwill of bourgeois politicians or imperialist governments. It could only be won by defeating capitalism. The Chinese view was that the Communist Party of the Soviet Union had been leading the majority of Communist parties along the road of capitulation to imperialism. Never in the recorded history of Communism had such an accusation been hurled by a leading member of a great Communist party at the citadel of Communist revolution. At other points in his speech Teng flayed the Soviet attitude of granting aid to nationalist leaders, such as Nehru and Nasser. This point was subsequently to emerge as an important issue of Chinese national interest.

Whilst many delegations were very disturbed, the only vociferous support for the Chinese came from Enver Hoxha, the leader of the Albanian Party of Labour. Hoxha delivered a wild and intemperate harangue. He said, " Anyone who does not see that imperialism is preparing for war is blind." And, in a reference intended for Krushchev, " Anyone who sees it, and refuses to recognise it, is a traitor." At another point he declared, " The socialist camp is encircled and Tito is part of the encirclement." The underlying reason for Albanian hostility to Krushchev as the wayward champion of Tito and support for Peking, Tito's opponent, had been made clear. Before returning again to Yugoslavia, Hoxha spoke of economic and other pressures upon Albania. " These were intolerable pressures," he cried. " The Soviet rats were able to eat while the Albanian people died of hunger! "

Maurice Thorez, the French Communist leader, summarised the position with succinctness, " We are now quite certain that it is not a question of a disagreement limited to two or three points in the statements proposed to this conference but of a whole line opposed to that of the international Communist movement." Thorez was later to make an appeal to the Chinese, " An abnormal situation full of dangers has been created. If this situation were to be continued, it must result in considerable damage for the world revolutionary movement. . . . Think again, comrades of the Chinese Communist Party. . . ."

The Chinese realised that they were in a very small minority in Moscow in 1960. The large majority of the conference had been taken aback by the virulence of their attack and, in particular, the delegates were shocked by the fact the Chinese did not rise to repudiate Hoxha's behaviour. But the Chinese did not walk out of the conference as Hoxha suddenly decided to do. Instead Teng Hsiao-ping decided to sign the lengthy and extremely vague conference document which left itself open to various interpretations and to continue the struggle against Krushchev later, after greater preparation. The Chinese also agreed to sign the document on the condition that there would be another conference in two years, by which time they hoped to have rallied more support.

Krushchev had also come to realise that an open breach would not be in his own interests. The agreed document contained the ambiguous phrase, " Communists have always recognised the pro-gressive revolutionary significance of national liberation wars." It claimed, " A new stage had begun in the development of the general crisis of capitalism." The Soviet Party was accepted as " the universally recognised vanguard of the World Communist move-ment, being the most experienced and steeled contingent of the international Communist movement." On paper all these repre-sented victories for Krushchev. Yet by the time the Moscow Conference concluded the Chinese had not retracted a single word. The departing delegates were soon to realise, if they had not done so already, that the Communist world now had two centres of doctrine, each bitterly and determinedly opposed to the other. And the Communist world could never be the same again because of what happened in Moscow in 1960.

The Sino-Soviet struggle entered a new phase after Moscow when Krushchev withdrew Soviet aid from Albania and the Chinese Communists, despite their own economic difficulties, promptly stepped into take the place of the Russians. The Soviet Union retorted by signing a five-year trade agreement with Yugoslavia on 30th March, 1961, and followed this by inviting the Yugoslav Foreign Minister to Moscow for talks in July. This was the first high-level Soviet-Yugoslav meeting for over three years. Later that same month, it was also learned that all Soviet technicians had left Albania. It was now obvious that the relative positions of Yugoslavia and Albania towards Russia and China were associated directly with the differences between Mao and Krushchev. Hoxha and Tito had become the favourites at two rival courts of power.

The Twenty-second Congress of the Soviet Communist Party was opened by Krushchev on 17th October, 1961, whilst the

Berlin crisis of that year was still uppermost in the Western Press. Krushchev, nevertheless, returned to the fight against Stalinism. After condemning the Yugoslav Communists for their "revisionism" in such mild terms that the criticism did not compare with earlier rebukes, Krushchev said, " On the eve of the Twentieth Congress, the issue facing us was: either the Party would openly, in Leninist fashion, condemn . . . the cult of Stalin's personality and reject the methods of party and government leadership that had become an obstacle to progress, or the forces which clung to the old and resisted all that was new and creative would gain the upper hand. The issue was as crucial as that! Was it really necessary to criticise so scathingly and so frankly . . .? Yes it was. . . . It was a moral requirement. . . . It was a correct decision and it had tremendous importance for the destiny of the Party and for the building of Communism."

Krushchev turned to attack the Albanians, implying that it was the Chinese that he was accusing also. He charged the Albanians with accepting the decisions of the Twentieth Congress only in appearance, and went on, " It would appear that in their hearts the Albanian leaders disagreed with the 1957 and 1960 meetings [in Moscow]." Krushchev said defiantly: " No one can divert us from the Leninist road," and told the Albanians they must renounce their erroneous views.

Chou En-Lai, who had come to Moscow to lead the Chinese delegation to the Twenty-second Congress made a very carefully worded fraternal speech on 19th October in which he claimed Chinese loyalty for the 1957 and 1960 decisions. He then turned to the Albanians, saying, " This unity of ours has stood the test of time. No force can destroy it. Our socialist camp, comprising twelve fraternal countries, is a single entity from the Korean Democratic People's Republic to the German Democratic Republic, from the Democratic Republic of Vietnam to the Albanian People's Republic. . . . Any public, one-sided censure of any fraternal party does not help unity and is not helpful to resolving problems. To lay bare a dispute between fraternal parties or fraternal countries openly in the face of the enemy cannot be regarded as a serious Marxist-Leninist attitude." It was a public rebuke to Krushchev.

The Chinese Prime Minister followed up his scathing references with an openly provocative act. Before leaving for Peking on 23rd October he went to the grizzly mausoleum in the Red Square where the embalmed bodies of Lenin and Stalin lay and placed wreaths at the feet of both. The wreath beside Stalin carried the inscription, " The great Marxist-Leninist." Chou En-Lai's return to Peking before the end of the Congress was the complete Chinese answer. It stung Krushchev in his final speech, on 27th October, into his first direct reference to the Chinese, " We share anxiety expressed by our Chinese friends, and appreciate their concern for greater unity. If the Chinese comrades wish to make efforts towards normalising the relations between the Albanian Party of Labour and the fraternal parties, there is hardly anyone who could contribute more to the solution of this problem than the Communist Party of China." Then, as Krushchev's most expressive reply of all, Stalin's embalmed body was dragged out of the mausoleum three days later and his remains were buried in a simple grave beside the Kremlin wall.

Hoxha replied to Krushchev on 7th November, 1961, and accused him of "blackmail" and attempting to overthrow the leaders of the Albanian Party. The *Peking People's Daily* carried the report of Hoxha's speech in full, as an expression of Chinese support. Krushchev demanded the withdrawal of the Albanian Ambassador to Moscow, saying he was distributing "offensive material" which was Hoxha's speech. A few days later, all diplomatic relations between Moscow and Tirana were severed.

The Sino-Soviet dispute appeared possible of containment right up to the Soviet Twenty-second Congress of 1961. Both sides still needed each other and neither could afford to break the alliance. Whilst many wishful thinkers in the West were forecasting a formal rupture and others, who were more fanciful, spoke of a possible Soviet alliance with the West against China, the basic political requirements of both Moscow and Peking made such ideas appear absurd. Nevertheless, the arguments at the Twenty-second Congress went so far that it was difficult to see how the former unity could be re-established in the lifetime of Mao Tse-tung and Krushchev. But both sides made another attempt in the first part of 1962 when letters passed between them about another possible meeting of Communist parties.

In the meanwhile, regardless of the Chinese, Krushchev pursued his strangely determined aim of enticing Tito back into the Communist bloc. Gromyko visited Belgrade in April 1962. A Yugoslav "parliamentary" delegation, it was announced in May, would visit the Soviet Union. Tito was also invited for a holiday, and so strong had his position become that he insisted that Leonid

Brezhnev, the Soviet President, must visit Yugoslavia first to make up for Voroshilov's rebuff of 1958.

This made no difference to the Chinese. The *Peking People's Daily* referred to the Yugoslav Communists on the eve of Brezhnev's visit as "out-and-out renegades" and to Tito as "singing in harmony with U.S. imperialism." Whilst Brezhnev was actually in Yugoslavia, Chen Yi, the Chinese Foreign Minister, made a speech saying, " The imperialists need the help of reactionaries in various countries and the latter are serving imperialism in a less disguised way. The modern revisionists represented by the Tito clique precisely meet these needs."

Another major point of difference had been developing. Whilst Krushchev was preparing his plans to establish rocket bases in Cuba, he was also flirting with the idea of supplying Soviet jet fighters to India. With the increasing tension between India and China over the Tibetan border, the Soviet action represented an overt threat to the Chinese. It presented the Chinese with an opportunity to expose the Soviet Union's position as "revisionist" and even "anti-Communist." In August 1962 Nehru claimed to have reached agreement with the Soviet Union to manufacture Soviet military aircraft in India. And Nehru's announcement received more prominence in the Chinese Press than it did in the Western countries.

The Chinese decided to forestall the arrival of the Soviet aircraft and launched their invasion in the Ladakh area and the North-East Frontier Agency on 20th October, 1962. It swept all before it and the Indians suffered a scalding humiliation, which was underlined yet further when the Chinese forces suddenly withdrew just when they appeared to have no opposition between them and an advance upon Calcutta. When the Chinese advance cut through the Indian positions both the United States and Britain immediately sent high-level missions to offer help. Krushchev, however, was in no position to do anything to help the Indians, partly because of the consequences to the Communist bloc but also because he had become involved within a matter of hours in his own crisis of Cuba.

The Chinese greeted the Soviet withdrawal in Cuba with derision. Two articles appeared simultaneously on 18th November, 1962: the *Peking People's Daily* said, " It is pure nonsense to say that 'peace has been saved' by withdrawing Soviet missiles," and *Pravda* declared, " Neither bourgeois propagandists nor other falsifiers can conceal the main fact that Soviet policy saved world peace and preserved the Cuban revolutionary movement."

Tito visited the Soviet Union at last in early December 1962 and was given the unique distinction of being invited to address the Supreme Soviet on 13th December. The day before he also heard Krushchev defend his Cuba policy before the Supreme Soviet. In the course of this Krushchev flayed the Albanian Communists who had gone even further than the Chinese in condemning his Cuba retreat. "The Albanians are like silly boys," he rapped. "Someone has taught them foul language and they go about and use it against the Communist Party of the Soviet Union. And yet it is their mother; and for using this foul language they get three kopecks; and if they use stronger and cruder language they get another five kopecks and praise." After asking, "How have we retreated?" Krushchev turned on the Chinese. "Macao is situated at the mouth of the Chu Chang River, on the coast of China. . . . There is also the British colony of Hong Kong. . . . The smell coming from these places is by no means sweeter than that released by colonialism in Goa. But no one will denounce the Chinese People's Republic for leaving intact these fragments of colonialism. It could be wrong to prod China into any kind of actions which she considers untimely. . . . But maybe this is a retreat from Marxism-Leninism? Nothing of the kind. It means that the government of the Chinese People's Republic takes into account the realities, the actual possibilities. . . ."

Krushchev also had cutting words to say on the sudden Chinese withdrawal from India, "Would it not have been better not to advance from the positions where these troops were at the time?" In the same speech the Soviet leader spoke of imperialism, "It is, of course, true that the nature of imperialism has not changed. But imperialism to-day is no longer what it used to be when it held undivided sway over the world. If it is now 'a paper tiger,' those who say this know that this 'paper tiger' has atomic teeth."

The Chinese retort to Krushchev was to deny vehemently that they had ever wanted to plunge the world into nuclear war. The *Peking People's Daily* on 31st December, 1962, said, "We neither called for the establishment of missile bases nor obstructed the withdrawal. . . . What we did strongly oppose, still strongly oppose, and will strongly oppose in the future, is the sacrifice of another country's sovereignty as a means of reaching a compromise with imperialism." The Chinese also began to press strongly again from early 1963, for a new meeting of Communist Parties at which Mao now hoped he would exploit Krushchev's Cuban disaster. For this very reason, the Russian leaders were equally determined not to concede it. Polemical letters passed. An extraordinary article of 50,000 words appeared in *Red Flag* in early March challenging the Russians to publish the Chinese case. Eventually, the two sides agreed to hold bilateral talks in Moscow in July 1963 with a view to leading on to a full conference.

The Moscow talks almost coincided with the closing stages of the Soviet-Western negotiations for the Nuclear Test Ban Treaty. The inevitable Teng Hsiao-ping and Peng Chen arrived in Moscow for the talks on 5th July. A week before this event the Soviet Government asked for the recall of three Chinese diplomats and two Chinese citizens who had been distributing copies of the last and the most important Chinese letter of 14th June. This was followed by the smashing of windows at the Chinese Embassy by the Russians. There were counter-protests by the Chinese who now resorted to the absurdity of organising so-called "shock brigades" to scatter copies of the 14th June letter from the Trans-Siberian express as it crossed the Russian countryside.

The Sino-Soviet talks were held in secrecy but it was soon apparent from articles in the Chinese Press that no progress was being made. Eventually, on 14th July, *Pravda* published the Chinese letter of 14th June, together with an open letter from the Soviet Central Committee to " Party organisations and all Communists in the Soviet Union." The Chinese letter asked, " If the general line of the international Communist movement is one-sidedly reduced to ' peaceful co-existence,' ' peaceful competition ' and ' peaceful transition ' this is to violate the revolutionary principles of the 1957 Declaration and the 1960 Statement, to discard the historical mission of proletarian world revolution and to depart from the revolutionary teachings of Marxism-Leninism." The Soviet retort described the Chinese letter as "slanderous" and went on to argue the well-known Soviet position. The Sino-Soviet Conference broke up quickly. Krushchev agreed, somewhat reluctantly, to see the Chinese delegation before they left.

It was not long before the issue was joined in even more bitter terms over the Nuclear Test Ban Treaty. The dispute was now moving more clearly into field of power politics and national interest. The Chinese issued on 15th August, 1963, a most revealing statement: " As far back as 20th June, 1959, when there was not the slightest sign of a treaty on stopping nuclear tests, the Soviet Government unilaterally tore up the agreement on new technology for national defence concluded between China and the Soviet Union on 15th October, 1957, and refused to provide China with an atomic bomb and technical data concerning its manufacture. This was done as a presentation gift at the time the Soviet leader went to the United States for talks with Eisenhower. . . ." According to the Chinese statement, the Russians had also attempted to get the Chinese to give up nuclear weapons on 25th August, 1962. To this request the Chinese had sent notes on 3rd September, 1962, 20th October, 1962, and 6th June, 1963, warning that what the Russians did was " a matter for the Soviet Government " but " the Chinese Government hoped that the Soviet Government would not infringe China's sovereign rights and act for China in assuming an obligation." The Chinese added, " We solemnly stated we would not tolerate the conclusion in disregard of China's opposition."

The Soviet retort was angry and bitter. *Soviet News* on 21st August, 1963, accused the Chinese of wanting to slander " this treaty which expresses the hope of the peoples." It went on, " They also want by means of fabrications and low tricks to use this major event in international life in order to impose upon other countries their adventurist platform on fundamental issues of war and peace. . . ."

Sino-Soviet tempers rose yet higher. The Chinese announced on 2nd September that the Soviet statement " plumbed new depths. Apparently the Soviet leaders have already become so degenerate that they now depend on telling lies for a living. The whole world knows that the tripartite [Nuclear Test Ban] treaty is designed to manacle all the socialist countries other than the Soviet Union and all the peace-loving countries and that it has no restraining effect whatsoever on U.S. imperialism. It does not hinder the U.S. from using nuclear weapons in time of war or manufacturing stockpiles."

It is easy to understand the Chinese anger at the treaty. They considered it was going to deny them great power status in an even more real way than China's exclusion from the United Nations. They went on to accuse the Soviet Union of giving military secrets to the Americans—a very grave charge indeed—and continued, " Even if we Chinese people are unable to produce an atom bomb for a hundred years we will neither crawl to the baton of the Soviet leaders nor kneel before the nuclear blackmail of the imperialists."

The Chinese statement pointed out that nuclear weapons " cannot hope to stop the people's revolutionary struggles " as their " massive destructiveness limits their use." Turning to the Caribbean crisis it accused Krushchev of " the error of adventurism and the error of capitulationism. . . . The crisis was the result of the rash action of the Soviet leader, who without consulting anybody wilfully embarked upon a reckless course and irresponsibly played with the lives of millions upon millions of people. . . . We were totally opposed to sending the rockets in."

The Chinese argument was summed up with sharp succinctness: " In fighting imperialism we are of the opinion that strategically and with regard to the whole one must despise the enemy, dare to struggle with him and dare to seize victory; at the same time tactically and with regard to each specific struggle we must take the enemy seriously and be prudent—failure to do so leads to errors of adventurism in tactics and capitulationism in strategy."

The consequences of the Sino-Soviet dispute had reached out far into the Communist parties bloc by the end of 1964. The East European leaders, with the possible exception of Gheorghia-Dej of Rumania, were all deeply concerned because they recognised immediately that any major internal dispute within the movement undermined their own insecure positions.

Ulbricht, of East Germany, an anachronism from the days of Stalin, may personally have retained many of his Stalinist views but he was too dependent upon the Soviet Union to risk challenging Krushchev's revisionist policies. Conversely, the Communist position in the German Democratic Republic was far too insecure for Krushchev to contemplate the removal of Ulbricht.

Gomulka, in Poland, had maintained the more independent line of 1956, but the first hopeful flush of de-Stalinisation in his country had faded. The Communist régime in Poland was making little progress and, whilst Gomulka naturally accepted Krushchev's policies as being more akin to his aspirations, he was deeply concerned about the Sino-Soviet dispute as a disruptive force.

The situation in Czechoslovakia was ironical. Anton Novotny, one of the more important survivals from the Stalinist era, had been involved deeply in the Slansky and Clements trials of 1952, after which the principal defendants had been executed for " Titoism." Throughout the 1956 upheavals, the Czechoslovak régime had been most careful to discourage an easement that could have led to a repetition of the events in Poland and Hungary. At the same time the Czech leadership, because of their dependence upon Soviet patronage, had been compelled to pay lip service to Krushchev policies and gradually to apply them. Stalinist by record and inclination, the Czech leaders were forced by circumstance and national interest to align themselves with the Russians in the dispute with China.

Hungary was the most closely aligned of all with the Soviet Union, as both the régime and its leader Kadar came nearest to being genuine supporters of Krushchev.

The great exception in Eastern Europe was Gheorghia-Dej in Rumania, a man who survived from the days of Stalinism and by so doing had proved his tough opportunism. The first issue upon which Soviet-Rumania differences appeared was economic co-operation. The Council for Mutual Economic Assistance, the economic body of co-operation within the bloc, met in June 1962 to co-ordinate its activities. A number of very important decisions were taken at this gathering which went a long way towards implementing the long-held theory of the organisation as a body to allocate complementary tasks to the different countries within the bloc and to avoid duplication. Krushchev, later that same year, advocated a supra-national planning body to enforce the decisions. Therefore, it came as a considerable surprise when the 17th Session of the Council for Mutual Economic Assistance meeting in December 1962 failed to endorse Krushchev's proposal. It was obvious that there had been considerable opposition. The leadership of that opposition was provided by Rumania.

The Rumanian position stemmed again from her national interest. It is a country rich in natural resources but comparatively underdeveloped. Gheorghia-Dej's fear was that closer economic integration of the bloc might prejudice his country's chances of industrial advancement. A protracted and at times heated debate followed. When Rumania remained adamant, the Council for Mutual Economic Assistance was forced in July 1963 to accept Rumania's rights to reject proposals that were in conflict with her national interests—an unheard of position in Stalin's day. Throughout the dispute with Rumania, the Soviet Union's position was prejudiced by the Sino-Soviet dispute and Krushchev was not in any position to incur further difficulties in confrontation with Gheorghia-Dej.

In the meanwhile the Sino-Soviet argument briefly appeared to recede into the background during the last quarter of 1963, only to flare up again in 1964. Krushchev made several attempts to contain the argument, but his overtures had little impression upon the Chinese who continued a sporadic attack upon the Soviet position through the Peking Press and radio. Early in 1964 the Soviet Communist Party Central Committee held a plenum to deal with the situation which had developed thus far. It took the form of a major speech by Suslov, the most important and carefully reasoned Soviet attack on the Chinese Communist Party that had yet taken place.

Suslov spoke on 14th February, 1964. His speech lasted about five hours. He set out the Chinese attitude as he saw it as being one of " great power chauvinism and petty bourgeois adventurism." He said, " The real aim of the Chinese leadership is to use all kinds of political splinter elements—renegades of communism, anarchists, Trotskyites, and suchlike—to split the united front . . . to hammer together as a counterweight to Communist movement, a bloc of pro-Chinese actions and groupings, to subordinate Communist parties to their own influence."

In a reference to the Indian frontier dispute Suslov said, " The Government of the U.S.S.R. repeatedly advocated a settlement of the border dispute. Military operations, nevertheless, developed in the Himalayas. The baleful effects of that conflict have now become apparent. It did a great service to the forces of imperialism. It did serious damage to the national liberation movement in India." In short, Suslov had exposed the Soviet sense of frustration at the way in which he considered Chinese policies were prejudicing Russian policies of subversion and penetration.

At various stages Suslov held up the Chinese position to ridicule. He also told a number of telling and malicious stories against the Chinese, including an account of an interview given by Tao Chu, a member of the Chinese Central Committee, to a Czech journalist who had pointed out that Czechoslovakia's population might be wiped out in a thermo-nuclear war. According to Suslov, Tao Chu replied, " In the event of a destructive war, the small countries of the socialist camp will have to subordinate their interest to the general interests of the entire camp as a whole."

Suslov's bitter attack led to an interesting Rumanian attempt at mediation. A Rumanian delegation hurried to Peking and travelled on to North Korea in March 1964. This delegation appears to have met with very little sympathy. The Chinese responded in early April by denouncing Krushchev as the greatest revisionist of all time and, in effect, called upon the Soviet people to depose him.

Krushchev was on the point of an important visit to Hungary when the sensational news of the Chinese attack calling upon the Russians to depose him arrived. The Soviet reaction was to describe the Chinese attitude as a terrible insult to the Soviet leader and people.

The argument had reached a point at which a new conference of the Communist Parties of the world had become essential from the Russian point of view. The Russians published Suslov's February speech to the Central Committee—hitherto a secret—and proceeded to make their preparations for the conference. They were sure of a massive victory on paper for, apart from the Indonesian, Albanian, North Vietnam, and North Korean Communist Parties, the Chinese Communists possessed little support—except from small bodies such as the New Zealand Communist Party and certain splinter groups.

Yet the Chinese challenge had grown in its long-term prospect, because it had forced Krushchev on to the defensive in a number of areas. His attitudes to Eastern Europe had been modified to the point at which he had been compelled to allow local Communist régimes a more free hand—without going as far as Yugoslavia. His tactical approach of subversion and penetration had suffered a number of setbacks, such as in India and Africa. And the very existence of the Chinese alternative pole of attraction had dealt a deep blow at the ethos of the monolith that had been Stalin's great legacy. For these reasons, the Chinese were in no hurry to hold a conference.

The Chinese challenge had begun in ideological arguments. By now it was an overt clash between two civilisations. Each of the Communist countries and parties was taking up its position along lines of national interests and political expediency. This was a new and profound development in the story of world communism, full of pregnant possibilities for the future.

CHAPTER 25

JENGHIZ KHAN WITH A TELEPHONE?

The most dangerous prospect that mankind may ever have to face is a Jenghiz
Khan with a telephone.   *Tolstoy*

Krushchev fell from power on 14th October, 1964. Kennedy was
assassinated almost a year earlier on 22nd November, 1963. The
same span of months broadly included Adenauer's unwilling and
long-delayed retirement, Macmillan's resignation—due in the
event to ill-health, Nehru's death and the emergence of a Labour
Government in Britain. New men in many countries suddenly confronted each other. The forces that had operated behind their predecessors remained and so did the many intractable problems
that were their legacies. Yet, new prospects of immense importance
for the world were dawning, the implications of which will only
become manifest with the passing of time.

The 1962 Cuba crisis, it could be seen even more clearly in
retrospect, had been a watershed in Soviet-Western relations. The
glint of American resolution had caused such a trauma of Communist policy that the impact of it continued to reverberate for
more than two years. As far as the Soviet Union and Eastern Europe
were concerned, there was a noticeable easing in the bellicosity of
anti-Western attitudes following the Cuba crisis, even to the extent
of the dropping of radio jamming of Western broadcasts. A significant example of the new trend towards a *détente* in Europe was
a visit by Aleksei Adzhubei, the editor of *Izvestia* and Krushchev's son-in-law, to Bonn in July, 1964. It was intended to prepare the way for a visit by Krushchev himself, to discuss the
German question. The Western leaders in general—and President
Johnson in particular—appeared at first to be incredulous and
somewhat apprehensive about the Soviet Union's new intentions.
With the passing of the months, however, the Johnson administration, that was conducting its own private dialogue with the Soviet

leaders, began to formulate fresh assessments of Russian policy. The major European countries—with the exception of France, who was following separatist policies—awaited American leadership in the Western Alliance on the specific issue of Soviet-Western relations, although the Alliance itself was facing major internal problems.

A different situation existed in the Communist countries where there was upheaval on the question of how to deal with the West. Mao Tse-tung continued to disagree profoundly, and at times violently, with Krushchev and the Soviet leaders. The East European Communist governments—whilst desiring a reduction in East-West tension—were often very apprehensive and increasingly opposed to a final rift between Russia and China because of its potential effect upon their own positions. The Sino-Soviet dispute mounted in intensity in Krushchev's last months of office and, as it grew, the authority of the Soviet Union as the leader of World Communism began to decline. Yet Khrushchev obstinately continued to press for a preliminary meeting of Communist parties on 15th December, 1964, to deal with the differences about Communist policy. Mao Tse-tung remained equally adamant that the time was not opportune for such a meeting.

Mao calculatedly exacerbated relations on 10th July, 1964. He delivered a savage attack upon the Soviet Union, that was later published, in the course of an interview to a Japanese delegation. What he said was really an indictment of Stalin himself. "The places occupied by the Soviet Union are too numerous," Mao told his visitors. "In the correspondence with the Yalta Agreement, the Soviet Union, under the pretext of guaranteeing the independence of Mongolia, actually put the country under its rule. . . . They have appropriated part of Rumania. Detaching parts of East Germany, they drove out the inhabitants to the Western area. Detaching parts of Poland, they included it in Russia and as compensation gave Poland part of East Germany. The same thing happened to Finland. They detached everything that could be detached. . . ." Although Mao's words might have been used by John Foster Dulles, they were intended to be a clarion call to the East European Communists to oppose Soviet policies on nationalistic grounds. His reopening of the Mongolian question showed also how far the two powers were in conflict on issues affecting their immediate boundaries.

The Soviet leaders replied angrily by adopting a similar tactic. *Pravda* accused China on 2nd September, 1964, of persistently publishing maps since 1954 showing as Chinese territory Burma, Vietnam, Thailand, Malaya, Nepal, Bhutan and Sikkim, as well as large tracts of Soviet territory. This was a parallel attempt by the Russians to create difficulties for Mao Tse-tung along China's marches. On the Mongolian issue, *Pravda* retorted, "China would like to deprive Mongolia of her independence and make her a Chinese province. . . . We are faced with an openly expansionist programme of far-reaching pretensions. History has known many cases where reactionary wars were started with a view to expanding *Lebensraum.*" *Pravda* accused the Chinese of mounting an attack that, in intensity, equalled "the Cold War of the Western Powers upon the Soviet Union." The Peking *People's Daily* retorted by opposing "all criminal designs to buy or sell-out East Germany"— a reference to Krushchev's proposed visit to Bonn. Thus the Sino-Soviet diatribe reached its crescendo on 11th October, 1964, just as the decisive steps to overthrow Krushchev were being taken in Moscow. A preface to two volumes of Krushchev's statement published in Peking accused Krushchev of having "usurped" the post of First Secretary and described him as "a conspirator, careerist and double-faced hypocrite in all his ugliness."

By now, the Soviet Communist party leadership had become increasingly alarmed by the consequences of Krushchev. Abroad, he had brought the Communist bloc to the point of fragmentation. At home, his industrial and agricultural policies were in a state of impasse—or on the brink of collapse, as in the case of the virgin lands. Finally, there were Krushchev's own impulsive and increasingly high-handed methods of working. There was the growing fear amongst certain Soviet leaders that if they did not act against Krushchev, he might act against them—that frightened feeling of self-preservation that has been one of the most potent stimulants to political conspiracy throughout history.

Important parts in the coup were played by Nikolai Podgorny and Alexander Shelepin, although nearly every member of the Praesidium appears to have been involved. Podgorny, with Shelepin's aid, laid the foundations for an anti-Krushchev majority in the Praesidium and for a selected anti-Krushchev quorum of the Central Committee to endorse its action. There was going to be no repetition of 1957. As in all palace revolutions in authoritarian states, secrecy was essential. Thus Shelepin, who was head of the K.G.B.—the state security organisation—before he became a member of the Central Committee secretariat, was now in a key position with the help he was able to give. It seems, too, that his successor at the K.G.B., Semichastny, aided him willingly.

Krushchev was on holiday at the time near the Black Sea resort of Sochi. Two of his closest associates, including Pavel Satyukov, the editor of *Pravda*, were abroad. Adzubei must have discovered what was happening too late. Almost certainly, he wrote an article in *Izvestia*, desperately attempting to rally support, as the paper failed to appear on time on 15th October. The final plans for the coup were actually made on 13th October, 1964. That night, certain of Krushchev's portraits in prominent places started to come down, indicating that the great decision had already been taken. Krushchev was summoned to Moscow on 14th October and left Sochi in a hurry. Upon arrival at Moscow, he was driven to a meeting of the Praesidium where he was confronted with their decision to remove him. As in 1957, he demanded the right to appeal to the Central Committee. This was the conspirators' moment of triumph. The selected quorum of the Central Committee had already been assembled. Krushchev defended himself at great length. It is said that at times he was blustering and, at other times, pleading. A substantial majority of those present voted against him. His defeat was complete.

The news of Krushchev's fall was announced to the world by *Tass* next day. His titular successors were Leonid Ilych Brezhnev, a fifty-eight-year-old Ukrainian, as First Secretary of the Soviet Communist party, and Alexi Nikolaevich Kosygyn, the new Chairman of the Council of Ministers. Brezhnev, a man of considerable capacity who rose to prominence in the war, had succeeded Voroshilov as Soviet President. He had given way on 15th July to the ageing Mikoyan and returned to party work. His part in the coup was limited, as he had been abroad in East Germany until a few days before. To some extent this was an advantage, as Brezhnev's acceptability was an important factor in retaining confidence in the Soviet Party itself. Kosygyn was a Leningrad bureaucrat with a long and distinguished service in government including the Economic Planning Commission. The parts played by Podgorny and Shelepin emerged in the next few days. Podgorny was strong enough to demand the task of "reorganising the party." Shelepin joined the Praesidium. The dual posts of membership of the Central Committee secretariat and the Praesidium now belonged only to Brezhnev, Suslov, Podgorny and Shelepin.

Thus Krushchev, the man who had destroyed the myth of

471

Stalin, passed abruptly from the scene. His role in world history, for ten years, had been immense. He had, in his term of office, bowed to the inexorable facts of the thermonuclear age. At home, he had recognised the tremendous pressures of the Soviet people towards a better material life and more freedom.

Krushchev's fall caused astonishment throughout the world and extreme concern in the various Communist parties. In Moscow, there were no tributes to him: only a biting *Pravda* article on 17th October referring to "hare-brained scheming, immature conclusions, hasty decisions, actions divorced from reality, bragging, phrase-mongering and commandism."[1] But his old friend Kadar, in Hungary, insisted that he deserved "considerable credit for exposing the Stalinist cult." In Czechoslovakia, too, there was "surprise and emotion." In China and amongst the pro-Chinese Communist parties there was open jubilation; the Chinese hailing the event as a victory and describing it as "the downfall of a buffoon."

Various Communist parties sent delegations to Moscow for the November anniversary celebrations of the Russian Revolution with explicit instructions to find out what had happened. Chou En-Lai also attended, for the first time since 1961, in a visit that was obviously a reconnaissance. The visiting Communists now discovered that a long list of charges had been drawn up against Krushchev. They fell under the headings of foreign policy mistakes, "personal feelings" and domestic policy. This document had been the basis of the denunciation of him at the Central Committee and included the mishandling of the Cuba crisis and the personalisation of the Sino-Soviet dispute, as well as his own increasingly difficult personality; and the widespread confusion in the economy. At the same time, Chou En-lai discovered that whilst the Soviet leadership wished to reduce Sino-Soviet tension—they decided immediately to postpone the preliminary Communist conference proposed for 15th December—they were not proposing to return to the Chinese concept of "perpetual revolution." Instead, Brezhnev went out of his way to affirm support for "the decisions of the 20th, 21st, and 22nd Congresses." In fact, there were indications that Soviet foreign policy would continue for the time being along Krushchev's course of a limited *détente* in the West.

In the meanwhile, an event of far-reaching implications for the world, as well as for Sino-Soviet relations, had taken place on 16th

[1] A Soviet term denoting "government by ordering people about."

October, 1964—two days after Krushchev's fall. The Chinese had exploded a low-yield nuclear device, typical of an early nuclear test. The explosion took place at three o'clock in the afternoon near Lop Nor, a lake in a remote and desolate part of Sinkiang. The Chinese promptly issued a statement calling for "a world summit conference to consider nuclear disarmament." Whilst this was an overt propaganda gesture it faced the world, at last, with the growing problem of China.

The hopes of a Soviet-American understanding and the intensity of the Sino-Soviet conflict had diverted attention from this and other issues. In the years 1962-5 many Western observers had gradually become fascinated by the political arguments, some open and some implicit, between Washington, Moscow and Peking, to the exclusion of much else that was vitally important. In Africa, a bitter struggle had been developing between African nationalist groups and the ex-colonial powers, with the Communist countries attempting to exploit the situation in a manner that was reminiscent of the Spanish Civil War. The wider East-West struggle had become divided, in its turn, into Russian and Chinese rivalry for the leadership of the local pro-Communist forces. A different and more complicated situation had been developing in Latin America, where corruption, frustration and reaction all contributed to political instability. Deep down, the Latin American upsurge was a revolt against the power exercised by foreign financial interests rather than against traditional colonialism.

The apparently orderly withdrawal in Africa over years by British imperialism, to the accompaniment of the pageantry and goodwill of various "Independence" days, had camouflaged the true social and political situation in this continent. The major awakening amongst Europeans as to the future possible course of African politics came first because of a local revolt against the British in Kenya; and then by the development of affairs in the former British colony of Ghana. Independence was granted to Ghana on 6th March, 1957. Within a comparatively short space of time, the constitution was amended. The rule of law, that had been the chief British legacy, fell into disrepute. Eventually, it was abandoned for all practical purposes. Although the African leader in Ghana, Kwame Nkrumah, had been a product of British education, he fell gradually under Communist influences that played upon his vanities and primitive fears. An effective campaign of Soviet infiltration followed, aimed at re-aligning Ghana's internal and

473

foreign policies. Ghana soon became a despotism on a new pattern in which the state of repression of part of the African population reached the point at which it was as bad as, indeed worse than, in South Africa.

An even more critical situation developed in the Belgian Congo. The Belgian administration withdrew on 30th June, 1960, leaving behind a leftist government under a former post office clerk, Patrice Lumumba, who was unable to impose the authority of his government upon the vast and primitive country. Again, the Soviet Union was quick to seize its opportunity. Lumumba appealed for help but was driven from power. In the confused situation that followed a series of conflicts developed: between the Central Congolese Government and the separatist state of Katanga; between the Congolese and the Soviet political and economic advisers, who were ordered out of the country; and between Congolese forces and the Europeans and Americans. Thus, both the Soviet Union and the Western Powers became involved in a running civil war in which appalling and primitive atrocities—including Lumumba's murder— were committed, mainly by the Congolese participants. The confusion was increased by the fact that President Tshombe—the President of the rebel state of Katanga that was eventually overrun by United Nations forces acting under doubtful authority, with the support of the Central Congolese Government—re-emerged as head of the Central Congolese Government, supported by the United States, and looked upon by African states as the agent of Western Imperialism. Tshombe also found that he had little more control over the country than Lumumba had in the early days of Independence, and was dependent upon a few white mercenary troops. His authority was defied in November, 1964, by a rebel force with Communist associations in Stanleyville, that massacred large numbers of their own fellow-Africans, as well as a number of white hostages. An American-aided drop by Belgian paratroops on 24th November, that was regarded by the European countries as a justifiable humanitarian rescue of the hostages, provoked the delegates of many African countries at the United Nations to language of astonishing frenzy and total disregard of truth. These latter events did more than any other circumstances to make Western opinion realise at last that the principle of "one man, one vote" would have different connotations in Africa than in Europe or North America, and that primitive and distorted political concepts in Africa would create problems for years to come. Similar uncertainties developed in East Africa during the year 1964. A Communist-inspired coup with Chinese and Cuban associations in Zanzibar in early 1964 threatened nearly all the other fledgeling régimes in the area. The temporary return of British troops at the request of two of the local governments restored the situation briefly. In the context of a major Imperial withdrawal, the Soviet Union and China were now making determined efforts to assert new national influences. By early 1965, Communism was seeking to ride in on the coat-tails of anti-white racialism. Whilst the Communist Powers were severely handicapped by lack of experience of African conditions, there could be no doubt that the Communist drive to displace the West in Africa was only in its infancy.

An even more successful Communist initiative was taken in regard to Egypt. The earlier Czech sale of arms and the Russian offer of 1956 to help finance the Aswan Dam, following upon Dulles's withdrawal of American aid, played a large part in extending Soviet influence in the Arab countries. The 1958 revolution in Baghdad brought in a new régime under General Kassim that developed close associations for a time with the Soviet Union. The Algerian revolution provided fertile opportunities for Communism.

The first stage of the Aswan project was completed in 1964. Krushchev, himself, went to Egypt to attend the opening ceremony and exploited the occasion very skilfully. He awarded both Nasser and the Egyptian Vice-President, Amer, the highest Soviet decoration—"Hero of the Soviet Union"—and promised a loan to Egypt of £100 millions on favourable terms. Krushchev was criticised for these actions, at the time of his fall, but there is no doubt that he helped to make Soviet influence strong in a country whose position was bound to affect the future course of the Middle East. As if to prove Krushchev's wisdom, Shelepin, who led a Soviet delegation to Cairo in December, 1964, confirmed the terms of the Soviet loan.

It is interesting to note, in passing, the major difference developing in the attitudes of the Soviet Union and China towards the developing countries. Whereas the Soviet Union's approach was that of the anti-colonial power that was both benevolent and wealthy, China, obviously, had much less to offer in the way of material aid. Therefore, she claimed instead to be the revolutionary nation whose experience was closest to that of the Africans and Asians. It was with this philosophy in mind that Chou En-Lai undertook a major tour of the area in early 1964, meeting with a varying reception. For example, he was received markedly less cordially in Egypt than was Krushchev, whose offers of aid were of much greater substance.

Farther east, around China's borders, East-West tensions continued apace and demanded Western reactions. By the early 1960s, the 1954 Geneva settlement in Indo-China was operating no longer. Communist infiltration and subversion increasingly threatened Laos and South Viet-Nam. Both were areas in which American policy was deeply committed. From 1962, the military position had worsened in South Viet-Nam. Also, the reactionary régime of President Ngo Dinh Diem became involved in major clashes with Buddhists in the summer and autumn of 1963. After heavy fighting in Saigon on 1st and 2nd November, 1963, the South Viet-Nam Government was overthrown by an uprising of militarists and Buddhists. Ngo Dinh Diem and his brother were taken prisoner and murdered. Whatever may have been his excesses, Ngo Dinh Diem's fall was a set-back to the American position and considered to be so by the Communists. As the latter saw it, the pattern was returning to the situation during the French struggles of 1950-4. The Americans feared that the pattern was more akin to China in the years preceding 1949. Chinese aid to the Communists quickly grew in intensity, taking full advantage of geography. By late 1964, four possible courses were facing Johnson. The Americans could continue broadly as they were doing, hoping that the South Viet-Nam administration would eventually establish a viable position. Alternatively, they could seek to neutralise the area—as De Gaulle had proposed at one stage—and negotiate a settlement. Or they could commit American arms directly to the struggle. Finally, the Americans could withdraw altogether, leaving Viet-Nam to the Communists. Of the various courses, the neutrality proposal was unpractical. The Communist concept of negotiation in the area was only too clear: "What's mine is mine and what's yours is negotiable." In any case, there was no assurance that any settlement would be respected. At the same time the Americans were finding that there was no way of "saving" a people who did not wish to be "saved." Therefore, the logic of the situation pointed increasingly either towards direct Western commitment and the possible extension of the fighting in Viet-Nam until the Communists had been defeated or withdrawal.

A significant incident took place in the Viet-Nam area in late summer, 1964, that indicated both American and Communist attitudes and how far each was prepared to go. The American destroyer *Maddox* of the U.S. 7th Fleet was attacked by three North Viet-Nam torpedo boats in the Gulf of Tonkin on 2nd August. The torpedo boats opened fire with 37-mm. guns and launched torpedoes. Four aircraft of the U.S. carrier *Ticonderoga* joined the *Maddox* and helped to drive off the torpedo boats, one of which appeared to be badly damaged. At first, it was considered in Washington that the attack might have been a mistake, or that it had been on the initiative of some irresponsible local commander. However, a second attack on the destroyers *Maddox* and *C. Turner Joy* at 10.30 p.m. on 4th August showed that it was much more. The second action lasted four hours in very bad weather and the attackers were driven off by gunfire. Johnson, in Washington, acted swiftly. He ordered bombing attacks by American aircraft on 5th August on the North Viet-Nam torpedo boat bases at Hon Gay, Loc Chao, Phuc Loi and Quang Khe and the oil storage depots at Vinh. It was a major operation and a great deal of damage was inflicted. The North Viet-Nam Government described the action as "an act of war." As in the case of Cuba, Western neutralists were quick to forecast that there would be Communist reprisals that might lead even to war. They were proved wrong again. Johnson's reaction had been the right one in the Western interest.

The problems facing the West by the beginning of 1965 were several. In strictly Soviet-Western terms, the Berlin and wider German issues had progressed little over the years, yet there were indications in the early post-Krushchev era that the Soviet Union wished to adopt a limited policy of genuine co-existence, as it was understood by the West. The Soviet request for the resumption of Four-Power contacts over Berlin was one case in point and the revival of the so-called Rapacki Plan for disengagement in Europe was another. On the whole question of disarmament, the problems remained largely as before. The seventeen-nation disarmament conference, which had begun on 14th March, 1962, had made little progress upon the practical issues. Whilst both sides loudly proclaimed their genuine desires for disarmament, the difficulties remaining were the problems of verification and control. Whilst the Western Powers demanded inspection rights and effective control, the Soviet Government insisted that the disarmament agreement itself must come first. In effect, its attitude was that if the West first accepted the Soviet Union's disarmament proposals, the Soviet

Union would accept the Western plans for control. The major problems were not technical or military but political.

In Africa, however, there were still no signs of a reduction in the East-West tensions that showed themselves from time to time as the cauldron of nationalism boiled and bubbled over. Nor did it appear that there would be any such reduction, as the appetites of both the Soviet Union and China remained undiminished in their desires to further their influences.

But the greatest challenges loomed in the Orient. The Western Powers faced new problems, hitherto largely confined to Europe, in situations that were both more complex and hazardous. The explosion of China's first nuclear weapon had reinforced the Peking Government's claim to be the greatest regional power in Asia. The magnetism of Mao Tse-tung's political concept was being felt over a very wide area. Militarily and politically, China posed a direct threat to the future survival of India as the democratic state constructed by Nehru. The growing ripples of Chinese expansionism were being aided strongly by the left-wing nationalism of Indonesia, whose aggressive foreign policies, in their turn, made new claims upon the Western Powers. The Western nations—particularly the United States and Britain—now foresaw their requirements for military alliances and forces in the area, nuclear as well as conventional, increasing rather than diminishing. Already on the political horizon were military threats to Japan and Australasia.

These new factors were really symptoms of the significant changes of the post-Krushchev era. The traditional concept of World Communism, conceived as a united movement for world domination, directed from a single point and based upon a common doctrine, had ended. The great idea, with which Lenin had embarked upon his original aim forty-seven years before, had been destroyed by the rival claims to leadership of the two major Communist Powers. Instead, there was now the Soviet Union, ruled by a Communist party exerting its influence abroad partly by political affiliations and partly by military and economic strength. Its Communist rival, China, was busy laying the foundations for a new strident, revolutionary international organisation whose principal appeal was directed to the developing countries, as opposed to Marx's original analysis that World Communism would succeed with the triumph of the industrial proletariat in the most advanced countries. It is the break up of the Communist monolith, and the emergence of China as the new leading champion of the under-privileged peoples that has also caused the geographical shift eastwards in the struggle for world supremacy by Communism.

Did this mean that the Soviet threat to Western civilisation was at last at an end? Such an assumption would have been premature. The Soviet Union's military position in Europe cast a long shadow across the West European nations. The division of Germany and the isolated vulnerability of West Berlin would continue for as long as the Red Army maintained Soviet influence in Europe. The true European settlement could not be achieved until the Red Army was withdrawn from Germany and the various East European countries that were overrun by the Russians in 1945. Various formulæ for limited disengagement, attractive though they may have been to the smaller countries concerned, such as Poland, and to some superficial thinkers in the West, were no substitute for the realities of removing the root causes of international political conflict in Europe. The acceptance by the Soviet Union of such a settlement would still take time, but eventually the time could come. In considering the future international prospect, therefore, it had to be remembered how far Soviet policy had been adapted already in a comparatively short space of time. Writing in early 1965, it had to be emphasised that it was still less than three years since the leadership of the Soviet Union had attempted the Cuban coup; and in the expected aftermath of American demoralisation the Soviet leadership had expected to seize West Berlin and eventually to subjugate Western Germany and perhaps other European countries. If Khrushchev's Cuban policy had succeeded in 1962, it was probable that the Soviet Union's leadership of World Communism would have been restored for a time. The will to resist of the Western Powers would certainly have been undermined to a point close to destruction, and a very different situation would have prevailed in the world. Equally, it had to be accepted that it was the existence of Western nuclear power—primarily American—and the knowledge that it could and would be used ruthlessly to destroy the Soviet Union's entire industrial society that had caused Krushchev and his immediate colleagues to quail before the implications of their aggressive course and to adopt policies that made inevitable the Sino-Soviet conflict. The frontal challenge of Soviet Communism had been halted frontally. In the last analysis there could be no other way—a simple fact that has always to be learned anew by the appeasers of each generation, whether they be those who once blithely advocated compromise with Hitler or later acted as the

479

dishonest and craven apologists of Soviet policies in the period of the Cold War.

The Chinese challenge, although a potential military challenge of great gravity, already differed from that of the Soviet Union's earlier drive. Mao Tse-tung's aim had been made clear for a number of years. He considered that Marx had been wrong in one fundamental and that Communism's best hope of extending its authority lay in the under-developed countries of Asia, Africa and Latin America. He claimed that the Chinese revolution was the true model for these areas of the world. He had believed also, ever since his surprised disappointment during the period of the so-called "Hundred Flowers" in 1957, that his rule could only be extended if the ideological militancy of Chinese Communism were fostered constantly in the closed climate of a besieged fortress. This did not mean that the Chinese were not prepared to practise "peaceful co-existence" where the policy was tactically advantageous. Chou En-Lai's journeys in 1954 and his appearance at the Bandung Conference of 1955 had shown this much earlier. Nor did it imply that Chinese Communism would eventually seek to establish the same rigid organisational control over other Communist parties as had been the case with the Soviet Union in the Third International. It was the *ideological leadership* of World Communism to which Mao had staked his claim, and his belief was that he would reap his full reward in the answering echoes of millions of peoples suffering from poverty and despair. It was a very formidable prospect, in some ways much more formidable than Stalin's and Krushchev's attempts to overrun Europe that both came so close to success.

What could be the Western answers to Mao's policy? In geopolitical terms China's military threats had to be matched by Western military strength. The Chinese leaders, whether they were of Mao's generation, or their heirs, would have to realise always that any frontal military attack on other Asian cities would meet with the same Western reactions as a Soviet attack upon Western Berlin. At the same time, the experience of Viet-Nam had shown that there were equally dangerous military threats that could not be answered in the crude terms of massive retaliation. The Western Powers, despite the tentative experience of S.E.A.T.O., had failed to meet successfully this latter threat by early 1965. Again, there was the internal threat of social collapse, upon which Mao based his greatest hope. As India had shown, this problem was so immense that it appeared almost insoluble. The Marshall Plan had saved the situation for the Western Powers in 1947 because the technological skills of the men and the industrial society of Western Europe had been sufficiently well established to enable Western Europe to be saved. No such conditions prevailed in Asia and Africa, nor even in Latin America where industrialisation was much more advanced. The Western Powers, and their allies in Australasia—and their potential ally, Japan—now faced their greatest task. They had to provide the leadership and support for viable, healthy societies in conditions that were akin to the impossible and in political circumstances where they were often unwelcome.

Could it be that the Chinese Communist revolution would succeed where Lenin's revolution had failed? New forces were on the march. No one knew the points they would eventually reach. Everyone grasped the conditions from which they were seeking to escape. They were impelled by the pressures of history. They were not the products of the wills of individual men. As Tolstoy wrote in *War and Peace*:

"The Napoleonic wars, though somewhat doubtfully, still appear to us as the products of the will of heroes; but in the crusades we already see an event which occupies a definite place. . . . In the migration of the peoples no-one in our day imagines that the arbitrary will of Attila had anything to do with it. The farther back in history we take the subject of observation, the more doubtful does the freedom of the event-producing men become, and the more manifest is the law of necessity."

BIBLIOGRAPHY
INDEX

BIBLIOGRAPHY

The following is a selective list; it does not pretend to be an exhaustive bibliography of source books for the many subjects dealt with in *Struggle for the World*.

ACHESON, DEAN: *Sketches from Life* (Hamish Hamilton) 1961

BARNET, A. DOAK: *Communist China and Asia* (Harper) 1960

BELOFF, MAX: *The Foreign Policy of Soviet Russia 1929-41* 2 vols: *1929-36* and *1936-41* (Oxford University Press) 1947 and 1949

Soviet Policy in the Far East, 1944-51 (Oxford University Press) 1953

BULLOCK, ALAN: *Hitler, A Study in Tyranny* (Odhams) 1952

CHURCHILL, W. S.: *The World Crisis*, 5 vols (Thornton Butterworth) 1923-31

The Second World War, 6 vols (Cassell) 1948-54; (Penguin) 1964

CONQUEST, ROBERT: *Power and Policy in the U.S.S.R.* (Macmillan) 1961

DALLIN, DAVID J.: *Soviet Foreign Policy After Stalin* (Methuen) 1962

DEGRAS, JANE: *The Communist International 1919-1943 Documents* (Oxford University Press) 1960

DEUTSCHER, ISAAC: *Stalin* (Oxford University Press) 1961

The Prophet Armed: Trotsky (Oxford University Press) 1954

The Prophet Unarmed: Trotsky (Oxford University Press) 1959

The Prophet Outcast: Trotsky (Oxford University Press) 1963

DJILAS, MILOVAN: *Conversations with Stalin* (Hart-Davis) 1962

EDEN, ANTHONY: *The Eden Memoirs*, 3 vols (Cassell) 1960-65

EISENHOWER, D. D.: *The White House Years*, vol 1: *Mandate for Change* (Heinemann) 1964

FEIS, HERBERT: *The China Tangle* (Oxford University Press) 1953

Churchill, Roosevelt, Stalin (Oxford University Press) 1957

Between War and Peace (Oxford University Press) 1960

Japan Subdued (Oxford University Press) 1961

FLOYD, DAVID: *Mao Against Kruschev* (Pall Mall Press) 1964

FORRESTAL, JAMES: *The Forrestal Diaries* (Cassell) 1952

GRIFFITHS, WILLIAM E.: *The Sino-Soviet Rift* (Allen & Unwin) 1964

JONES, JOSEPH M.: *Fifteen Weeks* (Viking Press) 1955

KARDELJ, EDWARD: *Socialism and War* (Methuen) 1962

KENNAN, GEORGE F.: *Russia and the West Under Lenin and Stalin* (Hutchinson) 1951

HULL, CORDELL: *Memoirs* 3 vols (Hodder & Stoughton) 1948

LABEDZ, LEOPOLD: *Revisionism* (Allen & Unwin) 1962

LECKIE, ROBERT: *The Korean War* (Pall Mall Press) 1963

LENIN, V. I.: *Collected Works* 20 vols (Foreign Languages Press, Moscow) 1960-4

LEONHARD, WOLFGANG: *Child of the Revolution* (Collins) 1957
  The Kremlin Since Stalin (Oxford University Press) 1962

LEWIS, J. W.: *Leadership in Communist China* (Cornell University Press, Oxford University Press) 1963

MACFARQUHAR, RODERICK: *The Hundred Flowers Campaign* (Stevens) 1960

MACKINTOSH, J. M.: *The Strategy and Tactics of Soviet Power* (Oxford University Press) 1962

MCNEILL, W. H. ed: *America, Britain and Russia* (Oxford University Press) 1953 (Survey of International Affairs vol 3)

MAISKY, IVAN: *Who Helped Hitler?* (Hutchinson) 1964

MAO TSE-TUNG: *Selected Works* (Foreign Languages Press, Peking; Lawrence & Wishart) 1954-56

MARX, KARL: *Capital* 3 vols (Foreign Languages Press, Moscow) Lawrence & Wishart 1954-60

MURPHY, ROBERT: *Diplomat Among Warriors* (Collins) 1964

REES, DAVID: *Korea: The Limited War* (Macmillan) 1964

SCHAPIRO, LEONARD: *The Communist Party of the Soviet Union* (Eyre & Spottiswoode) 1960

SETON-WATSON, HUGH: *Eastern Europe between the Wars* (Cambridge University Press) 1946
  East European Revolution (Methuen) 1950
  The Revolution of our Time (Phoenix House) 1955
  Neither War nor Peace (Methuen) 1960
  The New Imperialism (Bodley Head) 1961
  The Pattern of Communist Revolution (Methuen) 1961
  The Decline of Imperialist Russia (Methuen) 1964

SHERWOOD, ROBERT E.: *The White House Papers of Harry L. Hopkins* 2 vols (Eyre & Spottiswode) 1948

SHULMAN, M. D.: *Stalin's Foreign Policy Reappraised* (Harvard University Press) 1946

SNOW, EDGAR: *Red Star Over China* (Gollancz) 1937, 1963
  The Other Side of the River (Gollancz) 1963

STALIN, J. V.: *Collected Works*, 13 vols (Foreign Languages Press, Moscow) 1953-55

WALKER R. L.: *China Under Communism* (Yale; Allen & Unwin) 1956

WILMOT, CHESTER: *The Strnggle for Europe* (Collins) 1952

ZAGORIA DONALD S.: *The Sino-Soviet Conflict 1956-61* (Princeton University Press) 1962

INDEX

487